The Starr Evidence

The Complete Text of the Grand Jury Testimony of President Clinton and Monica Lewinsky

WITH ANALYSIS AND REPORTING BY THE STAFF OF

The Washington Post

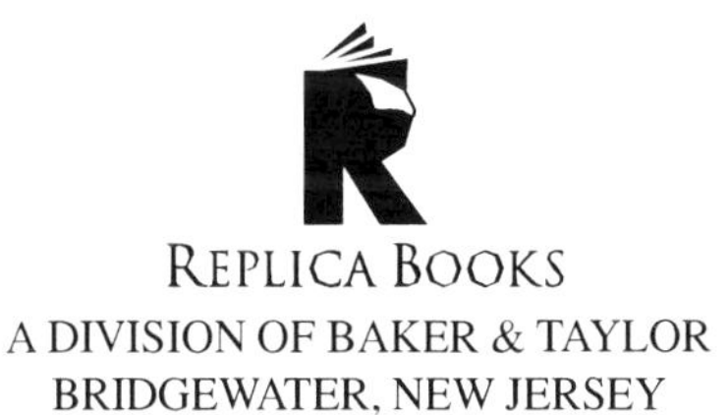

REPLICA BOOKS
A DIVISION OF BAKER & TAYLOR
BRIDGEWATER, NEW JERSEY

The Starr Evidence

THE STARR EVIDENCE

THE COMPLETE TEXT
OF THE GRAND JURY TESTIMONY
OF PRESIDENT CLINTON
AND MONICA LEWINSKY

WITH ANALYSIS AND REPORTING
BY THE STAFF OF

The Washington Post

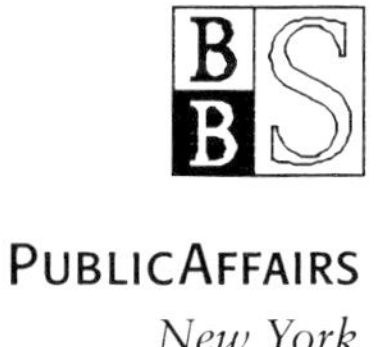

PUBLICAFFAIRS
New York

This edition of *The Starr Evidence* is based on the Communication from the Office of the Independent Counsel, Kenneth W. Starr Transmitting Appendices to the Referral to the United States House of Representatives Pursuant to Title 28, United States Code, Section 595(c) Submitted by the Office of the Independent Counsel, September 9, 1998, released by the U.S. Congress on September 21, 1998. The independent counsel neither authorized nor approved its publication. Any errors it may contain will be corrected in future editions.

Published by PublicAffairs™,
a member of the Perseus Books Group.

For information, address PublicAffairs,
250 West 57th Street, Suite 1825, New York, NY 10107.

ISBN: 1-891620-25-8

Contents

Publisher's Note

On September 21, 1998, the House Judiciary Committee released to the public 3,138 pages of documents that had been assembled by Kenneth W. Starr and the Office of the Independent Counsel. This book contains the most important of those documents, including the complete, unabridged testimony of both President Clinton and Monica Lewinsky. Also included are a number of crucial supporting documents, which have never before been made public. Omitted from this book are a number of lengthy, tangential documents, including information about press coverage of the current scandal, communication between the President's lawyers and the Office of the Independent Counsel, and the Paula Jones case. Information about these omitted documents can be found at http://www.washingtonpost.com. The reporting and analysis by *The Washington Post* places the testimony and other material in perspective and provides a background for understanding this phase of the historic impeachment process.

All information in this book appears exactly as it does in the original Starr referral. Typographical errors have not been corrected, and some documents (particularly several e-mail printouts) may be difficult to read because of this. Certain sections of the text have been blacked out by the House Judiciary Committee. Finally, it should be noted that much of the material is sexually explicit and graphic.

Clinton Decries Attempt to "Set Me Up"; Millions Across Nation See Videotape of August 17 Testimony

President Clinton vigorously defended himself during grand jury testimony broadcast to the nation, denying that he perjured himself about his affair with Monica S. Lewinsky and emphatically portraying himself as the victim of a politically inspired attempt to "set me up."

With millions of Americans tuned in, Clinton's four-hour session with prosecutors was released by the House Judiciary Committee and aired unedited on a half-dozen television networks, providing the public its first extended explanation from the president in an investigation that has Congress considering impeachment proceedings.

Clinton flared with controlled pique at times, but never displayed the pure rage some had forecast and stuck to his script "acknowledging inappropriate intimate contact" with the onetime White House intern while declining to elaborate. Forced to justify what he called his "jumbled" answers about the affair during the Paula Jones lawsuit, he engaged in tortuous debates with prosecutors over what counts as sex and the meaning of words such as "alone" and "is."

"My goal in this [Jones] deposition was to be truthful, but not particularly helpful," the president said during a heated finger-

By PETER BAKER *and* SUSAN SCHMIDT *Washington Post Staff Writers* jabbing exchange. "I did not wish to do the work of the Jones lawyers. I deplored what they were doing. I deplored the innocent people they were tormenting and traumatizing. . . . This was a bogus lawsuit."

The release of the Aug. 17 videotape and 3,183 pages of evidence collected by independent counsel Kenneth W. Starr marked an unprecedented moment in American history, allowing voters to watch for themselves as their leader was interrogated under oath about whether he broke the law and then evaluate the supporting documentation on the Internet.

The two-volume set of documents made public contained no new blockbuster revelations not included in Starr's previously released report to the House alleging 11 impeachable offenses by Clinton. But it amounted to a voluminous compendium of sometimes highly graphic grand jury testimony by Lewinsky as well as White House entry logs, telephone records, gift receipts, appointment diaries, electronic mail, love notes, letters, photographs, DNA test results and other material intended to bolster Starr's case that Clinton committed perjury, obstructed justice, tampered with witnesses and abused his power.

The huge mass of information—not even counting another 16 boxes of still-secret evidence sent by Starr—could help fuel or undercut the fledgling impeachment drive building on Capitol Hill, depending on the public reaction in coming days.

The White House hoped for a backlash to pointed questioning by prosecutors and exhaustive disclosure by Congress. Clinton spent the day in New York consulting with foreign leaders, while his spokesman Michael McCurry decried "the rank partisanship" that led to the release of lurid sexual tales, "most of which are irrelevant" to the issue. "That the president's conduct does not rise to the level of an impeachable offense should now be clear to everyone," he said.

Rep. John Conyers Jr. (Mich.), the top Democrat on the House Judiciary Committee, joined in protesting the release, saying, "Democrats and the public will not stand for the railroading of the president."

Because the contents of the videotape were already known, politicians evaluated the visual impact and many came away convinced that Clinton's performance did not further damage him and may have even helped. "Based on the expectations built up by both sides, the broadcast failed to register on the Richter scale," said Sen. Charles E. Grassley (R-Iowa).

Still, other Republicans said Clinton's sometimes evasive performance on the videotape made it more likely that the House will open an impeachment inquiry to weigh his credibility against Lewinsky's and determine whether the president committed perjury, not only in his Jan. 17 deposition but also in the Aug. 17 grand jury appearance.

"It does come down to that, whether the specific, detailed, corroborated testimony of Monica Lewinsky is true, or whether the president's testimony is true," said Rep. Lamar Smith (R-Tex.), a member of the Judiciary Committee. "They both can't be."

Beyond the videotape, the most important items released were 900 pages detailing Lewinsky's extensive accounts of her 18-month, on-and-off affair with the president, which remained strikingly consistent from her first handwritten, 10-page proposed testimony drafted Feb. 1 through numerous private interviews with prosecutors as recently as Sept. 6.

Lewinsky called Clinton "sort of my sexual soulmate" and described her feelings for him as "a little bit of obsession." But she was distraught by his Aug. 17 televised address to the nation after his closed-door grand jury session because he did not publicly acknowledge what she had gone through over the previous seven months and seemed to belittle the significance of their relationship.

Returning to the federal courthouse three days after his testimony, a grand juror asked her, "And today, Monica, do you still love the president"

"Before Monday, I would have said yes," she said. "It was very painful for me to watch his speech on Monday night . . . [and feel] that this was a service contract, that all I did was perform oral sex on him and that that's all that this relationship was. And it was a lot more than that to me."

VIEWING BEGINS

The torrent of evidence made its way into public view just after 9 A.M., when the Government Printing Office delivered 3,500 two-volume bound copies of the appendices to the Starr report to the clerk of the House of Representatives. Each member of Congress got a copy and the House Judiciary Committee kept 1,350 copies for itself. Others were distributed to news organizations, while 1,400 were sent to libraries around the country and another 1,500 made available for sale at $68 apiece.

At 9:25 A.M. Fox News began feeding the pool videotape of Clinton's grand jury testimony through the House recording studio in the basement of the Rayburn House Office Building. All six major broadcast and cable networks carried the feed live and, with few exceptions, stayed with it for more than four hours while flashing occasional warnings of sexually explicit material.

Although the Judiciary Committee in a fractious two-day meeting last week deleted 155 items it considered too graphic, private or irrelevant, it rejected Democratic efforts to redact another 19 sections with sexual content and five others on privacy grounds.

Among the items left in at Republican insistence was Lewinsky's testimony that Clinton sexually stimulated her with a cigar and that he rebuffed her attempt to initiate phone sex the night after Adm. Jeremy Boorda, the chief of naval operations, committed suicide. In another section Democrats failed to excise, Lewinsky described Clinton telling her that he had had hundreds of affairs, that his life was falling apart when he turned 40 and that he may have told her that at the time he "entertained thoughts about ending his life."

While the most important information has already surfaced publicly, the evidence released contained a wealth of detail about how Starr conducted the investigation, the legal sparring throughout and the meticulous way his prosecutors and FBI agents went about corroborating Lewinsky's testimony and establishing the facts of the relationship with Clinton.

Included is everything from a photograph of the infamous navy blue Gap dress that contained Clinton's semen stain to the president's own handwritten notes related to sexual harassment allegations by former White House volunteer Kathleen E. Willey to the calendar Lewinsky kept in her Filofax noting when she had encounters with Clinton. Starr retrieved e-mail and draft letters to Clinton from Lewinsky's computer hard drive and provided an inventory of the gifts that Lewinsky gave to presidential secretary Betty Currie to hide under her bed to prevent them from being turned over in response to a Jones subpoena. Starr even commissioned an appraisal of how much some of the gifts were worth—not much, in many cases, such as the much-discussed hat pin and gold brooch, each valued at about $3.

The material elaborated on Starr's suspicion that some of Linda R. Tripp's secret recordings of her conversations with Lewinsky were doctored. Tripp surreptitiously taped Lewinsky from Oct. 3 until Jan. 15, depositing tapes in a bowl in her house, but nine of the 27 tapes she turned over to Starr did not appear to be originals as she testified, according to FBI tests. Starr did not use those in his report and had Lewinsky authenticate the only ones he did cite.

Lewinsky also blamed Tripp for the idea of keeping the soiled dress, testifying that she was going to send it to the cleaners but that her friend told her to keep it "because it could be evidence one day." Starr asked for a blood sample from Clinton the same day he obtained the dress, July 29. Clinton rolled up his sleeve after 10 P.M. five nights later in the White House Map Room. The positive results came back just hours before Clinton's testimony.

First Account

Lewinsky's first official account to Starr of her dealings with Clinton came in a handwritten proffer that referred to herself in the third person and described the frightening 2 A.M. phone call from the president last December telling her she was on the Jones witness list.

"After Ms. Lewinsky was informed by the Pres. that she was identified as a possible witness in the Jones case," she wrote, "the Pres. and Ms. L discussed what she should do. . . . When asked what to do if she was subpoenaed, the Pres. suggested she could sign an affidavit to try to satisfy their inquiry and not be deposed. In general, Ms. L should say she visited the WH to see Ms. Currie, and, on occasion when working at the WH she brought him letters when no one else was around. Neither of those statments untrue."

Lewinsky said in the proffer that after she received the Jones subpoena Dec. 19, she went to Clinton friend Vernon E. Jordan Jr., who asked her if she had had sex with Clinton. She said no. Later, though, she "tried to make it clear to Mr. Jordan that she in fact did have a physically intimate relationship with the Pres. Ms. L made it clear she intended to deny the sexual relationship with the Pres."

At another point, she said she asked Jordan if he thought the Clintons would stay married and Jordan said yes. When she expressed disappointment, said Lewinsky, Jordan said perhaps she and Clinton would have an affair when he left office. "Ms. L replied that she and the Pres. had already had an affair minus having sex—but it included everything else," Lewinsky wrote.

Lewinsky said neither Clinton nor Jordan asked or encouraged her to lie in the affidavit and that she decided she could justify denying a sexual relationship with Clinton in the affidavit because they did not have intercourse.

But Lewinsky told the grand jury that she told Tripp some things about Jordan that were not true—things that ended up on an FBI tape recording and that she said "got him in a lot of trouble." Specifically, Lewinsky said she was lying when she told Tripp she flatly refused to sign the affidavit until Jordan got her a job offer.

Lewinsky said she lied about the quid pro quo because it was a course of action Tripp was urging on her and she "wanted her to feel . . . like I needed to hold her hand through this in order to try to get her to do what I wanted, essentially."

In her own accounts to authorities, Lewinsky emerges as a deeply hurt young woman who was in love with Clinton and could not accept that it was over when he called off their affair. She took antidepressant drugs throughout their affair and as it ended she and Tripp even tried to piece together what went wrong, making "a stupid spreadsheet on Microsoft Excel" to try to discern a pattern in her faltering relationship.

Even through much of this year's investigation, she remained devoted to him, she said, at least until she saw him describe their affair coldly on television. "I just thought he had a beautiful soul," she said. "I just thought he was this incredible person, and when I looked at him I saw this little boy and I don't know what the truth is anymore. . . . How could I know the truth of my love for someone if it was based on him being an actor?"

"A Good Girl"

Clinton sounded more caring in the testimony she did not see that day. During the broadcast, he described her as "charming" and "a good girl" burdened by a difficult childhood. "It wasn't her fault," he said. "It was mine." In the end, he said, he always knew she would talk about their relationship and it would become public. "It was a part of her psyche," he said.

Much of Clinton's testimony was already known through news accounts and Starr's reports, but the public never before has seen a president being grilled like this. The session took place in the Map Room beginning at 1:03 P.M. and broke at several points before finally ending at 6:25 P.M., after the president rejected requests to extend it past the prearranged time. Throughout, the camera stayed trained on him, but he was clearly aware that he was speaking to a larger audience, once explaining that he would not describe exactly what sexual activities he engaged in because he knew the statement would find its way into "historical annals."

Clinton bristled with indignation at several points, repeatedly assailing the motives of the Jones lawyers and, occasionally, the Starr team. More than once, he noted that Tripp had gone from consulting with Starr's prosecutors to advising Jones's lawyers on the same day just before his deposition, hinting at collusion between the two camps to trap him.

"It now appears . . . that there had been some communication between you and Ms. Tripp and them and they were trying to set me up and trick me," he said. "And now you seem to be complaining that they didn"t do a good enough job."

Under questioning by Starr and three of his deputies, Clinton denied he perjured himself in answering questions about sex with Lewinsky during the Jones deposition, asserting that he did not touch her breasts or genitals with an intent to arouse or gratify, despite her testimony to the contrary.

Clinton's interpretation of the definition of sex used in the Jones case, covered only his own actions, he said, not acts performed upon him. "My understanding of this definition is it covers contact by the person being deposed with the enumerated areas, if the contact is done with an intent to arouse or gratify," he said. "What I believed then is what I believe today."

Clinton said he believed the use of the words "cause contact" in the definition implied forcible behavior—a "rather strange" definition, he allowed, noting that no one had ever suggested he forced himself on Lewinsky. When asked specific questions about the nature of his relationship with Lewinsky, Clinton repeatly referred back to a three-paragraph statement he read at the outset acknowledging an inappropriate relationship without providing details. When asked whether he ever used a cigar as a sexual prop with the former intern, Clinton reddened but refused to provide any answer beyond that statement.

Clinton and prosecutors sparred repeatedly over his narrow interpretations of language to defend the truthfulness of his earlier testimony. The president defended allowing his lawyer to say during the Jones deposition that Lewinsky's affidavit in the case showed "there is absolutely no sex of any kind in any manner, shape or form, with President Clinton."

"In the present tense," Clinton told the grand jury, "that's an accurate statement. . . . I'm not at all sure this affidavit is not true." He went on to explain that both he and Lewinsky—along with most "normal Americans"—believed "sexual relations" would necessarily include intercourse. (A recent Time-CNN poll, however, showed that 87 percent of Americans consider oral sex to be sexual relations.)

While in the deposition Clinton said he had no specific recollection of being alone with Lewinsky, he acknowledged to the grand jury he had numerous private meetings with her, including several sexual encounters and a Dec. 28 conversation in which she told him of her reluctance to testify in the Jones case. He explained that he never really felt as if he was alone with Lewinsky because there was always someone else in the "Oval Office complex."

Prosecutors focused intently on whether Clinton lied in January when he did not reveal he had discussed Lewinsky's subpoena with Jordan. Asked by the Jones lawyers whether he had talked about it with anyone but his own attorneys, Clinton said he did not believe so. He then offered that deputy White House counsel Bruce R. Lindsey had first brought the matter to his attention and tried to turn the question into one about how he learned about the subpoena instead of who else he'd discussed it with.

In his testimony, Clinton admitted he talked to Jordan about the subpoena—and that in fact Jordan had come to the White House to discuss it on Dec. 19, less than a month before the Jones deposition. "I now know I had a conversation with Mr. Jordan about that," Clinton told the grand jury. He blamed imprecise questions for his answer in January.

This prompted one of the most tense exchanges. When prosecutor Solomon L. Wisenberg suggested he may have made "a false statement, presumably perjurious," Clinton snapped back.

"No, Mr. Wisenberg," he said tartly. "I have testified about this three times. Now I will do it the fourth time. I am not going to answer your trick question."

Clinton said he did not recall Lewinsky's concern that the Jones subpoena sought a hat pin he had given her. Clinton said he gives and gets hundreds of gifts as president, and did not see the gift issue as a dangerous area the way Lewinsky did. "It just was not a big deal," he said, adding that he told Lewinsky at some point in December that she would have to turn over any subpoenaed gifts that she had.

"I didn't see this as a problem. I never encouraged her to avoid complying with the subpoena." He flatly denied dispatching Currie to retrieve a box of gifts from Lewinsky that Currie then stashed under her bed. "I did not do that," he said.

As evidence that he would tell the literal truth, even if it embarrassed him, Clinton pointed to the fact that he admitted during the Jones deposition that he once had sex with Gennifer Flowers, despite his statements during the 1992 campaign. "I would have rather have taken a whipping rather than done that," he said.

Prosecutors briefly questioned Clinton about Willey, another woman on the witness list in the Jones case who claimed she was groped by the president when she went to see him about obtaining a paid White House job in November 1993. Willey has said Clinton got her phone number and called her from his hotel in Williamsburg, Va., during the 1992 presidential campaign and asked her to come to his hotel room that night. Prosecutors produced phone records that back up her claim that he called.

Clinton said in his testimony that, "I have no recollection of asking her to come to my room," but said he did recall some sort of conversation with her around the time of the trip to Virginia for a debate. He charged that her credibility had been "shattered" after the White House last spring released genial letters she wrote to Clinton after the alleged groping incident.

Clinton was questioned about why he did not produce those letters when they were subpoenaed by the Jones lawyers but waited to release them after Willey appeared on "60 Minutes." He said they were not in his personal files, but in White House files, and "I don't believe we were required to produce them."

Staff writers JULIET EILPERIN *and* GUY GUGLIOTTA *and researcher* JEFF GLASSER *contributed to this report.*

From The Brink; Video Release May Help More Than Hurt Clinton; Videotapes May Prove Beneficial To Clinton

It has happened time and again throughout Bill Clinton's political career: Just when he appears most vulnerable, an unexpected bit of luck yanks him back from the brink. The release [on September 21, 1998] of the videotape of his Aug. 17 grand jury testimony—a release pushed by his adversaries and fought by his allies—might someday be remembered as the unlikeliest and most ironic of his lifetime of lucky breaks, a potentially damaging event that helped more than hurt, due in large measure to misplaced expectations that the tape would do him in. There were, to be sure, palpably uncomfortable moments for Clinton during the four-hour grilling, and several exchanges where his wordplay seemed exceedingly cute or intentionally misleading, yet there appeared to be no single frame that will be burnished forever in public memory. Clinton, the ultimate survivor, somehow finished the ordeal laughing, a smile on his face, as though he realized at that moment that once again, following the eerily repetitive cycles of his life, his opponents might have overplayed their hand.

Though on a smaller scale and with less grave consequences, the closest ancestor to the grand jury videotape in Clinton's ceaselessly

By David Maraniss, *Washington Post Staff Writer*

melodramatic political biography was the release of what came to be known as "the draft letter" during the early stages of the 1992 presidential campaign. In February of that year, when Clinton's candidacy was already reeling from allegations of sexual infidelity and draft dodging, his enemies discovered and released a letter that he had written back in 1969 in which he had thanked an ROTC colonel at the University of Arkansas for "saving" him from the draft and allowing him to maintain his "political viability."

Conventional wisdom at the time held that the letter was a grievous embarrassment that might force the governor of Arkansas to drop out of the race. But Clinton's enemies, as it turned out, had utterly miscalculated how the letter would be interpreted by the public. While a paragraph-by-paragraph examination of the letter would reveal several points of deception, in its totality it came to be seen not so much as evidence of Clinton's duplicity as an eloquent expression of angst and uncertainty by a young man struggling to find the right thing to do under difficult circumstances.

In similar fashion, the grand jury videotape might have backfired. Even if a close reading of the transcript could reveal points where Clinton was not telling the truth, in its totality it made Clinton again appear to be a reasonable man struggling to survive in a difficult situation brought on by his political enemies.

This historic parallel was the first thing that came to the mind of one Republican operative viewing the videotape yesterday. "My God, I can't believe it, it's the draft letter all over again," said this consultant, who had been a campaign aide to President George Bush six years ago when the letter surfaced. Not only did the videotape show Clinton making "reasonable explanations" for everything he had said and done, this consultant concluded, but the close-camera cinematic style of the videotape only elicited sympathy: "Even I felt for him," the consultant acknowledged. "It was like the Gestapo."

What America saw on tape was the full Clinton. He was not just the character that his enemies sought to portray: an angry man trapped by his adversaries, a conjurer of semantic legerdemain trying to slip-side out of testimony in which he may have perjured himself. Instead, he was the protean president of many personalities—subdued and angry, humiliated and proud, evasive and persuasive—at once reminding the nation why he gets into trouble and also why he so often gets out of it, balancing traits that tend to exasperate his critics with rhetorical skills that make him, even amid all his troubles, a sympathetic figure to much of the public.

Clinton took some of the edge off the deceptive nature of his wordplay by presenting the context of his answers. He presented himself as the victim of a political vendetta hounded by hostile lawyers, both during his deposition in the Paula Jones case last January and again here before Kenneth W. Starr and his dogged deputies.

He went to the Jones deposition with a state of mind that her lawyers were "taking a wrecking ball to me to see if they could do some damage," Clinton explained at one point. During another exchange, turning to another violent metaphor, he said he was "determined to walk through the minefield" his enemies had set for him without violating any laws. He viewed the Jones deposition as "a gotcha game," he said, and in response decided that his goal should be "to be truthful" but "not particularly helpful."

In his deliberative answers, Clinton made it clear that he viewed the motivations of the independent counsel's office with the same measure of suspicion that he held for Jones's lawyers. He tried to turn the issue of evasiveness on its head. His careful answers—such as claiming that he could accurately deny an affair with Monica S. Lewinsky if he was talking in the present tense, since the affair was in the past—were nothing more than an effort to escape the equally manipulative word traps set by his legal adversaries. "I am not going to answer your trick questions!" he once declared with a tone of self-righteousness.

Whether the grand jury videotape proves to be a long-term boon to the president is still uncertain, of course, but it served at least one positive purpose on the first day: boosting the morale among Clinton's harried supporters and, for perhaps the first time, clearly defining his new line of defense.

Clinton's most outspoken defender, consultant James Carville, was in Brazil and had not even seen the videotape, but had received so many reports on the president's unlikely showing that he was yapping with more effusiveness than usual, if that is possible. "I wish I'd have had this tape before," Carville said in a telephone interview. "Nothing is more effective than when I can say, "As the president said . . . Now I can say it. I've been looking for him to lead the defense, and it appears he's done it."

DAVID MARANISS *is the author of* First in His Class: A Biography of Bill Clinton.

Clinton and the Kenneth Inquisition

In terms of what was promised or anticipated, President Clinton's videotaped grand jury testimony, aired on all the major networks, ranked with such fabled fizzles as "Godzilla." Clinton didn't breathe fire, grow red-faced with fury or stomp off in a huff, advance word to the contrary. Indeed, he seemed as civil and even-tempered as the humiliating circumstances would allow.

Why this video had to be rushed onto the air, and what Republicans thought they would gain from exposing it, remained a mystery after more than four hours of rigorous viewing by us beleaguered folks at home. The tapes were aired not only on the broadcast networks but also on such cable channels as CNN and MSNBC, and while as television this certainly had a morbid novelty value, the expected explosions never erupted.

It seemed a president of the United States was being needlessly harassed and insulted and that the country was suffering right along with him.

During the days leading up to the telecast, pundocrats on talk shows kept telling viewers they'd be shocked silly to discover that

By TOM SHALES, *Pulitzer Prize-winning Television Critic for* The Washington Post.

the Clinton we would see in these relatively unguarded moments would be in sharp contrast to the wily, silky smoothie who delivers slick speeches to Congress or chummy chats from the Oval Office. Imagine, a politician whose public and private demeanors are not exactly the same! Surely this has never happened before in the recorded history of civilization!

But in fact Clinton was much the same as in other televised appearances, even if he didn't know at the time that this particular performance would be seen on national TV as well as on the closed-circuit feed from the White House to the courthouse. Even the much-ballyhooed sexual candor that anchors kept warning viewers about never really materialized, at least not at great length. The Clarence Thomas hearings were a lot smuttier.

Clinton made a reference to the Thomas hearings, and the Anita Hill controversy, during his testimony. Thomas thought he was the victim of a "high-tech lynching." Clinton is beginning to look like the victim of a high-tech crucifixion.

While the televised testimony may have revealed little that was new about the ongoing Kenneth Starr investigation, viewers who sat through it may well have emerged with a new or renewed feeling of sympathy for the president. His having to sit there and try to remember whether he gave Monica Lewinsky a box of chocolate-covered cherries, in addition to being prodded for lurid details of their sexual activities, made Clinton seem vulnerable and victimized.

The fact that the camera remained stationary and glued to him and that no other participants could be seen—and that the questions came from the ominous, off-camera voices of creepy-sounding attorneys—made Clinton seem a bit like Joseph K, persecuted hero of Franz Kafka's "The Trial." At times the goal appeared to be to rob the president of whatever dignity he's been able to salvage from this torturous mess.

What does Starr have in mind next for him—an afternoon in the pillory, perhaps, with Clinton being pelted with fruits and vegetables? Network cameras would be there to transmit it all to the nation, whether the nation wanted to see it or not.

"I need to go to the restroom," Clinton said at one point, signaling one of several breaks in the testimony that required engineers to change to the next videotape. Dan Rather popped up on CBS to say the president had been "sometimes testy" in his responses so far, but had he? Rather was closer to the mark when he said Clinton seemed "aggressive but respectful."

It was appropriate somehow that the broadcast began with a lurch and a clunk. It seems the tapes arrived at the location for the pool feed without labels on them, so that engineers had to preview each tape to figure out the proper order before playback could begin. Network anchors vamped to fill the empty time. Tom Brokaw of NBC News joined Rather in warning that "a lot of explicit language" was coming down the tube and urging that all children be shielded from the dreaded onslaught.

Rather promised that CBS would air the tape on a 30-second delay so that offending words could be bleeped, but none were. ABC used a five-second delay as a safeguard. After about 20 minutes, the network news divisions received transcripts of the testimony so they could see if something wildly obscene lay ahead. Finally, about 25 minutes late, we saw an engineer's finger hit the "play" button of a professional-style VCR and the tape began unreeling. William Jefferson Clinton raised his right hand and took an oath to tell the truth, the whole truth and nothing but. The definition of "the truth" became something of an issue during the long sessions that followed, however, as of course did the definition of "sexual relations" and of "love." Fairly late in the proceedings Clinton even said, in response to a question, "It depends upon what the meaning of the word 'is' is."

Abbott and Costello Meet George Orwell.

There were indeed moments when Clinton could not conceal his resentment at the direction or repetitiousness of the questioning. Hammered and hammered about things he had failed to say during his deposition in the Paula Jones sexual harassment case, Clinton at one point snapped, "I'm not going to answer your trick questions" and later said he detected "some sort of 'gotcha' game at work in this deposition."

Certainly Clinton, who claimed he is "blessed . . . with a good memory" but at many other points couldn't remember what had happened when, came across as evasive, sometimes because he wouldn't indulge the prosecutors' lust for salacious details. Die-hard Clintonians could even interpret his reluctance to discuss the sex acts as sort of gentlemanly, and he pointedly refrained from saying anything mean about Lewinsky.

"She's basically a good girl, a good young woman with a good mind," he said near the end of the testimony. Earlier he said with an admiring smile, "Ms. Lewinsky has a way of getting information out of people." He smiled, too, when a lawyer asked a ridiculous question about Clinton "excluding" others from his trysts with Lewinsky. "It's almost humorous," Clinton said, "but I'd have to be an exhibitionist not to try to exclude everyone else." Throughout most of the testimony, during which he drank often from a glass of water or a can of soda, Clinton appeared patient and courteous. He never blew his top. When he put on a pair of glasses, halfway down his nose, to read from a brief prepared statement, he looked cute. Obviously Clinton stirs strong passions in people, but it's hard to imagine watching his performance and not feeling a certain sympathy—despite the bad things he did in the White House and the fact that during a previous TV appearance he lied right to our faces.

In Washington, viewers had many choices for coverage of the testimony, but they were deprived of the choice of ABC News by WJLA, the network's local affiliate. Station executives chose to preempt network coverage that featured Peter Jennings, Cokie Roberts, Sam Donaldson, George Stephanopoulos and others in favor of their own local coverage starring those two giants of journalism, Kathleen Matthews and Paul Berry.

Reached at his office in New York, ABC News President David Westin said of Channel 7's decision, "I'm not as angry as you might think." Westin said ABC News executives had been unable to promise WJLA that the network would stick with the testimony through all four-plus hours, and the station wanted to be sure it carried everything. As it turns out, ABC did broadcast the testimony in its entirety. There really wasn't much leeway in covering the story except to air the tapes as they became available and comment on them during brief breaks when it was time to switch to the next reel. Even so, CNN managed to muck things up. Anchor Bernard Shaw, who doesn't always know when to keep still, suddenly started speaking over Clinton at one point in the testimony, obscuring the president's words. "Greta Van Susteren, tell us what prosecutors are trying to do here," Shaw commanded, and soon her negligible babbling was heard over the president's voice. CNN still manages to be amazingly amateurish at times.

Commentators on all the networks tended to agree that the president's appearance wasn't likely to change the mind of anyone who already had an opinion about his guilt or innocence or what his fate should be. But even if Clinton had thrown a fit as was predicted ahead of time, there are some of us, perhaps millions, who would have empathized. It would seem he's more than earned the right to be ticked off. And so, for that matter, have we.

Members of the House Judiciary Committee now must wrestle with the Contradictory testimony; A formal impeachment inquiry by the panel looks increasingly probable

Rep. Christopher B. Cannon (R-Utah) heard "some pretty bizarre things" spoken "in a pretty reasonable voice." Rep. Thomas M. Barrett (D-Wis.), who braced for the worst, thought it might have been "a wash."

But these and other members of the House Judiciary Committee agreed that while the release of President Clinton's videotaped grand jury testimony did not decide the case against him, it made a formal impeachment inquiry increasingly more probable.

"The next big question is to justify whether there is enough evidence to make an inquiry," said senior committee member Charles T. Canady (R-Fla.). "I haven't made a final judgment, but there's a lot pointing in that direction."

The 37 members of the Judiciary Committee are reviewing the Independent Counsel's report on Clinton's relationship with former White House intern Monica Lewinsky. They had refused to discuss

By GUY GUGLIOTTA *and* JULIET EILPERIN

the videotape and the accompanying evidence until their formal release.

In general, committee members regarded the new material as a reinforcement for their previously held views. Republicans focused on whether Clinton committed perjury in his grand jury testimony. Democrats attacked the GOP for deliberately trying to embarrass Clinton and railroad him out of office.

Rep. Robert L. Barr Jr. (R-Ga.), one of Clinton's most ferocious critics, said that the videotaped grand jury testimony "to me presents a very strong case for obstruction of justice and perjury."

"For example," Barr said, "the president continually refers to this piece of paper, his so-called statement, instead of answering directly. Every time he does that it would be a separate count of obstruction of justice because he's impeding the work of the grand jury. He definitely knows exactly what happened. He not only fails to answer without justification, he refers to a document that misleads the grand jury and that impedes their work."

But Rep. Melvin L. Watt (D-N.C.) said that the videotape "is not the point." He described the committee's handling of the investigation as "a blatantly political process, and there is nobody stepping forward on the other side to say that our responsibilities are more important than the political agenda. There is a rush to have the press and the public try the president."

Despite predictable responses to the videotape, several committee members found a more complicated message. Cannon said reaction among his constituents in Utah was "interesting and relatively mixed." Those who watched the videotape "felt some sympathy" for Clinton, he said, but "are still looking for the truth and wondering where to find it."

And in contrast to pre-videotape efforts to gauge the temper of his district, voters had relaxed a bit, Cannon added. "I sensed some relief that there was nothing else ugly on the tape. For a lot of people, it wasn't as bad as they thought, and they thought "Thank God."

Barrett said parts of Clinton's testimony may help the president hold off an impeachment proceeding, but other parts would hurt him: "In general it may be a wash, and there may be a backlash" against Republicans, he said. "I talked to a number of people who said even prior to the release: "enough already."

Release of the videotape, added Rep. John Conyers Jr. (Mich.), the committee's top Democrat, shows "an unhealthy preoccupation with...unnecessary disclosure of salacious and lurid details of sex" and cautioned that "if we are not very careful, this inquiry itself may soon become more unpopular than the actual conduct of the inquiry."

Under the House resolution governing the Lewinsky evidence, the committee must complete its review of 18 boxes of material by Sept. 28. Besides the videotape, on September 22 the committee released 3,183 pages of appendices to accompany the main 453-page report.

Unless it decides to the contrary, the remaining 17 boxes of material will automatically be published Sept. 28. Rep. James E. Rogan (R-Calif.) said that there was no formal committee meeting scheduled this week and suggested that there might be none.

"It's premature for any of us to make a judgment" about whether the committee will open a formal impeachment inquiry, he added. He said the panel likely will hold "preliminary inquiries" early in October to determine what to do next.

At that point, several members said, the panel will have to come together to examine the evidence to determine what constitutes an "impeachable offense" and to decide whether to proceed further.

Refusal by the Republicans to deal with this question prior to releasing the videotape and the appendices prompted Democrats to cry foul and condemn the panel's procedures as GOP strong-arming: "We have the cart way out in front of the horse," Watt said.

But now, said Rep. Lindsey Graham (R-S.C.), it is time to take stock: "After watching most of the videotape, it leaves more things to be done," Graham said. "To bring this thing to closure, you're going to have to tie up some loose ends.

"My bottom line is that we are not going to have an inquiry based on an inappropriate sexual relationship by the president.

That would never result in impeachment, and it's a waste of our time . . .

But if there was an ongoing pattern of activity to deliberately orchestrate the testimony of other witnesses, manipulate the stream of evidence, or mislead or lie to a grand jury," Graham continued, "that would be very serious."

Staff writer EDWARD WALSH *contributed to this report.*

"You let me down"; Excerpts from evidence by and about Monica Lewinsky

From June 1995, when she came to Washington as one of hundreds of unpaid White House interns, to the public exposure of her most intimate longings and sexual secrets, Monica S. Lewinsky has made a long and tumultuous journey. What began as an improbable crush on the president of the United States has led her, at the age of 25, to be the single most important witness in an inquiry being considered in the House of Representatives that could result in the impeachment of President Clinton.

The documents released on Monday, September 21, 1998 by the House, part of the voluminous Evidentiary record submitted by independent counsel Kenneth W. Starr, tell Lewinsky's story through more than 900 pages of love letters to the president, interrogations by FBI agents, testimony to prosecutors and the grand jury, and the perspectives of White House aides and Pentagon supervisors on her conduct.

In this untidy collection of texts, her emotional highs and lows are charted in both minute legalisms and unguarded private notes. There was joy the night Clinton first kissed her, said one prosecutor's memo. And there was threatening rage: "I am begging you one last time to please let me visit briefly Tuesday evening," she wrote Clinton after the affair had long died.

The testimony contains a remarkable session between Lewinsky and Grand Jurors, its tone more like Oprah than a criminal inquiry. They asked if she still loved Clinton. They asked why she had another affair with a married man, Clinton, when her earlier relationship with her married drama teacher had caused so much pain. "I think it's a fair question. It's a hard one to answer. No one likes to have their weaknesses splayed out for the entire world, you know—you'd probably have to know me better and know my whole journey to how I got here from birth to now to really understand it. I don't even understand it."

On Jan. 7, Monica Lewinsky signed an affidavit saying she "never had a sexual relationship with the president." But unbeknownst to her, Linda Tripp had been tape-recording their phone conversations. On Jan. 12, Tripp contacted Starr's office and the following day, FBI agents equipped Tripp with a hidden microphone and recorded four hours of conversation between her and Lewinsky at the Ritz-Carlton Hotel in Pentagon City. Using the tape recordings, Starr sought an expansion of his investigation to include the possibility of subornation of perjury and obstruction of justice in the Paula Jones case. The next day, FBI agents lured Lewinsky and Tripp to another meeting at the Ritz. What follows is the Office of Independent Counsel's account of their efforts to persuade a reluctant Lewinsky to cooperate:

> LEWINSKY was advised OIC attorneys were waiting in the room and that the agents and the attorneys wished to discuss her culpability in criminal activity related to the PAULA JONES civil lawsuit. LEWINSKY was advised she was not under arrest and the agents would not force her to accompany them to the hotel room. LEWINSKY told SSA (redacted) he could speak to her attorney.
>
> Also present in room 1016, the adjoining room, were Associate Independent Counsel (AIC) BRUCE UDOLF, AIC MICHAEL EMMICK, AIC STEVEN D. BINHAK, Deputy Independent Counsel JACKIE M. BENNETT JR., AIC STEPHEN BATES AND Contract Investigator COY A.COPELAND, all members of the Office of the Independent Counsel staff. The chronology of the meeting, with all times approximate, is as follows:

1:02 P.M. The air conditioning in room 1012 was turned on at LEWINSKY'S request.

1:05 P.M. LEWINSKY arrived in Room 1012, AIC EMMICK entered Room 1012 and began talking to LEWINSKY.

1:10 P.M. LEWINSKY given bottled water.

1:33 P.M. SSA (redacted) began reading LEWINSKY her rights as found on the form FD-395, "Interrogation, Advice of Rights." SSA (redacted) was unable to finish reading the FD-395.

1:40 P.M. LEWINSKY was offered a towel.

1:47 P.M. LEWINSKY was offered water.

2:13 P.M. LEWINSKY was offered water. LEWINSKY said, "if I don't cooperate, I can talk to whomever I want."

2:29 P.M. LEWINSKY stated, "if I leave now, you will charge me now."

2:30 P.M. LEWINSKY said, "I don't know much about the law."

2:33 P.M. LEWINSKY asked and was allowed to go to the restroom.

2:36 P.M. LEWINSKY requested and was given her second bottle of water.

3:10 P.M. LEWINSKY asked if she could be escorted to New York to see her mother, Marcia Lewis.

3:20 P.M. LEWINSKY called her mother, MARCIA LEWIS, in New York.

3:36 P.M. LEWINSKY requested and was allowed to go to the restroom.

4:12 P.M. LEWINSKY called MARCIA LEWIS. LEWIS requested to speak with an OIC attorney. AIC EMMICK and SA (redacted) got on the phone and identified themselves to LEWIS. LEWIS advised she would travel to Washington D.C. via AMTRAK Metroliner.

5:00 P.M. LEWINSKY called her answering machine to retrieve messages

5:21 P.M. LEWINSKY requested and received aspirin.

5:40 P.M. LEWINSKY, AID EMMICK and SA (redacted) departed room 1012, en route to the Pentagon City Mall. LEWINSKY, AIC EMMICK and SA (redacted) walked in the mall.

6:03 P.M. LEWINSKY requested and was permitted to visit the restroom on the third level of the MACY'S department story in the mall.

6:30 P.M. LEWINSKY, AIC EMMICK and SA (redacted) dined at MOZZARELLA'S American Grill, within the Pentagon City Mall. LEWINSKY paid for her portion of the dinner.

8:19 P.M. MARCIA LEWIS telephoned room 1012, and advised she was on the "163 Northeast Direct", and was experiencing travel delays.

10:16 P.M. MARCIA LEWIS arrived and all members of the OIC staff left LEWIS and LEWINSKY alone.

10:20 P.M. A meeting was held in room 1018 between LEWIS, AIC EMMICK, SSA (redacted) and SA (redacted). LEWIS advised that this wasn't an emotional experience for LEWINSKY. LEWIS advised LEWINSKY was younger than her chronological age. LEWIS asked if tapes were admissible in court. LEWIS advised she wanted to protect LEWINSKY. LEWIS asked how she would know LEWINSKY would not be charged if she cooperated. LEWIS asked about LEWINSKY's safety if LEWINSKY cooperated. LEWIS advised that LEWINSKY talked about suicide six years ago. After LEWINSKY'S parents divorced, LEWINSKY saw a therapist, but she is not currently seeing one. LEWIS advised she alone could not take responsibility for convincing LEWINSKY to cooperate with the OIC.

11:06 P.M. LEWIS telephonically contacted BERNARD LEWINSKY [Lewinsky's father], her ex-husband, at (redacted.)

11:20 P.M. BERNARD LEWINSKY telephoned room 1018.

11:35 P.M. BERNARD LEWINSKY telephoned room 1014. BERNARD LEWINSKY advised AIC EMMICK that MONICA LEWINSKY was represented by counsel.

11:36 P.M. MONICA LEWINSKY talked to BERNARD LEWINSKY on the telephone.

11:37 P.M. AIC EMMICK spoke with BERNARD LEWINSKY. AIC EMMICK asked MONICA LEWINSKY if she had an attorney and LEWINSKY advised it was GINSBURG. MONICA LEWIN-

SKY asked if there was still a chance she would go to jail if she cooperated . MONICA LEWINSKY suggested she may not have told the truth in previous conversations. MONICA LEWINSKY asked, "what if I partially cooperate?" MARCIA LEWIS asked what would happen if MONICA LEWINSKY gave everything but did not tape anything. MONICA LEWINSKY asked if the PAULA JONES case went away would "this" go away and was advised by AIC EMMICK "no." MONICA LEWINSKY asked how the OIC would resolve the chance that MONICA LEWINSKY said something to LINDA TRIP (sic) that was not true. MARCIA LEWIS advised that she appreciated the OIC members waiting until she arrived to proceed. MONICA LEWINSKY advised she appreciated having her mother present.

11:55 P.M. BILL GINSBURG telephoned room 1018 and spoke to AIC EMMICK, who advised GINSBURG he was uncomfortable with the relationship between GINSBURG and MONICA LEWINSKY. MONICA LEWINSKY advised she was not 100 percent sure it was the right thing to do because GINSBURG was a medical lawyer.

11:59 P.M. MONICA LEWINSKY advised she was represented by GINSBURG.

12:08 A.M. GINSBURG was advised by AIC EMMICK that MONICA LEWINSKY always had the right to leave at any time.

12:17 A.M. MONICA LEWINSKY spoke with Ginsburg, outside the presence of the OIC staff.

12:23 A.M. AIC EMMICK ended the phone call with GINSBURG and advised MONICA LEWINSKY and MARCIA LEWIS they were free to leave.

12:30 A.M. MARCIA LEWIS and MONICA LEWINSKY thanked the Agents and the staff of the OIC for being so kind and considerate.

Between February and July of this year, as Starr and Lewinsky's lawyers remained locked in a stalemate over whether prosecutors would grant her immunity in exchange for her testimony, Lewinsky remained on hold, awaiting resolution. It came when she changed attorneys in June and her new lawyers, Plato Cacheris and Jacob Stein, began negotiations with the Office of Independent Counsel. On July 28, Lewinsky reached an immunity deal with Starr in which she agreed to testify in return for a guarantee that she would not face prosecution.

Beginning in late July, Lewinsky began preliminary interviews with Starr's lawyers and other investigators. Following are excerpts from a summary of those interviews, prepared by Starr's office, In the interviews, Lewinsky quotes the president as saying that "during his life, he had been two people" and that he had long struggled with the temptations of infidelity. Following are excerpts from a summary of those interviews: May 24, 1997, was referred to by LEWINSKY as "Dump Day." LEWINSKY had an idea she would see the President on that date. LEWINSKY went shopping with ASHLEY RAINES at VICTORIA's SECRET. CURRIE called LEWINSKY around 11:00 A.M. and told LEWINSKY to come to the White House at about 1:00 P.M.

LEWINSKY did not recall how the conversation started; however, the President stated that he did not feel right about their relationship; it was not right, and the President said he could not do it anymore. LEWINSKY was crying. The President said this did not have to do with LEWINSKY. The President told LEWINSKY that he had been with hundreds of women in his life until he was about 40 years of age. The President told LEWINSKY that when he turned 40 his life was falling apart. LEWINSKY recalled that the President may have told her that, at the above time, he entertained thoughts of ending his life. However, LEWINSKY was not sure about the recollection. [Redacted material follows.] The President told LEWINSKY that he had been good until he met her. LEWINSKY did not believe the President. The President told her how he was attracted to LEWINSKY and how the President thought LEWINSKY was a great person. The President told LEWINSKY that they could remain friends. The President pointed out to LEWINSKY that he could do a lot for her. The President told LEWINSKY that it was difficult for him to resist being with other women. The president struggled with it daily. The president told LEWINSKY that he kept a calender [sic] on how long he had been good. The President explained that during his life he had been two people, and kept up two fronts. The President said that starting in the third or fourth grade, he was a good boy with his mother and stepfather but also began telling stories and leading a secret life. LEWINSKY's impression was that the President was telling her he wanted to be right in the eyes of God. The President wanted the affair to be over, though he said it was not LEWINSKY's fault. LEWINSKY did not know if the President meant what he said.

Near the end of her many days of Grand Jury testimony, after Clinton told the nation on Aug. 17 that their relationship was wrong, and expressed no feeling for her, Monica Lewinsky told the grand jury she was hurt. "I thought he had a beautiful soul," she said. "I don't know what the truth is any more." At one point she was asked if she wanted, for any reason, to hurt the President. "No," she replied, "I'm, I'm upset with him right now, but I, no, that's the last thing in the world I want to do."

Compiled by LORRAINE ADAMS *and* LIZ SPAYD.

The Lewinsky File (Part 1)

Office of the Independent Counsel

1001 Pennsylvania Avenue, N.W.
Suite 490-North
Washington, DC 20004
(202) 514-8688
Fax (202) 514-8802

AGREEMENT

This is an agreement ("Agreement") between Monica S. Lewinsky and the United States, represented by the Office of the Independent Counsel ("OIC"). The terms of the Agreement are as follows:

1. Ms. Lewinsky agrees to cooperate fully with the OIC, including special agents of the Federal Bureau of Investigation ("FBI") and any other law enforcement agencies that the OIC may require. This cooperation will include the following:

A. Ms. Lewinsky will provide truthful, complete and accurate information to the OIC. She will provide, upon request, any documents, records, or other tangible evidence within her custody or control relating to the matters within the OIC's jurisdiction. She will assist the OIC in gaining access to such materials that are not within her custody and control, and she will assist in locating and gaining the cooperation of other individuals who possess relevant information. Ms. Lewinsky will not attempt to protect any person or entity through false information or omission, and she will not attempt falsely to implicate any person or entity.

B. Ms. Lewinsky will testify truthfully before grand juries in this district and elsewhere, at any trials in this district and elsewhere, and in any other executive, military, judicial or congressional proceedings. Pending a final resolution of this matter, neither Ms. Lewinsky nor her agents will make any statements about this matter to witnesses, subjects, or targets of the OIC's investigation, or their agents, or to representatives of the news media, without first obtaining the OIC's approval.

C. Ms. Lewinsky will be fully debriefed concerning her knowledge of and participation in any activities within the OIC's jurisdiction. This debriefing will be conducted by the OIC, including attorneys, law enforcement agents, and representatives of any other institutions as the OIC may require. Ms. Lewinsky will make herself available for any interviews upon reasonable request.

D. Ms. Lewinsky acknowledges that she has orally proffered information to the OIC on July 27, 1998, pursuant to a proffer agreement. Ms. Lewinsky further represents that the statements she made during that proffer session were truthful and accurate to the best of her knowledge. She agrees that during her cooperation, she will truthfully elaborate with respect to these and other subjects.

E. Ms. Lewinsky agrees that, upon the OIC's request, she will waive any evidentiary privileges she may have, except for the attorney-client privilege.

2. If Ms. Lewinsky fully complies with the terms and understandings set forth in this Agreement, the OIC: 1) will not prosecute her for any crimes committed prior to the date of this Agreement arising out of the investigations within the jurisdiction of the OIC; 2) will grant her derivative use immunity within the meaning and subject to the limitations of 18 United States Code, Section 6002, and will not use, in any criminal prosecution against Ms. Lewinsky, testimony or other information provided by her during the course of her debriefing, testimony, or other cooperation pursuant to this agreement, or any information derived directly or indirectly from such debriefing, testimony, information, or other cooperation; and 3) will not prosecute her mother, Marsha Lewis, or her father, Bernard Lewinsky, for any offenses which may have been committed by them prior to this Agreement arising out of the facts summarized above, provided that Ms. Lewis and Mr. Lewinsky cooperate with the OIC's investigation and provide complete and truthful information regarding those facts.

3. If the OIC determines that Ms. Lewinsky has intentionally given false, incomplete, or misleading information or testimony, or has otherwise violated any provision of this Agreement, the OIC may move the United States District Court for the District of Columbia which supervised the grand jury investigating this matter for a finding that Ms. Lewinsky has breached this Agreement, and, upon such a finding by the Court, Ms. Lewinsky shall be subject to prosecution for any federal criminal violation of which the OIC has knowledge, including but not limited to perjury, obstruction of justice, and making false statements to government agencies. In such a prosecution, the OIC may use information provided by Ms. Lewinsky during the course of her cooperation, and such information, including her statements, will be admissible against her in any grand jury, court, or other official proceedings.

4. Pending a final resolution of this matter, the OIC will not make any statements about this Agreement to representatives of the news media.

380

5. This is the entire agreement between the parties. There are no other agreements, promises or inducements.

If the foregoing terms are acceptable, please sign, and have your client sign, in the spaces indicated below.

Date: July 28, 1998

KENNETH W. STARR
Independent Counsel

I have read this entire Agreement and I have discussed it with my attorneys. I freely and voluntarily enter into this Agreement. I understand that if I violate any provisions of this Agreement, the Agreement will be null and void, and I will be subject to federal prosecution as outlined in the Agreement.

Date: July 28, 1998

Monica S. Lewinsky

Counsel for Ms. Lewinsky:

Jacob A. Stein

Plato Cacheris

709

1. Ms. Lewinsky had an intimate and emotional relationship with President Clinton beginning in 1995. At various times between 1995 and 1997, Ms. Lewinsky and the President had physically intimate contact. This included oral sex, but excluded intercourse.

2. When asked what should be said if anyone questioned Ms. Lewinsky about her being with the President, he said she should say she was bringing him letters (when she worked in Legislative Affairs) or visiting Betty Currie (after she left the WH). There is truth to both of these statements.

3. After Ms. Lewinsky was informed she was being transferred to the Pentagon, Mr. Clinton told her that a) he promised to bring her back to the WH after the election and (in a subsequent conversation), b) Evelyn Lieberman spearheaded the transfer because she felt the President paid to much attention to me and vice versa. Ms. Lieberman told the Pres. that she didn't care who worked there after the election, but they needed to be careful until then.

After the election, Ms. Lewinsky asked the Pres. to bring her back to the WH. In the following months, Mr. Clinton told Ms. Lewinsky that Bob Nash was handling it and then Marsha Scott became the contact person. Ms. L met with Ms. Scott twice. In the second meeting, Ms. Scott told Ms. L she would detail her from the Pentagon to her (Ms. Scott's) office, so people could see Ms. L's good work and stop referring to her as "The Stalker." Ms. Scott told Ms. L they had to be careful and protect the Pres. Ms. Scott later rescinded her offer to detail Ms. Lewinsky to her office.

Ms. Betty Currie asked Mr. John Podesta to take over placing me in the WH. Three weeks after that, Ms. Linda Tripp informed Ms. L that a friend of Ms. Tripp's in the NSC, Kate, had heard rumors about Ms. L; Ms. L would never work at the WH with a blue pass; and suggested to Ms. Tripp that Ms. L leave Washington, DC.

Following this conversation, Ms. Lewinsky requested of the Pres. that he ask Vernon Jordan to help secure her a non-government position in NY. He agreed to ask Mr. Jordan.

In an effort to help Ms. L, Ms. Currie asked Mr. Podesta to assist, as well. Ms. L believes that

711

the Pres. ~~asked~~ spoke with Mr. Erskine Bowles regarding Ms. L's employment in NY. Mr. Podesta arranged for Ms. L to interview with Amb. Richardson who later offered Ms. L a position in communications/Public Affairs at the USUN.

In the beginning of November 1997, Ms. L met with Mr. Jordan. He asked Ms. L why she was there to see him. Ms. L explained to him (in more detail) that she and the Pres. were friends and people got the wrong idea, resulting in Ms. L's 'banishment to the Pentagon. Ms. L said she was seeking Mr. Jordan's help to begin a new life; he agreed to help.

Ms. L met again with Mr. Jordan in the beginning of December '97, at which time he provided Ms. L with a list of three people to contact and suggested language to use in her letters to them. At some point, Mr. Jordan remarked something about Ms. L being a friend of the Pres. of the United States. Ms. L responded that she never really saw him as "the President"; she spoke to him like a normal man and even got angry with him like a normal man. Mr. Jordan asked what Ms. L got angry about. Ms. L replied that the Pres. doesn't see or call her enough. Mr. Jordan said

712

Ms. L should take her frustrations out on ~~the~~ him-- not the President.

The following week Ms. L had two interviews in NY in response to ~~as a result of~~ her letters.

4. After Ms. Lewinsky was informed, by the Pres., that she was identified as a possible witness in the Jones case, the Pres. and Ms. L discussed what she should do. The Pres. told her ~~to~~ he was not sure she would be subpoenaed, but in the event that she was, she should contact Ms. Currie. When asked what to do if she was subpoenaed, the Pres. suggested she could sign an affidavit to try to satisfy their inquiry and not be deposed. In general, Ms. L should say she visited the WH to see ~~B~~ Ms. Currie and, on occasion when working at the WH, she brought him letters when no one else was around. Neither of those statements untrue. To the best of Ms. L's memory, she does not believe they discussed the content of any deposition that Ms. L might be involved in at a later date.

5 After receiving a subpoena two days later, Ms. L contacted Mr. Jordan (because Ms. Currie's brother had been killed in a car accident). Mr. Jordan told Ms. L to come see him at 5pm because he couldn't understand Ms. L ~~through her tears~~ on the phone, through her tears. Upon Ms. L's request, Mr. Jordan arranged an appointment for her with an attorney, Mr. Frank Carter.

Ms. L expressed ~~any~~ anxiety with respect to her subpoena requesting the production of any gifts from the Pres., specifically citing hat pins which the Pres. had in fact given her. Mr. Jordan allayed her concerns by telling her it was standard language. Mr. Jordan asked Ms. Lewinsky two questions: Did you have sex with the Pres. and/or did he ask you for sex? Ms. L responded to both questions with "no."

Possibly later in that meeting but more probably the next meeting, Ms. L tried to make it clear to Mr. Jordan that she, in fact, did have a physically intimate relationship with the Pres. ~~On more than one occasion, Ms. L expressed concern about signing an affidavit~~

714

Ms. L made it clear she intended to deny the sexual relationship with the Pres.

On the day Mr. Jordan drove Ms. L to Mr. Carter's office, she showed Mr. Jordan the items she was producing in response to the subpoena. Ms. L believes she made it clear this was not everything she had that could respond to the subpoena, but she thought it was enough to satisfy. Mr. Jordan made no comment about whether or not what Ms. L brought was right or wrong. Mr. J drove Ms. L to Mr. Carter's office; introduced them; and left.

6. The Pres., through Ms. Currie, invited Ms. L to come see him to get her Christmas presents. They played with Buddy, he gave her the presents, they talked casually and spoke for a few minutes about the case. Ms. L asked him how he thought the attorneys for Paula Jones found out about her. He thought it was probably "that woman from the Summer... wit Kathleen Willey" (Linda Tripp) who lead them to Ms. L or possibly the uniformed agents. He shared Ms. L's concern about the hat pin. He asked Ms. L if she had told anyone that he had given it to her and she replied, "no."

715

Ms. L then asked if she should put away (outside her home) the gifts he had given her or, maybe, give them to someone else. ~~Betty~~

[Ms. Currie called Ms. L later that afternoon as said that the Pres. had told her Ms. L wanted her to hold onto something for her. Ms. L boxed up most of the gifts she had received and gave them to Ms. Currie. It is unknown if Ms. Currie knew the contents of the box.]

Ms. L told the Pres. she was planning to sign an affidavit. When Ms. L and the Pres. discussed when Ms. L was moving to NY, the Pres. thought it might be possible that they would not seek her deposition if she was in NY.

7. Ms. Lewinsky called Mr. Jordan several times concerning her employment in NY. When she called one day especially concerned about the case, Mr. Jordan suggested they meet for breakfast

At breakfast, Ms. L expressed concern about Ms. Tripp saying she (Ms. L) had trusted her before, but was now suspicious of her.

716

Ms. L said Ms. Tripp may have seen notes when she was in Ms. L's home. Mr. Jordan asked if the notes were from the Pres. Ms. L said That they were notes to the Pres. Mr. Jordan suggested to Ms. L she check to make sure They are not there (something to that effect). Ms. L interpreted that to mean she should get rid of whatever is there.

~~On the~~
In the car on the way to his office, Ms. L asked Mr. Jordan if he thought the Pres. would always be married to Mrs. Clinton. Mr. Jordan replied that he thought they would always be married, as they should be. ~~as~~ Ms. L expressed disappointment and then Mr. Jordan said, "well, maybe you two will have an affair when he's out of office. Ms. L replied That she and the Pres. had alread had an affair minus having sex -- but it included everything else. Ms. L believes They did not get into any more detail

After Ms. L received the draft of the affidavit, she called Mr. Jordan to ask that he look it over before she sign it. He instructed her to drop off a copy at his office. They spoke later by phone about the affidavit agreeing to make some changes.

That evening, Ms. L placed a phone call to Ms. Currie asking her to tell the Pres. that she wanted to speak with him before she signed something the next day. He returned Ms. L's call a few hours later. Ms. L told him Mr. Carter had asked her some sample questions that might be asked of her in the deposition and she didn't know how to answer them. Furthermore, she was concerned that if the answers involved naming people in the WH who didn't like her they would try to screw her over. Ms. L asked him how she should respond to the question, "How did you get your job at the Pentagon?" He replied "The people in Legislative Affairs helped you." This is, in fact, part of the truth -- but not the whole truth. The Pres. told Ms. L not to worry about the affidavit as he had seen 15 others.

718

9. Ms. L started to become wary of Ms. Tripp in the beginning of Dec. 1997, when Ms. Tripp told Ms. L she had received a subpoena in The Jones case and if asked about Ms. L or others, she would divulge all she knew.

10. Ms. L had a physically intimate relationship with the President. Neither the Pres. nor Mr. Jordan (or anyone on their behalf) asked or encouraged ~~me~~ Ms. L to lie. ~~I~~ Ms. L was comfortable signing the affidavit with regard to the "sexual relationship" because she could justify to herself that ~~they~~ she and the Pres. did not have sexual intercourse.

11. At some point in the relationship between Ms. L and the President, the President told Ms. L to deny a relationship, if ever asked about it. He also said something to the effect of if ~~two~~ the two people who are involved say it didn't happen -- it didn't happen. ~~[illegible]~~ Ms. L knows this was said some time prior to the subpoena in the Paula Jones Case.

12. Item #2 above also occurred prior to the subpoena in the Paula Jones Case.

721

UNITED STATES DISTRICT COURT
FOR THE DISTRICT OF COLUMBIA

\- - - - - - - - - - - - - - - - - - - x
IN RE: :
GRAND JURY PROCEEDINGS :
\- - - - - - - - - - - - - - - - - - - x

Grand Jury Room No. 3
United States District Court
for the District of Columbia
3rd & Constitution, N.W.
Washington, D.C. 20001

Thursday, August 6, 1998

The testimony of MONICA S. LEWINSKY was taken in the presence of a full quorum of Grand Jury 97-2, impaneled on September 19, 1997, commencing at 9:34 a.m., before:

SOLOMON WISENBERG
Deputy Independent Counsel
MICHAEL EMMICK
KARIN IMMERGUT
MARY ANNE WIRTH
Associate Independent Counsel
Office of Independent Counsel
1001 Pennsylvania Avenue, N.W.
Suite 490 North
Washington, D.C. 20004

Diversified Reporting Services, Inc.
1025 VERMONT AVENUE, N.W. SUITE 1250
WASHINGTON, D.C. 20005
(202) 296-2929

722

2

CONTENTS

Diversified Reporting Services, Inc.
1025 VERMONT AVENUE, N.W. SUITE 1250
WASHINGTON, D.C. 20005
(202) 296-2929

P R O C E E D I N G S

Whereupon,

MONICA S. LEWINSKY

was called as a witness and, after having been first duly sworn by the Foreperson of the Grand Jury, was examined and testified as follows:

EXAMINATION

BY MR. EMMICK:

Q Good morning.

A Good morning.

Q Ms. Lewinsky, this is the grand jury appearance that you'll be making or at least the first of the grand jury appearances, if there will be any more. What we routinely do with witnesses before the grand jury is that we begin the appearance by discussing your rights and your obligations and so that's what we'll do right now.

A Okay.

Q What I'd like to say first is that you have a Fifth Amendment right. That Fifth Amendment right is the right to refuse to answer any questions that may tend to incriminate you. Do you understand that right?

A Yes, I do.

Q Now, ordinarily, you could refuse to answer questions that would tend to incriminate you. As I understand it, here you have entered into an agreement with the government that provides you with immunity, in exchange for which you will be cooperating with the government. Is that right?

A Correct.

MR. EMMICK: What I would like to do is show you a copy of what has been marked as Exhibit ML-2.

(Grand Jury Exhibit No. ML-2 was marked for identification.)

BY MR. EMMICK:

Q Do you recognize this?

A Yes, I do.

Q On the third page of that document, there is a signature line that says Monica Lewinsky. Is that your signature?

A Yes, it is.

Q All right. You also have a right to counsel. What that means is that although your attorney cannot be in the grand jury room here with you, your attorney can be outside the grand jury room and available to answer whatever questions you might have. Do you understand that right?

A Yes, I do.

Q Do you have an attorney?

A Yes, I do.

Q Who would that be?

A Several.

Q All right.

A Jake Stein, Plato Cacheris -- do you want me to name all of them who are here or just the lead?

Q All right. Those are the lead counsel?

A Those are the lead counsel.

Q All right. And are they outside?

A Yes, they are.

Q You understand that if you need to speak with them, all you need to say is "I'd like to speak with my attorneys about something for just a minute"?

A Yes.

Q All right. In addition to those two rights that you have, you also have an obligation and that obligation is to tell the truth. That obligation is imposed on you because you have taken an oath and that is the oath to tell the truth. Do you understand that?

A Yes, I do.

Q Do you understand that if you were to intentionally say something that's false, in common parlance, if you were to lie, that would constitute perjury and perjury is a felony and it's punishable by up to five years in prison? Do you understand that?

A Yes.

Q Do you understand as well that because of the agreement that you have signed if you were to lie, if you were to intentionally lie, that would mean that the agreement that you have that gives you immunity could be voided and you could be prosecuted? Do you understand that?

A Mm-hmm.

Q All right. And that in simple parlance, what that means, is that you can retain immunity, but only if you do not lie. Do you understand that?

A Yes.

Q Okay. What I'd like to do is simply discuss with you briefly or clarify with you the fact that we have had interviews with you since the time when you signed this agreement. Is that right?

A Yes.

Q All right. We've had interviews with you, I believe, every day since the signing of the agreement.

A Correct.

Q Several hours a day?

A Yes.

Q Is that right? All right. I also wanted to ask you a question having to do with your mental state right now. How are you feeling?

A Nervous.

Q Okay. I wanted also to ask you, are you taking any medication at this time?

A Yes, I am.

Q What I'd like to ask about that is simply is that having any effect on your ability to recall or to communicate that in some way will hinder your ability to answer questions?

A I don't believe so, but it affects my short-term memory just a little bit.

Q Okay. That's fine. Understand, if you will, that your role today is simply to answer questions that we pose to you.

We have spoken with you for a number of hours, a number of days, and we're going to be asking you to talk about essentially three years of conduct. We are not going to be asking you to recount every detail of the last three years of your life and we are not going to be asking you to recount everything that you've told us over the last ten days or so. You'll just be answering questions and we understand that you have other details that you could provide on other occasions.

A Yes.

MR. EMMICK: All right. What I'd like to do next is to let you know what our approach is going to be today.

What we're going to do is we're going to start off talking about your internship at the White House and then we're going to ask you questions having to do with your relationship with the President.

Because we think that that will proceed more comfortably if those questions are asked by Ms. Immergut, I'm going to turn the questioning over to her and at some point, then, we'll collaborate in asking further follow-up questions. So without further ado --

BY MS. IMMERGUT:

Q Ms. Lewinsky, when did you start working at the White House?

A My internship began July of 1995.

Q And when you say "internship," could you just very briefly describe what it is you were doing and where you were working?

A Sure. I was interning for Mr. Panetta, who was Chief of Staff at that time, and I worked in his correspondence office preparing his correspondence, drafting some of the language.

Q Was there ever a time -- or I guess -- after beginning your internship, how long did you serve as an intern in the White House?

A About four, four and a half months. Four and a half months.

Q And was there ever a time that you then assumed a staff position that was not an intern position?

A Yes.

Q And when would that have been?

A In November of 1995.

Q When did you first notice the President of the United States?

A Our first encounter, I guess non-verbal encounter, was August 9, 1995.

Q And could you describe what that encounter was?

A Yes. It was a departure ceremony on the South Lawn and, as he was going by on the rope line shaking hands, we made eye contact and it was more intense eye contact than I had experienced before with him.

Q Okay. And did you have any further such contact sort of later, after that initial time?

A Yes. The next day the President -- I guess the staff had a birthday party for the President on the South Lawn and the interns were invited to that later in the day. And at that party, there was sort of a more intense flirtation that went on at a distance.

Q Okay. Did you feel that he was flirting with you as well? Or how would you describe the behavior that you both exhibited?

A It was intense eye contact and when he went by the rope line to shake hands, it was -- I mean, he -- he's a charismatic person and so -- just when he shook my hand and -- there was an intense connection.

Q Okay. And could you sort of just summarize the

early relationship that you had with the President before any first sexual contact?

A I think it was intense flirting.

Q Okay. Did you have conversations with him?

A Brief conversations that I think in passing -- if I saw him or -- at a departure ceremony, "Have a nice trip." I introduced myself at one point.

Q Okay. And how did you manage to run into him or even see him? Was that a common occurrence or how would that be accomplished?

A Before the relationship began, it was mainly at departure ceremonies, I think there were a few, and then on one occasion my best friend was in town and she was getting a tour of the West Wing and I was waiting for her in the basement lobby and met him that way. There were several other people there.

Q Okay. Was there ever a time that your relationship became more of a romantic and sexual relationship?

A Yes.

Q And when did that occur?

A On November 15, 1995.

Q Okay. And although as I've told you, I'm not going to go into a lot of specific dates, this is one that I wanted you to explain sort of how it came about.

A It was during the furlough. I was up in

Mr. Panetta's West Wing office answering phones. The President came down several times during the day.

There was the continued flirtation and around 8:00 in the evening or so I was in the hallway going to the restroom, passing Mr. Stephanopoulos' office, and he was in the hall and invited me into Mr. Stephanopoulos' office and then from there invited me back into his study.

Q Okay. And what happened there?

A We talked briefly and sort of acknowledged that there had been a chemistry that was there before and that we were both attracted to each other and then he asked me if he could kiss me.

Q And what did you say?

A Yes.

Q And did you kiss on that occasion?

A Yes.

Q And where in the -- you mentioned you went back to the study area.

A Mm-hmm.

Q Where exactly did the kiss occur?

A Right outside his bathroom, in the hallway, inside -- adjacent to the study, to the office.

Q Okay. And how did you end that -- was there anything more than a romantic kiss on that sort of first encounter?

A No.

Q Okay. Did you have any later encounter with him on that same date?

A Yes, I did.

Q Okay. Could you describe how that occurred?

A The President came down to Mr. Panetta's office, I think it might have been around 10 p.m., and told me that if I wanted to meet him back in Mr. Stephanopoulos' office in five minutes, that that would be fine. And I agreed. And I met him back there. We went back to his office again, in the back study area.

Q Okay. And what happened in the back study area?

A We talked and we were more physically intimate.

Q Okay. And on that occasion, did you perform oral sex on the President?

A Yes.

Q With respect to physical intimacy, other than oral sex, was there other physical intimacy performed?

A Yes. Everything up until oral sex.

MS. IMMERGUT: Okay. And just for the grand jury purposes, I have marked as an exhibit ML-6 and I'll just read it the grand jury and place it before you.

(Grand Jury Exhibit No. ML-6 was marked for identification.)

MS. IMMERGUT: It states "Definition of Sexual

Relations. For the purposes of this grand jury session, a person engages in 'sexual relations' when the person knowingly engages or causes contact with the genitalia, anus, groin, breast, inner thigh, or buttocks of any person with an intent to arouse or gratify the sexual desire of any person. Contact means intentional touching, either directly or through clothing."

BY MS. IMMERGUT:

Q Ms. Lewinsky, do you understand that definition?

A Yes, I do.

MS. IMMERGUT: And I do have copies to pass out to the grand jury.

BY MS. IMMERGUT:

Q When you described that you had other physical intimacy during your contact with the President on November 15, 1995, did that include sexual relations within the definition that I've just read to you?

A Yes, it does.

Q In that -- again, that second contact with him on November 15, 1995, where exactly did the sexual contact that you've described occur?

A In the same hallway, by the back study, and then also in his back office.

Q Okay. And the back office, would that be the study area?

A Yes.

Q Okay. Did you have any further sexual encounters with him after that first time on the 15th?

A Yes.

Q When was the next time?

A On the 17th of November.

Q And could you explain how that contact occurred?

A We were again working late because it was during the furlough and Jennifer Palmieri and I, who was Mr. Panetta's assistant, had ordered pizza along with Ms. Currie and Ms. Hernreich.

And when the pizza came, I went down to let them know that the pizza was there and it as at that point when I walked into Ms. Currie's office that the President was standing there with some other people discussing something.

And they all came back down to the office and Mr. -- I think it was Mr. Toiv, somebody accidently knocked pizza on my jacket, so I went to go use the restroom to wash it off and as I was coming out of the restroom, the President was standing in Ms. Currie's doorway and said, "You can come out this way."

So we went back into his back study area, actually, I think, in the bathroom or in the hallway right near the bathroom, and we were intimate.

Q Okay. And at that point, what sort of intimacy was it?

A I believe it was just kissing at that point.

Q Okay. And how did that encounter end?

A I said I needed to back and he said, "Well, why don't you bring me some pizza?" So I asked him if he wanted vegetable or meat.

Q Okay. And, actually, where did the kissing occur that time?

A It was -- I think it was in the bathroom or it was right outside the bathroom, in the hallway adjacent to the bathroom.

Q Okay. So did you go back and get him some pizza?

A Yes, I did.

BY MR. WISENBERG:

Q Pardon me. Sorry to interrupt. That's the bathroom adjacent to the hallway that leads from the Oval Office to the dining room. Is that correct?

A Correct.

MR. WISENBERG: Sorry for interrupting.

BY MS. IMMERGUT:

Q Did you go back and get pizza?

A Yes, I did.

Q And did you ever return to the President with the pizza?

A Yes, I did.

Q Could you describe what happened when you returned?

A Yes. I went back to Ms. Currie's office and told her the President had asked me to bring him some pizza.

She opened the door and said, "Sir, the girl's here with the pizza." He told me to come in. Ms. Currie went back into her office and then we went into the back study area again.

Q Okay. And what happened in the back study area?

A We were in the -- well, we talked and then we were physically intimate again.

Q Okay. And was there oral sex performed on that occasion?

A Yes.

Q Okay. And that would be you performing oral sex on him?

A Mm-hmm.

Q Okay. And, again -- and I have to sort of tell you, you can't answer "Mm-hmm" --

A Oh, sorry.

Q Just yes or no, just for the record. With respect to the physical intimacy again, does that fall -- when you say "physical intimacy," do you mean sexual relations within the definition?

A Yes, I do.

Q Now, without going into sort of a lot of details of specific dates, I wanted to ask you some general questions about the relationship and to make clear, although we've already -- Mr. Emmick already asked you whether or not you've met with us on several occasions, is it fair to say you've given us many, many details about each of the specific dates involved in the relationship?

A Yes.

Q Did the relationship with the President develop into or also have a non-sexual component to it?

A Yes, it did.

Q Could you describe sort of that aspect of the relationship for the grand jury?

A We enjoyed talking to each other and being with each other. We were very affectionate.

Q What sorts of things would you talk about?

A We would tell jokes. We would talk about our childhoods. Talk about current events. I was always giving him my stupid ideas about what I thought should be done in the administration or different views on things. I think back on it and he always made me smile when I was with him. It was a lot of -- he was sunshine.

Q And did he make you feel like he enjoyed your being there and talking to you about things?

A Yes.

Q Were there times that you visited him in the Oval Office where there was no sexual contact at all?

A Yes.

Q Was there sort of affectionate contact during some of those times?

A Very. Yes.

Q Okay. And how would you describe sort of affectionate but non-sexual contact?

A A lot of hugging, holding hands sometimes. He always used to push the hair out of my face.

Q Okay. Could you describe generally how those meetings were set up or how those encounters were actually set up as a general matter?

A After the first few incidents that sort of happened during the furlough, they were set up -- when I was working in Legislative Affairs, usually the President would call my office on a weekend.

He had told me earlier on that he was usually around on the weekends and that it was okay to come see him on the weekends. So he would call and we would arrange either to bump into each other in the hall or that I would bring papers to the office.

Do you want me to do after?

Q Okay. Then what happened after?

A Once I left the White House, Ms. Currie arranged

the visits.

Q Okay. And how would she arrange those, typically?

A I don't understand. I'm sorry.

Q When you say Ms. Currie would arrange them, how would it come about that they would be set up?

A Usually either through my talking to the President prior to and then him talking to Ms. Currie or me bugging Ms. Currie to ask the President.

Q Okay. All right. Did the relationship after the events you've described of November 15th and 17th, did it continue also to have a sexual component?

A Yes, it did.

Q After the two incidents that you've described, did you have further sexual contact with him?

A Yes.

Q And I'm going to ask you just some general questions about that. The grand jurors heard that there's a chart and we'll sort of go through a chart afterwards in less detail. Approximately how many times do you recall performing oral sex on the President?

A I think about nine.

Q Did he ever perform oral sex on you?

A No. We had discussed it and there were times when it almost happened, but mother nature was in the way.

Q Okay. How many times did he ejaculate when you

performed oral sex?

A In my presence?

Q In your presence.

A Twice.

Q Okay. And do you recall the dates of those times?

A Mm-hmm. February 28, 1997 and March -- I think it's the 29th, 1997.

Q Did you engage, other than oral sex, in other physical intimacy that would fall within the definition of sexual relations that we've read to you?

A Yes.

Q Were you alone with the President when you had these sexual encounters with him?

A Yes.

Q It seems like an obvious question, but I have to ask it. Did the President ever have telephone calls while you were actually engaging with oral sex with him?

A Twice.

Q And when those telephone calls occurred, did he ever talk on the phone while you were performing oral sex?

A Yes.

Q Do you have any recollection about when those occurred?

A I believe one was November 15, 1995, in my second visit with him, and I know April 7, 1996.

741

21

Q Okay. Did you ever have sexual intercourse with the President?

A No.

Q Was there ever a time when your genitals actually touched each other?

A Grazed each other, yes.

Q And do you remember when that occurred?

A Yes. February 28, 1997. Oh, no. I'm sorry. March 29th, not February 28th. Sorry.

Q Okay. And could you explain why you didn't have sexual intercourse with him?

A He didn't want to. The President said that he -- that at his age, that there was too much of a consequence in doing that and that when I got to be his age I would understand. But I wasn't happy with that.

Q Okay. I want to move away from that now.

A Okay.

Q And ask you whether or not you've ever spoken to the President on the telephone.

A Yes.

Q And can you estimate approximately how many times since the beginning of your relationship with him that you've spoken to him on the phone?

A Over 50, probably.

Q And has he initiated any of those calls?

A Yes.

Q Do you have any sort of idea how many times he's called you?

A Most of those phone calls were calls that he placed to me directly.

Q Okay. Did he ever leave any messages for you at your home?

A Yes.

Q And you remember about how many times he left messages?

A I think about four.

Q Did you save any of those messages?

A Yes, I did.

Q And have you provided any cassette tape of those messages to the OIC?

A Yes, I have.

Q Do you remember any particular messages that he left you?

A I remember them all.

Q Okay. Why don't you just tell the grand jury what they say.

A They're pretty innocuous. Sometimes -- or one time, it was, you know, "Sorry I missed you." One time, it was just "Hello." And then one time he called really late at night when I was not at home and it was whispered kind of loudly, you know, "Come on. It's me." Something like that. It was always nice to hear his voice.

Q Okay. Did he ever tell you how he felt about leaving messages on your home machine?

A Yes.

Q What did he tell you about that?

A I believe it was the beginning of 1996, at some point, he just remarked that he didn't like to do that, he just -- I think felt it was a little unsafe.

Q Okay. Did he ever call you late at night?

A Yes.

Q Can you tell us a little bit about that? Did that happen on many occasions?

A Yes. He's a night owl, so it would be customary for him to call sometimes 2:00 in the morning, 2:30 in the morning.

Q Okay. What sorts of things did you discuss with him generally of a non-sexual nature on your telephone calls with him?

A Similar to what we discussed in person, just how we were doing. A lot of discussions about my job, when I was trying to come back to the White House and then once I decided to move to New York. We told jokes. We talked about everything under the sun.

Q Okay. Was there ever a time that you began to

engage in phone sex on the telephone?

A Mm-hmm. Yes.

Q And do you remember when that started to occur?

A In the beginning of 1996.

Q Okay. Did he participate in that?

A Yes.

Q Okay. And about how many times did you have phone sex with him, if you know?

A Oh, maybe 10, 15. I'm not really -- I'm not really sure.

Q Okay. We can look at the chart after to refresh your recollection, but that sounds sort of ballpark?

A I think so.

Q More than 10, about? In your view?

A Yes, I think so.

Q Did the President ever tell you that he wanted to end the sexual relationship with you?

A Yes.

Q And did he tell you that more than once?

A Yes.

Q Could you tell us when he told you that?

A February -- it was Presidents Day of 1996. I think that's February 19th. And also on May 24, 1996 -- no, 1997. I'm sorry.

Q And just for the grand jury's information, on the

chart that we're going to show them in a little bit, how do you list -- do you have a term that you refer to the May 24, 1997 meeting with him?

A D-day.

Q And what does that stand for?

A Dump day.

Q And on those two occasions, what did he tell you about wanting to end the relationship? Just generally.

A Both were, I think, motivated sort of by guilt and just not wanting to -- more I think on the 24th of May in '97, just really wanting to do the right thing in God's eyes and do the right thing for his family and he just -- he didn't feel right about it.

Q Did you engage in sexual contact with him after those times?

A Yes. Kissing.

Q Okay. After the -- well, after the February 19, 1996 time?

A Yes. Yes.

Q And what about after the May 24, 1997 time?

A Just kissing.

Q Did your relationship involve giving gifts to each other?

A Mm-hmm. Yes. I'm sorry.

Q And did you give any gifts to him?

A Yes.

Q Do you have any sort of ballpark figure of how many gifts you've given to him since you've known him?

A About 30.

Q And what about him to you? Do you have any estimate of how many gifts he gave you?

A I think about 18.

Q Did you ever write him any notes or letters or cards?

A Yes.

Q And what sort of cards or letters or notes would you write to him?

A It varied on the occasion. It could be a funny card that I saw or a Halloween card. If I was angry, it could be an angry letter. If I was missing him, it was a missing him letter.

Q Okay. So were some of them -- is it fair to say some of them were romantic in nature?

A Yes.

Q And when they were angry, what would you be angry about in your letters or cards?

A Either job-related issues or him not paying enough attention to me.

Q Okay. Did he write you any letters or notes?

A No.

Q Did he ever say why he wasn't writing you any letters or notes?

A No.

MS. IMMERGUT: I'd now like to show you what I had previously marked as Exhibit 7, I believe. Perhaps somebody has the other original version.

(Grand Jury Exhibit No. ML-7 was marked for identification.)

BY MS. IMMERGUT:

Q I'm going to place this before you and ask if you recognize that chart.

A Yes, I do.

Q And have you seen that chart before?

A Yes, I have.

Q Did you assist the Office of Independent Counsel in preparing that chart?

A Yes.

Q Did you provide all of the information that's listed on that chart?

A Yes.

Q Could you describe for the grand jury just generally what is described by that chart?

A I think it's a chronology that marks some of the highlights of my relationship with the President. It definitely includes the visits that I had with him and most of the gifts that we exchanged. It reflects most of the phone calls that I remember.

Q And to the best of your knowledge, is the chart accurate?

A Yes.

Q Have you noticed anything that you would add or delete from the chart since you've reviewed it?

A Yes. On page --

MS. IMMERGUT: Do the grand jurors have the chart?

MR. EMMICK: They do. Yes.

THE WITNESS: On page 5, the last entry in the chart, on 10/23, I attended a Democratic fundraiser that you guys have all probably seen on T.V. lately.

BY MS. IMMERGUT:

Q Okay. Anything else that you've noticed?

A No.

Q Okay. Otherwise, would you say that the chart is a pretty accurate rendition or description of your memory of all of the events?

A Yes.

Q How is it that you remember all the events in such detail over really sort of what is a few years?

A I've always been a date-oriented person and I had a -- probably a habit of circling dates in my Filofax when I either talked to the President or saw him.

Q And did you provide those Filofax sheets to the Office of Independent Counsel?

A Yes.

Q And did that assist you in remembering the dates?

A Yes, it did.

Q And were these encounters important to you?

A Very.

Q And, again, on that chart there are various categories. In the visit category -- or descriptions in the visit category area that are described as physical intimacy. And with respect to all of those, do they fall within the definition of sexual relations that I've presented as Exhibit 6 to the grand jury?

A Yes.

Q So anywhere physical intimacy is listed on the chart, it falls within that definition. Is that correct?

A Right. I think the only thing that might be missing is kissing.

Q Okay. And kissing is separately described on the chart, is it not?

A No, not necessarily.

Q Okay.

A I mean, because the physical intimacy -- wherever there's physical intimacy, there was always -- there was always kissing.

Q Okay. But where there's physical intimacy, there was also then more than kissing.

A Correct.

Q Okay. So physical intimacy is never on the chart to describe only kissing.

A Correct.

Q Okay. There's one particular date also that I wanted to cover with you which is February 28, 1997.

A Okay.

Q Because at that time, as the chart demonstrates, you haven't really seen the President since April of the year before. Could you describe what the circumstances were leading up to your visit with him on February 28, 1997?

A The President had told me in December that he had a Christmas present for me and I ended up not getting it until the end of February. Ms. Currie called me at work during that week to -- or I guess it was that day, I'm sorry, that -- Friday, to invite me to a radio address that evening.

I went to the radio address and when I went to take my picture with the President, he said to go see Betty because he had something to give me after. So I waited a little while for him and then Betty and the President and I went into the back office.

Q Okay. And why did Betty come in the back office with you?

751

31

A I later found out that -- I believe it was Stephen Goodin who said to Ms. Currie and the President that the President couldn't be alone with me, so Ms. Currie came back into the back office with us.

Q And then what?

A And then left.

Q Okay. She left? And do you know where she went?

A I came to learn later, I believe she was in the pantry. In the back pantry.

Q Okay. And how did you learn that later?

A I think that Mr. Nelvis told me. Or Ms. Currie told me.

Q Okay. What happened when she went to the back pantry? Did you remain with the President?

A Yes, I did.

Q And could you describe what you and the President did?

A Mm-hmm. He gave me my hat pin and the book "Leaves of Grass" and I was pestering him to kiss me and so we moved -- that was in the back study and then we moved over to the back hallway by the bathroom and we were physically intimate.

Q Okay. And did you perform oral sex on that occasion?

A Yes.

Q And how did you -- do you remember what dress you were wearing on that occasion?

A Yes.

Q What dress was it?

A The navy blue dress from The Gap.

Q And after that incident, did you ever tell Linda Tripp that there might be the President's semen on that dress?

A Yes, I did.

Q And why did you tell her that? Or did you believe that that could be true?

A I thought it was possible.

Q Were you positive it was true?

A No.

Q Back to the incident with the President, how did you leave it with him on that occasion? Sort of once you finished the visit, what happened?

A Betty came back into the back study and then I think Ms. Currie walked me out.

Q Okay. How much about your relationship with the President did you tell Linda Tripp?

A A lot. Most everything.

Q Okay. And did you tell her about the sexual encounters that you had with him?

A Yes.

Q Did you also tell her about the emotional encounters and the gifts?

A Yes.

Q Were you truthful about the relationship when you told Linda Tripp about it?

A Most of the time, but sometimes -- there were occasions when I wasn't truthful.

Q Were you truthful about the sexual parts of the relationship with her?

A Yes.

Q And what about the emotional component, when you would tell her -- and why don't I say before December of 1997, were you truthful about the emotional components of the relationship?

A Yes.

Q I'm actually done with my questioning on that. Do you want to break now or continue to different subjects?

A A five-minute break? Could I --

THE FOREPERSON: We can take a ten-minute break.

MS. IMMERGUT: Okay. A ten-minute break.

MR. EMMICK: A ten-minute break.

MS. IMMERGUT: Would that be all right?

THE WITNESS: Okay.

MR. EMMICK: That's fine.

(Witness excused. Witness recalled.)

MS. IMMERGUT: Madam Foreperson, are there any unauthorized persons present?

THE FOREPERSON: No, there are none.

MS. IMMERGUT: Do we have a quorum?

THE FOREPERSON: Yes, we do.

Ms. Lewinsky, I would like to remind you that you are still under oath.

THE WITNESS: Thank you.

BY MS. IMMERGUT:

Q Ms. Lewinsky, the grand jurors had a few follow-up questions --

A Sure.

Q -- for you that I wanted to ask you before we move on to other topics. You mentioned that on the occasions where you had sexual contact with that were described, sexual contact with the President, that it occurred in the hallway, as you described, or sometimes in the back study.

A Mm-hmm.

Q Why did --

A JUROR: Pardon me.

BY MS. IMMERGUT:

Q Oh, excuse me. Why did you choose the hallway?

A Because I believe it was -- it was really more the President choosing the hallway, I think, and it was -- there weren't any windows there. It was the most secluded of all the places in the back office. Well, that's not true. The bathroom is the most secluded, I guess, because you can close the door.

Q And did you sometimes have sexual encounters in the bathroom?

A Mm-hmm.

Q And then next to the bathroom, would you say that the hallway is --

A Right.

Q -- off the study is the next most --

A He has a bad back and so I think a lot of times we ended up just sort of standing there and talking there because he could close the door to the bathroom and lean up against the bathroom and then he was -- I guess it made his back feel better and also made him a little shorter. So --

Q Did the President ever tell you he was concerned about being seen?

A I'm sure that came up in conversation.

BY MR. EMMICK:

Q Did he ever indicate to you looking outside that he might be concerned, for example?

A Yes, yes.

BY MS. IMMERGUT:

Q Can you describe that?

A Sure. I think the one that comes to mind was

actually December 28th of last year when I was getting my Christmas kiss. And he was kissing me in the doorway between the back study, or the office, and the hallway, and I sort of opened my eyes and he was looking out the window with his eyes wide open while he was kissing me and then I got mad because it wasn't very romantic. And then so then he said, "Well, I was just looking to see to make sure no one was out there."

Q Can you generalize about the locations where you had your sexual encounters with the President?

A I'd say they mainly took place in that hallway, but there were occasions on which we were intimate in the office and then also in the bathroom.

Q Okay. And when you say the office, do you mean the back study?

A Right.

Q So not the Oval Office?

A No, no, we were never physically intimate in the Oval Office.

Q Okay. Did you notice whether doors were closed when you were physically intimate with him in the back study or hallway?

A No, he always -- well, I'm not sure about the door going in the dining room but I know that the door leading from the back hallway to the -- into the Oval Office was always kept ajar so that he could hear if someone was coming.

BY MR. WISENBERG:

Q How ajar? How much ajar?

A Maybe this much (indicating).

BY MR. EMMICK:

Q You're indicating six to eight inches, something like that?

A I'm not very good with that.

Q A foot or less, something like that?

A A foot or less. I guess that's -- I would assume that's --

Q Enough so that one could hear more easily what was going on in the next room?

A Mm-hmm. Right, or if someone came in to holler for him.

BY MS. IMMERGUT:

Q Now directing your attention back to February 28th, -- 1997, the day that you wore the blue cocktail dress --

A It's not a cocktail dress.

Q Okay, I'm sorry.

A No, that's okay. I'm a little defensive about this subject. I'm sorry.

Q How would you describe the dress?

A It's a dress from the Gap. It's a work dress. It's a casual dress.

Q With respect to that dress --

A Right, I'm sorry.

Q -- you mentioned that you believe that there could be semen on it. Could you describe what you did with the President that led you to believe that?

A We were in the bathroom and -- can I close my eyes so I don't have to --

Q Well, you have to speak up. That's the only --

A Okay. We were in the bathroom and I was performing oral sex. I'm sorry, this is embarrassing. And usually he doesn't want to -- he didn't want to come to completion.

Q Ejaculate?

A Yes. And this has sort of been a subject that we had talked about many times before and he was always saying it had issues to do with trust and not knowing me well enough at first and then not feeling right about things, and not that he said this but I took away from that to sort of mean that maybe in his mind if he didn't come then maybe it wasn't -- he didn't need to feel guilty about that, that maybe with it not coming to completion that that was easier for him to rationalize.

And it was on this occasion that since we hadn't been alone together since April 7th of '96 that after we had engaged in oral sex for a while and he stopped me as he normally did, I said to him, you know -- this is so

759

embarrassing, I'm sorry. I said to him, you know, I really -- I want to make you come. I mean, this is --

Q Okay. Why don't you just describe the position that you were in once he had tried to stop you. What did you do that led you to believe there might get semen on your dress?

A I told him that I really cared about him and he told me that he didn't want to get addicted to me and he didn't want me to get addicted to him, and we embraced at that point and that's -- I mean, it was -- it's just a little tiny spot down here and a little tiny spot up here and --

Q Okay. And to get -- when you're pointing down here, you mean sort of your right lower hip area?

A Well, one of my -- I don't know if it was my right or left, but lower hip area.

Q Okay. And the chest area would be the second place that you thought you might have gotten some?

A Mm-hmm.

Q And is that from when you -- when you did actually continue to perform oral sex on him later?

A I believe so.

Q Did you ever see something that you thought was semen on the dress that led you to conclude that?

A The next time I went to wear the dress.

Q So at the time you didn't notice anything on the

dress?

A I don't believe so.

Q Okay. What happened then the next time you wore the dress that led you to conclude that?

A Well, I also -- can I say here? I also -- I think I wore the dress out to dinner that night, so which is why I'm not sure that that's what it is.

Q Okay.

A So it could be spinach dip or something. I don't know. I'm sorry, could you repeat the question?

Q Sure. When was the -- when was it that you at least began to believe that maybe there was semen on the dress?

A I really don't remember when it was the next time I went to wear the dress, but I gained weight so I couldn't wear the dress and it didn't fit. And I'm not a very organized person. I don't clean my clothes until I'm going to wear them again.

Q Did you notice there was something on the dress?

A Yes. And at that point I noticed it and I kind of thought, oh, this is dirty, it needs to get cleaned. And then I remembered that I had worn it the last time I saw the President, and I believe it was at that point that I thought to myself, oh, no. And it was -- it --

Q So at that point, you weren't positive what it was.

And why did you tell Linda that you thought there was semen on the dress?

A I think it just sort of came up in conversation somehow and then -- as kind of this funny, gross thing. And then the next time she was at my house I still couldn't fit into the dress and believe that I said to her, oh, look, you want to see this? You know, this is what I was talking about.

And but I just want to say because I know everybody here reads the newspapers and listens to TV that I didn't keep this dress as a souvenir. I was going to wear it on Thanksgiving and my cousins, who I always try to look skinny for because they are all skinny -- and I know it sounds stupid. And when I told Linda I was thinking about wearing the dress, she discouraged me. She brought me one of her jackets from her thinner closet. And so it wasn't a souvenir. I was going to clean it. I was going to wear it again.

Q Different topic. Where was Nel when you were -- or do you have any idea where Nel was when you were in the hallway or the study with the President?

A On which --

Q On any of the occasions. I mean, would Nel be around generally?

A There were some occasions that -- very few

762

42

occasions, I think, that Nel was there -- was at the White House. And I don't know where he would have necessarily -- I think he was in the pantry on the 28th of February.

Q Do you know where he was on any of the other occasions? And, again, where you had sexual contact with the President.

A I don't think so.

Q Did you ever use hand towels in the bathroom to wipe your lipstick?

A Hand towels, no.

Q What about tissues?

A I believe I used a tissue sometimes to wipe off my lipstick.

MR. WISENBERG: Karen, can I ask something really quick?

MS. IMMERGUT: Sure.

BY MR. WISENBERG:

Q How about, do you think Nel would have been around on renaissance -- right before the departure for renaissance weekend?

A New Year's Eve '95?

Q Yeah.

A Yes, he was.

Q Also, did you ever show -- did -- I don't -- it's my bad. Did you ever show the dress to Linda Tripp?

A Yes.

MR. EMMICK:

Q You mentioned that the President called you on a number of occasions. Some of those occasions included phone sex. Did he indicate where he was when he was placing those calls?

A Not always, but sometimes.

Q And where did he say he was when he did say where he was?

A At home.

Q Meaning the White House residence?

A Yes.

Q Where else might he have placed calls from?

A There were, I think, two times that he placed calls from the campaign term, from Florida I think.

Q Do you know whether he sometimes placed calls from the Oval Office or other places?

A Yes, yes.

Q How do you know that?

A Sometimes he would mention it and say he was in the office. I know one time I said -- I knew he was in the office and I asked him if he was in the back or could he go in the back.

Q Did he not only call you, what, at your home but also call you at your office?

A When I was working at the White House, yes.

Q But not while you were working at the Pentagon?

A He never directly called me when I was working at the Pentagon.

Q When you say didn't directly call, what do you mean?

A I mean he -- there were, I think, maybe two occasions when I was working at the Pentagon when Betty placed a call for him, and when that didn't occur he picked up the phone and dialed the phone number himself.

Q When he placed calls to you when you were at Leg Affairs, or Legislative Affairs, excuse me, was there anything that indicated on your caller ID?

A Yes. When he called from the Oval Office, the phones have a caller ID up at the top, and when he calls from the Oval Office it says POTUS and when he calls from the residence it has an asterisk.

Q And did you ever discuss with him the fact that you had POTUS on your ID?

A Yeah.

Q Tell us about that.

A I think one time when he called and I picked up the phone I said something that indicated to him that I knew who it was. And he said, "Well, how did you know it was me?" And I told him, "Well, don't you know that it lights up POTUS

765

45

when you call from the Oval Office?" And he said, "No, I didn't know that." So I thought that was funny.

Q When you --

A And he made an effort one time to call me from the residence on a line and called and said, "Did it show up a phone number instead of -- " So it had. He seemed proud of himself.

Q All right. You had mentioned earlier that on, I think it was February 28th, Steve Goodin spoke with Betty and the President about being -- about him being alone with you.

A Mm-hmm.

Q Could you give us a little more detail about what you saw and what you later learned and where you later learned it so that we can figure out what you know from personal knowledge?

A Okay. What I saw was Steve Goodin and Ms. Currie going into the Oval Office. I think --

Q Where are you at this time?

A Oh, I'm sorry. I was in Ms. Currie's office and I was waiting with Ms. Currie. And I believe Stephen was there at some point and he might have gone into the Oval Office first and then called Ms. Currie in a few minutes after or maybe the President called her in after. And they spoke sort of --

A JUROR: (Coughing.)

THE WITNESS: Do you want some water? Oh, okay So --

BY MR. EMMICK:

Q Was there anyone else in the Oval Office, as far as you know?

A It's possible I think I might have seen Rahm Emanuel in there at some point, but I'm not really sure that he was included in this conversation.

Q So they go into the Oval Office, and what do you next see or hear?

A I believe Betty came out to get me. I was really nervous because I hadn't been alone with the President since the elections so I was focused -- I was kind of internal, focused on being nervous.

Q Betty came out to get you and what did the two of you do?

A The three of us went into the back office.

Q You had mentioned earlier that you later came to learn that there was a discussion between them, between them, about you and the President and whether you should be alone. Tell us when you learned that approximately and what you learned.

A I think I learned it, I believe, maybe shortly after -- not on that day, maybe within the next few weeks, guess -- that Stephen had said to the President or maybe had

767

47

said to Betty, you know, she can't be alone with him. So, and I don't recall if I learned that from Ms. Currie or from Nel.

BY MR. WISENBERG:

Q But it -- was it when, based on what you were told, it was a conversation between -- it was a conversation in which Goodin, Ms. Currie and the President were there?

A Correct.

BY MR. EMMICK:

Q Let's focus a little bit about the Presidential aides. You mentioned Steve Goodin. Where are the aides at the time you are having your encounters, if we can call them that, with the President?

A Most of the time they weren't -- they weren't there. They weren't at the White House.

Q And how was that arranged?

A When I was working in Legislative Affairs, I don't think -- I don't know if it was ever verbally spoken but it was understood between the President and myself that most of the -- most people weren't in on the weekends so there was -- it would be safer to do that then.

And then after I left the White House, that was sort of always a concern that Betty and I had just because she knew and I knew that a lot of people there didn't like me.

Q So is it fair to say then that the Presidential aides, whether they be Steve Goodin or Andrew Friendly or whoever it might be, were not around at the time?

A Correct. They may have been but --

Q Mm-hmm. I wonder if you could expand a little bit on the nature of your relationship with Betty and then the nature of your relationship with Nel, and specifically what we mean to ask is to what extent were these relationships genuine relationships and to what extent were they, in part, based on an interest in cultivating their friendship because of your relationship with the President?

A I think that they -- both of them started out probably at the latter of what you said, as maybe a function of making my relationship with the President easier, or for me, I guess, getting information, but that they both came to have a very genuine component to them. I still care very deeply about Betty.

Q When you talk about getting information, could you expand on what you mean by that?

A I think sometimes if it was from Ms. Currie finding out what the President's schedule was, when he might be around, what might be a good time to come by or maybe for her to talk to him to let him know something.

With Nel, Nel and I developed a friendship that started during the furlough and I thought he was a really

769

49

nice guy and didn't get treated correctly or properly, I guess. And the kind of information, he sort of just would give me information about the President. I mean, I don't think that was the only -- that wasn't the only component of the friendship, but that was a component of it.

Q You have discussed how Betty helped arrange for you to come visit the President, especially in 1997, I think it would be fair to say.

A Yes.

Q When those arrangements were made, who initiated the arrangements? How did they start off? Did you ask? Did the President ask? Did Betty ask?

A I'd say most of the time it was probably me asking -- either asking the President directly or asking him through Betty or through sending a note of some sort. And there were occasions that he initiated, so it would come through Betty.

Q All right. Let me ask you the following question. You have described the ways that Betty helped let you in --

A Mm-hmm.

Q -- facilitate the relationship, if you will. Do you think Betty Currie knew about your relationship with the President?

A I don't know. It's possible she could have gleaned that from witnessing that the -- you know, that the President was having a relationship that caused -- with a 25 year-old woman or, at the time, younger -- you know, that made me emotional. But I really can't answer that question.

Q She saw you under circumstances where she realized you and the President had an emotional tie.

A I believe so. I'm not really -- I'm not really comfortable sort of answering questions about what -- you know, what Betty knew because --

Q Well, then let me focus more on what Betty was in a position to see.

A Okay.

Q Was Betty in a position to see that you and the President visited frequently and had a strong emotional attachment?

A I believe so, yes.

Q Did you ever expressly tell Betty about the relationship?

A What aspect of the relationship?

Q Well, let me separate it out for you.

A Okay.

Q Did you ever expressly tell Betty about the emotional aspect of the relationship?

A I believe I characterized that to her.

Q Did you ever expressly tell Betty about the sexual aspect of the relationship?

A No, I don't believe so.

Q Let me ask the question, why not?

A Because it's not appropriate. I mean, I think -- I don't think people necessarily talk about these things. I mean, there is a difference between a relationship that you have with someone who is sort of involved in a situation, and then the kind of relationship you have with a friend whom you talk to. I think with -- a little bit with Betty's age and it wasn't clear to me that the -- you know, the President didn't tell her so, if he didn't tell her, why should I tell her.

Q Let me ask similar questions about Nel. Do you think Nel knew?

A Nel knew --

Q About the emotional aspect of the relationship?

A Yes, I think so.

Q Is that based on what you told him or what you think he must have seen, or both?

A I think probably based more on what I told him.

Q Do you think Nel knew about the sexual aspect of the relationship?

A We never directly discussed it, so I don't know if -- I don't know how to answer that.

Q Did he ever say things to you that made you think that he must know about the sexual aspect of the

772

51

relationship?

A Not that I remember.

Q You mentioned earlier, perhaps an obvious thing, that you were alone with the President on the times that you had sexual contact with the President.

A Yes.

Q Were there also times when you were alone with the President that you did not have sexual contact with the President?

A Mm-hmm, yes.

Q Can you give us sort of a general description about how those encounters occurred and where they occurred?

A Okay. There were numerous that ranged from the beginning of our relationship till the end of our relationship.

Q Were some of them brief? Were some of them substantial in length?

A Mm-hmm, yes.

Q Where within the White House would those have occurred?

A One occurred in the Oval Office and then the others occurred -- oh, that's not true. Two occurred in the Oval Office and the others were in the back study area.

I should also just -- maybe I could just add right now that every -- that every time I had a visit with the

President when I was working there -- not after, but when I was working there -- we usually would -- we'd start in the back and we'd talk and that was where we were physically intimate, and we'd usually end up, kind of the pillow talk of it, I guess, was sitting in the Oval Office talking. So there's --

BY MR. WISENBERG:

Q And, again, when you say when you started in the back, that could either be the hallway or the back?

A Correct, yes.

BY MR. EMMICK:

Q I would like to ask you some questions about any steps you took to try to keep your relationship with the President secret.

A A lot.

Q All right. Well, why don't we just ask the question open-endedly and we'll follow up.

A Okay. I'm sure, as everyone can imagine, that this is a kind of relationship that you keep quiet, and we both wanted to be careful being in the White House. Whenever I would visit him during -- when -- during my tenure at the White House, we always -- unless it was sort of a chance meeting on a weekend and then we ended up back in the office, we would usually plan that I would either bring papers, or one time we had actually accidentally bumped into each other in the hall and went from that way, so then we planned to do that again because that seemed to work well. But we always -- there was always some sort of a cover.

Q When you say that you planned to bring papers, did you ever discuss with the President the fact that you would try to use that as a cover?

A Yes.

Q Okay. What did the two of you say in those conversations?

A I don't remember exactly. I mean, in general, it might have been something like me saying, well, maybe once I got there kind of saying, "Oh, gee, here are your letters," wink, wink, wink, and him saying, "Okay, that's good," or --

Q And as part of this concealment, if you will, did you carry around papers when you went to the visit the President while you worked at Legislative Affairs?

A Yes, I did.

Q Did you ever actually bring him papers to sign as part of business?

A No.

Q Did you actually bring him papers at all?

A Yes.

Q All right. And tell us a little about that.

A It varied. Sometimes it was just actual copies of letters. One time I wrote a really stupid poem. Sometimes I

775

55

put gifts in the folder which I brought.

Q And even on those occasions, was there a legitimate business purpose to that?

A No.

Q Did you have any discussions with the President about what you would say about your frequent visits with him after you had left Legislative Affairs?

A Yes.

Q Yes. What was that about?

A I think we -- we discussed that -- you know, the backwards route of it was that Betty always needed to be the one to clear me in so that, you know, I could always say I was coming to see Betty.

Q And is there some truth in the notion that you were coming to see Betty?

A Coming to see Betty, I don't know. Did I -- I saw Betty on every time that I was there.

Q What was your purpose though in going --

A My purpose was -- most of the time my purpose was to see the President, but there were some times when I did just go see Betty but the President wasn't in the office.

Q When the President was in the office, was your purpose in going there to see the President?

A Yes.

Q What about the writing of things down on paper?

Diversified Reporting Services, Inc.
1025 VERMONT AVENUE, N.W. SUITE 1250
WASHINGTON, D.C. 20005
(202) 296-2929

Was there any discussion between you and the President about the risks of writing things down and whether you should write things down?

A Yes.

Q All right. Tell us about that.

A There were on some occasions when I sent him cards or notes that I wrote things that he deemed too personal to put on paper just in case something ever happened, if it got lost getting there or someone else opened it. So there were several times when he remarked to me, you know, you shouldn't put that on paper.

Q We'll have occasion to get into some details about that in a bit. I don't know how to ask this question more delicately, so I'll just ask you. Did you take any steps to try to be careful with how loud you might be in sexual matters?

A Yes.

Q All right. Can you tell us, as discreetly as you can and as -- about that?

A I think we were both aware of the volume and sometimes I'd use my hand -- I bit my hand -- so that I wouldn't make any noise.

Q All right, that's fine. Let me ask another question. Did you try to take -- are you okay?

A Yeah, this is just embarrassing.

Q Did you try to take different routes in and out of the Oval Office area as part of your way of concealing the relationship?

A Yes, I did.

Q Could you tell us about that?

A I made an effort on my own to go out a different door than the door that I came in so that if there was a guard that was on duty in the front of the Oval Office he might see me going in but a different guard would see me leave, so no one would know exactly how long I had been in there.

Q Did you try to do that most of the time, all of the time?

A I'd say 90 percent of the time. I mean, I can't really recall a time that I didn't do that, but it's possible. That was the pattern.

Q Were there some people that you tried to specifically avoid when you were visiting with the President?

A Yes.

Q All right. Who were they, please?

A Pretty much everybody but Betty.

Q Okay. What about, for example, Nancy Hernreich?

A Yes.

Q All right. And how would you take steps to avoid Nancy Hernreich?

778

58

A Generally, coming in on the weekend. This is after I left?

Q Yes.

A Okay. After I left the White House it was coming in on the weekend or sometimes we -- I tried to see him but I don't think it actually ever occurred on Tuesday nights because Ms. Hernreich has yoga, I think -- I believe.

BY MR. WISENBERG:

Q Who told you that she had yoga?

A Ms. Currie.

BY MR. EMMICK:

Q Any discussion with the President about trying to make sure that there are fewer people around when you were to visit?

A When I worked in Legislative Affairs, I think that was sort of the understanding that the weekend was the -- there weren't a lot of people around. And there were times when I think that the President might have said, oh, there are too many people here because there was some big issue or some big event happening maybe.

Q Were there any occasions when you tried to make arrangements to see the President but for some reason or another Betty was not in a position to let you in?

A Sure, I think so.

Q Any occasions when you had actually planned to

visit and then for some reason or another she wasn't there, that you remember?

A No, not that I remember.

Q What about throwing away notes that you had written to the President? Was there any discussion of throwing out the notes or any notations that you would write on the notes to remind him to throw them out?

A Yes, I think that I may have had a discussion with the President about him throwing things away, I think, or making sure that they're not there. I know one specific occasion in one of the notes that I sent him I made a joke that really was reminding him not to -- to make sure he threw the -- make sure he threw it away.

Q I've asked you a number of questions having to do with how you tried to keep the relationship secret. Let me ask, did you tell some people about the relationship?

A Unfortunately, yes.

Q All right. Could you tell us some of the people that you've told about the relationship?

A Linda Tripp, Catherine Davis, Neysa Erbland, Dale Young, Ashley Raines, and my mom and my aunt. Everybody knew a different amount of -- had a different amount of information.

Q Natalie Ungvari?

A Oh, Natalie Ungvari, yes.

Q Did you tell any of your -- any counselors or therapists of any kind about your relationship?

A Yes, I did.

Q All right. Would you tell us who they would be?

A Dr. Irene Kassorla, and I believe it's Dr. Kathy Estep.

Q When you talked about your relationship with the President with these people, did you lie about your relationship?

A No. I may have not told them every detail, but I don't believe I ever lied. Oh, about the -- oh, wait, do you mean the doctors or was that in general?

Q I meant in general.

A Well, there were -- about my relationships -- I'm sorry, could you be more specific?

Q Sure. You listed a number of people that you had told about your relationship with the President.

A Right.

Q I'm just trying to figure out if you told the truth to those people when you described the relationship.

A Yes. There were some occasions when I wasn't truthful about certain things, but not having to do with, I think, the general relationship. Does that make sense?

Q Expand on that just a little. I'm just not sure.

A Well, I think with Linda Tripp, I mean there were

times that I was not truthful with her. I mean, I didn't know if that's what you were encompassing by saying relationship or not.

Q Let's put Linda Tripp aside for a bit because I think I know what you have in mind.

A Right.

Q Put Linda Tripp aside for a bit. Were you truthful with the others about your description of the relationship?

A Yes.

Q And since you mentioned Linda Tripp, were there occasions toward the end of, I guess it would be December or January, when you said some things to Linda Tripp that were not true?

A Yes.

Q All right. We'll have a chance to get to that in a bit.

A Okay.

Q What I would like to turn to next is the -- is April of 1996 and your transfer from the White House to the Department of Defense. When were you first told about the fact that you were being terminated from Legislative Affairs?

A On the 5th -- I think it was the 5th of April, Friday.

Q Did you later have a telephone conversation with the President about your being terminated?

A Yes, I did.

Q When was that?

A On the 7th, on Easter.

Q Easter Sunday, April 7th of 1996?

A Correct.

Q Would you tell us first what your reaction was when you were told that you were going to be terminated from Legislative Affairs?

A My initial reaction was that I was never going to see the President again. I mean, my relationship with him would be over.

Q You did not want to go to the Pentagon?

A No.

Q When you spoke with the President on April 7th, did you call him or did he call you?

A He called me.

Q Would you tell us how that telephone conversation proceeded and then we'll talk about the meeting.

A Okay. I had asked him how -- if he was doing okay with Ron Brown's death, and then after we talked about that for a little bit I told him that my last day was Monday. And he was -- he seemed really upset and sort of asked me to tell him what had happened. So I did and I was crying and I asked him if I could come see him, and he said that that was fine.

Q Did you go over to the White House?

A Yes, I did.

Q About what time of day, if you remember?

A I think it was around 6:00 p.m.

Q Who let you in?

A I had a pass at the time.

Q How long did you visit with the President that day?

A Maybe a half an hour. I'm not very good with the time estimates.

Q You've already had occasion to talk a little bit about the sexual aspect of your encounter with the President at that time and the phone call that you -- that came in in the midst. I'm not going to ask you about that. What I am going to ask you about instead was your discussions with the President about the termination and about what the future would hold for you.

A He told me that he thought that my being transferred had something to do with him and that he was upset. He said, "Why do they have to take you away from me? I trust you." And then he told me -- he looked at me and he said, "I promise you if I win in November I'll bring you back like that."

Q How were things left at the end of that meeting?

A I sort of ran out.

Q Right. I guess what I mean by that -- I'm sorry, I didn't mean to be that specific.

A Okay.

Q At the end of the meeting, were you going to go to the Pentagon?

A Well, he was going to see what he could do.

Q I see. All right.

A He said he'd try to see. He said he was going to ask -- try to find out what had happened. And I told him that I was going to be meeting with Ms. Hernreich the next day and he sort of said, "Let me see what I can do."

Q Did you later have a telephone call with the President where you discussed what he had learned?

A Yes.

Q When was that?

A The following Friday.

Q That would have been then April 12th?

A Yes, I think so.

Q Did he call you or did you call him?

A He called me.

Q Where were you?

A I was at home.

Q How long was the telephone conversation?

A Maybe about 20 minutes.

Q Tell us what the two of you talked about.

A He told me that he had asked Nancy and Marsha Scott to find out why I had been transferred, and that what he had come to learn was that Evelyn Lieberman had sort of spearheaded the transfer, and that she thought he was paying too much attention to me and I was paying too much attention to him and that she didn't necessarily care what happened after the election but everyone needed to be careful before the election.

Q Did he offer any of his views about what you should do with respect to this Pentagon job?

A He told me that I should try it out and if I didn't like it that he would get me a job on the campaign.

Q What was your reaction to that?

A I think I was disappointed. I didn't want to go to the Pentagon and I didn't really see what the difference on the campaign was going to be -- why I couldn't work -- if I could work at the campaign why I couldn't work at the White House. So --

Q Did you start working at the Pentagon?

A Yes.

Q What position did you hold when you worked at the Pentagon?

A Confidential Assistant to Ken Bacon, who is the Pentagon spokesman.

Q Let's talk generally, if you will, about what sort of contact you had with the President during the rest of 1996. Did you see him in person?

786

68

A Yes, I did.

Q Okay. Did you see him in person very often?

A No. I wasn't alone with him so when I saw him it was in some sort of event or group setting.

Q Did you continue to have telephone contact with him?

A Yes.

Q And those telephone contacts are set out in the chart that we've put together --

A Mm-hmm.

Q -- with your assistance?

A I guess. Yes. I'm sorry.

Q Let's then just turn to the first part of 1997. The election is over. Did you talk with the President about getting you back to the White House?

A Yes.

Q All right. Would you tell us about that?

A I believe the first time I might have mentioned it to him was in January of '97 in a phone conversation, and he told me that he would talk to Bob Nash, who is the head of White House or Presidential Personnel, I think it is, about bringing me back. In the next phone call he said he had spoken to Bob Nash and then -- do you want me to go as far as --

Q Just a bit more detail so that we can get a sense

of what efforts you thought were being taken and whether you came to be disappointed with those efforts.

A Very disappointed. He -- my understanding at first was that the ball had sort of been passed to Bob Nash to bring me -- to find a position for me to come back to the White House. I then came to learn maybe in March or so that the ball had been passed from Bob Nash to Marsha Scott. And then Marsha Scott was supposed to help me find a position at the White House, which didn't work out, then she was going to detail me to her office in the White House and then she later rescinded that offer.

Keep going?

Q Were you frustrated with all that?

A Very frustrated.

Q And did you communicate your frustration to the President?

A Yes, I did.

Q Tell us about how you communicated your frustration to the President.

A There were various occasions, different things that happened. Sometimes it was in our phone conversations, sometimes it was in a letter, sometimes it was in person.

Q Let me direct your attention to July 3rd of 1997. Did you cause some sort of a communication to be made to the President on that day?

788

68

A Yes.

Q Tell us about that.

A I had been trying to get in touch with him maybe since the latter part of June to discuss some of my meetings with Marsha Scott that had not gone as I had hoped they would and -- excuse me -- the President wasn't responding to me and wasn't returning my calls and wasn't responding to my notes. And I got very upset so I sat down that morning actually and scribbled out a long letter to him that talked about my frustrations and that he had promised to bring me back; if he wasn't going to bring me back that I -- you know, then could be help me find a job -- at that point I said in New York at the United Nations, and that I sort of dangled in front of him to remind him that if I wasn't coming back to the White House I was going to need to explain to my parents exactly why that wasn't happening.

Q And what was your purpose in sending a letter of -- that kind to the President?

A I think it was sort of had a few purposes, in that towards the end of the letter I softened up again and was back to my mushy self, but the purpose was -- one of the purposes, I think, was to kind of remind him that I had left the White House like a good girl in April of '96. A lot of other people might have made a really big stink and said that they weren't going to lose their job and they didn't want to do that and would have talked about what kind of relationship they had with the President so they didn't lose their job, and that I had been patient and had waited and that all of this had gone on. So I was frustrated.

Q Did you -- how did you get this letter to the President?

A I gave it to Ms. Currie.

Q Did you meet with the President on the 3rd of July?

A Mm-hmm. Yes, I'm sorry.

Q Did you meet with the President on the 4th of July?

A Yes, I did.

Q Would you tell us how that was arranged?

A I spoke with Ms. Currie later that afternoon on the 3rd and she told me to come to the White House at 9 o'clock the next morning.

Q You showed up at the White House?

A (Nodding.)

Q What I would like to do with respect to this meeting is just ask you to give a very general description of the meeting, whether it was emotional.

A It was very emotional.

Q I don't want to focus on the emotional aspect of that meeting. What I want to do is focus on the end of the meeting.

A Okay.

Q And whether or not you said anything to the President about Kathleen Willey.

A Yes, I did.

Q Can you tell us what happened in that conversation?

A Can I jump back a little to how I got the information or do you want me to just stick to what I told him?

Q Sure, why don't you. Okay, jump back to how you got the information and then we'll plug it in.

A Just so everyone understands. I believe it was in February or March of that year when I was friends with Linda, she had frantically come to me telling me that this reporter whom I had never heard of before that day, Michael Isikoff, had shown up in her office to question her about Kathleen Willey, who was this woman that you all know now but who was this woman who had -- that Linda had worked with in the White House and that I guess this woman had told Michael Isikoff that the President had sexually harassed her and that Linda would corroborate that fact.

And Linda was -- she had said to me that she was nervous and she responded that no -- I think she had sort of tried to lead Michael Isikoff away from the fact that it had been sexual harassment but, at the same time, had sort of confirmed to Michael Isikoff that something might have happened there.

I'm sorry, I'm going too long.

Q It's all right.

A Throughout the next couple months I had encouraged Linda to get in touch with someone at the White House to let them know that this was out here. Being a political appointee, I thought that was something that should be done.

Q Who at the White House did you encourage her to contact?

A Well, she said she would feel comfortable either getting in contact with Nancy Hernreich or Bruce Lindsey from her experiences at the White House. And I don't really remember how it came to be Bruce Lindsey but that -- I don't remember who encouraged what. She contacted Bruce, or she told me she contacted Bruce Lindsey and that Mr. Lindsey did not return her phone call or answer her page.

Q So jumping forward to July --

A Right.

Q -- what were you trying to convey to the President and what did you say to him?

A Just let me add that I think right -- at some point before July 4th, soon before July 4th, Michael Isikoff had again contacted Linda and so the story was sort of bubbling again. And I was concerned that the President had no idea this was going on and that this woman was going to be another Paula Jones and he didn't really need that.

792

So --

Q This is another grand juror who has just walked in.

A Okay.

Q So that you know.

A Thanks. So I wanted to inform the President about what he should sort of be aware of. And at the end of our meeting -- it had been a really emotional meeting -- I told him that I wanted to talk to him about something serious and that while I didn't want to be the one to talk about this with him, I thought it was important he know.

And I told him that a woman whom I was friendly with at the Pentagon had been approached by Michael Isikoff and sort of informed her that Kathleen Willey was claiming -- I know I didn't use the term sexually harassed because I would have felt uncomfortable saying that to the President, so I think I said something or another that indicated what Kathleen Willey was claiming, and that this woman had known Kathleen Willey when she worked at the White House and she -- I think I may have indicated that she had -- did not corroborate Kathleen Willey's story.

Q Did you identify Ms. Tripp by name?

A No, I did not.

Q Did the President ask who it was you were referring to?

A No, he did not.

Q Continue. I think you were --

A At that point -- I don't know if it was at that point in the conversation, then the President informed me that Kathleen Willey had actually called Nancy Hernreich during the week earlier and had said -- excuse me, sorry -- and had said that this reporter was chasing after her trying to find out her relationship with the President.

And so to me, what that meant was that when -- I thought that meant that when Kathleen found out Linda wasn't going to corroborate her story that she was trying to cover her tracks with the White House so that they wouldn't then find out or think that she was trying to encourage Michael Isikoff.

So I thought everything was over with and I later told that to Linda.

Q Why did you want to say anything to the President at all about that? What did you think the President might do to respond?

A I thought he -- I thought maybe, you know, my understanding from Linda was that Kathleen had been trying to get a job, and I could certainly understand the frustrations of being told someone is going to help you get a job and then you don't. And I thought at that point -- I didn't know too many details about what was going on. I don't think she was in the Paula Jones case and I thought, well, gee, maybe if you know someone who needs -- who would want to hire her you can make this go away for -- that's how I thought of it. Then I thought maybe there was something he could do to fix it or someone else could do to fix it, or just be aware of it.

Q He might get her a job, for example?

A He might. I mean, I think that was one of the things that crossed my mind.

Q At that time, did the President ask you whether you had disclosed anything about your relationship to anyone else?

A Not at that time.

Q Did he at some other time?

A Yes, he did.

Q When was that?

A I think there might have been several times throughout the relationship, but he specifically asked me about Linda Tripp on July 14th.

Q All right. Then we'll get to that in just a moment.

A Okay.

Q At the beginning of the meeting with the President on July 4th, you had sent him a letter in which you said that you were considering telling your parents. Did he ever say anything to you about, you know, you shouldn't be threatening the President or something like that?

A Yes. Our meeting started out with a fight, so he sat down and we sat down and he lectured me and, you know, "First of all, it's illegal to threaten the President of the United States and, second of all -- " I mean, it was just -- and then I started crying so --

Q All right, fine. After the meeting on July 4th concluded, did you leave the country?

A Yes.

Q All right. Where did you go?

A I think a few days after that. I went to Madrid.

Q When did you return, as best you can remember?

A On the 14th of July.

Q All right. Then let's turn our attention to the 14th of July. You got back from overseas. Did you get a call from Betty?

A Yes, I did.

Q Tell us about that.

A She called around -- I think it might have been around 7:30 -- I was already in bed because of jet lag and everything -- and told me that she thought the President either wanted to talk to me or see me later, and that I believe he was out golfing at the time, and that she'd call me back later to let me know what was going to happen. And she did. She called back maybe around 8:30 or so, 8:30, 9 o'clock, and asked me to come over to the White House. So I did.

Q When you got to the White House, did you see the President?

A Yes, I did.

Q Could you tell us how that meeting went?

A It was an unusual meeting, I mean, first because we -- he met me in Betty's office and we went into Nancy Hernreich's office, which is adjacent to Ms. Currie's office, and sat on the sofa and talked. It was very distant and very cold. And he asked me if the -- I don't remember the sequence of things necessarily, but at one point he asked me if the woman that I had mentioned on July 4th was Linda Tripp. And I hesitated and then answered yes, and he talked about that there was some issue with -- this had to do with Kathleen Willey and that, as he called it, that there was something on the sludge report, that there had been some information.

And what his main concern seemed to be was that Kathleen Willey had called Nancy again that week and was upset because Michael Isikoff had told her that he knew she had called the White House saying he was pursuing her and her story. Is that clear?

A JUROR: No.

THE WITNESS: Okay. Kathleen had called Nancy, and

the President had told me that Kathleen had called Nancy. This was on July 4th. And then that following week when I was in Madrid, I believe -- I know I was in Madrid, I think it was that following week -- Kathleen called Nancy again. And Kathleen was upset because Michael Isikoff had told Kathleen that he knew that she had called Nancy the previous week.

Does that make a little more sense?

A JUROR: Yes, thank you.

THE WITNESS: So what the President's concern was that the only people who knew that Kathleen had called Nancy originally were Nancy, Bruce Lindsey, the President and myself, and Kathleen. So he was concerned and had asked me if I had told Linda the information he had shared with me, and I had said yes, I did because I thought that meant it was over, that Kathleen was trying to backtrack.

So that alarmed me because, obviously, someone had told Michael Isikoff. And he was concerned about Linda, and I reassured him. He asked me if I trusted her, and I said yes. And he -- we had talked about -- oh, I had -- I'm sorry, I'm sorry. On July 4th I had mentioned that -- to the President that this woman had tried to contact Bruce Lindsey and that Bruce Lindsey didn't return her phone call.

So on July 14th, the President asked me if I thought Linda would call Bruce Lindsey again, and I told him that she is a really proud woman and that she was really offended that he didn't call her back and it was -- so I didn't think she would. And he asked me if I would just try to see if she would call, and so I said I would try.

BY MR. EMMICK:

Q Did he ask you whether you had told anything to Linda about your relationship with the President?

A Yes, he did.

Q All right. Tell us about that.

A He asked me just that, and I said no.

Q Where was this conversation taking place with the President?

A In Nancy Hernreich's office.

Q Did there come a time when he left to take a conference call?

A Yes, he did.

Q All right. Did you know who the conference call -- was with?

A That's a little murky for me. I believe it might have been with his attorneys, but I don't remember how I know that. So it's possible it was with his attorneys.

BY MR. WISENBERG:

Q How would you know it? I mean, how would you know it?

A I don't know. That's just what sounds -- that's

what came to my mind when I was recalling the event. And I don't recall how I knew that so I don't know if maybe that's just how I'm recalling it or that I knew it and I don't remember who told me.

Q Was there anybody there to tell you he was talking to his attorneys other than him that day?

A It could have been Betty. I sat with Betty when -- in her office when he was on the conference call in the Oval Office or in the back. I don't know where he was, actually.

BY MR. EMMICK:

Q Other than the President asking you to get a hold of Linda and have Linda call Bruce Lindsey, how were things left at the end of the meeting?

A He asked me to let Betty know the following day without getting into details with her, even mentioning names with her, if I had, you know, kind of mission accomplished sort of thing with Linda.

Q And did you?

A Yes, I got in touch with Betty the next day and I told her that I needed to talk to the President having to do with what he had asked me.

Q And did you follow up with that?

A Yes, he called me that evening.

Q Okay. And what did the two of you talk about?

A We discussed the -- I guess that I had tried to

800

80

talk to Linda and that she didn't seem very receptive to trying to get in touch with Bruce Lindsey again, but that I would continue to try. And I think I just gave him some more -- I think I gave him maybe the background information about what I knew when Linda worked there and gave him, I think, a fuller version of whatever it was I knew about this situation.

MR. EMMICK: I'm prepared to move on. Is this an appropriate time for another break?

THE FOREPERSON: Most appropriate.

MR. EMMICK: Okay. Good timing.

THE WITNESS: Me, too. Too much water.

MS. IMMERGUT: Ten minutes?

MR. EMMICK: Let's just take ten minutes.

THE FOREPERSON: Ten minutes, please.

(Witness excused. Witness recalled.)

THE WITNESS: So where are we?

MR. EMMICK: In fact, I'll even walk up and show you where we are, but first we have to clarify that there are no unauthorized persons present and we have a quorum.

THE FOREPERSON: That's correct.

And I need to remind you that you're still under oath.

THE WITNESS: Thanks.

MR. EMMICK: Just to make some reference here, we

are here at the end of July, but there are some questions. I'm going to circle back to April 7th.

THE WITNESS: Okay.

MR. EMMICK: We're going to ask some more detail on April 7th and we're going to talk a little bit about a call that you had from the President in -- I think it is April of '97 about some conversations that --

THE WITNESS: Okay.

MR. EMMICK: A call in that time period.

THE WITNESS: Okay.

MR. EMMICK: There were also some -- let's call them sort of a laundry list of follow-up questions.

THE WITNESS: Okay.

MR. EMMICK: So we'll focus there and a little bit on the 14th and a little bit on that phone call.

THE WITNESS: I thought I -- I also might just say that if, as happened before, if I'm saying something and I'm not clear, I'm not understanding, just let me know, because I do that a lot.

BY MR. EMMICK:

Q All right. Let's start off with some questions. First, let's focus on July 14th because the President wanted you to have Linda contact Lindsey. Why wouldn't Lindsey just contact Linda? Was there any discussion of that? Why did it have to go one way rather than the other way?

A I don't believe there was a discussion about it. I have my own thoughts on it, but there wasn't a discussion about it.

Q What were your own thoughts on it?

A That it would just -- I -- I think I sort of thought that it would probably be more proper -- not in a chain of command, necessarily, but -- it just seemed more appropriate for Linda to call Bruce Lindsey.

Q Did it look -- do you think it would have looked inappropriate for Lindsey to contact Tripp?

A I think it would have been awkward because I think -- how would -- you know, how would Bruce Lindsey have known to call -- you know, to call Linda at that point? If -- you know, the President thought at that point that -- you know, that Linda didn't know anything, so if Linda didn't know anything, then how -- wouldn't it be odd for Bruce Lindsey to just call her back out of the blue?

Q Okay.

A I mean, that was sort of how I thought of it.

Q But in either event, there wasn't any actual discussion about the strategy behind who would have to call whom?

A Not that I remember. No.

BY MR. WISENBERG:

Q Well, did you say to him anything like, "Hey, she

tried to call him before."

A Right.

Q "She isn't going to call him this time." I mean, anything like that?

A Yes. I think I had mentioned that before. I mean, that might have been -- you know, I think was sort of -- he was saying, "Well, just try to see."

BY MR. EMMICK:

Q Let me approach the question in just a little bit different way. When you talked to Linda and tried to convince Linda to talk to Bruce Lindsey, what did you say to her to try to convince her to talk to her? Do you understand what I mean?

A Right. Well, I didn't tell Linda that -- and this was unusual, I didn't tell Linda that I had seen the President on the 14th of July because I was somewhat wary of her, having learned that someone had told Michael Isikoff, and I knew it wasn't me, so sort of assuming that Linda had talked to Michael Isikoff and not really knowing where she was coming from on this, so I just kept encouraging her to call Bruce Lindsey again, that this was heating up more and you really should call Bruce Lindsey.

Q All right. Let me go to another question. You made a reference earlier to the fact that you felt that Nel hadn't been treated well or hadn't been treated respectfully.

Could you tell us what you meant by that?

A People in the White House -- I mean, Nel is stationed in the pantry, which is right -- I mean, which is even a part of the Oval Office area and he's always there and he takes very good care of the President and people just walk right past him, they don't say hi to him, a lot of people don't acknowledge him.

And they just -- you know, they kind of come to him when they need something, but aren't -- and I just -- I don't think people should be treated like that. I mean, I think anybody who -- and especially everyone who is working at the White House and who works -- I've always categorized people as people who are there to serve the President and people who are there to serve themselves through the President and I think Nel has a lot of loyalty to the President.

Q Would it be fair to say that it's no so much that they were affirmatively mistreating him, but they were treating him as a non-person almost? Or is that --

A I think that's a mistreatment.

Q Yes. That's a mistreatment. Okay. That's a fair characterization.

A In my opinion.

Q We had talked earlier about certain people that you wanted to avoid in order to help keep the relationship secret and you talked about Nancy Hernreich as being one of those people. Can you tell us what other people you wanted to sort of avoid in that same vein?

A Stephen Goodin. Let's see. I guess it's different from when I was at the White House to after. When I was there, Evelyn Lieberman, Harold Ickes, anybody who knew who I was, certainly. And after I left, I think it was mainly anybody who knew me from before. So --

Q All right.

A Does that -- does that answer it?

Q If that's the answer, then that's the best we can do.

A Okay.

Q We talked earlier about February 28th and about Steve Goodin going into the Oval Office with Betty and what you learned about that conversation they had.

A Mm-hmm.

Q The question is this: why would Steve Goodin, who is after all just a presidential aide, why would he be in a position to be able to tell the President, "You can't be with Monica Lewinsky alone"?

A I don't know. And that was a question that I -- that I posed -- I don't think I posed it as a question, but I sort of made a comment, you know, who is -- and then -- I don't remember if it was to Betty or to Nel, you know, why would -- you know, how inappropriate that was.

Q Right.

A And maybe Stephen made the comment to Betty. Maybe just Betty. I -- I -- I -- you know, I wasn't in the room, so I don't know what the course of the conversation was. Maybe Stephen said it to Betty and Betty told the President that Stephen had said that to Betty. So I'm not sure, but I thought it was inappropriate, too.

MR. EMMICK: Any other follow-up on that?

A JUROR: I think a point be is that did he feel that he had the authority do so because someone else was encouraging him to monitor that sort of activity, such as Evelyn Lieberman, for example?

THE WITNESS: That's a good thought. I don't know. I don't have any knowledge of that. I never thought of that.

BY MR. EMMICK:

Q You mentioned that during 1997 especially you frequently complained to the President that although he said he could bring you back (snapping finger) like that, it wasn't happening. How did the President respond when you complained about these things?

A You know, I mean, it was the -- "Bob Nash is handling it," "Marsha's going to handle it" and "We just sort of need to be careful." You know, and, "Oh, I'll -- " he would always sort of -- what's the word I'm looking for?

Kind of validate what I was feeling by telling me something that I don't necessarily know is true. "Oh, I'll talk to her," "I'll -- you know, I'll see blah, blah, blah," and it was just "I'll do," "I'll do," "I'll do." And didn't, didn't, didn't.

Q All right. You mentioned that in that July 3rd letter that you sent to the President through Betty you made a reference to the fact that you might have to explain things to your parents. What did you mean by that?

A If I was going to pick up and move from Washington -- first of all, I had told my -- well, my mom knew, you know, that I was having some sort of a relationship with the President. My dad had no idea. And I had told my dad that was I -- you know, I was told I could probably come back to the White House after the election, as Tim Keating had told me. And the President.

So I had sort of told him that course and I would -- have needed to explain to them why I was going to pick up and move to New York without -- what the point would be.

Q Were you meaning to threaten the President that you were going to tell, for example, your father about the sexual relationship with the President?

A Yes and no. I don't think I -- I know that I never would have done that. I think it was more -- the way I felt was, you know, you should remember that I sort of -- I've been a good girl up until now.

I mean, I kind of have -- that I think I tended to -- I know that I thought he tended to forget what I had gone through already and that -- and so that this wasn't an issue of, well, you know, "We can do this in a little while, this is maybe changing your job while you're in the White House," you know, if I had wanted to maybe do something different, it was a lot more significant. And I felt that he was giving me the runaround a bit, too.

Q Is it fair to say that it was in part an implied threat?

A Yes, but I think -- but I think if you want to look at it that way, it was a threat to him as a man and not a threat to him as president. Does that -- I mean --

Q What do you mean?

A Well, I think when I hear you say, you know, "Was that an implied threat" that that letter being sent to any man who is having an illicit relationship with someone would be a threat, and so it was irrelevant, the fact that he was president.

Q I see.

A So just because we had talked earlier about it and then that was what had upset me, when the President said, "It's illegal to threaten the President of the United States."

Q Right.

A And I just thought, you know, "I don't deal with you like the President, I deal with you as a person."

MR. EMMICK: All right.

MR. WISENBERG: Can I ask something about that?

MR. EMMICK: Yes.

BY MR. WISENBERG:

Q But you had said your mother by that time knew there was some of kind of a relationship.

A Right. He didn't know that, though.

Q But you hadn't told -- he didn't know that.

A I never told him that. No.

BY MR. EMMICK:

Q A question about lipstick and tissues.

A Okay.

Q You mentioned that a couple of times you used tissues to wipe lipstick off. Do you remember where you threw those tissues away and did it occur to you that somebody might see those tissues later and therefore might think of it as somehow evidencing the relationship?

A No, really the only -- the one time that I specifically remember doing that was on January 7th of '96. And -- no, I don't think that -- I mean, I had light lipstick on so I don't -- I think if it had been a darker colored lipstick that maybe I would have been concerned, I might have

810

96

thought about that, but that didn't cross my mind. I don't think people go through the trash.

Q Right.

A I hope not.

Q Do you recall where you threw the tissue away on that occasion?

A It was in the bathroom. I think there's a wastebasket right next to the sink.

Q All right. A question going back to the '96 period, because you had mentioned that on February 19th of '96 the President told you essentially we should break up, we shouldn't have any more of a sexual relationship, yet five or six weeks later, there was a continuation of the sexual relationship. How does that happen? How does it get broken off and then rekindled?

A Well, there continued to sort of be this flirtation that was -- when we'd see each other. And then one night, I -- don't -- I think it was maybe in the end of -- the end of February or maybe some time in March when he had -- I had seen him in the hall when I was leaving to go from work, and this was the night he was coming back from the Israeli embassy from something, and we didn't make any contact or anything because he was with Evelyn Lieberman. And I went home.

About 45 minutes later, he called me and had told

me he had gone back to his office and had called my office because he wanted me to come over and visit with him, but I was home now, you know, and then he had gone back upstairs.

So that had sort of implied to me that he was interested in starting up again and then when I saw him on the 31st of March -- when he kissed me, that pretty much --

Q Just, basically, people got back together.

A Yeah. There was never a discussion of, "Okay, now we're going to resume our relationship again." I didn't want to -- why bring up the memory of the guilt? So --

Q Okay. Then what I'd like to do next is turn our attention back to April 7th, which is the Easter Sunday, and we're going to ask some more detailed questions about that period. First, when you got to the White House, did you see a Secret Service agent and did the two of you talk?

A Yes.

Q All right. Tell us who it was and what the two of you said to one another.

A It was John Muskett, I believe. And I had brought some papers with me from home and so I believe I said something, "Oh, the President asked me to bring these to him." And John Muskett said, "Oh, I'd better check with Evelyn Lieberman." And I don't remember exactly what the rest of the exchange was, but I talked him out of doing that and then I just went in.

Q Were you nervous when he said, "I've got to talk to Evelyn Lieberman"?

A Oh, yeah. Yes. Also, it alarmed me that she was there. I didn't really expect her to be there on a Sunday evening.

Q You mentioned that a telephone call came in while you were with the President. Did you later come to believe you knew who that call was from?

A I made a speculation about who that call was from. I have no knowledge nor had no knowledge about who was on the phone call.

Q Let's take this a step at a time, then.

A Okay.

Q First, what do you remember about the content of the call and then what was the reason that you drew whatever conclusion you did later?

A The content was political in nature and I drew, you -- know, the possibility that it was Dick Morris just based on -- that it was campaign stuff. And I think that how it even came up that it could possibly be Dick Morris was in a joking way with Linda on the phone.

So I don't believe that I ever -- I don't think I would have ever categorically stated that it was Dick Morris on the phone, because I didn't know that.

Q All right. About how long after April 7th did you

813

93

draw the conclusion or develop the suspicion perhaps that it was Dick Morris?

A I don't remember.

Q Okay. All right. At some point, did you hear a voice that you believed to be Harold Ickes' voice?

A Yes.

Q Okay. Tell us how that happened.

A The President and I were in -- I believe it was the back study or the study and -- or we might have been in the hallway, I don't really remember, but I -- Harold Ickes has a very distinct voice and so he -- I heard him holler "Mr. President," and the President looked at me and I looked at him and he jetted out into the Oval Office and I panicked and didn't know that -- I thought that maybe because Harold was so close with the President that they might just wander back there and the President would assume that I knew to leave. So I went out the back way.

Q When you say you went out the back way --

A Through the dining room.

Q Where did you go?

A I went through the dining room exit, to the left, past the Chief of Staff's office, to the right, down the stairs.

Q Were you in a hurry?

A Yes.

Q All right. At some point afterwards, did you get a call from the President?

A Yes.

Q All right. And what happened in that phone call?

A He asked me why I left, so I told him that I didn't know if he was going to be coming back and so he -- he was a little upset with me that I left.

MR. EMMICK: All right. Before we move off that particular call, are there any follow-up questions that you have? Yes?

MR. WISENBERG: Yes. Yes. And I'll try to be delicate. I'm not known for delicacy.

THE WITNESS: I can see that everyone seems to agree with that.

BY MR. WISENBERG:

Q First of all, Ms. Lewinsky, when you went out the dining room, did you go out through Nel's pantry door or through the main dining room door?

A I would have gone out the dining room door.

Q Okay. I want to make sure that I get the sequence right, because this is partly based on stuff we discussed Monday in New York and you correct me if I get anything wrong.

A Okay.

Q We'll do it that way. As I understand it, there

is a -- you're back with the President that day and let me ask first if you recall, the more intimate sexual moments that day, were they in the hallway or the back study?

A Both.

Q Okay. Now, as I understand it, you're with the President. It's an intimate moment. A call comes in.

A Correct.

Q All right. And the President leaves.

A Mm-hmm.

Q You put your top back on. Your top had been off and you put your top back on.

A Mm-hmm.

Q And at some point he comes back. Is that correct?

A Mm-hmm.

Q Okay. And what I'm trying to do is distinguish between the Ickes event and the call, if there is a distinction in your mind. In other words --

A Yes.

Q The call is something different, as far as you know, from the Ickes event.

A Correct.

Q Okay. The President comes back and it's at some point later that you hear the voice of Harold Ickes.

A I'm sorry --

Q The President comes back from the phone call that

he takes --

A No. The -- someone came in to tell the President he had a phone call, so someone came in, hollered something, not Mr. Ickes.

Q Okay.

A The President went out, came back in and I think then they sent the phone call in.

Q All right. He took that in --

A He took the phone call in the back study.

Q Okay.

A Then we were -- and I think we had been in the hallway -- I know we had been in the hallway prior to that.

Q Okay.

A And he came back in and then the phone rang and he took the phone call in the back study.

Q Okay.

A Then it was much later in that same day that he heard the "Mr. President" voice.

Q Of Ickes.

A Right. And I'm going to -- I think that we were in the back study at that point because that's why he jetted so quickly, not wanting Harold, I think, to walk back there. That was --

Q Okay. Now, the voice you heard saying to the President that he had a call --

A Mm-hmm.

Q You never saw the President attached to that voice.

A No. And it wasn't a voice that was familiar to me.

Q Okay. And you never saw Ickes. Is that correct? When you later heard his voice, you didn't see him. You're just familiar with his voice.

A Correct.

Q As far as you know, did Ickes see you when you headed out the back way?

A He couldn't have.

Q Okay. Why do you say that?

A Because he was in the office.

Q Okay. And you said that Ickes was much later. I mean, much later within the whole time you were there with the President that day?

A Right. Correct.

Q Okay. I mean, not like several hours later.

A No. No.

Q Okay.

A Just much later within my visit.

MR. WISENBERG: Okay. Thank you.

BY MR. EMMICK:

Q What I'd like to do is turn our attention to a call that you got from the President some time, I believe, in April, but correct me if I'm wrong, where he asked you something about whether you had told your mother --

A Yes.

Q -- about the relationship. Let's first talk about -- can you place this in time as best you can?

A It was April. And this came about because -- I guess Marsha Scott, I think, had relayed some information to the President about her conversations, I think possibly with Walter Kaye, who is a friend of my family's, and that from that conversation, I think Marsha either directly said to the President or the President wondered from something Marsha said, if I had told my mom -- well, it must have been the President assuming from something that Marsha said.

The President asked me if I had told my mom or had my mom told -- and where that went was had my mom told Walter Kaye. And I said no.

Q What you're describing, is it all based on what the President said in this phone call?

A I don't understand.

Q Yes. You said that at some point it was based on the fact that Walter had spoken to Marsha Scott and I'm trying to figure out if you're learning that from a different source or if it's all from the President.

A No, I was learning that from the phone call with the President.

Q All right. How long was the phone call?

A You know, I'm thinking just now, I don't know if that was in April. It could have been in May.

MR. EMMICK: Okay.

A JUROR: Of 1997?

THE WITNESS: Yes. Sorry. Okay. I don't know if the month time is important or not.

BY MR. EMMICK:

Q In April or May, you have this discussion.

A Right.

Q The President asks you if you've told your mother about the relationship.

A Right.

Q What do you respond?

A "No. Of course not."

MR. EMMICK: Okay.

MR. WISENBERG: Mike?

MR. EMMICK: Yes?

MR. WISENBERG: Can I butt in?

MR. EMMICK: Yes.

BY MR. WISENBERG:

Q Do you know independently what, if any, conversation there was -- that is, whether -- did you later learn that Walter had said something to Marsha or that somebody had said something to Walter?

A In a way, that's too broad of a question because

I think Walter Kaye kind of comes in and out -- if you look at this whole few years, he comes in and out of this in a few ways, so -- did I learn independently that Walter had had a discussion with Marsha? No. Is that what you were asking me?

Q Well, that's one. How about with anybody else? I guess did you hear anything that struck you as this is kind of consistent with what the President had told me in that conversation or this fits together now? Walter had a conversation with somebody and could have actually talked to Marsha Scott and then that got relayed to the President.

A I don't think I'm following you 100 percent. I'm sorry.

Q Okay. Well, I'm not always very articulate. I'll just --

A It --

Q Do you recall -- let me be more specific. Are you aware of your aunt ever having made a comment to Walter Kaye?

A I'm aware of Walter Kaye having made a comment to my aunt.

Q Okay. And what was that?

A He remarked something to my aunt that he had heard from people that the reason I had left the White House or had been moved from the White House was because I had had this relationship with the President.

821

Q Do you know what your aunt responded to Walter Kaye?

A My understanding was she got up and walked out. She was having lunch with him.

BY MR. EMMICK:

Q After you had this telephone call with the President where he asked you whether you had told your mom, was the next time that you saw the President May 24th, I think, which you refer to as dump day?

A Yes. Either way, it would have been, whether it was in April or May.

Q Right. Because you didn't see him in April --

A Right.

Q -- and you only saw him once in May.

A Right. Correct.

Q All right. And you had -- that's fine. All right. What I'd like to turn our attention to next is as we're working down our outline here, we're finished up with the July 3rd, 4th and 4th period. I take it that you remained frustrated with the President's efforts to try to get you back to the White House.

A Mm-hmm. I mean, it always -- and I did make this clear to him, that it was always more important to me to have him in my life than to -- than to get the job, but the job was something that was important to me.

822

102

Q Did there come a time in about October when you gave up, more or less, on your efforts to get back to the White House and you turned your attention more to New York City?

A Yes.

Q All right. Tell us how that happened.

A Linda Tripp called me at work on October 6th and told me that her friend Kate in the NSC had heard from -- had heard rumors about me and that I would never work in the White House again and, if I did, I wouldn't have a blue pass and that her advice to me was "get out of town." So that meant to me that I wasn't going to be coming back to the White House and I was very upset by that.

Also, she, Linda, told me that Kate had said, "You know, they create jobs at the White House, you know, six days a week." And that Stephen Goodin's girlfriend had just gotten a job, so with these examples of how there had been all these other people receiving jobs that I could have done and I didn't get it.

Q Did you communicate your additional frustration and disappointment to the President?

A Yes, I did.

Q Tell us how and when.

A I believe I sent him a short note telling him that I really needed to talk to him in person having to do with

823

103

this subject matter and he and I had an argument in a conversation on the 9th of October.

Q And was that a telephone conversation?

A Yes, it was.

Q Did he call you or did you call him?

A He called me.

Q About what time, if you can remember?

A I think it was around 2:30, 3:00 in the morning.

Q Was it a long phone call?

A Yes. Yes. 2:00, 2:30 maybe.

Q Is it fair to characterize the phone call as involving an argument?

A Yes. And then we made up.

Q And then you made up.

A It was half argument, half making up.

Q Did the name Vernon Jordan come up in the course of that discussion?

A It's possible.

Q What do you have in mind about the first time that Vernon Jordan's name would have come up in conversations with the President?

A It was either in that phone call or on October 11th.

Q And tell us what was said about Vernon Jordan, whether it was in the phone call or on the 11th.

A I don't remember. I know that I had discussed with Linda and either I had had the thought or she had suggested that Vernon Jordan would be a good person who is a close friend of the President and who has a lot of contacts in New York, so that that might be someone who might be able to help me secure a position in New York, if I didn't want to go to the U.N.

Q And what was the President's response?

A "I think that was a good idea."

Q At some point, did you send the President something like a list of jobs or interests that you might have in New York?

A Yes. He asked me to prepare that on the 11th of October.

Q At some point, did you have an initial meeting with Vernon Jordan?

A Yes, I did.

Q Can you tell us when that was, as best you can recall?

A The beginning of November of last year.

Q How was that meeting arranged?

A Through conversations with the President and with Betty.

Q Without getting into a lot of detail about what happened there during the first meeting with Vernon Jordan,

825

105

what did you think were your job prospects after that? Did it look like things were going to happen?

A Yes.

Q All right. And what happened with respect to the job situation from that meeting with Vernon Jordan until, say, Thanksgiving?

A Nothing, really.

Q Okay. Then let's turn our attention to the month of December. We'll have to relate back a little bit to November in order to complete things, but on December 5th, did you return to Washington from overseas?

A I did. You know -- the question you just asked me before about until Thanksgiving, I did have a conversation with him before Thanksgiving, I think it was the day before.

Q Okay.

A So --

Q Then why don't you complete that, then.

A Okay. I had spoken to Betty about -- about not being -- being able to get in touch with Mr. Jordan because he was in and out of town and then wasn't necessarily returning my call. He's a busy man. And so Betty arranged for me to speak with him again and I spoke with him when I was in Los Angeles before -- right before Thanksgiving.

Q Okay. Let's just go back, if we might, to that early November meeting with Mr. Jordan.

826

106

A Okay.

Q Did he say anything indicating to you that he had spoken with the President recently about you?

A Yes. I believe he mentioned he'd had a conversation with the President.

Q And what did he say about that or what did he say that indicated he may have spoken with the President?

A I believe he mentioned that in the course of the conversation and as I was leaving, he remarked to me that I came highly recommended.

Q Okay. Let's turn our attention to December 5th, then.

A Okay.

Q Having in mind that you had had a meeting with Vernon Jordan and a discussion and were trying to get a hold of him, when you got back from overseas, sort of what was the status of the Vernon Jordan job effort?

A When I had spoken with Mr. Jordan right before Thanksgiving, he had asked me to call him the next week, either, I think, Thursday or Friday. And because I was out of town, I called him on Friday when I got back, and it was my understanding from his secretary he had gone out of town that day, so we had missed each other.

Q All right. Did you try to arrange a meeting with President Clinton?

A Yes.

Q Tell us what you did to try to arrange meeting with President Clinton.

A I sent a note to Betty much earlier in the week that I asked her to pass along to him which in that letter requested of him that I could come have a visit that Saturday.

Q Did you follow up that note with a call to Ms. Currie?

A Yes.

Q When was that call, if you remember?

A December 5th.

Q Okay. And what happened during the call?

A Well, there were several calls, actually. And so at first, it was -- the first few, she still hadn't given him the note.

So then finally she gave him the note, just, I think, right after the radio address or right before his radio address, and then she told me that he was meeting with his lawyers all day Saturday, but that she was coming in in the morning to give a tour and she would check and see with him then, you know, if maybe I could come by, but that the prospects didn't look good.

Q Was she focused on Saturday because you had asked whether Saturday would be a good time?

A Mm-hmm. Yes. I'm sorry. Maybe he was going out of town on Sunday. I'm not sure why I would have focused on Saturday versus Sunday.

Q In any event, what she said was he was busy with meetings with lawyers, something like that?

A Yes.

Q All right. Did you go to a Christmas party that night?

A Yes, I did.

Q Did you see the President?

A Yes, I did.

Q Let's turn our attention to December 6th.

A Okay.

Q Are you doing okay?

A Yes.

Q All right. December 6th. Let me ask as a background question, had you previously purchased for the President a Christmas present?

A Yes.

Q All right. What was that Christmas present?

A It was a sterling silver antique standing cigar holder.

Q You had been unable to arrange an actual visit with the President to give him that present in person. What did you do instead?

829

10?

A I had some other gifts for him as well that I had gotten on my trips and --

Q Tell us what those other gifts were, if you remember.

A A tie. A mug from Starbucks in Santa Monica. A little box that's called hugs and kisses and it's Xs and Os inside, it's really -- it's just a cute little chatchki. An antique book from the flea market in New York that was on Theodore Roosevelt. And -- I think that's it.

Q Okay. What did you try to do on the 6th in order to give those gifts to the President?

A Well, I had wanted to give them to him, if I was going to have a planned visit with him, and then through the -- just some course of events, I got upset and I decided that I was really tired of everything that was going on and I just -- it was clear to me that he was ignoring me and I just didn't want to deal with this anymore.

So I decided -- I had purchased these presents for him and I'm very -- I spend a lot of time and am very particular about the presents I give to people, so I didn't want to give them to someone else and I wanted him to have them, so I packaged them up with a note that I was going to drop off to Betty.

Q And where did you go?

A I went to the southwest gate.

Q What happened at the southwest gate?

A I paged Betty or I think I might have called her. I know I called her and she wasn't at her desk, so I paged her to let her know I was there. And then Marsha Scott drove up, so I ran away to the northwest gate because I didn't want Marsha to see me. Continue from there?

Q Yes. Did you have any trouble getting in at the northwest gate? What happened?

A Well, I wasn't trying to get in. I -- so --

Q What were you trying to do?

A I was trying to wait for Betty. So I called Betty from the northwest gate and she wasn't at her desk and then I saw someone go into the -- it was under construction at the time, so it was a different little hut than normal, and I saw someone who went in who I thought was John Podesta, so I thought I would -- since I knew that Betty had talked to John Podesta about me, I thought I would ask him, you know, maybe I would ask her -- I would give the gifts -- I would feel comfortable probably giving the gifts to John Podesta to give to Betty, just knowing that he knew I had a relationship with her.

So when I went in to ask this person who I thought was John Podesta -- it turned out to be Lanny -- I think Lanny Davis, and so then one of the guards said, "Oh, are you here to see Betty Currie?"

And I said, "No. I'm not here to see her, I'm trying to get her. She doesn't know I'm coming."

And then they told me she was giving a tour and that Eleanor -- do you want me to go into this detail?

Q Sure.

A Okay. That Eleanor Mondale had come recently and that she was giving a tour to Eleanor Mondale. Then I sort of -- wanting to know if the President was in the office, asked the guards, "Oh, well, is the President in the office? Because if he is, she's probably too busy to come out and get these gifts."

And they said, "Yes, he was."

Q What was you reaction to that?

A Not good.

Q Okay.

A Very upset. Hysterical.

Q Where did you go and what did you do?

A I turned around and walked out and I was livid. I had -- well -- are the grand jurors aware of the rumors about Eleanor Mondale that had been out? I mean, because it doesn't make sense if --

BY MS. IMMERGUT:

Q Well, why don't you say why you were upset.

A

832

112

BY MR. WISENBERG:

Q A question. Pardon me for interrupting. I just wanted to -- you said you were upset. Did you show your upsetness to any of the guards?

A No.

MR. WISENBERG: Thank you.

BY MR. EMMICK:

Q Did you contact Betty?

A Yes, I did.

Q Where did you contact her from?

A I called her from the pay phone at the Corcoran Gallery.

Q Did you have a fight with her?

A I think so.

Q Okay. You say you think so --

A I'm trying to remember if I -- if I actually got her on the phone, which I think I did. I'm pretty sure I did.

Diversified Reporting Services, Inc.
1025 VERMONT AVENUE, N.W. SUITE 1250
WASHINGTON, D.C. 20005
(202) 296-2929

Q All right. Did you eventually come to talk to the President on the telephone?

A Through a much more circuitous route, yes, I did.

Q All right. And where were you at that time?

A I was at home.

Q All right. And about what time of day was it?

A Maybe around noon or so.

Q How did the two of you come to be speaking on the phone? Who placed the calls?

A Well, I believe maybe I had called Betty or maybe Betty called me, one of the two, but she put him on the phone.

Q All right. And what happened in the conversation with the President?

A Well, we had a fight. And he was very angry with me.

Q Why was he angry with you?

A Because I had gotten so upset and I had made a stink to Betty and I had -- you know -- I -- what I came to learn, I think, is that as a result of me being upset with Betty and mentioning that I knew Eleanor Mondale was there, Betty called the guards at the northwest gate and so it had just caused a whole big commotion.

And he was just angry at me and he told me it was none of my business what -- you know, what he was doing and that -- you know, that -- that he had never been treated as poorly by anyone else as I treated him and that he spent more time with me than anyone else in the world, aside from his family, friends and staff, which I don't know exactly which category that put me in, but --

Q Okay. Was it a long phone call with the President?

A Maybe half an hour, 45 minutes.

Q Eventually, were arrangements made for you to visit him at the White House?

A Mm-hmm.

Q Are you doing okay?

A Yeah. Yes.

Q Were you surprised that he would let you come to the White House?

A Yeah, I was -- yes, I was a little bit surprised.

Q Why?

A Because none of the other times that we had really fought on the phone did it end up resulting in a visit that day.

Q All right. What about the fact that he was supposedly meeting with his lawyers all day? Did he say anything about that?

A He had in the fight. When we were fighting, he said -- you know, he was angry because he said, "I have one day to meet with my lawyers and, you know, I've got you

835

115

messing things up and being upset and blah, blah, blah."
So --

Q Did you go and did you meet with the President?

A Yes, I did.

Q Did Betty wave you in?

A Yes.

Q Can you describe for us in general terms how that meeting went? Did you give him the gifts, for example?

A I did. It was -- it was a really nice visit.

Q Okay. What do you mean by a "nice visit"?

A It was just sweet. He liked his Christmas presents and we were very affectionate and it just -- it was just nice to be with him.

Q Did you discuss the job search?

A I believe so.

Q At the time, how did you think the job search was going?

A Not very well. With respect to Mr. Jordan.

Q Right. And did you communicate that to the President?

A Yes.

Q Can you give us a little more detail? What would you have said to one another?

A I think I said that I -- that I was supposed to get in touch with Mr. Jordan the previous week and that things didn't work out and that nothing had really happened yet.

Q Did the President say what he was going to do?

A I think he said he would -- you know, this was sort of typical of him, to sort of say, "Oh, I'll talk to him. I'll get on it."

Q Okay. Did he say anything to you about whether he had a Christmas present for you?

A Yes, he did.

Q What did he say?

A He told me that on the phone, actually.

Q All right. What did he say about that?

A Well, I said to him, "Well, how do you have a Christmas present? I haven't read that you've gone Christmas shopping yet." And he said that he had bought it in Vancouver.

Q Okay. Did he say at any time on the 6th anything about a witness list or your being on a witness list?

A No.

Q How were things left when you left him on the 6th?

A That he would bring me -- oh, our meeting ended up -- or was cut short by the fact that he had to have a meeting with Mr. Bowles, so he told me that he'd give me my Christmas present another time and that he wouldn't jerk me around and abandon me.

You know, that -- because I think I remarked to

him, "Well, at the rate we go, I won't get it 'til Christmas of '98." So --

MR. EMMICK: I have no more questions about this date and I look at the time and it looks like it's 12:30.

THE FOREPERSON: Sol, I think, went to check on something.

MR. EMMICK: Oh, all right.

THE FOREPERSON: Did you check on something for lunch?

MR. WISENBERG: I have checked. It is here. It's been here.

MR. EMMICK: Okay. All right. Well, if this would be a good time to take a break for lunch --

THE FOREPERSON: It's fine with me.

MR. EMMICK: Okay. Let's take an hour-long break for lunch.

THE FOREPERSON: Hour-long.

MR. EMMICK: Okay.

THE WITNESS: Okay.

THE FOREPERSON: Okay.

MR. EMMICK: Thank you.

(Whereupon, at 12:34 p.m., a luncheon recess was taken.)

* * * * *

A F T E R N O O N S E S S I O N

Whereupon, (1:38 p.m.)

MONICA S. LEWINSKY

was recalled as a witness and, after having been previously duly sworn by the Foreperson of the Grand Jury, was examined and testified further as follows:

EXAMINATION (RESUMED)

THE WITNESS: Time for a nap?

MR. EMMICK: Madam Foreperson, do we have a quorum?

THE FOREPERSON: Yes, we do.

MR. EMMICK: Are there any unauthorized persons present?

THE FOREPERSON: There are none.

Monica, I'd like to remind you that you are still under oath.

THE WITNESS: Okay. Thanks.

BY MR. EMMICK:

Q Ms. Lewinsky, we just got through speaking about the December 6th meeting that you had with the President. What I'd like to do is turn our attention next to the date of December 11th.

A Mm-hmm.

Q Did you have a meeting with Vernon Jordan on that day?

A Yes, I did.

Q Would you tell us when that meeting was?

A Around lunchtime.

Q And how was that meeting arranged?

A By his secretary.

Q What was the purpose of the meeting?

A For him to -- I learned after we had the meeting, for him to give me some contact names and some suggestion of what to do with these contact names.

Q When you say --

A For a job.

Q When you say "contact names," these are names of potential employers?

A Yes.

Q What else did the two of you talk about?

A We talked about my -- the fact that my mom's fiance at the time knew Mr. Jordan. We talked about the President.

What else did we talk about? I think that's it.

Q All right. Did he at some point make a comment to you about your being a friend of the President?

A Yes, he did.

Q Would you tell us how the conversation transpired from that point?

A I don't remember how we got to this point, but at some point, Mr. Jordan said something to me, "Well, you're a friend of the President of the United States."

And I remarked that I didn't -- I didn't really look at him as the President, that I saw him more as a man and reacted to him more as a man and got angry at him like a man and just a regular person.

And Mr. Jordan asked me what I got angry at the President about, so I told him when he doesn't call me enough or see me enough.

We were sort of bantering back and forth about that and then he told me that I shouldn't get angry at the President because he's got a lot of -- it sounds so stupid -- obviously, he has a lot of other more important things and difficult things to deal with than someone getting upset with him. And he suggested that if I was upset that I should call and take my frustrations out on Mr. Jordan instead of the President.

I mean, I think I should just say that it was all -- this was all sort of in a light tone.

Q Is this a meeting during which the subject of your possibly being in love cropped up?

A Oh, yes. So after we had the conversation I was just talking about with Mr. Jordan, he said to me, "Well, you know what your problem is?"

And I said, "What?"

He said, "Don't deny it." And he said, "You're in love, that's what your problem is."

841

121

So I think I just -- probably blushed or giggled, something like that.

Q How did the meeting end? What were you going to do and what was he going to do?

A I was planning to send the letters that he had suggested I write to the list of people and he suggested that I cc him and keep in touch with him, keep him apprised of what was happening with my job search.

Q And did you send out those letters?

A Yes, I did.

Q And make arrangements for some interviews?

A Yes, I did.

Q What I want to do next, then, is direct your attention to a few days later, several days later, a week later, I guess. Did you come to have a telephone conversation with the President on December 17th?

A Yes.

Q Would you tell us how that telephone call was -- how that conversation took place?

A Okay. The phone rang unexpectedly at about maybe 2:00 or 2:30 and --

BY MS. IMMERGUT:

Q In the morning?

A Right. In the morning. And it was the President and he called and said he had two things to tell me and then he had to call me right back. So he called me right back.

BY MR. EMMICK:

Q Did he explain why he had to call and then call back?

A I don't know. He just was very brief with me and then he said, "I'll call you right back." And he hung up and called back about a minute later.

Q Before you get to the actual things that he says next, you mentioned that you unexpectedly go the call. Why were you surprised by the call?

A Normally, the President wouldn't call me when Mrs. Clinton was in town, so -- and I usually was aware when she was out of town, so I that I would sort of be expecting or hoping that he would call. And the call came as a surprise to me.

Q He called you back?

A Right.

Q Then what happened?

A And he told me that he had two things to tell me. The first was that Betty's brother had been killed in a car accident and that -- so I reacted that and we talked about that being -- that this was the same brother who had been beaten up just a few months ago and she had lost her sister and her mom was ill. We talked about Betty for a little bit.

843

123

And then he told me he had some more bad news, that he had seen the witness list for the Paula Jones case and my name was on it.

Q Did you get an impression from him about when he had found out your name was on the witness list?

A Yes. I mean, the impression I got based on the entire conversation was that he found out recently.

Q When he told you that, what did he say about having seen your name on the witness list?

A He told me it broke his heart.

Q Tell us how the conversation went from there.

A I was -- I'm sure, as you can imagine, I was upset and shocked. He told me that it didn't necessarily mean that I would be subpoenaed, but that that was a possibility, and if I were to be subpoenaed, that I should contact Betty and let Betty know that I had received the subpoena.

I believe that I probably asked him, you know, what should I do in the course of that and he suggested, he said, "Well, maybe you can sign an affidavit."

At some point in the conversation, and I don't know if it was before or after the subject of the affidavit came up, he sort of said, "You know, you can always say you were coming to see Betty or that you were bringing me letters." Which I understood was really a reminder of things that we had discussed before.

Q So when you say things you had discussed, sort of ruses that you had developed.

A Right. I mean, this was -- this was something that -- that was instantly familiar to me.

Q Right.

A And I knew exactly what he meant.

Q Had you talked with him earlier about these false explanations about what you were doing visiting him on several occasions?

A Several occasions throughout the entire relationship. Yes. It was the pattern of the relationship, to sort of conceal it.

Q When he said that you might sign an affidavit, what did you understand it to mean at that time?

A I thought that signing an affidavit could range from anywhere -- the point of it would be to deter or to prevent me from being deposed and so that that could range from anywhere between maybe just somehow mentioning, you know, innocuous things or going as far as maybe having to deny any kind of a relationship.

Q At some point, did you talk with him about possibly settling the Paula Jones case?

A Yes. I had -- I had had a thought and then had a conversation with Linda about this and just a way that he could settle the case and I suggested it to him.

845

125

Q And what was that way? Not in a lot of detail, but --

A The gist of it is, I thought that first Mrs. Clinton should do something publicly, maybe on a T.V. show or something, and talk about how difficult the case had been for her and on her daughter and that she just wished that he would settle it and it would go away. And then the President should unannounced and unexpectedly go into the briefing room, make a brief statement that he -- in an effort to put this behind him, you know, against his attorneys' advice, he was going to pay Ms. Jones whatever it was, however much she wanted, and so that this case would be over with.

Q Did the two of you talk about how much the settlement amount would be or might be?

A Yes. I believe at some point I had mentioned that I had recently read the -- I think she had lowered her -- the amount that she wanted to $500,000 or something lower and he said, "I thought it was a million or two million dollars."

And I thought that was very strange, that he wouldn't know she had -- you know, that her lawyers -- or his lawyers had not told him that she had lowered her request for money. Or I don't know how you say that legally, whatever it is that she did.

Q Right. Demand, probably.

A The demand was lower.

Q Right.

A We also talked in this conversation about he mentioned that -- he said he'd try and see if Betty could come in on the weekend to give me my Christmas presents and I told him that was out of the question, to -- you know, let Betty be.

Q Because her brother had just been killed, right?

A Right.

Q All right. About how long was the entire phone call? Or I guess technically it would be the second phone call.

A Maybe a half an hour. Maybe I could just say since you asked me earlier that it was him suggesting that I would contact Betty if I were subpoenaed that led me to believe he didn't think I would be subpoenaed that soon because he knew Betty was going to be out, you know, he assumed obviously that Betty would be out for the week or two weeks with the unexpected loss of her brother.

Q Right.

A So that was what led me to believe he had just found out.

Q After the call was ended, did you call anyone else?

A Yes. About a half an hour later, I called Linda.

Q What did the two of you talk about?

A My conversation with the President.

Q Right. It seems self-evident, but --

A I know. I'm sorry.

Q That's all right. What did you tell Linda?

A Well, if I could just jump back --

Q Yes.

A I mean, I had -- Linda had told me some time in -- I think the second week of December that she had been subpoenaed in the Paula Jones case and that she intended to rat on me, so up until this point, I had been trying to convince her not to tell, that it's not anybody's business.

So when I -- part of my telling her that the President had called; that I, too, may be pulled into this case was just sort of -- maybe assure her that if that happened, there would be someone else denying it, it wouldn't be just Linda out there alone saying "I don't know anything about any kind of relationship between the President and Monica."

Q Kind of a unified front or something like that?

A Exactly.

Q All right. How was the conversation left with Linda?

A I think that we'd talk about it the next day.

Q Did you get subpoenaed?

A Yes, I did.

Q When did you get subpoenaed?

A On Friday, the 19th of December.

Q Can you tell us about when you believe you were subpoenaed?

A I believe it was around 3:00, 4:00 in the afternoon. I think closer to 3:00, 3:30.

Q Okay. Where were you served?

A At the Pentagon.

Q Could you tell us how it happened? Did someone call you?

A Yes. I received a call in my office from the gentleman who was to deliver the subpoena to me. He informed me he had a subpoena for me. I made a stink to him, asking him why I was being subpoenaed and I had no idea what was going on.

When he gave me the subpoena, he suggested I call Ms. Jones' attorneys, which I made a comment to him that that's not something I would do.

Q When you actually did get served, what was your real reaction inside?

A I burst into tears. It was -- it was very scary. I mean, it just -- sort of my worst nightmare, or I had thought until that point, was being subpoenaed in this case. So I was pretty upset.

Q You couldn't call Betty because Betty was --

A Right.

Q -- in mourning herself. Who did you call?

A I called Mr. Jordan.

Q From what phone did you call Mr. Jordan?

A From a pay phone.

Q Close to where you were served, the nearest pay phone around?

A No, I think it was the pay phone which is down the hall from my office, which is kind of halfway between where I was served and my office.

Q And why did you use a pay phone?

A Because I was crying and I -- I mean, I -- my office, the way my office is set up is my desk was in the same room with four or five other people, so I couldn't very well have any kind of a private discussion.

Q What did you tell Mr. Jordan?

A Well, I don't remember what I told him. I was crying and he didn't seem to understand me, so he just -- he just told me to come to his office around 5:00.

BY MS. IMMERGUT:

Q Did you tell him you'd been subpoenaed?

A I probably did. I just -- I mean, I don't -- I don't remember, I just remember being on the phone crying and him saying, "I can't understand you. I can't understand you."

Q You got off the phone. What did you do next? Did you finally go to Vernon Jordan's office?

A Yes. I tried to compose myself and I went into the office. I told Mr. -- I believe I told Mr. Bacon or some other people in the office that I had an emergency and I needed to leave. I went home, sort of put myself together, and went to Mr. Jordan's office.

Q When you got to Mr. Jordan's office, did you have to wait outside for a bit?

A Yes.

Q In like a reception area?

A I waited in the lobby, like I always did.

Q About how long did you wait in the lobby?

A I don't really remember.

Q At some point, I take it, you did actually meet with Mr. Jordan?

A Yes.

Q How did the conversation with Mr. Jordan progress?

A First, I came in and I explained to him clearly that I had been subpoenaed and that I was upset and shortly after, I think maybe I said I didn't know what I was supposed to do, I didn't have an attorney, I think I was rambling.

Shortly after I had arrived at Mr. Jordan's office, he received a phone call and I stepped out of the office.

Q Did he ask you to step out of the office?

A I think I may have offered. That was sort of par for the course. And I waited for him while he was on the phone outside his office and when I came back in, he placed a call to -- I don't know if it was right after I came back in, but at some point, when I came back in, he placed a call to Mr. Frank Carter.

Q Now, when you stepped out, he took one call and then you stepped back in, did he tell you who he'd been on the phone with?

A No.

Q All right. He places a call to Frank Carter. Do you know whether he talked to Frank Carter in person or do you know whether he just left a message or do you recall?

A I don't really recall.

Q When --

A Oh, he said something about -- well, I know he referred to Mr. Carter as Mr. Carter, so I don't know if he was talking -- I don't really remember if he was talking to Mr. Carter or he was talking to someone else, but it scared me because I thought for Mr. Jordan to be referring to someone else as Mr. something, that -- I sort of thought he must be a big deal.

Q All right. When you went to the meeting with Mr. Jordan, did you bring the subpoena with you?

A Yes, I did.

Q Did you show it to Mr. Jordan?

A I believe so.

Q What most troubled you about the language of the subpoena and what the subpoena had called for you to produce?

A The thing that alarmed me was that it asked for a hat pin.

Q Okay. And why did that alarm you?

A Because I thought that was a very specific gift and in this list of gifts, everything else seemed to be somewhat generic and then it had hat pin, which screamed out at me because that was the first gift that the President had given me and it had some significance.

Q When you showed Mr. Jordan the subpoena, did he make any remark about any of the things that were called for?

A Yes. When I mentioned to him, I think, about the hat pin, he said, "Oh, don't worry about it. This is a vanilla subpoena, this is a standard subpoena," something like that. Generic subpoena, maybe.

Q Did you know what he meant, a vanilla or standard subpoena that asks for hat pins?

A Well, what I understood that to mean was that -- that what he was trying to say is there was nothing out of the ordinary about this subpoena.

Q I see. I guess what I'm trying to get at is do you

think he was trying to imply that all subpoenas ask for that or that all subpoenas in the Paula Jones case asked for that or all subpoenas -- what was he -- from your point of view, what was he trying to convey?

A I think what he -- I think what he was trying to convey was stop worrying, that this is not something out of the -- you know, out of the realm of possibility of what might be in a subpoena.

Q All right. Were you reassured by that?

A A little. I -- I sort of felt that he wasn't -- I mean, he didn't really understand what I was saying.

Q All right. Did you have any discussion with him about letting the President know that you'd been subpoenaed?

A Yes. I asked Mr. Jordan to inform the President.

Q How did you ask? How often? How vigorously?

A I -- I mean, I asked him to -- to please make sure that he told the President. He said he was going to see the President that night, so --

Q All right. Did the subject of a possible sexual relationship between you and the President come up in the conversation?

A Yes, it did.

Q Tell us how it came up.

A Mr. Jordan said to me that there -- "There are

two important questions" or "There are two important -- " I think, "Two important questions that are related to the case: Did you have sex with the President, you know, or did he ask?" And I said no to both of those.

Q What did you interpret him to be asking when he asked you those questions?

A Well, I thought he -- I guess -- can I step back for a minute?

Q Sure. Up until a point that we'll get to, which is December 31st, I sort of -- mainly, I think, from my discussions with Linda, I was under the impression that -- that Mr. Jordan kind of knew with a wink and a nod that I was having a relationship with the President, that it was never -- he and I never discussed it, but I thought it might be possible.

I'm, you know, a young woman, sort of coming to see him, the President's mentioned me. But I also was sort of under this influence of Linda saying to me, "Of course he knows. Of course he knows. Of course he knows."

So when he asked me those questions, I thought he was asking me, saying essentially "What are you going to say?" not necessarily asking me directly what -- you know, "What are the answers to these questions?" More "What are you going to reply in regard to the case?"

Q Now, was your interpretation of his questions based

entirely on your assumption about what he knew? Or was it based in part on how he asked the questions?

A I think it was based more in part on my assumptions of what he knew.

Q Was there anything unusual or suggestive about how he asked the questions?

A No.

Q And how did you answer the questions?

A No and no.

Q Okay. Did you try to make it clear to him at all that there was more to the story than just no and no?

A Not at that point.

Q At that time, did you make arrangements to meet with the attorney who you would get, Mr. Frank Carter?

A Yes. After Mr. Jordan made the arrangements with Mr. Carter, he told me to be at his office at -- I think 11:00 or 10:30 on Monday.

Q All right. How did the meeting with Mr. Jordan end? Was there any reference to a hug?

A Oh, yes. I'm sorry.

Q That's okay.

A When I was leaving, I asked him if he would give the President a hug for me. I bugged him again about making sure he told the President. And so he said, "I don't hug men." I said, "Well, okay."

Q All right.

A But --

Q All right. Did you call Linda Tripp afterwards?

A Yes, I did.

Q What was the purpose of your call?

A In a -- to let her know that I had been subpoenaed.

Q Tell us how that conversation went.

A It probably would be impossible for anyone who didn't -- who has listened to that tape to follow. I was beyond paranoid.

I had no idea how I had gotten onto the witness list and then, of course, been subpoenaed and I was thinking at that point that maybe my phone was tapped or someone had read my e-mails or something. But in thinking that my phone might be tapped, I sort of tried to explain to this to Linda that I had been subpoenaed in a veiled fashion.

Q How did you do that? What do you mean?

A I used different cover stories. I think like it was a movie or it was a book, trying to discuss things. I think I said something -- "I received the flowers," trying to intimate that I had received the subpoena. So --

Q Eventually, did you drop the sort of disguised way of talking and just talk about the subpoena, or do you recall?

A I don't believe I did. I don't really remember,

857

137

though.

Q How were things left with Linda?

A She was having a party the next day, so we made plans that -- or I suggested that I come early and we could discuss this and that I would help her set up for her dumb party. I'm sorry.

Q Her dumb party? All right. Well, we'll skip the dumb party for now.

A I'm sorry.

MR. EMMICK: That's all right.

MR. WISENBERG: I have a quick question.

MR. EMMICK: Okay. A dumb party question?

MR. WISENBERG: Not about the dumb party.

MR. EMMICK: All right.

BY MR. WISENBERG:

Q When you were doing the flowers bit, the book bit, how was she -- you're trying to speak in code to her, how was she responding?

A I don't really remember. I just sort of remember her not understanding and me being frustrated. "Hello? Understand. We just talked about this."

A JUROR: Excuse me. May I ask a question?

MR. EMMICK: Sure. Absolutely. Yes.

A JUROR: Did you ever find out how the Paula Jones lawyers knew about the hat pin, et cetera?

THE WITNESS: I -- from what I've read in the press, yes.

A JUROR: But just from any other source? Did you ever suspect maybe Linda or --

THE WITNESS: I had -- I came to start to suspect her, but not in any way that -- that it really has turned out to be. Not to that degree.

A JUROR: Thank you.

BY MR. EMMICK:

Q Let's turn our attention, then, to December 22nd, which is the day that you met with Frank Carter and I think you had said that you were going to meet with Vernon earlier.

A Mm-hmm.

Q Tell us about that. The Vernon part.

A Okay. With all the details?

Q Well, first, when were you supposed to meet with Vernon and then did you place another call to him?

A Right. I -- I -- I asked -- I called on the morning of the 22nd to see if I could come to see Mr. Jordan earlier. And I was -- I was a little concerned. I thought maybe he didn't really understand or -- fully understand what it was that was happening here with me being subpoenaed and what this really meant. So I came to see Mr. Jordan earlier and I also wanted to find out if he had in fact told the President that I had been subpoenaed.

Q Right.

A Which I found out he did. So I -- so I told Mr. Jordan that -- I said I was concerned that maybe -- that someone had listened in on phone calls and Mr. Jordan said, "Well, you know, so what? The President's allowed to call people."

And I said, "Well, we've had phone sex."

And so Mr. Jordan said, "Well, what's phone sex?"

And so I said, "Well, you know what phone sex is."

And he said, "No, I don't. I'm just an old man. I don't know what phone sex is."

And it was kind of this -- discussion that way.

Q Did you discuss the hat pin?

A We didn't discuss the hat pin, but I brought -- I had put together sort of an assortment of things that I was planning to hand over to Mr. Carter as being in response to the subpoena, sort of things that I would -- considered gifts, being the Christmas cards that I had received from the White House, I had a copy of the President's book, "Hope and History," which he had signed to me which had a very innocuous sort of inscription. And I think brought some innocuous pictures with me. So I showed those to Mr. Jordan.

Q What did you say about those items?

A I know that -- I think I was a little more specific in my proffer about what -- I mean, what I remember saying now was that -- you know, that I sort of showed him that this is what I was going to respond to for the subpoena.

Q Well, did you bring everything that could have responded to the subpoena that day?

A No. No.

Q Did you try to convey to Mr. Jordan the fact that it wasn't everything?

A I think I might have.

Q And do you remember how you would have conveyed it? Would it have been very expressly or would it have been more impliedly?

A More impliedly.

BY MS. IMMERGUT:

Q Did you tell Mr. Jordan that the President had indeed given you a hat pin?

A I did, but I had told him that on Friday and that was what prompted the sort of "this is a vanilla response."

MR. EMMICK: Let me show you the written proffer --

THE WITNESS: Okay.

MR. EMMICK: -- and see if that helps you recall or if you know whether or not when you wrote it it's accurate.

What we're looking at is the top of page 6 -- everyone else has a copy.

THE WITNESS: Okay. There's some spelling mistakes.

861

141

MR. EMMICK: Why don't I just read out loud. This paragraph starts, "On the day Mr. Jordan drove Ms. Lewinsky to Mr. Carter's office, she showed Mr. Jordan the items she was producing in response to the subpoena. Ms. Lewinsky believes she made it clear this was not everything she had that could respond to the subpoena, but she thought it was enough to satisfy. Mr. Jordan made no comment about whether or not what Ms. Lewinsky brought was right or wrong. Mr. Jordan drove Ms. Lewinsky to Mr. Carter's office, introduced them and left."

BY MR. EMMICK:

Q Now, having read that to you, does that refresh your recollection about what was said to him?

A I think I would have implied it.

Q Yes.

A That this wasn't everything. I -- I don't really remember if I specifically said -- and from reading this, it doesn't make me think I necessarily specifically said, "This isn't everything, but it's enough to satisfy," but I could have said that.

Q At the time you wrote this, were you trying to be completely truthful and accurate?

A I was trying to be completely -- yes, I was completely truthful and accurate. I'm just also while I'm reading this now, it doesn't necessarily indicate to me that -- that what I'm saying here is sort of a direct quote of what I said.

Q Do you remember what Mr. Jordan's reaction was? There it's written that he didn't indicate whether he thought it was right or wrong, but more generally, how did he react when you tried to convey to him that this may not be everything?

A There were often times when I was with Mr. Jordan that he would have no reaction at all. He would kind of do this "Mmmph" thing.

Q I'm not sure how the court reporter is going to get that. Is that a grunt?

A And so -- I remember feeling in general with Mr. Jordan and this sub t matter, just not knowing. Do you understand what I'm trying to say? Is this clear? And not really ever getting much of a reaction from him.

Q Did you take from his lack of reaction that he did understand or was it still ambiguous in your mind?

A I think sometimes I thought he understood and sometimes I thought it was ambiguous.

Q Okay. Did the subject of phone sex come up again in your conversation with Mr. Jordan?

A Aside from what I mentioned before?

Q Yes. Did you explain to him what phone sex was at some point?

A I think it -- at -- I don't think I said it. He might have said -- know, is it -- uh -- this is embarrassing. Hmm. I think he -- it's hard. I think he -- uh -- might have given some suggestion as to what he thought phone sex was and I agreed. Is that --

Q That's fine.

A -- fair?

Q That's fine.

A By this time, had you expected the President to call you?

A Mm-hmm. Yes.

MR. EMMICK: I'm sorry?

A JUROR: Before you go on, can you ask her what does that mean?

MR. EMMICK: What does phone sex --

A JUROR: No, what did he say?

MR. EMMICK: I think the grand juror is asking for more detail.

THE WITNESS: If I remember correctly, I believe that he said -- or maybe I said something like -- you know, "He's taking care of business on one end and I'm taking care of business on another." Does that --

BY MR. WISENBERG:

Q Do you remember which one of you said it?

A When I'm saying that now, I think I said it,

because that sounds more familiar to me.

Does that answer your question?

A JUROR: (Nods affirmatively.)

BY MR. EMMICK:

Q Did you expect the President to call you?

A Yes, I did.

Q Is that why you were bugging or asking Vernon so much about whether he had told the President?

A I don't know. Maybe.

Q All right.

A I think I just wanted to make sure the President knew.

BY MS. IMMERGUT:

Q That you had been subpoenaed.

A Right. Because I was supposed to call -- you know, in the event that I was subpoenaed, I was supposed to have called Betty and -- so --

BY MR. EMMICK:

Q I'm going to ask a question that will suggest what assumptions you were making about what Vernon knew or didn't. Why would you feel comfortable talking with Vernon Jordan about phone sex?

A I wasn't comfortable talking to Vernon Jordan about phone sex.

Q Okay.

A I was scared.

MR. EMMICK: Okay.

MR. WISENBERG: Questions?

MR. EMMICK: Yes?

BY MR. WISENBERG:

Q Did you say on the 22nd that you showed to Vernon Jordan the gifts you bringing to Frank Carter?

A Yes.

Q Okay. Was a hat pin among the things you showed to Vernon Jordan?

A No.

Q But you had indicated to him on the 19th that the President had given you a hat pin.

A Yes.

MR. WISENBERG: Thank you.

BY MR. EMMICK:

Q At some point, you went to Frank Carters's.

A Mm-hmm. Yes.

Q Tell us what happened when you got to Frank Carter's.

A We arrived at Mr. Carter's office and Mr. Jordan and I sat down on the sofa. Mr. Carter came out. Mr. Jordan introduced us and left.

Q In your discussions with Mr. Carter, what was the major point that you were trying to make? What was the big thing you were trying to convey to Mr. Carter?

A That there was absolutely no reason why I should have been subpoenaed in this case.

Q Okay. And --

A And that I certainly did not have a relationship with the President.

Q You said that to him.

A I don't think I said those words, but that was what I was trying to convey and certainly when asked those questions, that's what I answered.

Q Did you discuss with him how you could get out of the deposition?

A Yes.

Q Tell us what you talked about. Maybe that would be the easier way to go.

A Okay. I told Mr. Carter I really didn't want to be dragged into this, I didn't -- I thought Paula Jones' claim was bunk and I didn't want to be associated with the case. believe I suggested maybe that I could -- maybe I asked him if I could sign an affidavit or is that something to do.

He said that the first step -- to hold off on that and that the first step is he would try to talk to the attorneys for Paula Jones and find out what it is, why they're subpoenaing me and where it is that they're going with this and that maybe one option might be is he could arrange for them to interview me, just kind of do a brief interview, versus a deposition.

Q Did you discuss with him the subpoena insofar as it requested items? Did you, for example, go through and talk about what items were called for?

A Yes, we did. Yes. And I said no to everything until we got to the gifts and then I sort of turned over what it was that I had brought with me that I thought responded to the gifts. And that was it.

Q Was there any mention made by either of you of Bob Bennett?

A Yes.

Q Tell us what was said.

A I requested of Mr. Carter that he get in touch with Mr. Bennett and just to be in touch with him and to let him know that I had been subpoenaed in this case and I didn't know why.

Q Why did you request that Mr. Carter contact Mr. Bennett?

A Because I thought in the -- how do I explain this? Sort of in the story or role, the story that I was giving to Mr. Carter and being a low level political appointee and, in general, even if I hadn't been a low level political appointee, I thought it was probably appropriate to align myself with the President's side, being that that's whose side I was on and there was no question in my mind.

Q Is another way of saying that you were trying to send a message to the President or to Mr. Bennett?

A Not to the President. He knew. I mean, the President knew, you know? So --

Q So it was more a message to Mr. Bennett?

A I just -- to me, that seemed -- I mean, I think -- you have to look at this from the point of view that I was a political appointee. And so --

Q What does that imply for you?

A For me, that means that the reason you're in this job is you work for this administration and that you're politically aligned with this administration and everything you do is in the best interests of the administration and, ultimately, the President. And that's where your goal and your focus should be.

Q How were things left? What was he going to do and what were you going to next?

A Mr. Carter was going to get in touch with the attorneys for Paula Jones and get in touch with Mr. Bennett. And he was going to send me a retainer letter. And we'd be in touch.

Q Let me then ask you the following. You had earlier indicated that the President said that he had a Christmas present for you.

A Mm-hmm. Yes.

Q Did you ever make contact with Betty Currie in order to make arrangements to pick up the present?

A Yes.

Q Tell us about that.

A I called Betty after Christmas to see how she was doing and find out how her holiday was and to ask her -- or to let her know that the President had mentioned to me that he had a Christmas present for me and, you know, to touch base with him to see if he -- what he wanted to do, if he wanted to get together.

So she called me back and told me to come to the White House at 8:30 in the morning on Sunday, the 28th of December.

Q Did you?

A Yes, I did.

Q All right. Betty waved you in?

A Yes.

Q At about what time was it, if you can remember?

A 8:30.

Q When you got there, what happened?

A I think the President was already there. He was just coming to the Oval Office and Betty and the President and I were in the Oval Office and this was the first time I got to meet Buddy.

So we played with Buddy in the office and he was running around the carpet. And I had brought a small Christmas present for Buddy. And so the three of us were just talking and goofing off. And then the President and I went into the back study and he gave me my Christmas presents.

Q How long were you in the back study with the President?

A Maybe about 45 minutes to an hour.

Q What was the Christmas present or presents that he got for you?

A Everything was packaged in a big Black Dog -- or big canvass bag from the Black Dog store in Martha's Vineyard. And he got me a marble bear's head carving, sort of -- you know, a little sculpture, I guess, maybe.

Q Was that the item from Vancouver?

A Yes. Then he got me a big Rockettes blanket from Christmas of '95 or '96, I think. He got me a Black Dog stuffed animal that had a little Black Dog T-shirt on it.

He got me a small little box of chocolates, cherry chocolates, and then he got me some sunglasses that were a joke because I had -- I had teased him for a long time about the different sunglasses that he was wearing in public.

And so then I bought him a normal pair of sunglasses, and so we had just sort of had -- this was a long running joke with us, so he bought me these really funny looking sunglasses and we both were putting them on and joking around goofing off.

So -- I'm trying to think what else. Can I look at the list?

MR. EMMICK: Sure. Feel free.

THE WITNESS: Oh. He got me a pin that had the most of my Christmas presents were sort of New York themed, so he got me a pin that had the New York skyline on it. I think that's it. Well, it's a lot, so -- not just that's it.

BY MR. EMMICK:

Q Now, you had mentioned earlier that you were concerned about the fact that the subpoena covered this hat pin.

A Mm-hmm.

Q Did you discuss that concern with President Clinton?

A Yes. We -- we really spent maybe about five -- no more than ten minutes talking about the Paula Jones case on this day and -- do you want me to talk about the hat pin or that period of time?

Q The whole period of time, I suppose.

A I brought up the subject of the case because I was concerned about how I had been brought into the case and been put on the witness list. So I asked him how he thought I got put on the witness list and he told me he thought that maybe it was that woman from the summer with Kathleen Willey, which I knew to be Linda Tripp, or maybe -- he said maybe some of the uniformed -- maybe the uniformed officers.

We talked about that. I mentioned that I had been concerned about the hat pin being on the subpoena and he said that that had sort of concerned him also and asked me if I had told anyone that he had given me this hat pin and I said no.

Q That was false.

A Correct. Yes. When in fact I had told people about the hat pin.

Q Right.

A Let's see. And then at some point I said to him, "Well, you know, should I -- maybe I should put the gifts away outside my house somewhere or give them to someone, maybe Betty." And he sort of said -- I think he responded, "I don't know" or "Let me think about that." And left that topic.

Q When you said "the gifts," what did you mean by "the gifts"?

A I meant all the gifts that he had given me.

Q All right. Do you think that you're the one who came up with Betty's name?

A I'm not 100 percent sure, but when I received the

call from Betty, I wasn't surprised that it was Betty calling, so that's what leads me to believe that I might have suggested it.

Q Okay. Did you discuss with the President the fact that you were planning to sign an affidavit?

A I might have mentioned it, but I don't think -- we really didn't spend very much time on this subject.

Q All right. So you walked in without many gifts, you were going to walk out with a bag of gifts.

A Mm-hmm.

Q Okay. Did it strike you as unusual that when you had a subpoena calling for you to produce gifts the President is giving you a bag of gifts?

A At the time, it didn't strike me as unusual.

Q Okay. And why is that?

A I never thought about it. I mean, I was -- I was -- I had struggled for a long time before the 28th -- or I should just say -- I guess a few days before the 28th, that if I was going to see the President, if I should tell him or not that Linda knew. And I decided not to.

And so I -- I thought this might be the last time I saw him before I went to New York and I wanted it to be a really nice visit, so I was -- I -- having decided not to tell him about Linda, I kind of didn't even want to go too far there in getting mired down in the discussion of the case.

Q All right. When you left the White House, did anything unusual happen with respect to your E-pass?

A Yes. Well, I had a visitor's pass.

Q Visitor's E-pass, I guess.

A Is that what --

Q A visitor's pass?

A Visitor's -- I don't know. I know it is a visitor's pass. Betty escorted me out and I realized that I left the pass in the office, so Betty told me that she would call down to the guard station and let them know that I was fine and I had just left the pass somewhere.

Q Do you remember what gate you used when you left the White House?

A I believe it was the southwest gate.

Q Did you hear from Betty later that day?

A Yes, I did.

Q Were you surprised to hear from her?

A No. I mean, I wasn't surprised that I was hearing from Betty. I think I was a little surprised to sort of get the nature of this phone call when the President could have just said right then and there, "Well, yeah, I think, you know, why don't you give them to Betty, that's a good idea." But I wasn't terribly surprised. No.

Q What did she say?

A She said, "I understand you have something to give

875

155

me." Or, "The President said you have something to give me." Along those lines.

Q How long after you had left the White House did Betty call you?

A Several hours.

Q When she said something along the lines of "I understand you have something for me," or "The President says you have something for me," what did you understand her to mean?

A The gifts.

Q Okay.

A Kind of -- what I was reminded of then a little bit was jumping all the way back to the July 14th incident where I was supposed to call Betty the next day but not really get into details with her, that this was maybe along those same lines.

Q That actually anticipates my next question.

A Oh.

Q Did you feel any need to explain to her what was going to happen?

A No.

Q What arrangements did you make for transfer of the something?

A I think we discussed some things and Betty mentioned she was on the way to the hospital to visit her mom and she'd swing by and, you know, pick up whatever it was I was supposed to give her.

Q Now, at the time you had that conversation, were you already packing up the gifts at all?

A No.

Q When was she going to come by, then? That day?

A Yes.

Q What did you do after the phone call ended?

A I put all the gifts that he had given me on my bed and I got a big box from The Gap and went through each item and decided if I needed to give it to them or not.

Q Can you explain what you mean by that?

A It sort of was a difficult -- I -- I wasn't sure if I was going to get this box back, so I didn't want to give everything in the event that I didn't get the box back for some reason.

And I kept out some innocuous things and I kept out -- the -- really the most -- the most sentimental gift he had given me was the book, the "Leaves of Grass" book, so -- and it was just -- it's beautiful and it meant a lot to me, so I kept that out.

Q What other -- it sounds to me like you had one category of more sentimental gifts that you kept out of the box.

A Mm-hmm.

877

157

Q And kept for yourself. What other items were in that category, other than the "Leaves of Grass"?

A Not necessarily sentimental ones, but just -- I think I kept out the marble bear head, the bag, the canvass bag, the blanket, the sunglasses, the chocolates. And I think that's it. Oh, wait. And I might have kept out some of the Martha's Vineyard stuff that I had gotten in the fall.

Q Those were items that you've recently turned over to our office.

A Yes.

Q Which items did you put into the box? If you remember.

A The hat pin, the pin that I had received that day for Christmas, a pin that he had given me for my birthday, a picture that he had signed for me for my birthday that I had framed, a picture he had signed for me of him wearing the first tie I gave him.

Q Any other Black Dog items?

A I think there was a Black Dog hat that I put in there. And I'm not -- I'm not really sure what else was in there. Oh, I also put the copies that I had left of the Valentine's Day ad that I had put in the paper for him.

Q The Romeo and Juliet quote?

A Mm-hmm.

Q All right. Did Betty come by?

878

158

A Yes, she did. I met her outside.

Q How did you know when she was going to come by? Was there a prearranged time she was going to come by or did she call you from --

A I think she called me on her way out.

Q You met her outside, you had the box with you?

A Mm-hmm. I had taped it up and I wrote "Please do not throw away" on it.

Q Were you concerned that she might throw it away?

A Mm-hmm. Yes. Sorry.

Q Okay. Let me just ask you some questions. Did you ever discuss with her the contents of the box?

A I don't believe so.

Q Did she ever ask about the contents of the box?

A No.

Q Did she ever say anything indicating that she knew from a prior discussion the contents of the box?

A Not -- no, not that I remember.

Q Sounds like it was a short conversation.

A We talked about her mom a bit and Christmas. I think maybe I had elaborated on what I got for Christmas from him.

Q Now, you could have just thrown these items out, rather than putting them in a box. Why didn't you just throw them out?

879

159

A Because I -- they meant a lot to me.

Q Okay. You could have given the items to someone else, a friend of yours, Ashley Raines, or to your mother or just hidden them somewhere. Why didn't you do that?

A I think -- I've come to sort of see this now. I don't know that I necessarily saw it then, but I feel now a little bit that me turning over some of these things was a little bit of an assurance to the President or reassurance that, you know, that everything was okay.

Q In your mind, then, were you giving these items not just to Betty, but really to the President as well, in a manner of speaking?

A I think that was even more directly what I thought it was. Not that they were going to be in his possession, but that he would understand whatever it was I gave to Betty and that that might make him feel a little bit better.

Q Did Betty say where she was going to put the box of gifts?

A I think she said she was going to keep them in a closet. Or, you know, she'd keep the box in a closet.

Q Right.

A You asked me -- never mind.

Q The gifts. Right. I understood. I understood. All right. What I'd like to do now is ask a few questions --

880

160

MR. WISENBERG: Mike?

MR. EMMICK: Yes?

MR. WISENBERG: Before you leave that topic, I have a few on that. Do you mind?

MR. EMMICK: No. Not at all.

BY MR. WISENBERG:

Q You've said here today, Ms. Lewinsky, and I think you told us earlier in some of your sessions with us, that you were -- the non-innocuous items were going to go to Frank Carter and --

MR. EMMICK: You mean the innocuous items.

MR. WISENBERG: What did I say?

MR. EMMICK: The not innocuous items.

MR. WISENBERG: Boy. Thank you. I stand corrected.

BY MR. WISENBERG:

Q The innocuous items were going to go to Frank Carter, the non-innocuous items were not, but that one of the reasons, one of the criterion for stuff that didn't even go in the Betty Currie box that you would keep would be sentimental value.

A Mm-hmm.

Q Is that -- have I described that accurately?

A Sort of.

Q Okay. How not sort of?

Diversified Reporting Services, Inc.
1025 VERMONT AVENUE, N.W. SUITE 1250
WASHINGTON, D.C. 20005
(202) 296-2929

A I didn't really give any gifts to Mr. Carter. Nothing that I turned over to Mr. Carter was a gift from the President. And I think the way you described the dividing of the actual gifts was sort of innocuous, you know, not innocuous -- sentimental value, I think that was more accurate.

Q Well, as between the gifts you put in the box and the gifts you kept?

A Mm-hmm.

Q All right. How would you describe today the difference between the two? I just want to make sure I understand, between the ones you kept and the ones you put in the Betty box.

A You know, I don't have a perfect memory of what the criteria was at the time. I know I kept the book out because that was the most sentimental thing to me.

And I believe that the things I put in the box were -- also in the box was a dress he gave me from Martha's Vineyard, so the things that went into the box were, I think, more along the lines of some of the things that really complied with the subpoena, that were maybe specifically named, although I think books might have been specifically named in the subpoena, but I kept the "Leaves of Grass."

Q They complied with the subpoena, but they're going to Betty Currie.

A Correct.

Q Now, my question is, and I've asked you this before, but I want to ask you in front of the grand jury, since you were basically trying to keep some sentimental things but you told us that the hat pin was sentimental to you, why is the hat pin going into the Betty box?

A Because the hat pin was the alarm of the subpoena, so -- I -- I -- to me, it seemed logical that putting the hat pin in the box -- I mean, it was what had been named in the subpoena.

MR. EMMICK: All right. Should we take a break?

THE FOREPERSON: Yes, we should.

THE WITNESS: Oh, thank goodness.

MR. EMMICK: Okay. All right. Ten minutes.

THE WITNESS: Okay.

THE FOREPERSON: Ten minutes.

(Witness excused. Witness recalled.)

MR. EMMICK: All right. Do we have a quorum?

THE FOREPERSON: Yes, we do.

MR. EMMICK: Any unauthorized persons present?

THE FOREPERSON: None at all.

THE WITNESS: Let me guess. You're going to remind me I'm still under oath.

THE FOREPERSON: There you go.

THE WITNESS: Fast learner.

BY MR. EMMICK:

Q Ms. Lewinsky, this is what we're going to do. We're going to go over some questions that we'd like to ask and then we're going to turn our attention to the December 31st meeting, the breakfast meeting with Vernon Jordan.

A Okay.

Q Let's go to questions first. One question is Betty comes by and gets this box of gifts. Is there any other way Betty would have known to call and pick up this box of gifts except for the President asking her to?

A The only thing I can think of is if he had asked someone else to ask Betty.

Q Do you have any reason to think that happened?

A No, but, I mean, I wasn't there, so I don't know -- I don't know what he said, how -- maybe he left her a note. I mean, I don't know. So --

Q Another way of asking it is did you tell someone else about this and they might have asked Betty?

A No.

BY MR. WISENBERG:

Q Did you think it as a coincidence that she called you?

A No.

BY MR. EMMICK:

Q Let me ask you a couple of questions about the

December 20th dumb party.

A Okay.

Q Okay? First, why is it a dumb party.

A Oh. Really? You want me to answer that?

Q Yes.

A Well, because it was Linda Tripp's party and -- well, that should be enough, but just that I got there and I got stuck having to do all this stuff and I had really wanted to talk to her about the predicament we were in and -- I now look back on it and just -- she had spent all this money on food and a month before she had had no money for the bus and was trying to sell her clothes and somehow she had $500 to spend on food and had money to spend on presents underneath her tree and it was just dumb.

Q Let's focus on the discussions you had with Linda at the dumb party or before the dumb party about the situation.

A I really didn't sort of get into, I think, a full discussion with her until after -- well, until I was leaving and I asked her to walk me out to my car.

Q Let's talk first then about the efforts you made to talk with her about the subpoena in the house. Did you try to?

A Probably. It was -- I got there maybe -- the -- I think the party was supposed to start around 7:30 and I got there at 5:00 and she had made no food, had done nothing. mean, she just had this fridge stuffed with food.

So I was trying to help prepare all this stuff. There was a lot more work to do than I thought there would be and then her daughter had this obsession with vacuuming that night, so there were just a lot of people and I don't really remember trying to get a chance.

I may have tried to or sort of said "I need to talk to you," kind of a thing, but I don't recall having any discussions with her before the party.

Q Okay. And then you mentioned that you were able to talk to her a little bit outside, I think you said?

A Mm-hmm.

Q Tell us about that.

A The main -- the main feeling I had had at that point, once I had received my subpoena was that -- that now she didn't need to worry about denying that she knew anything about this relationship, because I was going to deny it under oath as well.

And so sort of just -- I figured that conversation would kind of just be mapping out what our next steps would be. But it ended up being much shorter and I -- she looked at the subpoena -- excuse me -- sorry -- and I think she -- she kept talking about how weird, "Isn't the hat pin strange? Isn't it strange that they're asking about the hat pin?"

And we talked about that. And I think that -- I -- I was -- I was -- I don't think that I was left with the feeling that she was going to continue on this path of insisting she would rat on me. So -- is that clear? I'm sorry -- no? Okay.

When I left that night, I felt a little more -- I think I felt a little more reassured that she and I would be saying the same thing in the Paula Jones case. Is that -- okay. But I wasn't 100 percent sure and I think that we left it that we'd have some more discussions about this.

Q Okay. One of the things we wanted to get back to was the whole situation on the 28th where there's a subpoena that calls for you to turn over gifts and the President is giving you gifts.

A Mm-hmm.

Q What do you think the President is thinking when he is giving you gifts when there's a subpoena covering the gifts? I mean, does he think in any way, shape or form that you're going to be turning these gifts over?

A You know, I can't answer what he was thinking, but to me, it was -- there was never a question in my mind and I -- from everything he said to me, I never questioned him, that we were ever going to do anything but keep this private, so that meant deny it and that meant do -- take whatever appropriate steps needed to be taken, you know, for that

887

167

to happen, meaning that if I had turned over every gift he had given me -- first of all, the point of the affidavit and the point of everything was to try to avoid a deposition, so where I'd have to sort of -- you know, I wouldn't have to lie as much as I would necessarily in an affidavit, how I saw it.

So by turning over all these gifts, it would at least prompt them to want to question me about what kind of friendship I had with the President and they would want to speculate and they'd leak it and my name would be trashed and he would be in trouble. So --

Q So your impression, then, was in the same way that the two of you were going to deny the relationship, you would also deny or conceal the gifts that were personal that passed between you.

A And the phone call -- I mean, I think that it was everything. I think it was kind of -- at least for me, I don't know what he did, for me, this had to be thought through. You know, I had to anticipate everything that might happen and make sure -- you know --

Q You did what was necessary.

A Exactly.

BY MS. IMMERGUT:

Q Although, Ms. Lewinsky, I think what is sort of -- it seems a little odd and, I guess, really the grand jurors

Diversified Reporting Services, Inc.
1025 VERMONT AVENUE, N.W. SUITE 1250
WASHINGTON, D.C. 20005
(202) 296-2929

wanted your impression of it, was on the same day that you're discussing basically getting the gifts to Betty to conceal them, he's giving you a new set of gifts.

A You know, I have come recently to look at that as sort of a strange situation, I think, in the course of the past few weeks, but at the time, I was -- you know, I was in love with him, I was elated to get these presents and -- at the same time that I was so scared about the Paula Jones thing, I was happy to be with him and -- I -- I didn't think about that.

He had -- he had hesitated very briefly right before I left that day in kind of packaging -- he packaged all my stuff back up and I just sort of -- you know, remember him kind of hesitating and thinking to myself -- I don't think he said anything that indicated this to me, but I thought to myself, "I wonder if he's thinking he shouldn't give these to me to take out." But he did.

Q And he had already told you he had some gifts for you for Christmas.

A Correct.

BY MR. EMMICK:

Q You mentioned earlier when I asked who was on the list in your mind of people who should be avoided like Nancy Hernreich or Steve Goodin, you mentioned Mr. Ickes.

A Mm-hmm.

889

169

Q That name came up. Why was Mr. Ickes on the avoid list?

A He -- well, he -- he's just strange. And he -- I'm sorry. He would -- you know, you could be the only person in the hall and you would pass Mr. Ickes in the hall and he would just glare at you. You know.

And I'd say, "Hello," you know, as you would imagine you're supposed to do and he'd just glare at you and walk past you. And I thought that was strange. Call me weird.

Q Okay. And that's the reason that you mentioned him on the list of people to avoid?

A And I think just -- his name is sort of in my mind for having to do with things that we're discussing today and what's been in the press of it, but it really was most every senior person in the White House, I mean, except for Betty who knew who I was that would concern me.

Q Right.

A I mean, I had -- you know, I had had a lot of interaction with these people during the furlough, so --

Q Let me ask you a question about Tim Keating. Did Tim Keating tell you or imply to you that you could come back after the election?

A He told me that I could probably come back after the election.

Q Okay. Do you remember when he said that to you?

A Yes. On --

Q Go ahead.

A I'm sorry. On the day that he informed me of the transfer.

Q So that would have been the 5th of April? Does that sound right? Friday, the 5th of April?

A Correct. It was Good Friday, I remember.

Q Did he say anything about any problem of an appearance of impropriety during that conversation with you? Something like there might be an appearance before but it doesn't matter after the election, anything like that?

A No. No. No.

Q That subject didn't come up at all?

A Not with Mr. Keating.

Q You mentioned that when -- oh, I'm sorry. Go ahead. Sure.

A JUROR: I'm sorry. What would have prompted him to make a comment like that, that you could come back after the election?

THE WITNESS: I was crying and I just kept telling him, I -- you know, I didn't really want to leave and why did I have to leave and wasn't there -- you know, weren't there other openings rather than me having to go to the Pentagon because he had --

Do you want me to get into a little bit about what was said there?

MR. EMMICK: If it will help answer the question, sure.

A JUROR: Yes. Please.

THE WITNESS: Okay. There had been problems with my supervisor, Jocelyn Jolley, and so when I was called in to Tim's office, I had thought he was -- he had just spoken with Jocelyn and I thought he was going to tell me they had fired Jocelyn and instead he told me that they were -- that for reasons having to do with some of the workload not -- things with the letters from the Office of Management and Budget, that they had to blow up -- quote-unquote, blow up the correspondence office and they were eliminating my position.

My transfer had nothing to do with my work, I shouldn't see this as a negative thing. He told me I was too sexy to be working in the East Wing and that this job at the Pentagon where I'd be writing press releases was a sexier job.

And I was crying and --

BY MR. EMMICK:

Q What do you think he meant by "too sexy"?

A I think he meant that -- he -- I think he was trying to -- you know, trying to conceal the fact that -- you know, that I now know, the real reason I was being transferred. And so I think he was trying to not maybe anger me. And thought that somehow by -- maybe he thought I'd think that was a complement.

A JUROR: Did you think he was patronizing you?

THE WITNESS: A little bit. Yeah. That's a good way to put it. I -- I just -- I just remember thinking that I was -- I was never going to see the President again and that all of a sudden that this -- you know, the end of this -- this relationship.

And I kept -- I've always sort of -- I'm the kind of person that always thinks that I can fix everything and so it was kind of this -- feeling of wait, this train's going too fast and I can't stop it and that it had already passed and -- and -- so when Tim said that, I think he sort of said that -- I don't think he meant to say that. I think that was probably more than he was supposed to say.

A JUROR: Thank you.

BY MR. EMMICK:

Q Going back again to the 17th of December when the President called you and let you know about the witness list, you said he used the phrase, "It broke my heart to see you on the witness list." What was your reaction when he said that?

A I believed him. I think I also --

Q You thought he was being sincere?

A JUROR: Can I ask another follow-up question?

MR. EMMICK: Sure.

A JUROR: Because you had nothing to do with formulating this witness list, why do you think it breaks his heart, that your name was on there? Because you're innocent of having formulated this list. Do you have -- or in your opinion, what is it that hurt him?

THE WITNESS: I think it was the idea that -- that -- this was going to -- that this was going to be a bad thing for me. I mean, if you imagine what's happened now hadn't happened and let's just say the Paula Jones thing had gone ahead and I had somehow been dragged into that, just being associate with it and it being difficult and maybe he -- maybe it was going to seriously alter any kind of friendship or relationship that we had, you know?

BY MR. EMMICK:

Q I want to ask a question about computer e-mails or files. Did you arrange for the deletion of files or e-mails that might have related to you and the President?

A Did I arrange?

Q Or did you delete them. Sorry.

A Yes, I did.

Q Okay. Did you ask Linda Tripp if she would delete e-mails relating to the President?

A Yes.

Q Did you speak with someone at the Department of

Defense in order to learn something about those deletions or to make sure that they would be more longstanding?

A Not about deletions.

Q Okay. Well, what was it that you spoke with him about?

A I asked him -- I asked Floyd, I think it is, if -- if -- sort of how easily someone could break into the computers. And I couldn't imagine how I had come to this witness -- come to be on this witness list, so one of the things I thought was maybe someone had broken into my computer and was reading my e-mails. And he told me that that was really difficult.

And then I asked him about -- then with the thought in mind of getting rid of the e-mails, I asked him what the sort of saving procedure was with the e-mails. I know at the White House, they back them up and put them in the archive forever and he told me that at the Pentagon, they sort of stay on the server for four weeks and then they're dumped into e-mail heaven or something.

Q All right. Did you ever ask Catherine Allday Davis to delete e-mails that you had sent relating to the President?

A No.

Q At any time, did you create anything like a spreadsheet that contained on it information relating to your relationship with the President?

A Yes.

Q Okay. Tell us about that.

A Linda and I had been talking and she had been talking about she's really good at coming up with patterns of things or -- I think that was the word she used.

And so she was wanting to see -- you know, I think in an effort to aid her in trying to figure out what the pattern of my relationship with the President was, I made a stupid spreadsheet on Microsoft Excel that just had the -- the numbered days of the month and the months and determined on what day was there a phone call or did I see him or see him at an event or something like that. So --

Q Is that something that you ultimately printed out and showed to her?

A Yes.

Q I take it that was on the DOD computer?

A Yes.

Q Were the entries that you made, would they have revealed that you were talking about Clinton?

A No.

Q Okay. Did you ever have an extra copy of that -- let's call it a spreadsheet?

A No.

Q Did you save the file of the spreadsheet?

A No. I don't believe so.

Q All right. Going back also to the night of the 17th, December 17th, just so that we can get clear on the date of that, it was at 2:30 in the morning. Is it literally on the 17th or is it --

A Nineteen -- eighteen -- it is literally the morning, 2:30 in the morning of the 17th. So, yes.

Q Okay. Good. When the President gave you the Vancouver bear on the 28th, did he say anything about what it means?

A Mm-hmm.

Q What did he say?

A I think he -- I believe he said that the bear is the -- maybe Indian symbol for strength, just -- you know, and to be strong like a bear.

Q And did you interpret that as be strong in your decision to continue to conceal the relationship?

A No.

MR. EMMICK: All right. Any follow-up on that?

MS. WIRTH: Can I ask one question?

MR. EMMICK: Sure.

BY MS. WIRTH:

Q Did he say something like "This is when you need to be strong," or "This is for when you need to be strong"? Beyond saying that it was a symbol of strength?

A I think he -- he held it and he said, you know, "You can hold onto this when you need to be strong."

MS. WIRTH: Thank you.

BY MR. EMMICK:

Q What I'd like to do is ask you about a passage from the proffer and I'm looking at page 5.

A Okay.

Q And you'll see at the bottom, and I'll read the passage, this is relating to the meeting on the 19th, just after you've gotten the subpoena, meeting with Vernon Jordan, and what the passage says is "Possibly later in that meeting, but more probably the next meeting," I assume that's a reference to the 22nd?

A Correct.

Q "Ms. Lewinsky tried to make it clear to Mr. Jordan that she in fact did have a physically intimate relationship with the President." And then let's go to the next page. It says, "Ms. Lewinsky made it clear she intended to deny the sexual relationship with the President."

So I guess what I want to talk about is the portion of the passage on page 5.

A Mm-hmm.

Q Tell us how you tried to make it clear to Mr. Jordan that you had a physically intimate relationship with the President.

A I think by mentioning the phone sex.

Q I see. All right. Any other way that you tried to make it clear to him?

A Not that I remember.

Q All right. And then is it your recollection now that it was on the 22nd that you were trying to make this clear to Mr. Jordan?

A Yes.

Q As opposed to the 19th?

A Yes.

MR. EMMICK: Any other follow-up on that?

BY MS. IMMERGUT:

Q Ms. Lewinsky, how did you make it clear to him that you intended to deny the relationship with the President on the 23rd? Excuse me. The 22nd.

A This is, I think, as I mentioned to you guys before, this is -- I don't have a memory of this. I know when I wrote this I was telling the truth, so I'm sure I did do this, but I don't remember.

MR. WISENBERG: Ms. Lewinsky --

Mike, do you mind if I ask some questions?

MR. EMMICK: Go right ahead.

BY MR. WISENBERG:

Q I think, you can correct me if I'm wrong, you've done it previously today, so I'm sure you will again if I am, you told us when we first met with you in the proffer meeting that you couldn't specifically remember that item. Is that correct?

A Yes.

Q And I think you said you couldn't specifically remember any more of the item that Mike just read to you on the bottom of the previous page about the physically intimate relationship.

A Right.

Q But that you had no doubt that it's true. Is that correct?

A I was being truthful in my proffer. Yes.

Q And the proffer, written proffer, is accurate. Is that correct?

A Yes.

Q But -- and I think you also said you feel some -- I don't know if this is the reason you don't remember it, but you have expressed to us that you feel some guilt about Vernon Jordan. Is that correct?

A Mm-hmm.

Q That's a yes?

A Yes.

Q Okay. Can you tell us why that is?

A He was the only person who did what he said he was going to do for me and -- in getting me the job. And when I met with Linda on the 13th, when she was wearing a wire, and even in subsequent or previous conversations and subsequent conversations, I attributed things to Mr. Jordan that weren't true because I knew that it had leverage with Linda and that a lot of those things that I said got him into a lot of trouble and I just -- he's a good person and --

Q Is one example of -- and then I'll leave this topic, is one example of one of the things you told Linda that isn't true, "I told Vernon Jordan no job, no affidavit"? Something along those lines?

A Yes. Because Linda made me promise her that on the 9th.

Q Okay. Of January?

A Of January.

MR. WISENBERG: Okay.

THE FOREPERSON: Do you need a minute?

THE WITNESS: I'm okay. Thanks.

A JUROR: I'm a little confused. When you said that you said certain things because you know Linda had the mike, right?

THE WITNESS: Oh, I didn't know Linda had the mike. I now know that she was wearing a wire.

A JUROR: Okay. But so why would you say these things about Mr. Jordan that were not true? What was the reason?

901

181

THE WITNESS: Because -- I had -- from some of my conversation with Linda, I started to think that she was a little bit jealous that Mr. Jordan was helping me get a job in New York and that I was leaving the Pentagon and that -- she had remarked one time that -- that, you know, Mr. Jordan who is the most powerful, you know, man in this city got me my attorney and she -- she thinks that she only had -- you know, this dinky attorney or something like that.

And I was -- I was so desperate for her to -- I was -- for her to not reveal anything about this relationship that I used anything and anybody that I could think of as leverage with her. I -- her, the President, my mom, everybody. I mean, not her, but Mr. Jordan, the President, my mom. Anybody that I thought would have any kind of influence on her, I used.

Does that answer your question?

A JUROR: Well, it doesn't. I guess what I'm trying to figure out, okay, is what was that going to accomplish? Was that going to make her -- what?

THE WITNESS: Well, specifically, with the statement about I won't sign the affidavit until I get the job, is that I had a conversation with Linda, which we'll probably get to --

MR. EMMICK: I hope.

THE WITNESS: Oh. On January 9th and in that

conversation, she had told me she had changed her mind, she was going to be vague on the truth about Kathleen Willey and then she told me -- at that point, I had told her I hadn't signed an affidavit when I had and I told I didn't have a job yet and I knew I was probably going to be getting a job that day.

And she said, "Monica, promise me you won't sign the affidavit until you get the job. Tell Vernon you won't sign the affidavit until you get the job because if you sign the affidavit before you get the job, they're never going to give you the job."

And I didn't want her to think that I had gone ahead and done anything without her and that I was leaving her in the dark. I wanted her to feel that -- sort of Linda and myself against everyone else because I felt like I needed to hold her hand through this in order to try to get her to do what I wanted, essentially.

BY MR. EMMICK:

Q We can get into that in more detail when we talk about the 13th.

A Okay.

Q Why don't we do the following. I wanted to ask some -- rather than just jumping into the 31st which is a Vernon Jordan meeting, why don't we ask some questions about which of your gifts to the President you have ever seen in the White House itself, either in the dining room or the study or the Oval Office generally.

A Does that include gifts that I gave him that I've seen him wear?

Q All right. Well, let's just start with the things that you've seen in the area itself.

A Okay. Okay. I -- can I go through -- just go through the list?

Q Sure.

A That would probably be easier. On page 6, I've seen the two little books.

Q Two little books?

A The "Oy Vey" book, which is jokes and the little golf book.

Q Do you remember when you saw those books?

A Yes. On -- I think it was November 13th.

Q Zadilla day?

A Zadilla day.

Q All right.

A I saw a copy of the Washington Post ad that I had given him in a book on his desk.

Q You gave him a smallish copy of the --

A I gave him an actual copy that I cut out from one of the papers and I glued it into a little cardboard thing.

Q And where did you see it on his desk.

A It was inside a book.

Q And the book was on the desk in the study?

A Yes.

MS. WIRTH: Mike, could I ask a question?

BY MS. WIRTH:

Q Did you see the ad in a particular book?

A Yes.

Q Which one?

A "Vox."

Q Okay. And was that on the desk in the study?

A Yes.

Q And was "Oy Vey" on the desk in the study?

A Yes.

Q What about the little golf book?

A I think it was. I -- I -- I'm not 100 percent sure it was a golf book, I'm 99.9 percent sure.

Q And about how many books does the President have on his desk in the study?

A He has maybe about 15 or 20 little books that are on his desk and he has more books over there and more books on the bookshelf.

MS. WIRTH: Thank you.

BY MR. EMMICK:

Q How about the opener?

A Right. The -- right. The wooden frog letter

opener that I gave him. I'm just trying to go through this way, so --

Q All right. Go ahead.

A I saw the -- well, I lent him the book "Disease and Misrepresentation."

Q And did you see it in the Oval Office somewhere?

A No, I saw it in the back study.

Q The back study? And that would have been on page 8, I believe?

A Right. And then the letter opener that I was mentioning a moment ago was on page 9. I saw the antique paperweight.

Q Okay. Where is it that you saw the opener?

A It was on top of -- I think it's a cigar box on his desk in the back office. I saw the antique --

BY MS. IMMERGUT:

Q When did you see that, Monica?

A Zadilla day. I saw the antique paperweight on his -- he has a collection of antique political memorabilia in the dining room on top of sort of a chest sort of thing, and I saw that there on -- I think on December 6th or December 28th.

BY MR. EMMICK:

Q Okay. Do you remember which?

A No. I saw the standing cigar holder, I think, it

was on his Oval Office desk. Or it might have been in the back. I think it was on the Oval Office desk. On the 28th of December. And that's it.

Q All right. Let's turn our attention to the 31st of December. You had indicated earlier that at some point you started to get more and more concerned about Linda Tripp and whether she was going to rat on you, I think was the way you put it. What did you do with respect to Vernon Jordan in that concern?

A Since Linda had stopped returning my calls around the 24th of December, by the end of December, I realized I'd kind of better come up with some sort of strategy as to how -- if Linda Tripp comes out and says all these things where this is coming from and try to prepare the President.

And since I couldn't find it within myself to bring it up to him directly, I called Mr. Jordan and told him that I needed to talk to him, I had some concerns about something.

Q When did you call him?

A I think it was the 30th of December.

Q Did you speak with him directly?

A I think I might have spoken with his -- with his secretary.

Q Do you remember her name?

A Gail. There was another one, too, but I've forgot

907

187

her name. And I met Mr. Jordan for breakfast on -- no, not Sunday but December 31st, the morning of the 31st, at the Park Hyatt Hotel.

And in the course of the conversation I told him that I had had this friend, Linda Tripp, who was sort of involved in the Paula Jones case with, I think, the Kathleen Willey stuff. I don't know if I went into that much detail, but I did tell him her name.

And I said that she was my friend, that I didn't really trust her -- I used to trust her, but I didn't trust her any more and I was a little bit concerned because she had spent the night at my home a few times and I thought -- I told Mr. Jordan, I said, well, maybe she's heard some -- you know -- I mean, maybe she saw some notes lying around.

And Mr. Jordan said, "Notes from the President to you?" And I said, "No, notes from me to the President." And he said, "Go home and make sure they're not there."

Q What did you understand him to mean when he said, "Go home and make sure they're not there"?

A I thought that meant that -- to go home and search around and if there are any copies of notes or anything that I sent or drafts, to throw them away.

Q Did you have any further discussions with Mr. Jordan about Mr. Clinton and the Clinton's marital status?

A Yes. After breakfast, in the car, I asked Mr. Jordan if he thought the President would always be married to the First Lady and he said, "Yes, as he should be." And gave me a quote from the Bible. And a few -- maybe a minute or so later, he said, "Well, maybe you two will have an affair when he's out of office."

And at that point, I was shocked because I thought Mr. Jordan had known that we had already had this affair and I think I alluded to this earlier today when I saying until the 31st I didn't know, and I said, "Well, we already had an affair. We just -- you know, we didn't have sex or did everything but sex," or something like that. And he just kind of went -- one of those "Mmmph." You know --

Q A grunt?

A And didn't really respond to me. So I took that as my cue to drop the subject. But -- so --

MR. EMMICK: All right.

BY MR. WISENBERG:

Q What did you eat for breakfast at the Hyatt?

A I had an -- I had an egg white omelet.

BY MR. EMMICK:

Q What did he have?

A I think he had cereal with yogurt.

BY MR. WISENBERG:

Q Do you remember who paid?

A Mr. Jordan. He's a gentleman.

Q Do you remember how he paid?

A No.

Q Has anyone from the Office of Independent Counsel or the FBI shown you any paperwork of any kind with reference to that breakfast?

A No.

MR. WISENBERG: Thank you.

BY MR. EMMICK:

Q Let's turn back to the topic of gifts.

A Okay.

Q Did you give a gift to the President in early January?

A Yes, I did. Well, I guess -- I gave it to Ms. Currie for the President.

Q What was the gift?

A It was an antique book on the various presidents with sketchings. A history book.

Q Where did you buy the book?

A At an antique bookstore in Georgetown.

Q Was there anything along with the book?

A A note.

Q Okay. What kind of a note?

A An embarrassing mushy note.

Q Okay. Did you attach the note to the book in some

way?

A I don't really -- I might have put it inside the book or I may have put it outside. I wrapped the book.

Q And how did you try to get this book to the President?

A I called Betty over the weekend and asked her if I could drop it off so I didn't have to waste money on a courier.

Q And when you say "the weekend," are you talking about that first weekend in January?

A Yes.

Q Do you remember if it was Saturday, the 3rd, or Sunday, the 4th?

A I believe it was Sunday the 4th.

Q You called Betty and what again did you say to Betty?

A I don't -- I think I said something -- you know, "I have something for him, could I drop it off to you so I don't have to waste money on a courier."

Q Okay. And what did you do?

A So she said that was fine. So I went over to her home and --

Q Had you been to her home before?

A Yes.

Q Had you ever dropped anything off at her home for

the President before?

A No.

Q What did you do when you got her home?

A Well, she was sitting on the porch, so we sat on the porch and I gave her the package and we talked for a little while.

Q Did you talk at all about the gift that was for the President?

A We might have. I might have mentioned it. Probably did. I'm not --

Q Was there any discussion about the fact that the President was himself under subpoena and was going to be deposed in a couple of weeks?

A No.

Q Were you concerned about giving him a book, a gift, under those circumstances?

A No.

Q Okay. Did you ever talk to the President and learn whether he got the book and the note?

A Yes, I did.

Q All right. When did you talk with him and learn about that?

A On the 5th of January. I think it was the 5th of January. You know -- can I just --

Q Sure. Take a look.

A Yes. It was the 5th of January.

Q And that would have been Monday?

A Correct.

Q Why don't we try to proceed through Monday because Monday started with a meeting with you and Frank Carter and then there was the phone call afterwards, so let's go first to the meeting with Frank Carter.

A Okay.

Q Feel free.

A I met with Mr. Carter to go over in more detail where we stood at that point with the Paula Jones case and he went over -- he went over what was going to happen if an affidavit wasn't going to satisfy the Paula Jones attorneys and I did have to get deposed and what the room looks like, what -- you know -- everything that happens in a deposition and he threw out a bunch of different questions.

You know, they'll probably ask you who your first grade teacher was and they'll ask you -- you know, some things and then some of the questions that concerned me were questions like "How did you get your job at the Pentagon?" And how did -- you know, and he said, "They'll ask things like did you find out about the opening on a bulletin board or did someone tell you about it? Who recommended you for the job? How did everything get facilitated for the transfer?"

913

193

And that alarmed me because I didn't really know how to necessarily answer that. I didn't express that to Mr. Carter, but --

Q Well, when you say you didn't know how to answer it, what do you mean, you didn't know how to answer it?

A Well, I was concerned that if I said in -- you know, if possibly that was going to come up in the affidavit which hadn't bee written yet or in a deposition, if I had said -- mentioned certain people that had been involved in helping me secure the position over at the Pentagon or forcing me to go there, really, that because these people didn't like me, if they were ever questioned by the Paula Jones attorneys, that they might say something contrary to what I said just because -- to get me in trouble because they didn't like me.

So I was concerned that -- I wanted to -- I wanted to have some sort of feeling of protection, that -- you know, that I wouldn't be screwed over by these people.

Q Were you concerned that they were going to say nasty things about you or were you concerned that they were going to say things that might ultimately lead to the revealing of the relationship in some way?

A No, I was just concerned that they would purposefully say something different from whatever I said just because they had the opportunity to screw me.

I mean -- not -- never mind.

Q Okay.

A To cause trouble for me. How's that?

Q Did you discuss with Mr. Carter the affidavit that you were considering?

A Yes.

Q What did you talk about?

A I think he -- he said he would work on a draft and he'd get a draft of the affidavit to me.

Q Okay. At the time, did you want anyone else to review that affidavit before you ultimately signed it?

A At first, I didn't think about it, but then I did. I decided I wanted Mr. Jordan to look at it.

Q All right. Why did you want Mr. Jordan to look at it?

A I think I felt that -- that he being the President's best friend and having a -- a clearer understanding of my relationship with the President than Mr. Carter did, that I just would feel that it sort of had been blessed.

MR. EMMICK: Okay.

BY MS. IMMERGUT:

Q And would that be blessed by the President as well?

A Yes, I that's what I -- I mean, I -- I think I felt that -- excuse me. That, you know, if Mr. Jordan thought something was okay, that I'm sure the President would think it was fine.

MS. IMMERGUT: Okay.

BY MR. EMMICK:

Q Did you discuss the subpoena and the items that might be responsive to the subpoena anymore? I think you had talked about it earlier.

A You know, there's been a little bit of confusion for me when I gave Mr. Carter those items, so it's possible.

Q All right. You mentioned that Mr. Carter asked you some hard questions about like how you got your job. Did you want to talk with anybody about that afterwards?

A Yes. I placed a call to Ms. Currie and asked her to let the President know I needed to speak to him and it was important.

Q Did you say anything to Ms. Currie about signing something?

A I think I might have sort of said, just, you know, hoping that she might pass that along, I think.

BY MS. IMMERGUT:

Q Do you remember saying that you wanted to or needed to speak to the President before you signed something?

A I think so.

BY MR. EMMICK:

Q All right. Did you explain to her what you meant

when you said that?

A No.

Q Okay.

A I'm pretty sure I did say that to Ms. Currie.

Q Did you finally get in contact or did you at some time shortly thereafter get in contact with Mr. Clinton?

A Yes.

Q How did that happen?

A Ms. Currie called me back a few hours later and then she put the President on.

Q Before we talk about what the President and you talked about, as background, I guess, were you upset or in a mood that day from a photograph you had seen?

A Oh, you really want to embarrass me, don't you?

Q Well, I just want to get the mood right.

A I had been peeved by the photo and the footage that was in the media from the President and First Lady being romantic on their holiday vacation. So I felt a little bit like -- I -- I was just annoyed.

I was jealous and it just seemed sort of something he had never -- an aspect of their relationship that he had never really revealed to me and it made me feel bad.

So I was -- I don't know if anyone here has ever done this, where you -- you're annoyed with someone so you kind of want to pick a fight with them and you want to be a little bit hostile so that -- you know, you just rub them the wrong way.

Q Okay.

A So that was how I was feeling.

Q That's how you exhibited the annoyance or anger or whatever.

A Mm-hmm.

Q Okay. Tell us about your conversation with the President.

A Because of those feelings, I was a little bit curt with him and so I told him that I had had this meeting with Mr. Carter and that I was concerned, you know, from the questions he asked me that if, you know, if I at some point had to kind of -- under oath, answer these questions and in the course of answering a question I mentioned people at the White House who didn't like me, that somehow I would end up getting -- they'd get me in trouble.

And so he -- so when I told him the questions about my job at the Pentagon, he said, "Well, you could always say that the people in Legislative Affairs got it for you or helped you get it."

And there was a lot of truth to that. I mean, it was a generality, but that was -- I said, "Well, that's a good idea. Okay."

Q Was there any discussion of the book?

A Yes. I had asked him if he had gotten the book that I sent with Betty and he said he did, he really liked it, and then -- I had written him this -- this note that I had sort of -- wrote -- I think it was Saturday night when I got home from the movies and I had seen the Titanic that weekend and it just was -- just brought up a lot of feelings and thoughts for me that I put on -- that I put on paper.

And so I sort of said something about, "Oh, well, I shouldn't have written some of those things in the note." Because I was angry about seeing the picture with them romantic, it made me feel really stupid for having sent this letter.

And he said, "Yeah, you shouldn't have written some of those things." Kind of along the ways he had said before, about not writing particular things on paper, you know, putting things to paper. So --

Q About how long was your telephone call with the President?

A Maybe 15 minutes.

MR. EMMICK: Anything else on that?

THE WITNESS: I see you trying not to laugh.

MR. EMMICK: What about break-wise? Where are we? Is this a good time for a break or do we want to keep going?

THE FOREPERSON: Yes. Yes.

MR. EMMICK: All right.

THE FOREPERSON: I would say only five minutes.

MR. EMMICK: All right. Five minutes it is.

THE FOREPERSON: A five-minute break. I'm sorry, guys. Okay.

(Witness excused. Witness recalled.)

MR. EMMICK: Madam Foreperson, do we have a quorum?

THE FOREPERSON: Yes, we do.

MR. EMMICK: Are there any unauthorized persons present?

THE FOREPERSON: There are none.

Monica, it's my responsibility --

THE WITNESS: I know.

THE FOREPERSON: -- to remind you you're still under oath.

THE WITNESS: Okay. Thank you.

BY MR. EMMICK:

Q We just finished talking about January 5th. Why don't we turn to January 6th. On January 6th, did you pick up a copy of the draft affidavit from Frank Carter?

A Yes, I did.

Q You had mentioned earlier that you wanted Vernon Jordan to look at it. Did you contact him?

A Yes, I did.

Q Did you speak with him personally or did you speak with someone on his staff?

A I don't really remember.

Q And did you try to get a copy of the draft affidavit to Mr. Jordan?

A Yes. I dropped off a Xerox copy in his office.

Q In his office?

A In the lobby of his -- of Akin Gump.

Q Did you make any arrangements to contact him in order to talk about the draft affidavit?

A I believe -- I think I remember Gail saying he was in a meeting and something about 4:00, that he was going to be out and he would call me at 4:00.

Q Did you talk with him on the 6th about the draft affidavit?

A Yes, I did.

Q All right. Tell us what the two of you talked about.

A I had had some concerns from looking at the draft affidavit and addressed those concerns with him and he agreed.

Q What were the nature of the concerns, if you remember?

A I think that the general concern was that Mr. Carter had inserted some information about me having possibly been alone with the President for a few minutes, bringing him a letter in Legislative Affairs.

Q Would it help you if I showed you a copy of the draft with some of your handwriting on it?

A Oh. Yes.

MR. EMMICK: I'm placing before the witness what is marked as Grand Jury Exhibit ML-3.

(Grand Jury Exhibit No. ML-3 was marked for identification.)

BY MR. EMMICK:

Q Can you tell us what this is?

A Sure. Do the grand jurors have a copy of this?

Q They do.

A Okay. This is a draft of my affidavit that Mr. Carter drew up based on his conversations with me.

Q And the handwriting on it? Whose is that?

A That's my handwriting.

Q There's also some underlining and some scratch-outs.

A Mm-hmm.

Q Did you do all of that?

A Yes.

Q Can you remember looking at that now what the two of you talked about?

A I think that -- I think that it was -- I think the two main things were this last sentence in paragraph 6 and the -- the concern was, for me at least, was not wanting to

922

202

give the Paula Jones attorneys any thought about why they might need to want to talk to me. So if I had mentioned that I had been in there alone, it would kind of make them think, oh, well, what happened and did he proposition or blah, blah, blah.

And then the second thing was in the -- towards the end of paragraph 8 on page 2, the idea of with crowds of other people, I think to me was too far from the fake truth?

Q Okay.

A Does that -- is that clear? Sort of -- that that seemed to be too out of the realm of possibility, so --

Q Too implausible?

A Exactly. Thank you. So I believe that, you know, that this statement, "There were other people present on all of these occasions," was something that I discussed with Mr. Jordan.

Q Did he agree with the suggestions or thoughts that you had on those two passages?

A Yes, I believe so.

Q Was there any discussion with Mr. Jordan about the portion of paragraph 8 saying that there was no sexual relationship?

A No.

Q At any time, did Mr. Jordan say that he didn't want to speak to you about the affidavit?

923

203

A No.

Q How long was your conversation with Mr. Jordan?

A I don't remember. Not long. We may have also talked about job stuff, too. But --

Q All right, then. Let's turn our attention to the next day, which is the 7th. That's the day when you finalized and signed the affidavit. Is that right?

A Yes.

Q And you notarized it under penalty of perjury.

A Yes.

MR. EMMICK: I believe you have -- this is the final version and it is Grand Jury Exhibit ML-4.

(Grand Jury Exhibit No. ML-4 was marked for identification.)

BY MR. EMMICK:

Q I'm placing that before you.

A Okay.

Q And it says "Affidavit of Jane Doe No. 6" at the top and it has your signature, right?

A Mm-hmm.

Q When you spoke with Frank Carter that morning in order to finalize the affidavit, do you remember what changes were made?

A When I spoke with him before I arrived at his office or in his office?

Q Either time.

A I believe that I sort of dictated to him the changes -- I think that's possible or I gave them to him in person, I don't really remember. Mr. Carter had prepared three different versions of the affidavit for the significant portion related to this case, I guess, they were all denying sexual relations, all three of them. And we discussed various things about it and eventually decided on this affidavit.

Q All right. Let me ask you a straightforward question. Paragraph 8 at the start says, "I have never had a sexual relationship with the President." Is that true?

A No.

Q All right. The next logical follow-up is, and maybe it's self-evident, but why were you willing to say something that was false under penalty of perjury?

A. I don't think that it's anybody's business.

Q Okay. Let me turn the page for you. At the end of paragraph 8, the statement, "The occasions that I saw the President after I left my employment at the White House in April 1996 were official receptions, formal functions or events related to the U.S. Department of Defense, where I was working at the time. There were other people present on those occasions." That's not correct either, is it?

A No, it's misleading.

Q Okay. In what respect?

A For me, at the time, I said -- well, it doesn't say the only occasions, but it's misleading in that one reading it would assume that the only occasions on which I saw the President were those listed.

Q Right.

A But I did some justifying in signing the affidavit, so --

Q Justifying -- does the word "rationalizing" apply as well?

A Rationalize, yes.

Q All right. All right. On the 7th, after you signed the affidavit, did you keep a copy of the affidavit?

A Yes, I did.

Q Where did you go later on the 7th?

A To New York.

Q Did you take a copy of the affidavit with you?

A Yes.

Q Why?

A If I remember correctly, I was in a rush and I kind of wanted to have it, if I wanted to look it over again or --

Q Why were you going to New York?

A A job interview.

Q Did you have a job interview?

A Yes, I did.

Q Was that the next day?

A Yes.

Q All right. Let's turn our attention to the job interview on the morning of the 8th. Now, was that with McAndrews & Forbes?

A Yes. This is my -- I had -- I mean, just to remind everyone, I had had some job interviews on the 18th of December up in New York at McAndrews & Forbes and Burson-Marsteller. I also took a test on the 30th, I think, of December at Burson-Marsteller and this is now another interview at McAndrews & Forbes on the 8th.

Q Do you remember who you interviewed with that morning?

A Jamie Dernan.

Q How did the interview go?

A Very poorly.

Q Okay. Tell us why it went poorly. What do you mean?

A I think it started off on the wrong foot because I was in a waiting room downstairs and I had thought they would let me know when he was available and I'd go to his office and instead he just walked in unannounced and the interview started, so I was -- I didn't have my wits together at the moment. And I was -- I just was sort of flustered from that moment on. I think everyone can relate to having a bad

927

207

interview. Maybe.

Q How long was the interview?

A Maybe 20 minutes.

Q Was that the only interview that morning?

A Yes.

Q What was your reaction afterwards?

A I was upset. I felt horrible. I might have even cried. I was embarrassed. I thought that I had sort of embarrassed Mr. Jordan, I think, in such a bad interview.

Q After having a bad interview like that, did you expect an offer?

A No, I didn't think so. My first interview with McAndrews & Forbes had been really, really good, so I wasn't sure exactly what was going to happen, but I didn't think it was --

Q Not a good sign.

A Correct.

Q What did you do after you had that bad interview?

A At some point, I called Mr. Jordan to just let him know that it had gone poorly.

Q Do you remember whether you placed one call or several calls to try to get a hold of him?

A I'm sure I placed several. It was -- he's difficult to get a hold of.

Q Did you eventually talk to him on the 8th?

Diversified Reporting Services, Inc.
1025 VERMONT AVENUE, N.W. SUITE 1250
WASHINGTON, D.C. 20005
(202) 296-2929

A Yes, I did.

Q What did you tell him?

A I told him that it hadn't worked out and that I was asking his advice on whether I should contact Burson-Marsteller or not and that I was concerned that the McAndrews & Forbes hadn't gone well.

Q At the time you were talking to him, were you still upset about the interview?

A I don't really remember. I'm sure I was. It was kind of a depressing thing all day.

Q And did he say what he was going to do because the interview had not gone well?

A Yes.

Q What did he say?

A He said he'd call the chairman. I thought he was kidding.

Q Okay. And did he call you back some time shortly thereafter?

A Yes, he did.

Q About how long after he called -- excuse me. About how long after he said he was going to call the chairman did he call you back? If you remember.

A I don't remember. I don't think it was very long after, but --

Q What did he say when he called back?

A That not to worry -- you know, I don't remember the exact words that he used. The gist of the conversation was that, you know, the were going to call me and everything was going to be okay.

Q Did he say that he had gotten a hold of the chairman or did he mention that at all or --

A I don't remember.

Q Did Revlon or McAndrews & Forbes personnel get a hold of you later after Mr. Jordan called?

A Yes. They called to set up an interview for me with someone directly at Revlon for the next day.

Q Do you remember about when it was that you were called later on the 8th?

A I think it was some time early evening.

Q Early evening?

A Or evening.

Q Were you surprised by the call?

A From having heard from Mr. Jordan, not 100 percent.

Q All right. They set up an interview for the next day?

A Yes.

Q Did you have an interview the next day?

A Yes.

Q Who did you interview with?

A Ellen Seidman.

930

210

Q And what was the tone of that interview?

A It went very well. It was --

Q Better than with Jamie Dernan?

A Yes.

Q All right.

A It was a very good interview.

Q Did you interview with others at Revlon as well?

A Yes.

Q Do you remember about how many interviews there were?

A Two others, aside from Ms. Seidman's.

Q And you mentioned that the interviews went well. After the interviews, did you give a call to Vernon to let him know how things were going?

A I think so.

Q Later that day, did you have another call from Revlon?

A From Revlon?

Q Mm-hmm.

A Yes, I did.

Q Tell us about that.

A They sort of informally offered me a position and I informally accepted it.

Q Do you remember who it was you were speaking with at the time?

931

211

A I believe it was Ellen Seidman.

Q Okay. You made a reference earlier in this grand jury appearance to a conversation you had with Linda Tripp on the 9th.

A Yes.

Q We're now on the 9th and I can tell you would like to talk about this conversation. Tell us about your conversation with Linda Tripp on the 9th. Let's start with when it happened.

A Well, I was returning Linda's call from earlier in the week and I think I made a couple of attempts to get a hold of her at her office and when I did get in touch with her, I told her I was on a pay phone because I was concerned about the phones.

And I just -- I -- I didn't -- I was very distrustful of her at this point, especially when I first got on the phone with her. I didn't really know why we were going to be in touch at this point, from what had happened the few weeks before.

So she started out the conversation, I think, asking me, you know, what was going on with my job stuff and everything and I told her I didn't have a job yet and that I hadn't heard from Betty, the President, or Mr. Jordan since December and I didn't know what was going on and so we were discussing that. And that was not true, obviously.

And then she told me that she had gone up to New York over Christmas to be with -- I think Norma Asness is her name, and that while she was in New York during the holidays she was shopping with Ms. Asness and this other woman on Madison Avenue buying shoes and that this woman had told Linda she was really savvy and Linda should move to New York and get a PR job in New York. Which I thought was a little strange, since I was in the process of moving to New York for a PR job.

That was just one of the indications that made me think she was a little bit jealous of the help I was getting, that I was talking about earlier.

So when we started to discuss the case, she told me that -- that because of this experience she had had in New York, she decided that maybe it would be best for her to be really vague on the truth about Kathleen Willey. You know, she really didn't know anything, she didn't really remember much, and that -- you know, led me to -- and I believe she may have even said directly that she wasn't going to tell about me or that I was -- you know, my understanding of that was that she wasn't even going to mention me and that I was safe.

Q Did this come as a surprise to you?

A Yes, it did.

Q In what way?

933

213

A Because she had -- I mean, she had stopped returning my phone calls, we had left everything in a very bad note a few weeks prior to that. So --

In the course of this conversation, when we talked about my job, she said, "Well, Monica -- " Oh. Oh. She asked me what I was going to do in the case and I told her that I was planning on signing an affidavit. Even though I had already signed the affidavit, I didn't want Linda to think that I would have gone ahead and done such a bold thing without her approval.

So she made -- that's when, as I mentioned earlier, she made me promise her that I wouldn't sign the affidavit until I got the job. She also went into this whole long story about her friend --

Am I getting into too much detail?

MR. EMMICK: Close.

JURORS: No. No.

MR. EMMICK: Okay.

THE WITNESS: Okay. All right. She told me about her -- this friend, I don't remember her name, but she's this -- she's an Indian woman who Linda goes to the gym with and that this Indian woman had gone to a psychic and the psychic had essentially said that one of her friends was in imminent danger having to do with the words she would speak.

So that that led Linda to believe, you know, along with this event in New York that she should -- you know, she's kind of going to go the good route -- well, what I considered the good route in the Paula Jones case. And it was really based on this conversation that I had with her and this sort of change that I agreed to meet with Linda on the 13th of January.

BY MR. EMMICK:

Q Then let's go to the 13th of January. Let me first cover some of the job-related items. On the 13th, did you get a formal offer from Revlon?

A Yes, I did.

Q And did you accept that offer?

A Yes, I did.

Q How was the matter left about references or recommendations?

A Well, she -- I can't remember her name, something with a J, I think. The woman in human resources with whom I was dealing about the job offer said, you know, I needed to send her some references, so this had been in -- oh. So I called Betty to ask her to remind the President or to check out for me what Mr. Hilley would say to -- I'm not saying this clearly. I'm sorry.

Q That's all right.

A One of the people that I needed to get a reference

935

215

from was John Hilley, who was the head of Legislative Affairs and had been my boss when I was there the latter half of my tenure at the White House. I was concerned that if I put him down as a reference, he might not say flattering things about me.

So I asked -- I had mentioned this to the President on October 11th and he said he'd, you know, make sure everything was okay, so I wanted to -- so I checked with Betty to ask her to kind of find out what was happening, what the status of that was. So --

Q Did you get a message later from Betty on that subject?

A Yes, I did.

Q Okay. What was that message?

A She had me page her and then later I came to find out from her that afternoon that it had been -- I think Mr. Podesta took care of it and that everything would be fine with Mr. Hilley.

Q Now, when the two of you were paging each other on this day, the name Kay was used rather than either Betty or Monica. Where did that name come from?

A This has sort of become a kind of strange area for me. I had not -- and I do not specifically remember discussing with Betty the fact that I had been subpoenaed in the Paula Jones case and anything surrounding that, but sort of I now know from -- from sort of things that I've been reminded of or shown that I must have. And one of them that indicates that to me is this notion that she -- I -- she and I had started -- I suggested that we use sort of the code name Kay in her paging me and in me paging her. And --

Q And where does the name Kay come from?

A Because Betty and I, our first encounter and our first connection was through Walter Kaye.

Q Now, had you and Betty had earlier conversations about the fact that her message indicator, I guess it would be her beeper or her pager?

A Her pager.

Q Her pager.

A Her text message pager.

Q Her text message pager on some occasion might have indicated Monica?

A Yes. There had been -- I think there had been at least one time when Betty's pager had been sitting on her desk when she was in with the President or had stepped away and someone else had picked up her pager when it went off and there was a message from me.

And so from -- you know, Betty kind of covered it, I think, by saying -- or she did actually have another friend named Monica or something or another, but it was -- you know -- Rebecca Cameron was the person who picked up the pager and so it was sort of a -- not a good thing to happen.

Q Why use any fake names, Kay or any other name? What's the reason you've got to use fake names at this time?

A I was beyond paranoid. I mean, I -- and obviously in denial. I think the -- I could not understand how I had been dragged into the Paula Jones case and so I was very wary of everything.

Q What did Betty say, if you can remember, when you suggested that you refer to one another as Kay?

A Okay.

Q Okay. Did she ask why or --

A I don't remember having this conversation with her.

Q All right. Were you also using names to refer to others? For example, the name Mary?

A Yes.

Q Who did Mary refer to?

A Linda.

Q And why were you using the name Mary to refer to Linda?

A Because that's what she chose.

Q And why were you using any name other than Linda to refer to Linda?

A Because Linda and Betty were the two people who paged me that were involved -- you know, somehow fell into this circle of the Paula Jones story. Is that -- it's not clear. I'm sorry. Okay.

Q When you were speaking with Linda about the President, did you sometimes refer to the President as "her" rather than "him"?

A Linda? No. I don't believe so.

BY MS. IMMERGUT:

Q So that was Betty?

A Yes.

BY MR. EMMICK:

Q Okay. And why did you use "her" to refer to the President?

A I believe that that was only in pages to her and it was just -- you know, I knew that the WAVES -- from having worked at the White House, I knew that people had access to the WAVES pages, let alone that someone types them, so it just was another measure of caution that I used throughout.

Q All right.

A I don't think I ever referred to the President on Betty's pages.

Q When we were talking earlier about your clarifying whether John Hilley would give you a recommendation, you indicated that you had a page from Betty. Does it refresh your recollection about what the page said if I were to read the following?

We have a page indicating that it says, "Will know something soon, Kay." Does that remind you about any pages that you got from Betty?

A Yes, I think I mentioned earlier that she paged me and then I talked to her later that day and found out about John Hilley.

Q All right. Did you -- at some point, did you send to Revlon a letter giving them the two recommendations, one of which was John Hilley?

A Yes.

Q Do you remember when that was?

A I believe I faxed it on the 14th of January.

Q So that would be the next day.

A Correct.

BY MR. WISENBERG:

Q Pardon me. Were they recommendations or references? Just as a technical matter, in other words, were they names or were they actual letters of recommendation?

A Oh. They were references, then.

BY MR. EMMICK:

Q All right. Let's go back to the 13th for just a moment because you met with Linda Tripp that day, I think you said, on the 9th you had --

A I also met with Mr. Jordan.

Q Okay. All right. Okay. Well, let's go back to Mr. Jordan, then.

A Well, I -- I mean, I was just thinking about the day. I'm sorry.

Q No, that's fine. That's fine.

A Just I stopped in to see him for five minutes, to thank him for getting me the job, and I gave him a tie and a pocket square.

MR. EMMICK: Okay.

BY MS. IMMERGUT:

Q Did you ever provide Mr. Jordan with a signed copy of the affidavit?

A I did not provide him with a copy. No.

Q Do you know whether or not he ever received a copy?

A I believe I showed him a copy. I don't know that he received a copy.

BY MR. EMMICK:

Q On this same meeting on the 13th?

A I -- I -- you know, I have to say I know I brought the copy with me to show him and I may have said, you know, "Do you want to see it?" And I think he may have not even -- I think he may have said, you know, "I don't need to see it." Or -- I --

BY MS. IMMERGUT:

Q So you don't specifically recall handing it over to

941

222

him or even showing it to him specifically.

A No.

Q But you brought it for him to --

A I did bring it.

MS. IMMERGUT: Correct.

BY MR. EMMICK:

Q All right. So that's the Vernon Jordan part of the 13th.

A Right.

Q What about the meeting with Linda Tripp?

A It was long. I was -- I was very nervous. I was wary of her. I actually thought she might have a tape recorder with her and had looked in her bag when she had gone up to the restroom. I told her a whole bunch of lies that day.

Q What were you trying to accomplish in meeting with her?

A I was trying to -- I was trying to make Linda continue to feel comfortable that she and I were sort of on the -- that we were on the same side, we were on the right side.

We -- and that -- when I had agreed to meet with her, I thought we were going to go over kind of her strategy for what she was going to do in the case and then once we got together, she kind of started wavering about what she wanted to do and then -- so I just was using everything I knew to try to convince her that -- that this is the right thing to do.

Q I think you mentioned earlier that you told her lies.

A Yes.

Q What lies do you have in mind?

A I mean, I think -- throughout that month of December, after I knew she was subpoenaed, there were various things that I think I said that were untrue, but I specifically remember from this meeting the thing that I had -- what I said to Linda was, "Oh, you know, I told -- I told Mr. Jordan that I wasn't going to sign the affidavit until I got the job." Obviously, which wasn't true.

I told her I didn't yet have a job. That wasn't true. I told her I hadn't signed the affidavit. That wasn't true. I told her that some time over the holidays I had freaked out and my mom took me to Georgetown Hospital and they put me on Paxil. That wasn't true.

I think I told her that -- you know, at various times the President and Mr. Jordan had told me I had to lie. That wasn't true. That's just a small example. Probably some more things about my mom. Linda had an obsession with my mom, so she was a good leverage.

Q Let's turn our attention back to the 14th, then.

On the 14th, the next day?

A Okay.

Q Right.

A Okay.

Q There's three pieces of paper that have come to be referred to as the talking points.

A Yes.

MR. EMMICK: I think we have them marked as Grand Jury Exhibit ML-5.

(Grand Jury Exhibit No. ML-5 was marked for identification.)

BY MR. EMMICK:

Q I'll place them in front of you.

A Okay.

Q And they are three pages. I wonder if you would tell us how those came to be written and on what computer and the like.

A Okay. First of all, they're out of order.

Q Okay.

A So the last page was actually the first page.

Q All right. Well, let's clarify. What is now the first page says "Points to make in affidavit." And the second page says, "The first few paragraphs" at the top. And the third page says, "You're not sure you've been clear." The third page should be the first page?

A Yes.

Q All right. Let's go to first the mechanics of how these got generated.

A Mm-hmm.

Q Were those printed from your printer?

A Yes.

Q Were they typed on your computer?

A Yes.

Q Was anyone present with you when they were typed?

A No.

Q When were they typed?

A On the 14th.

Q Did you talk with anyone in an effort to get assistance editing or writing or getting approval for what is in the talking points?

A No.

Q How did the -- where did you get the ideas that are reflected in the talking points?

A They were based on conversations I've had with Linda from the moment Kathleen Willey and Michael Isikoff ever entered into the picture until the conversations I had with her the morning of the 14th on the phone.

Q Tell me what you mean by that.

A At various times, especially early on, around March or so when -- when Kathleen Willey first came up, Linda talked about how -- you know, that -- that -- what Kathleen was saying to Michael Isikoff was not true. And so, you know, we had had -- I remember having this discussion with her where we were saying, well, if -- you know, if she's lying to Michael Isikoff, how do you know she didn't lie to you?

Linda said, "Yeah, that's a good point. Maybe she did." You know?

And I said, "Yeah, sure. She could have, you know, smeared her own lipstick and untucked her own blouse."

And Linda said, "Yeah, it's true."

That was very early on and throughout my discussions with Linda, especially when she was saying -- saying things about how to be vague on the Kathleen Willey issue in the Paula Jones case, we had these sorts of discussions.

Q What did you do with the talking points? How did you relay them to Linda Tripp?

A I took a copy of them to her.

Q And how were the arrangements made to give her that copy?

A She had told me she was going to go see her attorney, Kirby, that afternoon and was going to talk to him about signing an affidavit, which is why this was all generated. And so I offered to drive her there so that we could just talk on the way because we -- we had had some time to talk that morning, but not as much as I wanted.

Q Who was driving? You were driving?

A Yes.

Q And Linda has the talking points in her hands?

A I handed them to her in the parking lot of the Pentagon.

Q Did she read them?

A Yes, she did.

Q What was she saying or doing as she was reading them?

A She was going through it and she was sort of reading and going, "Yeah. Mm-hmm. Uh-huh. Well, that's true. Oh, good point."

I think she may have said, "Oh, these are -- this is really -- that's true." You know. "Did you write this?" Sort of a thing.

Q Okay. What did you think would happen after you dropped the talking points off to Linda and then you dropped Linda off? How were things left, I guess is another way to ask that question.

A I believe that it was in the car ride home that she said -- made some comment to me about -- that, well, she -- she feels okay -- and this might have been on the 13th when she said this, she feels okay about, you know, kind of not telling the truth or being vague on the truth when she talks to me, but then when she doesn't talk to me, she -- her mind starts to wander to different things, so I just remember feeling -- oh, like I had to hold her hand through everything and I constantly had to talk to her. So I may have said, "I'll call you tonight" or something like that.

Q Have you ever talked to Bruce Lindsey?

A No. I may have said hello to him in the hall, but I -- but -- just in passing.

Q Did you ever talk with the President about the talking points?

A No.

Q Did you ever talk with anyone at Bob Bennett's firm about the talking points?

A No.

Q Did you ever talk with anyone associated with the White House in any way about the talking points?

A No. And that would include Mr. Jordan.

Q Okay. Let's turn our attention, then, to the next day, which is January 15th. Did Betty call you that day about a call she had received from Mike Isikoff?

A Yes.

Q Okay. Tell us about that telephone call.

A I had learned earlier from my attorney that the Paula Jones people had -- had -- well, I guess my attorney had asked me something about if I had ever received any courier packages from the White House and I hadn't, but I told him I did -- I did send things to Betty and he said, oh, well, he had heard -- I think through -- maybe through Bennett's people -- Mr. Bennett's firm, the attorneys, I'm sorry, I don't mean to be so informal, that there was some issue with these courier -- with a courier service.

So I called the courier service and was able to find out that the records could be subpoenaed and then I spoke with Betty later that day and she told me that -- that Michael Isikoff had called her or had called for her intern and Betty had answered the phone and in the course of that he had asked her about the courier, my sending things to her through a courier.

And that she sort of said she didn't really remember or know what he was talking about and that he'd get back to her. Or she'd get back to him. I'm sorry.

Q And then she called you and related this to you?

A Yes. Yes.

Q What was your reaction to that?

A I was very shocked and very -- feeling very strange, that somehow this was closing in more and I -- I didn't know how they could have gotten this information about the courier because there was -- the first person that I thought of that knew about the courier was Linda and the only other person I thought of was this gentleman in my office who was a Clinton hater, Mark Huffman. So I thought that maybe -- I thought, well, maybe he had been the one who had sort of turned me, trying to cause trouble.

Q All right. What did you and Betty talk about doing in response to the Isikoff calls?

A The President was out of town that day and so I think she said she was going to try to get in touch with the President and I believe that Betty and I may have discussed that, you know, they were -- the courier packages were always sent to her and that some of the things were for her, you know.

Q Did Vernon Jordan come up?

A Yes. I know later -- and I don't know if maybe she mentioned to me earlier in the day that she wanted to try to get in touch with Mr. Jordan, but I do know that -- that later in the evening Betty called me and asked me if I could give her a ride to Mr. Jordan's office because Bob, her husband, had the car that day and it was raining. So --

Q So you drove her to Vernon Jordan's.

A Yes.

Q Describe what happened when you drop her off.

A Well, actually, I parked the car and I decided to wait for her downstairs in the restaurant. I think it's The Front Page. And she went up to Mr. Jordan's office and was there maybe 15, 20 minutes. I'm not very good with time.

Q Why didn't she just take a taxi there? It's a three, four dollar taxi ride up there.

A I don't know.

Q Okay. How long did you wait?

THE WITNESS: You know, I need to use the restroom.

MR. EMMICK: Okay.

THE WITNESS: I'm sorry.

MR. EMMICK: The witness needs a break.

THE FOREPERSON: Yes.

MR. EMMICK: Okay. Thank you.

THE WITNESS: Two minutes.

MR. EMMICK: That's all right.

(Witness excused. Witness recalled.)

MR. WISENBERG: Let the record reflect the witness has reentered the grand jury room.

Madam Foreperson, do we have a quorum?

THE FOREPERSON: Yes.

MR. WISENBERG: Any unauthorized persons present?

THE FOREPERSON: None.

MR. WISENBERG: Anything you want to say?

THE FOREPERSON: Monica Lewinsky, I just wanted to let you know that you are still under oath.

THE WITNESS: Really?

THE FOREPERSON: Mm-hmm. Yes, I mean.

BY MR. WISENBERG:

Q I have, I hope, just one or two questions about your proffer.

A Okay.

Q Your written proffer. Can you grab a hold of that?

A Sure.

Q And what are we calling that? That is ML-1.

A Okay.

(Grand Jury Exhibit No. ML-1 was marked for identification.)

BY MR. WISENBERG:

Q If you'll take a look at page 4, paragraph 4, that has to do with the President's call to you.

A Yes?

Q At two a.m. on the 17th of December telling you, among other things, that you're on the witness list, correct?

A Correct.

Q Going to the middle portion, starting with "When asked." "When asked what to do if she was subpoenaed, the President suggested she could sign an affidavit and try to satisfy their inquiry and not be deposed."

A Mm-hmm.

Q The next sentence says, "In general, Ms. L. should say she visited the White House to see Ms. Currie and, on occasion, when working at the White House, she brought him letters when no one else was around."

Have I read that correctly? Have I read that sentence correctly?

A Yes.

Q Okay. And I think you have earlier described that as a -- maybe not in these exact words, but you saw it as a continuation on his part of the pre-established pattern of things he had said in the past. Is that correct?

A Yes.

Q All right. And would you agree with me that that is -- that if you said that to the Jones people or to anybody else that that is misleading in a sense because it doesn't tell the whole story of what you were doing when you visited the President.

A Yes.

Q Take a look at -- then I would like you to take a look at page 10, I think it's page 10, it's paragraph 10, whatever page it is.

A Okay.

Q Mine's cut off. It's the last -- I think it's the last page.

A Right.

Q I'll read it. "Ms. L. had a physically intimate relationship with the President. Neither the President nor Mr. Jordan or anyone on their behalf asked or encouraged

Ms. L. to lie." I would like you for us to reconcile if you can that statement in your proffer with statements like the ones in paragraph 4 where you talk about specific things the President said or did that were kind of continuations of this pattern.

A Sure. Gosh. I think to me that if -- if the President had not said the Betty and letters cover, let's just say, if we refer to that, which I'm talking about in paragraph 4, page 4, I would have known to use that.

So to me, encouraging or asking me to lie would have -- you know, if the President had said, "Now, listen. You better not say anything about this relationship, you better not tell them the truth, you better not -- "

For me, the best way to explain how I feel what happened was, you know, no one asked or encouraged me to lie, but no one discouraged me either.

Q Okay. So you said what you would have done if the President hadn't said that, but he did say that, what you mentioned in paragraph 4, correct?

A Right.

Q And I guess -- and you had a conversation with him about what to do gifts that you both knew were under subpoena, then you get the call from Betty. Those things happened. When we discussed this on Monday in the proffer session, I think you said something to the effect of or that in paragraph 10 you were being pretty literal. Is that accurate? When you say that no one encouraged you -- told you or encouraged you to lie?

A Yes and no. I mean, I think I also said that Monday that it wasn't as if the President called me and said, "You know, Monica, you're on the witness list, this is going to be really hard for us, we're going to have to tell the truth and be humiliated in front of the entire world about what we've done," which I would have fought him on probably. That was different.

And by him not calling me and saying that, you know, I knew what that meant. So I -- I don't see any -- I don't see any disconnect between paragraph 10 and paragraph 4 on the page. Does that answer your question?

BY MS. IMMERGUT:

Q Did you understand all along that he would deny the relationship also?

A Mm-hmm. Yes.

Q And when you say you understood what it meant when he didn't say, "Oh, you know, you must tell the truth," what did you understand that to mean?

A That -- that -- as we had on every other occasion and every other instance of this relationship, we would deny it.

MR. WISENBERG: That's all I have on that. And

probably not anything else. Maybe.

MS. IMMERGUT: I had a couple of quick questions.

THE WITNESS: Sure.

BY MS. IMMERGUT:

Q Back for just a moment to January 15th with the visit when you took Betty to Vernon Jordan after she had been called by Michael Isikoff.

A Mm-hmm.

Q Did you ever tell Ms. Currie that you had been called by Michael Isikoff?

A No.

Q Had you ever been called by Michael Isikoff before January 15th?

A No. I'm trying to remember now -- I know that I had seen the Newsweek thing light up on my caller ID, but I don't remember if that was around that time or if that was later, once the scandal started.

Q Do you recall any calls from Michael Isikoff that you would have told Betty about, calling about gifts from the President?

A No. Absolutely not.

Q You mentioned, obviously, that you've given the President several gifts. Have you given him any ties?

A Yes.

Q How many ties have you given him, just

approximately?

A Six.

Q Have you had any conversations with the President about wearing your ties?

A Almost all of our conversations included something about my ties.

Q Could you just briefly describe what things that you've said to him and he to you about wearing the ties?

A I used to bug him about wearing one of my ties because then I knew I was close to his heart.

Q And did he ever say anything about -- after he had one of your ties or to alert you when he had worn any of your ties?

A Yes, there were several occasions.

Q And what kind of thing would he say to you?

A "Did you see I wore your tie the other day?"

Q So was he aware based on things you had told him that you would be looking out for when he would wear ties on various occasions?

A Yes.

MS. IMMERGUT: I'd like to show you now what's marked as Grand Jury Exhibits ML-8, 9 and 10.

(Grand Jury Exhibits No. ML-8, ML-9 and ML-10 were marked for identification.)

MS. IMMERGUT: And, unfortunately, I don't have copies yet for the grand jury because we got them at the last --

MR. WISENBERG: I'll pass them around afterwards.

MS. IMMERGUT: Okay. And I'll spread them out for you here.

THE WITNESS: Okay.

BY MS. IMMERGUT:

Q Directing your attention first to ML-8, it's a photograph of the President, obviously. Do you recognize the tie that he's wearing in that photograph?

A Yes, I do.

Q Had you actually seen that on television on June 24, 1998?

A Yes, I did.

Q Do you recall what that's in relation to or what event is being depicted on that photograph?

A He was leaving for China.

Q And now directing your attention to Exhibit 9, do you know what that's a photograph of?

A I don't know where it's from, but it's the President wearing my tie.

Q And this one states it's Monday, July 6, 1998. Do you remember watching any of the media on that date?

A Yes, I do.

Q And do you remember seeing him wearing your tie on that date?

A Yes, I do.

Q Do you remember what event was taking place on that date that he was wearing your tie?

A I don't, but I just saw it says "Medicare costs," so --

Q Okay. And then finally, ML-10. Do you recognize what that's a photograph of?

A Yes.

Q And what is that?

A The President wearing the same tie.

Q And do you know what date that is?

A Date? It was a few days after, he wore the tie when he came back from China, so it's July 9th.

Q Okay. And what -- I guess -- did you reach any conclusions from the fact that he was wearing your tie on those days?

A I -- I -- I think -- the first time he wore the tie, I thought maybe it was a coincidence, but I didn't really think so. And then when he wore it when he came back from China on the 6th, I thought maybe it was a reminder of July 4th, because that had been the first workday after July 4th and we had had a really intense, emotional meeting July 4th of '97. And then when he wore it a few days later,

I thought he's trying to say something. I mean, the President doesn't wear the same tie twice in one week, so -- I didn't know what it meant, but it was some sort of a reminder to me.

MS. IMMERGUT: Okay. Nothing further on that.

BY MR. WISENBERG:

Q This is well after the scandal broke, is that correct?

A Yes.

BY MS. IMMERGUT:

Q This is this summer, right?

A Correct.

BY MR. WISENBERG:

Q You've told us something about seeing a picture of Nelvis, Bayani Nelvis, I think coming to the grand jury.

A Yes.

Q Can you tell us -- and you noticed something about some neckwear he was wearing?

A I think it was on Nel's maybe third appearance or his last appearance. He was wearing the first tie that I ever gave to the President.

Q Did you know that the President had ever given that tie to Mr. Nelvis?

A No.

Q And what is -- can you recall the last time the

President had ever worn that tie?

A No. I didn't see him every day, so -- I mean, I know he -- I know some of the times he wore that tie, but I don't know the last time he wore the tie.

Q Okay. Is there any question in your mind that the President knew that both these ties, the one that we're putting around pictures of and the one that Nel wore to the grand jury, were ties you had given him?

A Not in my mind, but I can't -- I can't answer that.

MR. WISENBERG: Okay.

MR. EMMICK: There's a question? Yes?

A JUROR: Did you know the President after a while gave his ties to the people who worked for him? Did you know that?

THE WITNESS: Yes, I did know that.

MR. WISENBERG: Pardon me just a minute.

(Pause.)

MR. WISENBERG: I'm going to ask the witness to be excused very briefly and we'll possibly call you back in a couple of minutes.

(The witness was excused.)

(Whereupon, at 4:45 p.m., the taking of testimony in the presence of a full quorum of the Grand Jury was concluded.)

* * * * *

1057

UNITED STATES DISTRICT COURT
FOR THE DISTRICT OF COLUMBIA

\- - - - - - - - - - - - - - - - - x
IN RE: :
GRAND JURY PROCEEDINGS :
\- - - - - - - - - - - - - - - - - x

Grand Jury Room No. 2
United States District Court
for the District of Columbia
3rd & Constitution, N.W.
Washington, D.C. 20001

Thursday, August 20, 1998

The testimony of MONICA S. LEWINSKY was taken in the presence of a full quorum of Grand Jury 97-2, impaneled on September 19, 1997, commencing at 9:51 a.m., before:

MICHAEL EMMICK
KARIN IMMERGUT
Associate Independent Counsel
Office of Independent Counsel
1001 Pennsylvania Avenue, N.W.
Suite 490 North
Washington, D.C. 20004

P R O C E E D I N G S

Whereupon,

MONICA S. LEWINSKY

was called as a witness and, after having been first duly sworn by the Foreperson of the Grand Jury, was examined and testified as follows:

EXAMINATION

BY MR. EMMICK:

Q Good morning, Ms. Lewinsky.

A Good morning.

Q As we did with your earlier grand jury testimony, my job is to advise you of your rights and obligations here at the beginning.

First off, you have a right under the Fifth Amendment to refuse to answer any questions that may tend to incriminate you. In this case, that right is qualified by the fact that you've signed an agreement to provide truthful testimony in connection with our investigation. Do you understand that?

A Yes, I do.

Q In addition, you have the right to have counsel present outside the grand jury to answer any questions that you may have. Do you have counsel outside?

A Yes, I do.

Q Who is that?

1059

3

A Preston Burton.

Q And you understand that if you'd like to speak to your counsel, all you have to do is say "Could I take a break and speak with my counsel?"

A Yes.

Q All right. You also in addition to those two rights, you have an obligation and that obligation is to tell the truth. That obligation is imposed on you because you have been put under oath and also because in connection with your agreement you're required to tell the truth. Do you understand that?

A Yes, I do.

MR. EMMICK: What I have placed in front of you is what is marked as ML-7. This is a chart that you have earlier testified about of contacts between yourself and the President.

As I indicated to you informally beforehand, this grand jury session today is for you to answer questions from the grand jurors.

And so without any further ado, I will ask the grand jurors if they have any questions of Ms. Lewinsky.

A JUROR: I think I'm going to start out.

MR. EMMICK: Okay.

A JUROR: Ms. Lewinsky, in your testimony when you were with us on the 6th, you mentioned some of the steps that you took to maintain secrecy regarding your relationship: that you would bring papers or he'd have papers or either you would accidentally bump into each other in the hallway; you always used Betty as the excuse for you to be waved in; and on many occasions you would go in one door and out of the other door.

THE WITNESS: Yes.

A JUROR: Are there any other methods you used that I've missed? That you used to maintain your secrecy?

THE WITNESS: Hmm. I need to think about that for a minute.

A JUROR: And the second part to that question is were these ways to maintain your secrecy your idea or were they recommended to you by anyone?

THE WITNESS: I can answer the second part first.

A JUROR: Okay.

THE WITNESS: If that's okay.

A JUROR: That's fine.

THE WITNESS: Some of them were my idea. Some of them were things that I had discussed with the President. I think it was a mutual understanding between us that obviously we'd both try to be careful.

A JUROR: Do you recall at all specifically which ones he may have recommended to you as an idea on maintaining the secrecy?

1061

5

THE WITNESS: Yes and no. The issue of Betty being the cover story for when I came to the White House, it became my understanding I think most clearly from the fact that I couldn't come to see him after the election until -- unless Betty was there to clear me in and that one time when I asked him why, he said because if someone comes to see him, there's a list circulated among the staff members and then everyone would be questioning why I was there to see him. So --

MR. EMMICK: Let me try to ask some follow-ups in response to your question.

BY MR. EMMICK:

Q Were there ever any discussions between you and the President about what should be done with letters that you -- letters or notes that you had sent to him? That is to say, for example, did you ever write on the bottom of any letters what to do with those letters?

A It was my understanding that obviously he would throw them away or, if he decided to keep them, which I didn't think he did, he would put them somewhere safe.

I think what you're referring to is on the bottom once of a sort of joke memo that I sent to him I in a joking manner reminded him to throw the letter away, that it wasn't -- you know, that was a joke. So --

Q What about whether on your caller ID on your telephone the word POTUS would appear and whether anything

1062

6

was done in order to make sure that POTUS did not appear on your telephone?

A My caller ID at work, it would -- when the President called from the Oval Office, it would say POTUS and when he'd call from the residence, it was an asterisk. And I told him that. I didn't know if he knew that it said POTUS when he called from the office, and I assumed he didn't, because otherwise that would be sort of silly.

So I informed him of that and then one time he called me from the residence and he -- he called on a hard line -- I don't know. I shouldn't say "hard line" because I know that has some different terminology to it, but he called on a line that had a phone number attached to it and so when he called, he said, "Oh, did it ring up, you know, phone number? It didn't say my name, did it?"

And so it was -- that was something that I was concerned about.

Q Did he ever express to you a reluctance to leave messages on your telephone voice message system?

A At home?

Q Yes.

A Yes.

Q All right. Tell us about that.

A One time in a conversation he just said he didn't like to leave messages.

1063

7

Q Okay. What about the times that you would visit him? Were those times selected in a way so that there weren't people around or that certain people weren't around?

A Yes.

Q Okay. Would you tell us about that?

A There were obviously people at the White House who didn't like me and wouldn't -- wouldn't be understanding of why I was coming to see the President or accepting of that and so there was always sort of an effort made that either on the weekends -- when I was working in the White House he told me that it was usually quiet on the weekends and I knew that to be true. And after I left the White House it was always when there weren't going to be a lot of people around.

Q And what about particular individual people? Would there be particular individual people who would be -- staffers in the oval area that you would try to avoid in order to help conceal the relationship?

A Yes. Nancy Hernreich, Stephen Goodin, Evelyn Lieberman. Pretty much anybody on the first floor of the West Wing.

A JUROR: How did all these people come to not like you so much? What were you doing? Were you breaking the rules of the White House? What were you doing to draw their attention to not liking you so much? Before the relationship.

From the time you got there all the way up to the time -- what I'm saying is what did you do to deserve for them not to like you?

THE WITNESS: Before the relationship started?

A JUROR: Yes. What did you do from --

THE WITNESS: I don't think there was anything I did before the relationship started that -- the relationship started in November of '95. I had only been at the White House as an intern in the Old Executive Office Building for -- for a few months, so most of my tenure at the White House I was having a relationship with the President.

I think that -- the President seemed to pay attention to me and I paid attention to him and I think people were wary of his weaknesses, maybe, and thought -- in my opinion, I mean, this is -- I think that people -- they didn't want to look at him and think that he could be responsible for anything, so it had to all be my fault, that I was -- I was stalking him or I was making advances towards him. You know, as they've said, I wore inappropriate clothes, which is absolutely not true. I'm not really sure.

A JUROR: But you do admit a lot of the places that you weren't supposed to be you were always found. You do admit that there were things that you were doing, too, in order to see him that they were feeling that was going against the rules of the White House?

THE WITNESS: Uh --

A JUROR: You know, places that you were that you weren't supposed to be and hallways that you weren't supposed to be, you were seen in those places?

THE WITNESS: Yes and no. There really weren't any of these staffers who saw me in the places that I wasn't supposed to be. And that was part of the effort to conceal the relationship. So -- does that make sense?

I mean, when I was in the Oval Office with the President, no one else knew except for the Secret Service, no one else knew that I went in there. So for them to know -- for them to be disliking me for that reason, I don't think that they were really -- I don't know if they were aware of that or not.

I did make an effort, I think, to try to -- to have interactions with the President and I -- and I think that -- that was probably disturbing to them. I know that if the President was in the hall and he was talking to people and I passed by he'd -- he'd stop talking and say hi to me. I'm not really sure.

A JUROR: Just a follow-up to that.

THE WITNESS: Sure.

A JUROR: If they didn't see you, well, how did they know?

1066

10

THE WITNESS: I don't know what they knew. I -- you know, I -- I'm not sure -- I --

A JUROR: Because if you said you made an effort to hide yourself, you know, so you wouldn't see them, the Secret Service are the ones that saw you --

THE WITNESS: Mm-hmm.

A JUROR: Okay. So, I mean, how would they -- how did they know that you were there, you know, to want to keep you away from being there?

THE WITNESS: I don't know. Maybe -- I -- I mean, I've heard reported in the newspapers and on TV that the Secret Service, someone said something to Evelyn Lieberman and I had had an -- I don't know if I went over this the last time I was here, I had had a real negative interaction with Nancy Hernreich early on in my tenure at the White House and so --

I think there was also -- I'm a friendly person and -- and I didn't know it was a crime in Washington for people -- for you to want people to like you and so I was friendly. And I guess I wasn't supposed to be.

A JUROR: So that interaction that you had with Evelyn Lieberman was when she was telling you what?

THE WITNESS: She stopped me in the hall and she asked me where I worked, in which office I worked, and I told her Legislative Affairs in the East Wing.

1067

11

And she said, "You're always trafficking up this area." You know, "You're not supposed to be here. Interns aren't allowed to go past the Oval Office."

And she -- she really startled me and I walked away and I went down to the bathroom and I was crying because -- I mean, when -- you know, when an older woman sort of chastises you like that, it's upsetting.

And then I thought about what she said and I realized that, well, I wasn't an intern any more. I was working there. And I kind of believe in clear communication, so I went back to Evelyn Lieberman, to Ms. Lieberman, and I -- I said, "You know, I just wanted to clarify with you that I work here, I'm not an intern. So, you know, I am allowed to go past the Oval Office." I don't think I said that, but I had a blue pass.

And she looked at me and said, "They hired you?" And I was startled and then she said, "Oh, well, I think I mistook you for someone else or some other girl with dark hair who keeps trafficking up the area." And ever since then -- and that was maybe in December or January of '95 or '96. So --

A JUROR: Ms. Lewinsky, were you ever reprimanded or chastised by your immediate supervisor in Legislative Affairs for trafficking up the area or being where you weren't supposed to be or being away from your desk too much?

Anything like that?

THE WITNESS: Being away from my desk had been mentioned to me, but trafficking up the area and being where I'm not supposed to be, no.

I -- the -- I had a view of -- and this is sort of my view with work is that you get a lot more done and people are a lot more willing to help you when you have a personal interaction with them. And so the person who held the job before me would fax the drafts of his letters to the staff secretary's office and then at some point during the day when someone got the draft they would make the changes and then fax it back.

And I found it to be much more effective to take things over to the staff secretary's office and interact with the person -- I can't remember her name -- Helen -- to interact with Helen and have Helen edit the letters right then and there and then I could go back and to me it was a faster process.

So there was also -- you know, I also wanted to try to see the President. So, I mean, I did make efforts to try to see him in the hall or something like that because --

A JUROR: So the route to the staff person's office was a route that you could still veer off and see the President?

1069

13

THE WITNESS: No. It -- it wasn't necessarily in front of the Oval Office or anything. There were -- we also had -- let me see if I can explain this. I'm sure you guys know by now that the West Wing is three stories. There's the basement, the first floor and the second floor. Legislative Affairs has an office on the second floor of the West Wing.

There are two ways to get to that office -- or three ways, I guess. There's the West Wing, you can cut across the West Wing lobby, which is where people coming to visit someone in the White House sit. There's going the back way, which you pass the Oval Office, but the door's always closed when the President's in there. And then you can go all the way down the stairs and all the way around and then all the way up two flights of stairs.

When I first started working there, it didn't seem appropriate to walk through the West -- to me, it didn't seem appropriate to walk through the West Wing lobby with papers when there were people who were visitors coming to sit and wait. I just -- I didn't think that was appropriate during the business time.

So I went the other way, behind -- which went past the Oval Office, not knowing that -- I guess you're not supposed to do that. It seemed silly. The door's closed and it's locked. And there wasn't this intention to see the

1070

14

President that way.

So -- am I -- did I answer your question?

A JUROR: Yes.

THE WITNESS: Okay. I'm sorry.

MR. EMMICK: You know, one thing I might do is circle back to try to pick up some more concealment methods.

A JUROR: Okay.

MR. EMMICK: Because you asked the question are there any other methods.

A JUROR: Yes.

MR. EMMICK: And I can ask a few more questions that might direct us in that area.

THE WITNESS: Okay.

BY MR. EMMICK:

Q For example, you have indicated earlier that it was Betty Currie who waved you in all the times during 1997 that you saw the President. Did you ever talk with the President about whether he could wave you in instead or whether it would be a good idea for him to wave you in personally?

A Yes. I think that that's what I mentioned earlier.

Q Oh, okay.

A That he and I had discussed it and he said he couldn't do that because then it would be on a list.

Q Okay. What about -- you had mentioned that you took a different route into the Oval Office than you would take out of the Oval Office. In addition, did you ever take routes to get to the Oval Office that seemed calculated to avoid certain Secret Service or White House personnel?

A Not Secret Service, but I -- I liked or I preferred to sort of meet up with him and then we'd walk in together. And I preferred to go in through the Rose Garden because then I wasn't going -- I wasn't risking the possibility of running into someone in the hall right outside the Oval Office. So --

Q What about the routes that Betty would walk you in from the gates?

A Oh. When -- there were certain Secret Service officers who were friendly with Debi Schiff who Betty wanted to try to avoid because I guess they chatted with Debi Schiff a lot and there's a whole long story with Debi Schiff, so --

Q And would that be another way that you would help conceal your meetings with the President?

A Yes.

A JUROR: Just to back up for a minute. When you would meet the President and go in through the Rose Garden or meet the President before going into the Oval Office, did you discuss that with him ever about sort of what -- that that would be a way that would sort of be more concealing or --

THE WITNESS: We only did that, I think, twice. And the first time, it really was an accident. And so then the next time that we did that, I said -- you know, before -- he would call me in my office before I would come see him and we'd figure out what we were going to do.

And I think I -- I know I suggested to him, I said, "I really like that because then it's just easier, it seems." And also, I -- for me personally, I didn't -- I didn't always want to be the one that was being seen going in. Does that make sense?

So that I wasn't always bringing in the papers and it was me going to him, that in this instance if someone saw it, being the Secret Service, he invited me. So -- for me, that just made me feel better.

BY MR. EMMICK:

Q All right. I have a number of other questions about these alternative methods of concealment. Let me ask you this. I think you've testified earlier that most of the sexual contact that you had with the President tended to occur in the hallway, rather than in the study, although sometimes it was in the study itself.

Did that have anything to do with whether or not it would be easier to see you in the study as opposed to the hallway?

A I think so, but I don't specifically -- I don't

1073

17

specifically remember discussing that with the President, but there were circumstances that that sort of was obvious to me.

Q And would that include the fact that windows in the study tended to be uncurtained?

A Just that, windows. Yes.

Q Right. Yes, there were windows there.

A Yes.

Q And so you might be seen there.

A Yes.

MR. EMMICK: All right.

BY MS. IMMERGUT:

Q In that regard, you also mentioned that you would move from the oval area or that sometimes you'd start in the Oval Office and then you'd move towards the hallway. Did the President ever initiate that move?

A I think we both did. I mean, it just depended on the day. It wasn't --

Q Was it understood that you wouldn't actually have a sexual encounter in the Oval Office?

A I'm sure it was understood. I -- I -- I wouldn't have done that. I mean -- so -- I'm sure he wouldn't have done that.

BY MR. EMMICK:

Q Are there windows all around the Oval Office?

1074

18

A There are windows all around and it just -- I know this may sound silly, but it wouldn't be appropriate. You know.

Q What about any discussions with the President about not acknowledging one another at parties or photographs, for example?

A He called me in my office the day of Pat Griffin's going away party and had asked me if I was going to go. I said yes and he said, "Well, maybe we can get together after that."

And I told him I didn't think that was a good idea, that people were going to be watching. I was paranoid anyway and -- so I said, "I think it's a good idea if we just sort of ignore each other at the party and don't really say anything." And that's what we did.

Q And what about with respect to a photograph that was taken at the party and whether --

A I mean, we didn't discuss this. I didn't know there was going to be a picture taken. But I made an effort to stand on the -- I was the last person sort of on the outside of this picture so that -- I didn't want anyone to think that I was trying to get close to the President, I was trying to -- whatever it was.

Q So in that case, that would be a concealment effort, but not one that the President and you had collaborated on.

A No.

Q All right. What about an occasion when the President suggested that the two you might attend a movie and sort of bump into each other outside the movie? Tell us about that discussion.

A He told me he was going to watch a movie with some friends of his and that if I wanted to I could bump into him in the hall outside and then he'd invite me into the movie.

And I asked him if -- I think he said there were some friends and maybe some of his staff or I asked him if some of his staff was going to be there.

And he said yes and I don't remember who he said was going to be there, but I said I didn't think that was a good idea.

Q And why would you have to make prior arrangements for you to bump into each other rather than having sort of a -- you know, walk down the hall together to the movie?

A Well, I --

Q I know it's kind of obvious.

A For obvious reasons, I guess, because it wouldn't be appropriate. It -- people would -- people would wonder what was going on.

Q Right. Right. Okay. What about the fact that you made -- that you sent gifts and notes through Betty rather

1076

20

than directly to the President?

Was that something that was done in order to make it less obvious that the notes were actually to the President?

A Well, yes and no. You really -- if you send something directly to the President, if you send a gift to the President, if I sent something right now, well, I don't know, right now, but before this, it -- it -- it goes to the gift unit.

Q Right.

A And so I knew that Betty was the way -- I think that that's -- Walter Kaye would, you know, go through Betty, I think. And that's --

Q So it's yes and no, is the answer to that.

A You can't -- I mean, you can't send a courier thing to the President, you know, a courier to President Clinton, so --

A JUROR: I have a question to follow up on that. When you would send gifts and notes and what have you to Betty, as you had testified, sometimes you'd have a funny card in there, sometimes it would be something sentimental.

Did you ever give Betty license to read any of them because you thought, "Hey, take a look at this, tell me what you think," any of the cards or notes or anything?

1077

THE WITNESS: I don't think so. Maybe I told her about a funny card or something. Not that I really remember. I don't -- I think especially if it were something that was ultra-sensitive, I don't -- you know, I don't --

A JUROR: Yes. That would probably be sealed.

THE WITNESS: Exactly.

A JUROR: But for any of the other little --

THE WITNESS: Might have been the jokes. Sometimes I would put together jokes I got on the Internet or e-mail jokes that I put together for him because, you know, everyone needs to laugh, so -- I think maybe -- maybe there was a time that I said, "Oh, you should look at these jokes, they're really funny."

A JUROR: Okay.

MR. EMMICK: Other questions? Yes, ma'am?

A JUROR: Ms. Lewinsky, did you ever discuss with the President whether you should delete documents from your hard drive, either at the office or at home?

THE WITNESS: No.

A JUROR: Nothing like that?

THE WITNESS: No.

A JUROR: Did you ever discuss with the President whether you should deny the relationship if you were asked about it?

THE WITNESS: I think I always offered that.

1078

22

I think I've always --

A JUROR: In discussions with the President?

THE WITNESS: In discussions -- I told him I would always -- I would always deny it, I would always protect him.

A JUROR: And what did he say when you said that? What kind of response did you receive?

THE WITNESS: I said that often. I -- in my head, I'm seeing him smile and I'm hearing him saying "That's good," or -- something affirmative. You know. Not -- not -- "Don't deny it."

A JUROR: Thank you.

THE WITNESS: Sure.

BY MS. IMMERGUT:

Q Ms. Lewinsky, with respect to the weekend visits, did the President ever initiate that idea or say anything about it's good if you come on the weekends?

A Yes. The -- I don't remember if it was the Wednesday or the Friday when the relationship first started, he said to me at some point, you know, "You can come see me on the weekends. I'm usually around on the weekends." So --

Q And did you understand what that meant?

A Yes. To me, it meant there aren't as many people around on the weekends, so --

A JUROR: Ms. Lewinsky, when you -- now, this is a

1079

23

different kind of subject. When you first made the determination that you were moving to New York and you wanted to explore the possibilities of a job in private industry, can you recall how you first got the recommendation about Vernon Jordan's assistance in this endeavor?

THE WITNESS: I can't. I know that it was -- what I don't remember was if it was my idea or Linda's idea. And I know that that came up in discussions with her, I believe, before I discussed it with the President. I know that I suggested to the President or I -- I didn't suggest, I asked the President if Mr. Jordan might be able to assist me.

A JUROR: To go back from the job search to what we were talking about before, I seem to recall, and I may be mistaken, when you were here before you said something about Tim Keating when you were fired, said something to you like maybe you can come back after the election.

THE WITNESS: Mm-hmm.

A JUROR: And I wanted to just hear sort of a fuller explanation about that. Was it your understanding at the time that Tim Keating was sort of -- that he understood and was telling you that you were fired because of an appearance problem around the time of the election?

THE WITNESS: Not at all.

A JUROR: No?

THE WITNESS: No.

1080

24

A JUROR: The other question I have, and I apologize, it's a little bit sensitive, but did you and the President in sort of discussing cover stories and, you know, how -- you know, your desire to protect him from sort of what's going on now, did you ever talk about sort of -- you know, that you weren't really having sex?

I mean, you said that he made this comment to you about not having -- you know, that certain actions have consequences at his age.

THE WITNESS: Yes.

A JUROR: Was there ever sort of an understanding that, well, oral sex isn't really sex? Or did you talk about that?

THE WITNESS: We didn't talk about it. Something that I thought on my own was one of the reasons that it -- at first that he didn't want to -- that he wouldn't let everything come to completion in terms of oral sex was I thought that that sort of had to do with maybe that was his way of being able to feel okay about it, his way of being able to justify it or rationalize it that, well --

A JUROR: But you never discussed that.

THE WITNESS: No.

MR. EMMICK: Yes, ma'am?

A JUROR: Ms. Lewinsky, getting back to -- I think you have a copy there of contacts between the President and

1081

25

Monica?

THE WITNESS: Yes.

A JUROR: After you left the White House, it seems as if you attended a number of public functions where you came in contact with him.

Was that by chance? Was that something you wanted to do? Was it a way to see him? Was it something that he suggested?

Could you just tell us a little about that?

THE WITNESS: Sure. No. Those were all ways for me to get a chance to see him. I'm an insecure person and so I think -- and I was insecure about the relationship at times and thought that he would come to forget me easily and if I hadn't heard from him -- especially after I left the White House, it was -- it was very difficult for me and I always liked to see him and it -- and usually when I'd see him, it would kind of prompt him to call me. So I made an effort. I would go early and stand in the front so I could see him, blah, blah, blah.

BY MR. EMMICK:

Q Let me ask a follow-up question to that because I think it may have been in about October of '96 when you had a telephone conversation with him just prior to you going to Billy Shaddock to get a photograph.

A Right.

1082

26

Q During the conversation before, did you and the President have any discussion about your dropping by and seeing him at a public departure?

A Yes.

Q All right. Would you tell us about that?

A Let's see. I spoke with him -- I think it was October 22nd, and then I saw him at an event October 23rd and he called that night and I had mentioned to him on -- I think it was a Tuesday, the first phone conversation, that I was going to be at the White House on Thursday.

And when he called me Wednesday night, he said -- I was upset with him and so then he said, you know, "Don't be mad. Don't be mad." You know. "Are you coming tomorrow?"

And I said yes.

So he said, "Well, why don't you stop by Betty's office, stop by to see Betty and then maybe you can come see me for a few minutes before I leave." So --

Q Okay. All right. The reason I was asking that as a follow-up is that's sort of a prearranged semi-public occasion for the two of you to see each other.

A Right. I don't -- I don't know necessarily that I was going to go to the departure.

Q I see.

A But that was maybe kind of a cover story.

1083

27

Q I understand.

A Or I'm not -- I know he had a departure and I know that I was going to see him for a few minutes before the departure because I thought -- I remember thinking that I might get to kiss him, so --

MR. EMMICK: All right.

A JUROR: Now to follow up on your follow-up of my question --

MR. EMMICK: Yes

A JUROR: Did you get to see him that day?

THE WITNESS: No, I didn't.

A JUROR: Okay. Could you tell us a little about that?

THE WITNESS: Sure. I -- the short of it is that I didn't end up seeing him because Evelyn Lieberman was hanging around and left with him that day.

A JUROR: She was someplace where she didn't belong.

THE WITNESS: Right. So Betty had -- I was waiting in the West Wing lobby with Billy, actually, after we had gone to look at the photos and Betty finally came out and it was really just as he was walking to the helicopter and she took me to see it, but she said that -- and it was at that point when she sort of confirmed for me that Evelyn didn't like me. So -- that --

A JUROR: The contacts with the President, on page 5, for the 18th of August --

THE WITNESS: I'm sorry, I can't hear you.

MR. EMMICK: Page 5.

A JUROR: Okay. Page 5, 18th of August, it says "Public function, President's 50th birthday party, limited intimate contact."

A JUROR: I couldn't hear her.

MR. EMMICK: Okay. Let me repeat it. There is a reference on page 5 to August 18th of '96, a Sunday, "Public function, President's 50th birthday party, limited intimate contact."

Your question about that was?

THE WITNESS: What does that mean?

MR. EMMICK: What does that mean?

THE WITNESS: It's stupid. There was a cocktail reception for his -- he had this big 50th birthday party at Radio City Music Hall and there was a cocktail reception and at the -- when he came to do the rope line and he -- after he greeted me and talked to me, he was talking to a whole bunch of people in and around my area and I had -- can I stand up and show you?

MR. EMMICK: Sure. Sure.

THE WITNESS: Okay. If this is the rope line and here are all the people and the President's standing here, as

1085

he started to talk to other people, I had my back to him and I just kind of put -- put my hand behind me and touched him. This -- so --

BY MS. IMMERGUT:

Q Touched him in the crotch area?

A Yes.

A JUROR: I didn't hear that.

MS. IMMERGUT: Touched him in the crotch area.

A JUROR: Oh.

MS. IMMERGUT: And the response was yes.

A JUROR: Okay.

A JUROR: Did anybody see you?

THE WITNESS: What? No. What's the question?

A JUROR: Did anybody see you?

THE WITNESS: No.

A JUROR: But there were people around.

THE WITNESS: There were, but it was -- he was talking -- everybody was enamored with him. I'm sure everybody saw from Monday that -- and he was talking to different people and he -- he was always very close to me when -- whenever he'd do these rope lines and would sort of make a point of talking to me around -- you know, with other -- while other people were there and he'd usually hold my hand -- you know, sort of shaking hands and just -- would continue to just touch me somewhere. I mean, not -- not

1086

intimately, not --

BY MR. EMMICK:

Q Right. Just to set the scene, are there a lot of people kind of bunched together at the time?

A Oh, they're -- they're -- I mean, if we -- if everybody in the room came and stood in this one small corner, that's -- I mean, that's how crowded it was. So it was -- and my back was to him and he was -- he was holding onto my -- I think he was holding onto one of my arms or something, I had a sleeveless dress on. So --

Q So it sounds to me like -- it's almost a situation where there are so many people that you can't really see that kind of --

A Exactly. And it wasn't -- it wasn't a -- it was -- maybe sort of a grazing over of that area, but it wasn't -- it wasn't how you might imagine it if someone described this, from a scene from a movie, it wasn't like that, but it was -- you know. I don't even know if he remembers, so --

MR. EMMICK: Okay.

A JUROR: So on this paper we have here with sexual relations, would that qualify as -- what, contact? Sexual contact? Because if I remember -- where's my paper --

THE WITNESS: Let me look at the definition.

MR. EMMICK: Sure.

A JUROR: Yes. Contact with -- number 1 --

1087

31

MR. EMMICK: Just to clarify, the witness is looking at Grand Jury Exhibit ML-6.

THE WITNESS: I'm not really sure, because I don't think it was to necessarily gratify him or arouse him.

A JUROR: What was it for?

THE WITNESS: It was just -- I thought it was funny and it was sort of a -- I don't know how to explain it.

A JUROR: Contact.

BY MR. EMMICK:

Q Would it be better described as perhaps affectionate or playful?

A Playful, I think. It was just -- playful, not something I'd ever thought I'd have to discuss publicly.

A JUROR: While we're on this, I wanted to like finish it up, but I had a couple of questions with regards to the definition.

THE WITNESS: Sure.

A JUROR: Because I want to be sure in my own mind. At the bottom it says -- it says "Contact means intentional touching, either directly or through clothing."

THE WITNESS: Mm-hmm.

A JUROR: Out of all of the times you had intimate contact, were there times when the President would touch you either on the breasts or in the genital area directly to the skin or was it always through clothing?

1088

32

THE WITNESS: Directly to the skin. Both.

MR. EMMICK: Yes, ma'am?

A JUROR: I have some questions about the 50th birthday. That's when you gave the President the yellow tie. Is that when you gave the President the yellow tie?

THE WITNESS: Not on that date.

A JUROR: But just before that.

THE WITNESS: But before that. Correct.

A JUROR: When it shows on the chart here, it says "Some time before August 16, 1996."

THE WITNESS: Correct.

A JUROR: And that tie is the same tie that at the end of your appearance here we saw some evidence that the President has worn a number of times this summer.

THE WITNESS: Yes.

A JUROR: There's been some press accounts about that tie, last night and today.

THE WITNESS: Sure.

A JUROR: My question to you is have you authorized your attorneys or any other spokesperson through you to discuss that evidence?

THE WITNESS: Gosh. I don't think I've necessarily given a direct authorization.

A JUROR: Do you know that they have?

THE WITNESS: Do I know if they -- I -- I don't

1089

33

know if they necessarily directly have. I know there have been questions about it. I shouldn't say I know, I'm sure there have been questions about it, but there have been a lot of instances since the beginning of this thing that there's been information that's come out from places where I hadn't expected it and that includes my own -- the people on my team. So I can't -- I don't know.

A JUROR: So you don't know whether that information is coming from people that you have discussed it with?

THE WITNESS: I think that there -- there probably might have been -- I really -- I -- I wouldn't be surprised to find out that there was confirmation or some of that information came from there.

So -- but I know that also -- I'm sure it was somewhat limited because with my agreement, we're not allowed to talk to the press. We're not supposed to. So -- without prior approval.

BY MR. EMMICK:

Q So I guess there's -- let me just rephrase it. It sounds like you wouldn't be surprised by it, but do you have any direct knowledge that it occurred?

A I know that there have been calls about this tie and I know that -- that I don't think that we've been 100 percent silent about that. So -- I don't -- I mean -- I know

Diversified Reporting Services, Inc.
1025 VERMONT AVENUE, N.W. SUITE 1250
WASHINGTON, D.C. 20005
(202) 296-2929

1090

that we didn't cause this story to come out or I don't believe that we did. So --

A JUROR: Ms. Lewinsky, it says on the chart that you received a thank you note saying that the tie is really beautiful.

THE WITNESS: Mm-hmm.

A JUROR: And that was in the President's handwriting?

THE WITNESS: It's a typed letter and then he hand signed the letter and then "The tie is really beautiful" is handwritten.

A JUROR: Did you ever discuss the tie with him in person or was it just a note?

THE WITNESS: No, we discussed it a lot on the phone.

A JUROR: And did he like the tie?

THE WITNESS: Mm-hmm.

A JUROR: Thank you.

THE WITNESS: He called me the first day he wore it. The first time he wore it.

A JUROR: All right. Thank you.

A JUROR: I have another question.

THE WITNESS: Sure.

A JUROR: On the day you were here testifying, there was a report on the TV --

1091

35

THE WITNESS: Right.

A JUROR: The President in the Rose Garden wearing that tie. Did you see that?

THE WITNESS: That evening I did.

A JUROR: When you saw him with the tie, what did that say to you?

THE WITNESS: I understand you had to do what you had to do. That's what it meant to me. I had looked -- because I had seen him wear this tie prior -- a few other occasions since January, I had looked the day before my testimony because I thought he's just the kind of person that's going to wear this tie to tug on my emotional strings one last time before I go into the grand jury and say this under oath. And he didn't.

And him wearing it the day I came to testify sort of having to know that I wasn't going to see it until the end of the day, to me was just kind of -- you know, hey, you had to do what you had to do. But --

MR. EMMICK: Yes, ma'am?

A JUROR: Ms. Lewinsky, not to make a big issue about the tie, but is this tie something -- one of the ties that perhaps the President really liked, is a favorite tie?

THE WITNESS: I think so because he wore it during the campaign. He wore it once -- sometimes even twice a week. So I think he liked it a lot.

1092

36

A JUROR: Do you think that he would remember that it's from you? I mean, you know, I don't know, but do you think he would?

THE WITNESS: Ties were a big issue with us and I used to bug him all the time on the phone, "Well, when are you going to wear one of my ties?" You know. Or he'd say, "Did you see -- " On one occasion, I remember specifically he said, "Did you see I wore your tie the other day?"

There's a pretty big correlation between the times when he would wear one of my ties and we either spoke the night before or that night.

And I used to say to him that "I like it when you wear my ties because then I know I'm close to your heart." So -- literally and figuratively.

A JUROR: So you think he would know, then, that that was your tie.

THE WITNESS: He should know.

A JUROR: Which brings to mind when the first appearance by Nel, when he came testify --

THE WITNESS: Yes.

A JUROR: Can you tell me what your thoughts were when you saw the pictures of Nelvis wearing the first tie that you gave the President?

THE WITNESS: Yes. Actually, you know what? I think my cup's leaking. I'm sorry.

1093

A JUROR: Do we have another cup up there?

THE WITNESS: Am I allowed to know people's names in here?

MR. EMMICK: The answer to that is no.

THE WITNESS: Oh --

MR. EMMICK: I know it seems --

THE WITNESS: It's so awkward.

MR. EMMICK: It does seem awkward, but I think it's better if --

THE WITNESS: Okay.

MR. EMMICK: -- the record not have any identifications.

THE WITNESS: Okay.

MR. EMMICK: We didn't intentionally get you a dribble glass.

THE WITNESS: Oh, sure. At least it's water and not grape juice.

I had two very different thoughts. My first thought was "You jerk. You're trying to show me how little you care about me and how little this meant to you by giving it -- to show me that you gave it to someone else, it meant so little to you now."

And my second thought was that it was sort of some sort of message of some sorts. I don't know what. Because I could see the President kind of saying to Nel, you know, "Oh, why don't you -- " I could even see him spilling something on Nel on purpose and -- that morning and then sort of saying, "Oh, here, just wear this tie," or something like that. I mean, that's -- it's -- he's funny that way. But I thought there was some sort of deliberateness to it.

I don't know that Nel knew that, that that was the tie I gave the President but -- I don't think it was a coincidence.

MR. EMMICK: Yes, ma'am?

A JUROR: Could one of your thoughts perhaps have been that maybe he just gave him a batch of ties to Nelvis? And maybe he didn't remember?

THE WITNESS: No.

A JUROR: You really think he would have remembered that first tie?

THE WITNESS: I know he did. I mean, we -- we -- that was -- I don't know if you all know this or not, but I worked in a men's necktie store when I was in college for four years and so that was my thing, that was part -- you know, my spending money, a lot of it came from working. And so I love ties.

And I -- I mean, I can pick out -- you know, different designers and stuff. And so that was a big thing for me. And then -- and I liked to give him ties and I liked to see him wearing them.

1095

39

A JUROR: Do you know how much impact Nel had on what the President wore each day?

THE WITNESS: None. To my understanding. Nel was. My understanding is that Nel's strictly in the -- while he would go to the residence on occasions, that he was usually in the oval area.

MR. EMMICK: There's a question waiting for a bit here. Yes.

A JUROR: Ms Lewinsky, was it the President's nature to give his ties away?

THE WITNESS: Yes. I knew that -- I knew that he had given Nel ties, his ties in the past. But ties were such a big issue between the President and me that I really couldn't have imagined that he didn't -- that he didn't know.

A JUROR: Other people other than Nel as well, in terms of giving his ties away?

THE WITNESS: I don't know.

A JUROR: Okay. You just --

THE WITNESS: I'm not aware of anyone else, but that doesn't mean there aren't.

A JUROR: Okay.

THE WITNESS: Right.

A JUROR: But you did know about that.

THE WITNESS: Yes.

A JUROR: Do you happen to know whether the

1096

40

President had a valet to assist him in his dressing?

THE WITNESS: Assist him in his dressing, I don't know. I know that there's a valet.

A JUROR: Or like prepare -- Mr. President, this suit goes with this tie, kind of thing?

THE WITNESS: I don't know that necessarily, but I have seen -- I had seen evidence enough that he could wear my ties when he wanted to. You know. That if he wanted to, he could go pick it out, so I don't know what his getting dressed routine is.

A JUROR: Okay. Thank you.

A JUROR: Okay. I have a question that's a bit on the delicate side.

THE WITNESS: Okay.

A JUROR: But this is just something that I need to know.

THE WITNESS: Sure.

A JUROR: Did you and the President ever engage in sexual relations using cigars?

THE WITNESS: Yes.

A JUROR: Okay.

A JUROR: Okay. I'd like to change the subject now.

THE WITNESS: Thank you. Just once. Just once.

A JUROR: When you last testified, you told us that

1097

41

photographs that you saw of the President and First Lady when they were away that were romantic in nature upset you.

When you had an opportunity to speak with the President about those photographs or any film that was taken during these romantic moments, what did he say? Why they were -- because I'm just curious as to whether or not they were staged because of the legal things that were going on with the President at that time.

THE WITNESS: Right. I don't believe we discussed them. I know that that upset me and sort of put me in a bit of a contentious mood when I spoke with him on the 5th. I think it was the 5th of January of this year. And I may have said something in passing about them, but we didn't have a discussion about the pictures.

A JUROR: Okay. I was just wondering if there were --

THE WITNESS: Sure. No. I wondered, too.

A JUROR: Did you think any conversations to him about his wife were inappropriate?

THE WITNESS: I don't know if inappropriate is the right word. I tried not to. I -- there were very few discussions and I tended to say things like, "Well, when you're alone," you know, "Call me when you're alone," kind of a thing or, you know, that was how we discussed sort of Mrs. Clinton maybe not being there, was, "Well, I'll be alone on this day. Shall I -- " I think we were careful -- or I was careful, I know I was.

MR. EMMICK: Yes, ma'am?

A JUROR: Ms. Lewinsky, I wondered if you ever had any trouble with the Secret Service in trying to be near the President.

THE WITNESS: No. The only time that I remember was when I went to see him on the last time in '96, I guess it was April 7th, Easter. And when John Muskett was outside and he said he was going to check with Evelyn if I could go in and then I don't remember exactly how it happened, but I sort of -- I don't remember the exact discussion, but it ended up he ended up not talking to Evelyn and I went in. So --

A JUROR: I have a question about Linda Tripp.

THE WITNESS: Ugh. Sorry.

A JUROR: In your conversations with Ms. Tripp, was her opinion always that she must be truthful or was there a time where your impression was that she was going to provide you with cooperation as far as keeping the secrecy?

THE WITNESS: There are two areas of that, I guess. Linda always told me she would always protect me and she would never tell anybody and keep my secret, up until the Paula Jones case came about.

1099

43

And I had never had any reason to think that she would ever need to discuss this under oath because I was certainly always going to deny it and I couldn't even imagine a situation where that would really come up.

But there was a point in the period prior to my learning about her being subpoenaed in the Paula Jones case, most specifically, January 9th, when she led me to believe that she was not going to tell about my relationship and that she was going to be vague on the truth about Kathleen Willey and was just not going to really remember anything else and that was why I agreed to meet with her on Tuesday the 13th.

A JUROR: In your conversations with her as you were making your move to move to New York and what have you, did you ever get the sense that she was fishing for offers of benefits or the protection of her job? You know, or where she was hoping that nothing would affect her job or if there was something in it for her?

THE WITNESS: Yes and no. When you asked me the question, the first thing that comes to my mind was it may not be directly related to that.

When the Kathleen Willey incident had come out in Newsweek, there was a period after it, Bob Bennett had referred to -- or had made that comment about Linda Tripp and she made some off-comment about if she loses her job she's going to write a tell-all book.

And so I sort of -- that was an instance where I felt I needed to assure her that that wasn't going to happen, she wasn't going to lose her job, and that -- I certainly tried to make assurances. I mean, I -- I promised -- I would have promised her the moon if I could deliver it.

And then also -- then when I spoke with her on the 9th, she talked about that she had spent some time in New York during Christmas and that she -- that someone had suggested to her that she get a job doing public relations in New York.

And that seemed a little bit strange to me, in that that was exactly what I was in the process of doing, and that maybe that was what she thought, that somehow then -- you know, I think I told her, oh, I'd try to help her come to New York and try to help her that way, but I don't know that -- that I ever said anything directly about who would help her.

A JUROR: Okay. Thank you.

BY MR. EMMICK:

Q I'd like to ask a clarifying follow-up because I wasn't sure I understood all of the sort of ins and outs, if you will, of when Linda was going to maintain the secret and when she was going to reveal it. It sounded like prior to the time when Linda got a Paula Jones subpoena, your understanding was she was doing to keep the secret.

A Correct.

1101

Q And then after she got the Paula Jones subpoena, then she told you that she was going to disclose things and tell the truth. Is that right?

A Yes. Yes.

Q Okay. And then in this conversation on January 9th, she indicated some willingness to consider keeping the secret a bit longer.

A No, considered that she was going to do that.

Q That she was going to. All right. That's what I wanted to clarify.

A Sure.

MR. EMMICK: Thank you.

A JUROR: When you said that in your conversations with Linda Tripp you kind of had to exaggerate some things about the President to her, you exaggerated on some of the things you said to her about the President --

THE WITNESS: I'm not sure about that. I -- I don't know if exaggerate is the right -- is maybe the word I would choose.

A JUROR: Okay.

THE WITNESS: But go on. I'm sorry.

A JUROR: Well, no, I just used that word.

THE WITNESS: Okay.

A JUROR: Exaggerate. You didn't use it, but I couldn't think of the exact words you used.

THE WITNESS: Sure.

A JUROR: But were you -- why do you think that you had to not tell her some things that din actually happen, true things, in talking to her?

THE WITNESS: That really came about in relation to the Paula Jones case. I think that I was -- there were some occasions, one in particular that I remember, when I didn't disclose a contact that I had with the President -- I'm sorry, here -- I'll scoot over -- contact that I had with the President to her for some reasons, but after the Paula Jones case, I was scared to death. I mean, I was panicked that she was going to tell.

So, I mean, I -- I -- you know, along the lines of, you know, some of the things I said about Mr. Jordan, I said, you know, "Oh, the President told me I have to lie," I don't even remember everything I said, but I know that there were certainly lies at that point, not even exaggerations.

MR. EMMICK: Actually, I was going to ask that clarifying follow-up to that.

THE FOREPERSON: And then after that, we have to take a break.

MR. EMMICK: And then we'll take a break.

BY MR. EMMICK:

Q The clarifying follow-up was that I had understood that during that January period when you were talking to

1103

47

Linda Tripp you were lying to her on occasion, but I wasn't clear whether those lies related to times that you had been with the President or whether they related to other things generally. Do you understand what my question is?

A No.

Q What were the nature of the lies that you were telling to Linda Tripp during that January period?

A Oh, gosh. They went from -- I guess a non-disclosure of my meeting with him on the 28th, nor my phone call with him on the 5th of January, to -- ranging to things that he said I had to do or told me to do.

I haven't -- I haven't seen transcripts of those days, thank goodness, but I just know that I was -- I was scared to death. And I thought any influence that anybody would have, my mother, Mr. Jordan, the President, anybody, would -- I used.

MR. EMMICK: All right.

THE FOREPERSON: It's break time.

MR. EMMICK: Break time.

THE FOREPERSON: It's break time. It's break time.

A JUROR: I have a follow-up to that as well.

THE FOREPERSON: Okay. So we're going to take ten minutes.

THE WITNESS: Okay.

THE FOREPERSON: And we'll come back.

1104

48

A JUROR: I hope I remember my question.

THE WITNESS: Can you guys call me Monica?

Are they allowed to call me Monica instead of Ms. Lewinsky? I was just --

THE FOREPERSON: If you say so.

THE WITNESS: Okay.

MR. EMMICK: Sure.

THE WITNESS: I'm just 25. Please.

A JUROR: But you'll always be Ms. Lewinsky, whether you're 25 or 28 or --

THE WITNESS: Not if I get married.

(Witness excused. Witness recalled.)

THE FOREPERSON: Monica, I'd like to remind that you are still under oath.

THE WITNESS: Thank you.

MR. EMMICK: We have a quorum and there are no unauthorized persons present. Is that right?

THE FOREPERSON: You are absolutely correct.

MR. EMMICK: Lucky this time.

THE WITNESS: Thank you.

MR. EMMICK: Did you want to ask some follow-up questions?

MS. IMMERGUT: Yes.

BY MS. IMMERGUT:

Q Ms. Lewinsky, there are two things I wanted to

1105

49

clarify. First, with respect to the tie disclosure issue --

A Yes.

Q -- you were asked about before, I believe you mentioned something to the effect that there have been things that have come out of your team that you were surprised about before. Are you referring to your current legal team?

A No. My first legal team.

Q Okay. And that's Mr. Ginsberg?

A Yes.

Q Okay. You're not aware of any unauthorized disclosures from your current camp?

A No. Nor have I authorized any disclosures.

Q Okay. So you didn't authorize a disclosure about the tie.

A No.

Q With respect to -- to switch gears -- to what we were speaking about right before the break about the things that you said to Linda Tripp at the very end, particularly on January 13, 1998, I believe --

A Yes.

Q You mentioned that an example of things that you were not truthful about was, for example, the fact you had seen the President on December 28th and that you had spoken to him on January 5th. Is that correct?

A Right. Yes. And I didn't disclose that to her.

Diversified Reporting Services, Inc.
1025 VERMONT AVENUE, N.W. SUITE 1250
WASHINGTON, D.C. 20005
(202) 296-2929

Q Right. You did not disclose that to her.

A Quite to the contrary.

Q Okay. In fact, you told her that you hadn't seen or spoken to the President for two months.

A Or since the 17th of December.

Q Okay.

A Exactly.

Q You mentioned that there was -- you also said things about what the President had said to you to Ms. Tripp that were not true on January 13th. Do you remember any specific things that you said that the President had told you that in fact were not true?

A No. I don't remember any specifics, I just wanted to leave open the possibility. Does that clarify it?

MR. EMMICK: On the right here?

A JUROR: Monica, why did you keep that black dress?

A JUROR: Blue.

A JUROR: Blue dress.

A JUROR: Did you have a reason to keep it?

THE WITNESS: Pardon?

A JUROR: The blue dress.

A JUROR: The blue dress.

THE WITNESS: No. I didn't have a reason. The -- reason -- the dress -- I didn't realize -- if I remember correctly, I didn't really realize that there was anything on it until I went to go wear it again and I had gained too much weight that I couldn't fit into it.

And it seemed sort of funny and I -- it may sound silly, I have a lot of clothes. I don't clean all my clothes right after I wear them, I usually don't clean them until I know I'm going to wear them again. And then I was going to wear it for Thanksgiving because I had lost weight and I had -- I had shown the dress to Linda at that point and had just sort of said to her, "Well, isn't this -- " You know, "Isn't this stupid?" Or, you know, "Look at this, isn't this gross?" Or whatever. I don't really remember exactly what I said.

And she told me that I should put it in a safe deposit box because it could be evidence one day.

And I said that was ludicrous because I would never -- I would never disclose that I had a relationship with the President, I would never need it.

And then when Thanksgiving time came around and I told her that I was going to wear it for Thanksgiving, she told me I looked fat in the dress, I shouldn't wear it. She brought me a jacket from her closet as to try to persuade me not to wear the dress.

So I ended up not wearing it and then I was going to clean it. I took it with me up to New York and was going to clean it up there and then this broke, so --

A JUROR: Okay. Your relationship with the President, did your mother at any time try to discourage the relationship?

THE WITNESS: Oh, yes.

A JUROR: Well, what kept it going? I mean, what kept it -- you keeping it active or whatever?

THE WITNESS: I fell in love.

A JUROR: I beg your pardon? I couldn't hear you.

THE WITNESS: I fell in love.

A JUROR: When you look at it now, was it love or a sexual obsession?

THE WITNESS: More love with a little bit of obsession. But definitely love.

A JUROR: Did you think that the President was in love with you also?

THE WITNESS: There was an occasion when I left the White House and I was pretty stunned at how I felt because I did think that.

A JUROR: You did?

BY MR. EMMICK:

Q Do you remember the date?

A It was July 4, 1997.

A JUROR: Were you aware that he was having problems in his marriage? Did this ever spill over in the

1109

53

times that you were together? Did you get a feeling that something was not right, that --

THE WITNESS:

A JUROR:

THE WITNESS:

A JUROR:

THE WITNESS:

A JUROR:

THE WITNESS:

A JUROR:

MR. EMMICK: I thought there was a question in the front here.

A JUROR: And today, Monica, do you still love the President?

THE WITNESS: Before Monday, I would have said yes.

1110

54

A JUROR: So then it is no?

THE WITNESS: I don't know how I feel right now.

MR. EMMICK: A question in the front?

A JUROR: I guess I would like to know what happened Monday to make you just by Thursday change your mind so completely.

THE WITNESS: I don't think it's so much changed my mind. I think -- it's -- it was very painful for me to watch his speech on Monday night. I -- it's -- it's hard for me to feel that he has characterized this relationship as a service contract and that that was never something that I ever thought it was. And --

A JUROR: I'm sorry, you lost me already.

THE WITNESS: I'm sorry. I'm sorry. It's -- from my understanding about what he testified to on Monday, not -- just from the press accounts, is that this was a -- that this was a service contract, that all I did was perform oral sex on him and that that's all that this relationship was. And it was a lot more than that to me and I thought it was a lot more than that.

And I think I felt -- I was hurt that -- that he didn't even -- sort of acknowledge me in his remarks. And even also -- I mean, that has to do with directly with me, but I thought he should have acknowledged all the other people that have gone through a lot of pain for seven months.

I feel very responsible for a lot of what's happened, you know, in the seven months, but I tried -- I tried very hard to do what I could to not -- to not hurt him. I'm still not answering your question.

A JUROR: Well, let's -- you said the relationship was more than oral sex. I mean, it wasn't like you went out on dates or anything like that like normal people, so what more was it?

THE WITNESS: Oh, we spent hours on the phone talking. It was emotional.

A JUROR: Phone sex?

THE WITNESS: Not always. On a few occasions. I mean, we were talking. I mean, interacting. I mean, talking about what we were thinking and feeling and doing and laughing.

We were very affectionate, even when -- after he broke the relationship off in May, I mean, when I'd go to visit with him, we'd -- you know, we'd hug each other a lot. You know, he always used to like to stroke my hair. He -- we'd hold hands. We'd smile a lot. We discussed a variety -- you know, a wide range of things.

So, I mean, it was -- there was a real component of a relationship to it and I just -- I thought he had a beautiful soul. I just thought he was just this incredible person and when I looked at him I saw a little boy and -- I

1112

56

don't know what the truth is any more.

And that's, I think, what I took away on Monday, was that I didn't know what the truth was. And so how could I know the truth of my love for someone if it was based on him being an actor.

A JUROR: I'd like to ask you about Bayani Nelvis.

THE WITNESS: Okay.

A JUROR: How much about your relationship with the President did Bayani Nelvis know?

THE WITNESS: I think he knew that -- that we were friends and that I would come to see the President and I gave him things. I don't know -- I don't remember ever getting into any specific details. Might he have thought that from -- you know, from how much I kind of liked the President? I'm not sure.

But -- and I don't mean this in a racist way, you know, Nel's from another country and so his English is -- while his English is good, it's not perfect, not that anyone's is perfect, so I think that sometimes there was a little bit of a language barrier there, too, so I think he -- you know, Nel was just a -- is a really nice guy. He's a sweet guy and he -- he's very loyal to the President.

A JUROR: Did you ever tell him at any time that you loved the President?

THE WITNESS: I don't think so, but I might have,

1113

57

but I don't think so.

A JUROR: Okay.

MR. EMMICK: Yes? A question?

A JUROR: You just mentioned real components, the relationship was -- like a real component, you mentioned things like truth. But sometimes I go back and forth not understanding because you yourself were living a lot of secrets, a lot of lies, a lot of paranoia, but yet you wanted truth, a real component?

I'm not understanding these two different things because one time you're sentimental but then again you do just the opposite of what you say you're thinking.

Did you ever think that nothing real could come of this relationship?

THE WITNESS: Did I ever thing nothing real --

A JUROR: Anything real, that anything real could -- and truthful and honest could have come from this relationship?

THE WITNESS: Yes.

A JUROR: With this married man?

THE WITNESS: I did.

A JUROR: But I have a question for you about that.

THE WITNESS: Mm-hmm.

A JUROR: It's been reported in the papers that you had a relationship before similar to this, where a lot of hurt and pain came out of this, you know, a lot of hurt and pain toward a family.

And then you turn around and you do it again. You're young, you're vibrant, I can't figure out why you keep going after things that aren't free, that aren't obtainable.

THE WITNESS: Well, there's sort of two parts to that and just to clarify, the -- the way Andy and Kate Bleiler portrayed everything on TV and through their lawyer was pretty inaccurate, so I don't know how much of that is part of your question.

A JUROR: The only part I know is that he was a married man with a wife and a family.

THE WITNESS: That's true.

A JUROR: Like I know about the President.

THE WITNESS: Mm-hmm.

A JUROR: He was a married man and it wasn't no secret of that fact. But yet you want to talk about truth, a real component, honesty. It all seems so -- like a fantasy. That's why I asked you earlier about obsession.

THE WITNESS: That's a hard question to answer because obviously there's -- there's work that I need to do on myself. There are obviously issues that -- that -- you know, a single young woman doesn't have an affair with a married man because she's normal, quote-unquote. But I think most people have issues and that's just how mine manifested

1115

59

themselves.

It's something I need to work on and I don't think it's right, it's not right to have an affair with a married man. I never expected to fall in love with the President. I was surprised that I did.

And I didn't -- my intention had really been to come to Washington and start over and I didn't want to have another affair with a married man because it was really painful. It was horrible. And I feel even worse about it now.

A JUROR: Monica, I'd like to change the topic, if I can.

THE WITNESS: Did I answer --

A JUROR: Yes.

THE WITNESS: Okay.

A JUROR: And I also -- I want to let you know that we're not here to judge you in any way, I think many of us feel that way.

THE WITNESS: I appreciate that. But I understand that every -- you know, this is -- this is a topic that -- there are a lot of people think it's wrong and I think it's wrong, too. I understand that.

A JUROR: I had to ask that you question because I've had to ask other questions and it wouldn't have been right for me not to ask you the question --

THE WITNESS: Sure.

A JUROR: -- that I've had to ask --

THE WITNESS: I think it's fair and I think you should -- I think it's a fair question. It's a hard one to answer. No one likes to have their weaknesses splayed out for the entire world, you know, but I understand that. And I'd rather you understand where I'm coming from, you know, and you'd probably have to know me better and know my whole journey to how I got here from birth to now to really understand it. I don't even understand it. But -- I understand. I respect your having to ask that question and I appreciate what you're saying, whatever your name is.

A JUROR: We're here only to assess the credibility of your testimony.

THE WITNESS: Sure. But I -- I can see how that would be a factor.

A JUROR: I wanted to go back to the issue of ties. It's my understanding that you testified earlier this morning that your agreement, your immunity agreement, with the Office of the Independent Counsel includes an understanding that you -- that you and your legal team need prior approval to disseminate information to the press.

THE WITNESS: Mm-hmm.

A JUROR: And in looking over Exhibit ML-2, I don't see that provision. Can you look at that?

1117

THE WITNESS: Is that my agreement?

A JUROR: Yes.

THE WITNESS: Sure.

MR. EMMICK: Sure.

THE WITNESS: I know that portion of it very well.

A JUROR: I may be missing something.

THE WITNESS: There have been many times I've wanted to defend myself and the lies that have been spewed out.

MR. EMMICK: I think the reference is to part 1B.

A JUROR: Okay.

MR. EMMICK: Where it says "Will not make any statements -- " "Neither Ms. Lewinsky nor her agents will make any statements about this matter to witnesses, subjects, or targets of the OIC's investigation or their agents or to representatives of the news media without first obtaining the OIC's approval."

A JUROR: Okay. Thank you.

THE WITNESS: Sure.

MR. EMMICK: Other questions? Yes, ma'am?

A JUROR: I'd also like to return for a minute -- if you have that package out -- to something that was discussed this morning, earlier this morning, and that refers to your proffer. Do you have a copy of the proffer? The proffer?

MR. EMMICK: We do. Sure.

THE WITNESS: Okay.

MR. EMMICK: I'm placing Exhibit ML-1 before the witness.

THE WITNESS: Thank you.

A JUROR: Monica, if you could look at paragraph 11, I'm not sure what page it is, but it's paragraph 11.

THE WITNESS: Okay. Yes. Okay.

A JUROR: As I understood our discussion this morning, you said that you offered to deny the relationship and the President didn't discourage you, but said something like "That's good."

As I read your proffer here, it says "The President told Ms. L to deny a relationship if ever asked." And that seems to me slightly different.

THE WITNESS: I forgot this. So that's true.

A JUROR: Is this proffer statement correct, that he did tell you to deny a relationship?

THE WITNESS: Yes. I don't -- I don't -- when I answered the question earlier, that was what first came to my mind. But, I mean, I know that this is true.

I just at that point -- and I -- really reading it, I know it's true because I was truthful in my proffer, but sitting here right now, I can't remember exactly when it was, but it was something that was certainly discussed between us.

1119

63

A JUROR: And what about the next sentence also? Something to the effect that if two people who are involved say it didn't happen, it didn't happen. Do you recall him saying that to you?

THE WITNESS: Sitting here today, very vaguely. I can hear -- I have a weird -- I'll explain to you guys that I have a weird sense of -- for me, my saying I remember something, if I can see it in my mind's eye or I can hear him saying it to me, then I feel pretty comfortable saying that that's pretty accurate, that I remember that. And I can hear his voice saying that to me, I just can't place it.

A JUROR: Is it --

THE WITNESS: And this was -- I mean, this was early -- this was all throughout our relationship. I mean, it was -- obviously not something that we discussed too often, I think, because it was -- it's a somewhat unpleasant thought of having to deny it, having it even come to that point, but --

A JUROR: Is it possible that you also had these discussions after you learned that you were a witness in the Paula Jones case?

THE WITNESS: I don't believe so. No.

A JUROR: Can you exclude that possibility?

THE WITNESS: I pretty much can. I really don't remember it. I mean, it would be very surprising to me to be

1120

64

confronted with something that would show me different, but I -- it was 2:30 in the -- I mean, the conversation I'm thinking of mainly would have been December 17th, which was --

A JUROR: The telephone call.

THE WITNESS: Right. And it was -- you know, 2:00, 2:30 in the morning. I remember the gist of it and I -- I really don't think so.

A JUROR: Thank you.

A JUROR: I have some questions about the Paula Jones lawsuit. Going back to the period before you even had any idea that you might be a witness in that, did you follow the Paula Jones lawsuit fairly closely?

THE WITNESS: I followed it. I don't know "fairly closely," but -- I think it maybe depended more on was there something in the paper and that happened to be a day that I sat and read all the papers because I had nothing to do.

I did follow it, but I wasn't -- I didn't follow it as much as I follow this case. I mean, in terms of -- no, but I mean, I'm just saying as a gauge, you know.

A JUROR: So you were holding down a full-time job and everything at that time, but you did read the papers --

THE WITNESS: I did read the papers every day and it was -- sure, I followed it. I didn't know the ins and outs of it, but I followed it.

A JUROR: Did you -- in that period again, even before anyone knew that you would be a witness, did you discuss that with the President? Was he aware that you followed it? Was that something --

THE WITNESS: No. Really, the time that I remember we discussed it was on the 17th.

A JUROR: December 17th?

THE WITNESS: And when I told him my sort of stupid idea for how he should settle it. So that was -- but, no. He wasn't -- we didn't -- I -- and I think in general just to give you guys a flavor, because there have been different subjects that have come up, when we spent time together, I know I certainly made an effort -- unless I was angry with him about something, that there were topics that I wanted to stay away from and the time that I spent with him was precious to me. So things that were unpleasant I didn't bring up unless I had to.

A JUROR: Exactly what date again did you get your subpoena to be a witness?

THE WITNESS: The 19th of December.

A JUROR: The 19th? Okay. Now, when -- and if you could retell for me the conversation you had with the President about the gifts.

THE WITNESS: Okay. It was December 28th and I was there to get my Christmas gifts from him. Excuse me. I'm

1122

66

sorry. And we spent maybe about five minutes or so, not very long, talking about the case. And I said to him, "Well, do you think -- "

What I mentioned -- I said to him that it had really alarmed me about the hat pin being in the subpoena and I think he said something like, "Oh," you know, "that sort of bothered me, too. That bothered me," you know, "That bothers me." Something like that.

And at one point, I said, "Well, do you think I should -- " I don't think I said "get rid of," I said, "But do you think I should put away or maybe give to Betty or give to someone the gifts?"

And he -- I don't remember his response. I think it was something like, "I don't know," or "Hmm" or -- there really was no response.

I know that I didn't leave the White House with any notion of what I should do with them, that I should do anything different than that they were sitting in my house. And then later I got the call from Betty.

A JUROR: Now, did you bring up Betty's name or did the President bring up Betty's name?

THE WITNESS: I think I brought it up. The President wouldn't have brought up Betty's name because he really didn't -- he didn't really discuss it, so either I brought up Betty's name, which I think is probably what

1123

happened, because I remember not being too, too shocked when Betty called.

Somewhat surprised, I guess, that he hadn't said -- you know, it would have seemed easier to sort of have said something maybe then, but I wasn't too surprised when she called.

A JUROR: Thank you.

MR. EMMICK: I think there was a question in the front. Did you have a question?

MS. IMMERGUT: Did you have a question?

A JUROR: Yes. Back to the contacts?

THE WITNESS: Yes.

A JUROR: On page 7, on the 29th of March --

THE WITNESS: On the -- sorry, what date?

A JUROR: The 29th of March. Sunday.

MR. EMMICK: Then 29th of March.

THE WITNESS: Okay.

A JUROR: "Private encounter, approximately 1:30 or 2:00 p.m., study. President on crutches. Physical intimacy including oral sex to completion and brief direct genital contact." Brief direct genital contact, could you just elaborate on that a bit?

THE WITNESS: Uh --

A JUROR: I understand --

THE WITNESS: Oh, my gosh. This is so

1124

68

embarrassing.

A JUROR: You could close your eyes and talk.

A JUROR: We won't look at you.

THE WITNESS: Can I hide under the table? Uh -- I had -- I had wanted -- I tried to -- I placed his genital next to mine and had hoped that if he -- oh -- this is just too embarrassing. I don't --

A JUROR: Did you think it would lead to intercourse?

THE WITNESS: Not on that day.

A JUROR: Was that sort of the reason for doing the gesture --

THE WITNESS: Yes.

A JUROR: -- or trying to -- moving his closer to yours?

THE WITNESS: Then I -- not that we would have intercourse that day, but that that might make him want to.

A JUROR: Okay. Were you wearing clothes at the time or underwear at the time?

THE WITNESS: No.

A JUROR: And was he? Or his were pulled down?

THE WITNESS: Correct.

A JUROR: So was there direct skin-to-skin contact between your genitals and his?

THE WITNESS: I think very briefly. It was --

1125

he -- he's really tall and he couldn't really bend because of his knee, so it was --

A JUROR: It was more of a grazing?

THE WITNESS: Yes.

A JUROR: About how many encounters did you have in the study? If you can recall.

MR. EMMICK: What do you mean by "encounters"?

A JUROR: Sexual encounters. I'm sorry.

THE WITNESS: Do you include kissing or not?

A JUROR: No kissing. According to the definition.

THE WITNESS: Okay. Two.

A JUROR: Okay. Thank you.

BY MS. IMMERGUT:

Q And why don't you give us the dates of those.

A The -- well, let me look. The 29th of March and the 28th of February. There might have been -- I mean, in terms of the clothes and stuff, there might have been playful touches here and there, but not -- nothing that I would have considered sexual encounters.

Q And that's not listed as an intimate encounter?

A No. No, it's not. No, it's not.

Q And just to clarify again, are those the two times that the President actually came to completion during the oral sex?

A Yes.

1126

70

BY MR. EMMICK:

Q And I'm actually obliged to ask one follow up that I don't think will be too bad, but directing your attention to August 16th, did you attempt to touch the President on that day?

A Yes.

Q And did you actually touch him? In his groin area?

A Over his clothes.

Q Over his clothes. And did he say that's not -- "We can't do that"?

A Yes.

MR. EMMICK: Okay.

A JUROR: Did you feel any rejection the times that he wouldn't go all the way with you?

THE WITNESS: Yes.

A JUROR: Monica, I had one question to go back to the gifts. You had said that the President had called you initially to come get your Christmas gift, you had gone there, you had a talk, et cetera, and there was no -- you expressed concern, the President really didn't say anything. How much later in the afternoon did you get a call from Betty? It was that same day, is that correct?

THE WITNESS: Yes, that's correct. Let me just clarify real quickly that I had made the arrangements to go there on Sunday through Betty, just that you had said he

1127

called me.

A JUROR: So you had initiated the contact on that day?

THE WITNESS: He had -- he had told me on the 17th that he -- you know, he still had these Christmas gifts for me and then -- just shortly after Christmas and I called Betty and said, you know, "He said he had something for me," something like that, you know. And then she arranged it. So I just wanted to clarify.

A JUROR: And then how much of a time gap --

THE WITNESS: A few hours, maybe.

A JUROR: A few hours?

THE WITNESS: Maybe -- I think it was around 2:00 p.m. or so, around 2:00 in the afternoon, and I had gone there at 8:30 in the morning and left -- I'd say maybe four or five hours time span.

A JUROR: So what exactly happened? You went home and you packaged these gifts? Or had you already had them packaged?

THE WITNESS: No. I went home and I -- I think I went to New York that evening, possibly, so I was getting ready to go to New York, I think, or something.

But when Betty called, then she said, you know, "I understand you have something to give me." It was very vague. And I understood -- I mean, to me, that meant from this conversation that we had had that I should sort of -- you know, give some of the gifts.

So I put them all out on my bed and -- it's sort of been difficult to kind of explain why I put some things in and why I didn't put others in.

The things that seemed to be directly called for in the subpoena, I put in a box: the hat pin, the dress from Martha's Vineyard, some of the pictures and things, the ad to him from Valentine's Day. Not that that was directly called for, but some of the more intimate -- I guess personal things, except that I kept the "Leaves of Grass" book because that just -- I was worried, I didn't know if I would get the gifts back or not, ever, and so I -- that just -- that meant the most to me of anything he gave me.

A JUROR: And I believe your testimony last time was that you did not believe that Betty knew the contents of the package?

THE WITNESS: I don't believe so.

A JUROR: She just came and picked them up and that was it?

THE WITNESS: We chit-chatted for a little bit. She was on the way to see her mom in the hospital, so I got her a small plant to just take to her mom and --

BY MS. IMMERGUT:

Q Did she seem at all confused when you handed over

the box?

A No.

Q Did she ask you what was in it?

A No. Not that I remember. I don't believe so.

MS. IMMERGUT: Thank you.

A JUROR: And just to back up for a second on your conversation with the President that you already discussed a little bit where you said you were concerned about the subpoena and some of the items that it called for such as the hat pin which indeed the President had given you, you testified previously, I believe, that the President said he was concerned about that also when he saw the hat pin. Is that correct?

THE WITNESS: I don't know that he saw -- I don't know that he saw the hat pin on the -- I don't know that he saw the subpoena, so -- I know that the hat pin was a concern to him.

A JUROR: Okay. Do you remember what he said in response when you said you were concerned about the things called for in the subpoena?

THE WITNESS: I think he said something like "That concerned me, too."

A JUROR: Okay.

THE WITNESS: So I don't know if he saw it or someone -- you know, I don't know he learned that.

A JUROR: Okay. But he appeared to have some prior knowledge of --

THE WITNESS: I think so. I think so.

A JUROR: I have another question about that conversation on the 28th. You had already discussed with him earlier the subpoena and the fact that all of your gifts from him were under subpoena and then --

THE WITNESS: We hadn't discussed that. I wasn't -- I hadn't -- the 28th was the first time that I saw him or spoke to him since I had been subpoenaed. When he called me on the 17th, I wasn't yet subpoenaed.

A JUROR: Okay. Okay. So that conversation took place on the 28th?

THE WITNESS: Correct. The only conversation about gifts and the subpoena, really -- yes.

A JUROR: And on that same day, he gave you Christmas gifts.

THE WITNESS: Yes.

A JUROR: What was your thinking at that time about that? Did that concern you or --

THE WITNESS: No.

A JUROR: No?

THE WITNESS: I was --

A JUROR: Did you -- what did you plan to do with those gifts? Did it cross your mind that some -- that you

1131

should maybe give some of them to your attorney as responsive to the subpoena or --

THE WITNESS: No.

A JUROR: No?

MR. EMMICK: I have a quick clarifying question because you said that the only conversation you had with him about gifts after the subpoena was on the 28th. You also had a conversation with him on the 5th that related to the later gift of the book, if I remember it right.

THE WITNESS: Right. I meant my gifts that he gave to me.

MR. EMMICK: Right. Right. Right. I just wanted to clarify that.

THE WITNESS: Okay. Sure.

MR. EMMICK: Other questions?

A JUROR: Going back to your conversation with Linda Tripp --

MR. EMMICK: Which one?

THE WITNESS: Yes. Which tape are you referring to?

A JUROR: No, I'm just going to be general.

MR. EMMICK: Okay.

A JUROR: If you had to put it like percentage-wise, what you told her as being truthful and not truthful, what percentage will be not truthful?

THE WITNESS: I would say before the subpoena, before I found out she had been subpoenaed, so for argument's sake maybe saying before December of '97, I'd say 95 percent accurate. There were some things that I didn't tell her, but I usually pretty much told her everything.

A JUROR: You started talking to her when? In '95 or '96?

THE WITNESS: I first told her -- when I first told her about the relationship or when I started talking to her as a person?

A JUROR: The relationship.

THE WITNESS: The relationship, I told her in November of '96. After the election.

A JUROR: Okay. So from November '96 to December '97 --

THE WITNESS: Pretty truthful.

A JUROR: And then after '97?

THE WITNESS: Oh --

BY MR. EMMICK:

Q Could I ask just one clarifying matter about that answer? Because you had said that it was 95 percent accurate and then you also said because sometimes I didn't tell her everything. And I just want to make sure we're being clear on whether you're talking about being complete or being accurate.

In other words, are you not telling her things or are you saying things to her that are inaccurate, sort of in that 5 percent, if you will?

A Well, I don't remember the exact situations or the times that I didn't tell her something, if she had asked me about it, I would have been inaccurate about what I said.

Q All right. I see.

A So --

Q So there's kind of a blending of those two concepts.

A Correct.

BY MS. IMMERGUT:

Q And, again, to clarify, did you ever lie about your sexual relationship with the President?

A No.

MR. EMMICK: I'm sorry. I interrupted. I didn't mean to.

A JUROR: So after '97, then --

THE WITNESS: After December '97, I don't even know how to -- how to put a percentage to that.

A JUROR: Any truth at all after '97?

THE WITNESS: Yes. There were some truths in December of '97. There certainly were some true statements, but there were a lot of untrue statements. Probably the untrue statements stick out in my mind more because they

1134

caused so much trouble.

A JUROR: Which ones stick out in your mind as having been untruthful?

THE WITNESS: Stuff about my mom. Just -- a lot of different things about my mom. That I had -- that I told Mr. Jordan I wouldn't sign the affidavit until I got a job. That was definitely a lie, based on something Linda had made me promise her on January 9th. Some of the other things --

A JUROR: Did you tell Linda Tripp at any time that you had heard or understood that people don't go to jail for perjury in a civil case?

THE WITNESS: Yes, I believe -- I think I said that.

A JUROR: Did anybody tell you that?

THE WITNESS: Well, hmm.

A JUROR: Do you want to talk to -- I know there's -- is there an attorney issue there?

THE WITNESS: There's an attorney issue.

A JUROR: I see.

MR. EMMICK: Do you want to take a break and talk about the attorney issue? Because I think that may be a way to figure out if we can answer that question any more fully.

THE WITNESS: Do you want me to go talk to my attorney?

1135

79

MR. EMMICK: Well, I just think it might be -- I think your attorney would like it if he were to talk to you.

THE WITNESS: Okay.

MR. EMMICK: That's the way to answer it.

THE WITNESS: Okay. So just to be clear, you're --

A JUROR: Well, maybe I can help. Just -- if I could confine it to did anyone other than your attorney ever suggest to you that perjury in a civil case would not be prosecuted?

THE WITNESS: Uh --

MS. IMMERGUT: If you need to talk to your attorney, go ahead.

A JUROR: I just thought -- did anyone other than your attorney tell you that?

THE WITNESS: No.

MR. EMMICK: I think it still would be advisable to have a more complete answer, to at least let them talk.

THE WITNESS: Okay.

MR. EMMICK: Yes.

THE WITNESS: Excuse me.

(The witness was excused to confer with counsel.)

MR. EMMICK: Do we have a quorum?

THE FOREPERSON: Yes, we do.

MR. EMMICK: And are there any unauthorized persons present?

THE FOREPERSON: Not a one.

MR. EMMICK: All right.

THE WITNESS: And I'm still under oath.

THE FOREPERSON: Yes, you are.

BY MS. IMMERGUT:

Q And just to clarify a couple of things that were right before the break, when you sort of asserted a privilege or had some questions about whether there was a privilege, I did want to ask you just to clarify that with respect to the statement about your lawyer having -- or somebody telling you whether or not you can be charged with perjury in a civil case, just to be clear, did Mr. Jordan ever tell you that?

A No.

Q Did Mr. Carter ever tell you that?

A No.

Q And otherwise, I think the question was was it another attorney and I believe that you would like to assert the attorney-client privilege.

A JUROR: No, I think I excluded attorneys from my question.

THE WITNESS: Okay. You know, can I just address -- I think sort of the -- one of the questions that you had asked me before and I just -- about --

A JUROR: Myself?

THE WITNESS: Yes. That you had asked me about the

1137

relationship and being untruthful and things like that. And I just -- this is something that's sort of been on my mind since this whole thing started.

I have never -- I don't -- I certainly believe I have ever told a lie to hurt anybody, that I sort of -- some of the ways in which I grew up, it was -- there were secrets and inherent in a secret is a lie and so I just -- you know, I -- I just thought I'd tell you that.

A JUROR: Okay.

MR. EMMICK: Other questions?

A JUROR: Ms. Lewinsky, we're going to try, because we feel that we have been jumping around and you've done a very good job of sort of jumping from topic to topic, we're going to try to bunch our questions together around a few topics and our forelady is going to try to play traffic cop, so --

A JUROR: A little bit. No, you go ahead. This is your record. But I'll play traffic cop just a little.

A JUROR: Ms. Lewinsky, before you go into that, I just remember you saying something with Linda Tripp, you know, what was not the truth, okay? And I just remembered, was one of the things that you told her, that you gave your mother the blue dress, one of the untruths or was that true?

THE WITNESS: I don't know if I ever told Linda I gave my mom the blue dress. One of the things I did say was that I gave everything to my mom, so that probably included that and that was not true. I didn't give the evidence to my mom. My mom never hid the dress. She didn't know it was in New York.

A JUROR: Okay.

THE WITNESS: So she didn't know anything about it.

A JUROR: I've got one of those questions that goes along with what she just said.

A JUROR: Okay. Fine. That's the idea. The topic.

A JUROR: How much did your mom really know?

THE WITNESS: She knew -- she knew that I was having a relationship with the President. She knew that -- she knew that I was certainly emotional about it and that it made me miserable a lot and that sometimes I was elated and sometimes I was miserable, but I didn't -- you know, I -- I might have said something to her like, "We fooled around," but I -- not -- she didn't know as much as I led Linda to believe she knew. Is that --

A JUROR: Yes.

THE WITNESS: Okay.

A JUROR: Okay. Any other Linda Tripp questions?

A JUROR: Yes, there's one.

A JUROR: Did you ever suggest to Linda Tripp that she delete e-mails or anything like that from her computer?

THE WITNESS: Yes, I did.

A JUROR: And did you tell her that you had done the same thing?

THE WITNESS: Yes, I believe so.

A JUROR: And did anyone ever suggest to you or tell you that you should do that?

THE WITNESS: No.

A JUROR: Did you tell Linda Tripp that anyone had suggested that to you?

THE WITNESS: I don't think so.

A JUROR: Okay. Thank you.

A JUROR: Any others?

A JUROR: In that end of the year timeframe, did you ever tell Linda Tripp that you felt physically at risk?

THE WITNESS: I think so. I think I told her something about -- that -- that -- I said something about Mary Jo what's-her-name.

A JUROR: Kopechne.

THE WITNESS: Kopechne. And so -- I really didn't feel threatened, but I was trying to use anything I could to try to convince her not to tell. So that I thought that if she thought I was threatened and that was part of the reason, then she would maybe do the same.

A JUROR: So you did not at any time feel that your personal security was at risk from the White House or anyone in the White House?

THE WITNESS: No. I think that maybe there -- there -- maybe once or twice it had crossed my mind in some bizarre way because everybody's heard about the different -- you know, sure, there's the Marilyn Monroe theory. And so it -- but it was not -- it was not any factor of -- that related to my actions.

A JUROR: So any discussion that you had about the whole topic with Linda Tripp would fall into what you were describing before as a little bit of fabrication?

THE WITNESS: Yes. Yes.

BY MR. EMMICK:

Q If I could ask a follow-up on that, did your mother ever express any concerns about your safety?

A I think she might have, but it was sort of the -- I think it was more general. It might have been a more general sense.

A JUROR: Are there any other questions about personal safety?

A JUROR: Are we still on December? December, January?

A JUROR: Yes.

A JUROR: I have one follow-up question if this is

an appropriate time about the gifts. And, again, if you have your proffer there?

THE WITNESS: Yes.

A JUROR: At the top of page 7, where you say in your proffer that when Ms. Currie called later that afternoon she said, at least I think you mean that she said that the President had told her Ms. L wanted her to hold on to something for her. Do you remember Betty Currie saying that the President had told her to call?

THE WITNESS: Right now, I don't. I don't remember, but when I wrote this, I was being truthful.

The other thing, and this is something that I was thinking about this morning in relation to the proffer, that I had written this proffer obviously being truthful, but I think that when I wrote this, it was my understanding that this was to bring me to the step of getting an immunity agreement, and so I think that sometimes to -- that I didn't know this was going to become sort of this staple document, I think, for everything, and so there are things that can be misinterpreted from in here, even from me re-reading it, the conditions -- some of the conditions maybe under which I wrote it.

So I just thought I should sort of say that, that where -- I mean, I know -- I certainly was not untruthful or trying to be misleading in this. I didn't think it was going

1142

86

to be -- this was my understanding of a written thing that I would -- that I would attest to under oath and that it wouldn't be number 7, read this, is this -- do you --

BY MR. EMMICK:

Q So it may not be written with legal precision?

A Exactly.

Q But there's no intentional falsehoods in it?

A No.

Q You were trying to be truthful throughout?

A Exactly.

A JUROR: And my purpose in raising it really is to just see whether this might jog your recollection at all as to something you might have recalled back in February that you don't recall today.

THE WITNESS: It doesn't.

A JUROR: It does not?

THE WITNESS: It's possible, but -- I -- I -- it's not my -- you know --

A JUROR: Okay.

THE WITNESS: -- my memory right now.

A JUROR: Any other questions on that subject?

A JUROR: If we don't have any other questions, I guess the other thing that we wanted to ask you a little bit about is when you were first approached by Mr. Emmick and his colleagues at the OIC.

Can you tell us a little bit about how that happened? That's not a happy topic, either, I apologize.

MR. EMMICK: Maybe if I could ask, what areas do you want to get into? Because there's -- you know -- many hours of activity --

A JUROR: Well, one specific -- okay. One specific question that people have is when did you first learn that Linda Tripp had been taping your phone conversations?

THE WITNESS: I believe that I didn't learn the extent to which she had taped my conversations, until I read it in the press.

I learned that day that she had worn a wire at the lunch and that I -- and that there had been other people, I think, in the restaurant that had been listening in and -- so I knew -- she had -- she had said that -- that -- when I was first apprehended, she was -- she had said that they had done the same thing to her and she tried to hug me and she told me this was the best thing for me to do and -- oh.

MR. EMMICK: Any other specific questions about that day? I just -- this was a long day. There were a lot of things that --

A JUROR: We want to know about that day.

A JUROR: That day.

A JUROR: The first question.

A JUROR: Yes.

1144

88

A JUROR: We really want to know about that day.

MR. EMMICK: All right.

THE WITNESS: Linda was supposed to go see this new attorney that she had claimed she had gotten and was going to try to sign an affidavit so she paged me in the morning, I called her back and she told me she wanted to meet me before she went to see the attorney. So we planned to meet at the Ritz Carlton in the food court at -- I think it was quarter to one.

She was late. I saw her come down the escalator. And as I -- as I walked toward her, she kind of motioned behind her and Agent [redacted] and Agent [redacted] presented themselves to me and --

A JUROR: Do you want to take a minute?

THE WITNESS: And flashed their badges at me. They told me that I was under some kind of investigation, something had to do with the Paula Jones case, that they -- that they wanted to talk to me and give me a chance, I think, to cooperate, maybe.

I -- to help myself. I told them I wasn't speaking to them without my attorney.

They told me that that was fine, but I should know I won't be given as much information and won't be able to help myself as much with my attorney there. So I agreed to go. I was so scared.

1145

89

(The witness begins crying.)

A JUROR: So, Monica, did you go to a room with them at that time?

THE WITNESS: Yes.

A JUROR: And at that time, did you talk to anybody or what did you do? Did you want to call your mother?

THE WITNESS: Can Karen do the questioning now? This is -- can I ask you to step out?

MR. EMMICK: Sure. Okay. All right.

MS. IMMERGUT: I guess, Monica, if Mike could just stay -- do you mind if Mike is in here?

THE WITNESS: (Nods affirmatively.)

MS. IMMERGUT: Okay. Would you rather --

THE WITNESS: (Nods affirmatively.)

MR. EMMICK: Okay. That's fine.

BY MS. IMMERGUT:

Q Okay. Did you go to a room with them at the hotel?

A Yes.

Q And what did you do then? Did you ever tell them that you wanted to call your mother?

A I told them I wanted to talk to my attorney.

Q Okay. So what happened?

A And they told me -- Mike came out and introduced himself to me and told me that -- that Janet Reno had sanctioned Ken Starr to investigate my actions in the Paula

Jones case, that they -- that they knew that I had signed a false affidavit, they had me on tape saying I had committed perjury, that they were going to -- that I could go to jail for 27 years, they were going to charge me with perjury and obstruction of justice and subornation of perjury and witness tampering and something else.

Q And you're saying "they," at that point, who was talking to you about that stuff?

A Mike Emmick and the two FBI guys. And I made Linda stay in the room. And I just -- I felt so bad.

Q Now, when you say you felt bad, because you felt responsible somehow for pulling the President into something?

A Yes.

Q And is that something that still weighs heavily on you, that you feel responsible?

A Yes.

Q And is it -- do you feel responsible because you told Linda about your relationship?

A Yes.

Q I guess later just to sort of finish up, I guess, with the facts of that day, was there a time then that you were -- you just waited with the prosecutors until your mother came down?

A No.

Q Okay.

1147

91

A I mean, there was, but they -- they told me they wanted me to cooperate. I asked them what cooperating meant, it entailed, and they told me that -- they had -- first they had told me before about that -- that they had had me on tape saying things from the lunch that I had had with Linda at the Ritz Carlton the other day and they -- then they told me that I -- that I'd have to agree to be debriefed and that I'd have to place calls or wear a wire to see -- to call Betty and Mr. Jordan and possibly the President. And --

Q And did you tell them you didn't want to do that?

A Yes. I -- I -- I remember going through my mind, I thought, well, what if -- you know, what if I did that and I messed up, if I on purpose -- you know, I envisioned myself in Mr. Jordan's office and sort of trying to motion to him that something had gone wrong. They said that they would be watching to see if it had been an intentional mistake.

Then I wanted to call my mom and they kept telling me that they didn't -- that I couldn't tell anybody about this, they didn't want anyone to find out and that they didn't want -- that was the reason I couldn't call Mr. Carter, was because they were afraid that he might tell the person who took me to Mr. Carter.

They told me that I could call this number and get another criminal attorney, but I didn't want that and I didn't trust them. Then I just cried for a long time.

1148

92

A JUROR: All while you were crying, did they keep asking you questions? What were they doing?

THE WITNESS: No, they just sat there and then -- they just sort of sat there.

A JUROR: How many hours did this go on?

THE WITNESS: Maybe around two hours or so. And then they were -- they kept saying there was this time constraint, there was a time constraint, I had to make a decision.

And then Bruce Udolf came in at some point and then -- then Jackie Bennett came in and there were a whole bunch of other people and the room was crowded and he was saying to me, you know, you have to make a decision. I had wanted to call my mom, they weren't going to let me call my attorney, so I just -- I wanted to call my mom and they --

Then Jackie Bennett said, "You're 24, you're smart, you're old enough, you don't need to call your mommy."

And then I said, "Well, I'm letting you know that I'm leaning towards not cooperating," you know.

And they had told me before that I could leave whenever I wanted, but it wasn't -- you know, I didn't -- I didn't really know -- I didn't know what that meant. I mean, I thought if I left then that they were just going to arrest me.

1149

And so then they told me that I should know that they were planning to prosecute my mom for the things that I had said that she had done.

(The witness begins crying.)

MS. IMMERGUT: Do you want to take a break, Monica?

THE WITNESS: Yes.

(Witness excused. Witness recalled.)

THE FOREPERSON: Okay. We have a quorum. There are no unauthorized people and Monica is already aware that she is still under oath.

MS. IMMERGUT: We just have a couple more questions and then I think we'll break for lunch.

THE WITNESS: Okay.

A JUROR: Monica, I have a question. A minute ago you explained that the reason why you couldn't call Mr. Carter was that something might be disclosed. Is that right?

THE WITNESS: It was -- they sort of said that -- you know, I -- I -- I could call Frank Carter, but that they may not -- I think it was that -- you know, the first time or the second time?

A JUROR: Any time.

THE WITNESS: Well, the first time when I asked, that I said I wasn't going to talk to them without my lawyer, they told me that if my lawyer was there, they wouldn't give me as much information and I couldn't help myself as much, so that --

A JUROR: Did they ever tell you that you could not call Mr. Carter?

THE WITNESS: No. What they told me was that if I called Mr. Carter, I wouldn't necessarily still be offered an immunity agreement.

A JUROR: And did you feel threatened by that?

THE WITNESS: Yes.

A JUROR: And you said they offered you a chance to call another attorney?

THE WITNESS: Yes.

A JUROR: And did you take them up on that offer?

THE WITNESS: No.

A JUROR: Why not?

THE WITNESS: Because I didn't trust them.

A JUROR: I see. And at some point in this meeting, did you -- you did obtain an attorney? Mr. Ginsberg?

THE WITNESS: Well, like at 11:00 that night.

A JUROR: So it was seven hours or eight hours or more later?

THE WITNESS: They -- they finally let me call my mom, so I went to call my mom and then -- and I saw Linda again. She had been shopping or something like that. But I called my mom and then Mike had said that she could call him, so they called her or she called him or something like that and then they agreed to let her come down.

So she took the train and then -- and then he just sort of -- I shut down and I kind of -- you know, I thought maybe I should try and make these people like me, so I tried to be nice and I told jokes and I asked if we could walk around the mall because I couldn't sit in that room any more. And I just --

BY MS. IMMERGUT:

Q So did they let you do that?

A Mm-hmm. So Mike and Agent [redacted] took me and we walked around the mall and we ate dinner and then we went back to the room and I read Psalm 21 about a million times. And my mom's train had been -- there were problems with her train and then finally she got there and they told me they were going to want to talk to my mom alone for a little bit, but I got to talk to her.

And I was -- I didn't -- I didn't want to cooperate. I mean, I didn't -- I just kept thinking to myself, well -- well, I'll just say I made it all up, I'll just -- I'll just -- I -- I couldn't imagine -- I couldn't imagine doing this to the President. And I felt so wrong and guilty for having told Linda and that she had done all this.

But -- so then they took my mom into another room for a really long time and she had -- then when she came back, they called my dad. And then we finally -- and then I talked to my dad and then -- then -- Ginsberg came on the scene. And he --

A JUROR: So if I understand it, you first met the agents, Agents [redacted] and [redacted], at around 1:00 and it wasn't until about 11 p.m. that you had an opportunity to talk to a lawyer?

THE WITNESS: Yes.

BY MS. IMMERGUT:

Q Although you were allowed to -- the thing with Frank Carter was that they were afraid he would tell Vernon Jordan? Is that what they expressed to you?

A Right. And I had -- I had -- I think that someone said that Frank wasn't even -- Frank was a civil attorney and so that he really couldn't help me anyway, so I asked him if at least I could call and ask him for a recommendation for a criminal attorney and they didn't think that was a good idea.

And then I said, well, what about -- if I want to get in touch with Mr. Carter later, if I decide that's what I want to do, you know, and he's not there, because it's Friday and it was a holiday weekend, so then Agent Fallon went in the other room to find out if he had a service or something or another, a pager, I don't know --

Q Some way for you to reach him later?

A Mm-hmm.

1153

A JUROR: Sounds as though they were actively discouraging you from talking to an attorney.

THE WITNESS: Yes.

A JUROR: Is that a fair characterization?

THE WITNESS: Yes.

BY MS. IMMERGUT:

Q Well, from Frank Carter.

A From Frank Carter, who was my only attorney at that point.

MS. IMMERGUT: Right. Right.

THE WITNESS: So I could have called any other attorney but --

A JUROR: You didn't have another attorney.

THE WITNESS: I didn't have another attorney and this was my attorney for this case, so -- I mean, this was --

A JUROR: And this is the attorney who had helped you with the affidavit.

THE WITNESS: Yes. And that -- the affidavit -- well, the affidavit wasn't even filed yet. It was Fed Ex'd out on that day. So --

A JUROR: Monica, when you called your mother, how much were you able to tell her over the phone? Very little or --

THE WITNESS: I was hysterical. She didn't understand what I was saying, but I told her that -- that the

1154

98

FBI had me and there was something with the Paula Jones case and Linda and then she -- she -- I said that -- that the guy said you could call her -- you can call him and so she just told me to calm down and I was screaming that, you know, "They want me to cooperate and I don't want to cooperate, don't make me cooperate, don't make me do this," and she -- she said it was okay, don't worry, don't worry, and then she talked to Mike Emmick and they let her come down. So, I mean, she -- I don't know.

A JUROR: Did you feel better after you talked to your mother?

THE WITNESS: Oh, yeah.

A JUROR: Gained that support?

THE WITNESS: Yeah.

A JUROR: Okay.

THE WITNESS: Yeah. I mean --

A JUROR: And what were you thinking about Linda at this time?

THE WITNESS: Linda? Did you say --

A JUROR: Mm-hmm. Did you know exactly what had happened? That you had been --

THE WITNESS: No. I was under the impression that -- what I was thinking at that point was that they had -- that they had listened in on our conversation on the phone and that then they came to her and said she was in trouble for something and that then she let them listen in on this lunch conversation because she had said "They did the same thing to me. They did the same thing to me." So I didn't understand what she meant by that.

And then she said, "This is the best thing for you," as if I was left to believe that she had -- this was somehow something she had done and that she was trying to help me.

And I thought, "Why did she tell them? Why didn't she just say it was nonsense, it wasn't true? Why did she tell them that I had had this relationship with him?" And so -- you know -- and they had pictures of me at lunch with her. So --

A JUROR: The pictures were the taped lunch?

THE WITNESS: Yes. The wire lunch.

A JUROR: The wired lunch.

THE WITNESS: Yes. So that -- because they -- because I had said on one of the tapes that -- you know, if there was a tape of me -- I had -- I had -- I didn't know how the Paula Jones people had gotten my name and I thought maybe they had tapped my phone or maybe they had broken into my computer and read my e-mails.

I didn't know how I had gotten involved in this case and so I had said to Linda, "Well, if they have me on tape, I'll just say it's not me. I'll just say it's not me.

1156

100

I'll deny it. I'll deny everything."

A JUROR: So they took pictures.

THE WITNESS: Right. So they said, "We have you on tape saying that you'd deny it and we have pictures to prove that you were there." So --

A JUROR: During this time in the hotel with them, did you feel threatened?

THE WITNESS: Yes.

A JUROR: Did you feel that they had set a trap?

THE WITNESS: I -- I -- I did and I had -- I didn't understand -- I didn't understand why they -- why they had to trap me into coming there, why they had to trick me into coming there. I mean, this had all been a set-up and that why -- I mean, that was just so frightening. It was so incredibly frightening.

And they told me, you know, over and over again I was free to leave whenever I wanted, but -- I -- I didn't -- I didn't know that there's a grand jury and indicted and then you go to jail. I mean, and a trial and everything. I didn't understand that.

And so I didn't -- you know, then there was something that, well, if I partially cooperate, they'll talk to the judge, some -- you know, we're prepared to indict you or something like that for all these things. And I just didn't --

1157

101

BY MS. IMMERGUT:

Q So you didn't know what would happen if you left.

A No. And then it wasn't until my mom was there that Mike Emmick cleared it up and said to my mom, "Well, it's not that we'll arrest you tonight when you leave the hotel." You know. Because I didn't -- I didn't know.

Q And you didn't end up cooperating that evening.

A No, I didn't. Because -- well --

A JUROR: Excuse me. When you said they trapped you, you went there on the invitation of Linda for lunch or something?

THE WITNESS: Yes.

A JUROR: So, I mean, how did -- I mean, in your mind, how did you get to the fact that they were the one? Wasn't it just Linda?

THE WITNESS: No, because they were with Linda. When I met Linda in the food court at Pentagon City, the two agents were with her.

A JUROR: Oh, okay.

THE WITNESS: Yeah. And that's where -- so it was right -- have you ever been to Pentagon City mall?

A JUROR: Mm-hmm.

THE WITNESS: So it was right down in the food court, you know the escalator to come down is over here?

A JUROR: Mm-hmm.

THE WITNESS: So -- see, they were with her when she met me right -- right in the middle.

A JUROR: Okay.

THE WITNESS: And that's where -- and then --

(Pause.)

A JUROR: I think that's all the questions on that topic. There is one other question.

Going back to Monday night and the President's speech, what did you want or expect to hear from the President?

THE WITNESS: I think what I wanted and expected were two different things. I had -- I had been hurt when he referred to me as "that woman" in January, but I was also glad. I was glad that he made that statement and I felt that was the best thing for him to do, was to deny this. And -- but I had been hurt. I mean, it showed me how angry he was with me and I understood that.

And his -- the people who work for him have trashed me, they claim they haven't said anything about me, they have smeared me and they called me stupid, they said I couldn't write, they said I was a stalker, they said I wore inappropriate clothes, I mean, you all know.

I mean, you've heard them in here, you've read the papers, you've seen on TV, and yet -- and then when it came out about the talking points, then somehow no one ever asked

1159

103

the question, well, how could -- if she was so stupid and she couldn't write, how is it possible that she wrote the talking points? So then it was, well, someone must have helped her with that. Oh, it's okay, though, it wasn't someone in the White House.

So I just -- my family had been maligned because of a lot of their tactics and I felt that -- I had wanted him to say that I was a nice, decent person and that he was sorry this had happened because I -- I tried to do as much as I could to protect him.

I mean, I didn't -- I didn't -- I didn't allow him to be put on tape that night and I didn't -- and I -- I felt that I waited, you know, and I would have gone to trial had -- had -- in my mind, had there never been a point where the Office of the Independent Counsel and myself could come to - they could come to accept the truth I had to say, that that was the truth I had to give, and I'm only 24 and so I felt that I -- this has been hard for me and this has been hard on my family and I just wanted him to take back -- by saying something nice, he would have taken back every disgusting, horrible thing that anyone has said about me from that White House. And that was what I wanted.

What I expected him to do was to just acknowledge in his -- either in his apology -- you know, that first of all I think he should have straight out apologized and I think that he could have acknowledged that -- you know, apologized to me, I think, to the other people who were involved in this and to my family.

My -- my dad didn't know anything about the relationship and when he went on his -- the few interviews he did, he was telling the truth when he said he didn't know. But out of respect for the President and the presidency, he didn't say -- he could have easily said if this is true; X, Y and Z about the President, and I think that because my family didn't start a huge uproar about how wrong or improper or inappropriate it was for a 50-year-old man to be having a relationship with a young woman, we afforded him that, that was one less headache that he had to deal with, and I think he could have acknowledged that. That was what I expected. Does that --

A JUROR: Monica, none of us in this room are perfect. We all fall and we fall several times a day. The only difference between my age and when I was your age is now I get up faster. If I make a mistake and fall, I get up and brush myself off. I used to stay there a while after a mistake. That's all I have to say.

THE WITNESS: Thank you.

MS. IMMERGUT: Let me just check with Mike.

THE FOREPERSON: We do want to share something with her.

1161

105

MS. IMMERGUT: Okay. So do you want to -- why don't we hold off for just a second and let me check with Mr. Emmick.

THE FOREPERSON: Okay.

(Pause.)

MS. IMMERGUT: We don't have any further questions.

A JUROR: Could I ask one?

Monica, is there anything that you would like to add to your prior testimony, either today or the last time you were here, or anything that you think needs to be amplified on or clarified? I just want to give you the fullest opportunity.

THE WITNESS: I would. I think because of the public nature of how this investigation has been and what the charges aired, that I would just like to say that no one ever asked me to lie and I was never promised a job for my silence.

And that I'm sorry. I'm really sorry for everything that's happened. (The witness begins to cry.) And I hate Linda Tripp.

A JUROR: Can I just say -- I mean, I think I should seize this opportunity now, that we've all fallen short. We sin every day. I don't care whether it's murder, whether it's affairs or whatever. And we get over that. You ask forgiveness and you go on.

There's some that are going to say that they don't forgive you, but he whose sin -- you know -- that's how I feel about that. So to let you know from here, you have my forgiveness. Because we all fall short.

A JUROR: And that's what I was trying to say.

A JUROR: That's what it's about.

THE WITNESS: Thank you.

A JUROR: And I also want to say that even though right now you feel a lot of hate for Linda Tripp, but you need to move on and leave her where she is because whatever goes around comes around.

A JUROR: It comes around.

A JUROR: It does.

A JUROR: And she is definitely going to have to give an account for what she did, so you need to just go past her and don't keep her because that's going to keep you out.

A JUROR: That's right.

A JUROR: And going to keep you from moving on.

A JUROR: Allowing you to move on.

BY MS. IMMERGUT:

Q And just to clarify, and I know we've discussed this before, despite your feelings about Linda Tripp, have you lied to this grand jury about anything with regard to Linda Tripp because you don't like her?

A I don't think that was necessary. No. It wouldn't

1163

107

have been necessary to lie. I think she's done enough on her own, so --

Q You would not do that just because of your feelings about her.

A No.

THE FOREPERSON: Basically what we wanted to leave with, because this will probably be your last visit to us, I hope, I hope I'm not going to have to do this any more and I hope you won't have to come here any more, but we wanted to offer you a bouquet of good wishes that includes luck, success, happiness and blessings.

THE WITNESS: Thank you. (The witness begins to cry.) I appreciate all of your understanding for this situation and your -- your ability to open your heart and your mind and -- and your soul. I appreciate that.

THE FOREPERSON: So if there's nothing else?

MR. EMMICK: Nothing else.

THE FOREPERSON: We'd like to excuse you and thank you very much for your testimony.

THE WITNESS: Thank you.

(The witness was excused.)

(Whereupon, at 12:54 p.m., the taking of testimony in the presence of a full quorum of the Grand Jury was concluded.)

* * * * *

1281

OFFICE OF THE INDEPENDENT COUNSEL

```
-------------------------x
                         :
  DEPOSITION OF          :     Wednesday, August 26, 1998
                         :
  MONICA S. LEWINSKY     :     Washington, D. C.
                         :
-------------------------x
```

Deposition of

MONICA S. LEWINSKY

before the Independent Counsel, held in the Conference Room of the Office of the Independent Counsel, Suite 490-North, 1001 Pennsylvania Avenue, N. W., Washington, D. C. 20004, beginning at 12:35 p.m., when were present:

For the Independent Counsel:

KARIN IMMERGUT, ESQUIRE
Associate Independent Counsel

MARY ANNE WIRTH, ESQUIRE
Associate Independent Counsel

Court Reporter: Elizabeth A. Eastman

1282

PROCEEDINGS

MS. IMMERGUT: We are on the record. Ms. Lewinsky, could you please state and spell your full name for the record?

MS. LEWINSKY: Monica Samille Lewinsky, M-O-N-I-C-A S-A-M-I-L-L-E, L-E-W-I-N-S-K-Y.

MS. IMMERGUT: For the record, I am Karin Immergut from the Office of Independent Counsel. Seated with me is Mary Anne Wirth, also from the Office of the Independent Counsel.

WHEREUPON,

MONICA S. LEWINSKY

having been called for examination by the Office of the Independent Counsel, and having been first duly sworn by the notary, was examined and testified as follows:

EXAMINATION BY COUNSEL FOR THE INDEPENDENT COUNSEL

BY MS. IMMERGUT:

Q Before we begin the deposition, I do want to advise you of certain rights that you have in connection with this deposition. You have already, I know, testified twice before the grand jury, and essentially the same rights do apply.

First, you have a right to have an attorney present outside of the room. Do you have an attorney present?

A Yes, I do.

Q Who is that attorney?

1283

3

A Plato Cacheris.

Q You have the right to consult with Mr. Cacheris any time during the testimony, and I simply ask that you just request a break when you need to consult with him. Do you understand that you have that right?

A Yes, I do.

Q You also generally as a witness in a deposition, or before a grand jury, have a Fifth Amendment right not to incriminate yourself. Obviously, that now is modified pursuant to the agreement that you have with the Office of the Independent Counsel.

Do you understand that?

A Yes.

Q Have you seen the agreement that you have, giving you immunity for your cooperation in this case?

A Yes, I have.

Q That also is a grand jury exhibit in this case, is it not?

A Yes, it is.

Q Do you have any questions about what your rights are not to incriminate yourself as part of that agreement?

A No, I don't.

Q In addition, as always, you are required to tell the truth during this procedure and are subject to the penalties of perjury if you do not tell the complete truth.

1284

Do you understand that?

A Yes, I do.

Q Any other questions that you have before we proceed?

A No.

Q First I just want to ask you a general question. I know you have testified in two other proceedings about various aspects of your relationship with the President. Can you characterize whether or not your relationship was one that started with sex and then evolved into a friendship, or the other way around?

A It started with a physical attraction, which led to a sexual relationship, and then the emotional and friendship aspects of that relationship developed after the beginning of our sexual relationship.

Q I would like to place before you what I will mark as Deposition exhibit No. 1.

(Deposition Exhibit No. 1 was marked for identification.)

BY MS. IMMERGUT:

Q This is also a chart that was previously marked as Grand Jury Exhibit ML #7. You can see the Xerox copy of that sticker on this exhibit, and I will place that before you, and ask if you recognize what that exhibit is?

A Yes, I do.

Q What do you recognize it to be?

A A chart that I helped develop with the Office of Independent Counsel to describe and enumerate the -- my relationship with the President, the contacts between the President and myself.

Q As you've testified before, did you provide the information that is on this chart?

A Yes, I did.

Q And is it accurate to the best of your recollection of the events?

A Yes, it is.

Q What I would like to do is go through the events that are written in bold, which deal with the private encounters you had with the President that involved, for the most part, some sort of physical intimacy that we have listed as physical intimacy, including oral sex. I did want to get into some more detail about each incident.

Basically, with respect to each incident, I would like you to describe the circumstances leading up to the actual visit, who initiated it, how it was set up, and then I would like to ask you some details about the sexual encounters themselves that occurred during each of those visits.

So, why don't we start with the very first one, which is the second encounter that you had on November 15th,

1286

6

1995 that you've already testified some about. If you can, could you just tell us how that visit was set up, and then what occurred during the visit?

A The President came back to Mr. Panetta's office and I was the only person in the office at the time, and believe it was maybe around, I think, 10 p.m. or so, and asked me, or told me that if I wanted to meet him back in Mr. Stephanopoulos' office in about 5-10 minutes, that I could. And I told him I was interested to do that.

Q At that time, did you understand what it was he wanted to meet with you about?

A I had an idea. I, I, I had assumed that since we had been intimate in our previous encounter that evening, that we would again be intimate.

Q And just to clarify for the record, the intimacy that you had earlier that night was just kissing, is that correct?

A Yes.

Q So, did you, in fact, go meet with the President?

A Yes, I did.

Q And could you describe where you went to meet him?

A I met him back in Mr. Stephanopoulos' office and he invited me into the back study again, and we were in the hallway. And we were -- I don't remember exactly how it started. But I know that we were talking a bit and kissing.

I remember -- I know that he -- I believe I unbuttoned my jacket and he touched my, my breasts with my bra on, and then either -- I don't remember if I unhooked my bra or he lifted my bra up, but he -- this is embarrassing.

Q Then touched your breasts with his hands?

A Yes, he did.

Q Did he touch your breasts with his mouth?

A Yes, he did.

Q Did he touch your genital area at all that day?

A Yes. We moved -- I believe he took a phone call in his office, and so we moved from the hallway into the back office, and the lights were off. And at that point, he, he put his hand down my pants and stimulated me manually in the genital area.

Q And did he bring you to orgasm?

A Yes, he did.

Q Back to the touching of your breasts for a minute, was that then through clothing or actually directly onto your skin?

A He touched my breasts through clothing, being my bra, and then also without my bra on.

Q On that occasion, did you perform oral sex on the President?

A Yes.

Q Who actually initiated your performing oral sex?

1288

8

A I did.

Q Was the President wearing pants?

A Yes, he was.

Q Who unzipped his pants?

A I believe I went to go unbutton his pants and I had trouble. So, he did that. So, but --

Q So, you started it?

A If I remember correctly.

Q And he helped complete opening his pants?

A Yes.

Q Did the President at that time do anything to stop you from doing that?

A No. I think he asked me if I was sure I wanted to do that.

Q Did you have any other discussion with him while the sexual encounter was occurring, about the sex or what you were doing?

A No. Actually, I don't think he asked me if I were sure I wanted to do that, because he was on the telephone. So -- I'm sorry.

Could you repeat what you just asked me?

Q Did the President have any discussion with you about sex, or you with him, while the sexual encounter was occurring?

A Not at this time. He was on the telephone for the

second half when we were in the office.

Q So, he was on the telephone while you were performing oral sex?

A He was on the telephone while he was --

Q Touching you?

A Touching me, and was also on the telephone when I was performing oral sex.

Q For any part of this sexual encounter, was he then off the telephone?

A Yes, I believe towards the end of my performing oral sex.

Q Did he say anything about the oral sex or anything about the sex at all when he got off the phone, that you can remember?

A He stopped me before he came, and I told him that I wanted to, to complete that. And he said that, that he needed to wait until he trusted me more. And then I think he

A Yes.

Q Did he ejaculate in your presence that time at all?

A No.

Q How did you depart from the office, or how did you end that visit?

1290

10

A I believe we spoke for awhile and I know at some point in that conversation I -- oh, that might have been Friday. Hmm. I really don't remember how it ended.

Q Can you estimate at all how long the sexual part of your encounter with him lasted?

A Maybe 20 minutes?

Q How long --

A I'm not a very good estimator of times.

Q How long did the entire encounter last, if you can recall?

A The second one of that evening?

Q Yes.

A Maybe half an hour or 40 minutes?

Q So, the entire encounter did not involve simply the sexual part of it?

A No, it didn't.

Q Did you have talking beforehand or was most of the talking afterwards?

A It was before and after.

Q If I can direct your attention again back to Deposition Exhibit No. 1, the chart, the next date where you do have two encounters with the President is November 17th, 1995. Although you've described it somewhat for the grand jury, if you could now just describe in detail -- again, I'll direct your attention to that second contact where there was

1291

11

physical intimacy, including oral sex listed -- how that contact came about and what occurred during the contact?

A Yes. I had brought the President pizza, as he had asked. And when I brought it into him at the Oval Office, then he took me into the, to the back office and said that I could leave through that way. I believe we were talking for a little bit and he then, he got a phone call and he took the phone call in his bathroom.

Oh, it might have been before the phone call that -- I don't, I don't remember who, who unbuttoned my jacket or anything like that. But we were kissing and he was fondling my breasts with his hands and with his mouth.

Q Was that through clothing or not through clothing?

A It was both.

Q Okay. So, was there a point that your bra is removed?

A Yes.

Q But you don't remember who actually removed it?

A No. I think, I think he -- rather than necessarily removing my bra, sometimes he would just expose my breasts.

Q By lifting the bra over your breasts?

A Yes, or sometimes lifting my breasts out of the bra. Oh, God.

Q So, on that occasion though, you do recall that he touched you not just through your bra, but also directly on

1292

12

the skin?

A Yes.

Q

A

Q

A

Q Was there any discussion about sex while you were in this encounter with him?

A I don't remember the specifics of it, but I know there was another discussion, I think, about him not letting me make him come, and then I had to get back to -- I'm sorry.

Could you repeat the question?

Q Was there any discussion during the November 17th encounter about sex during the encounter?

A I don't know exactly what you mean. I mean, do you mean either about --

Q Talking --

A I mean, saying things, or --

Q Well, either about what he wanted or what you wanted, or anything like that, in terms of sex?

A No. I mean, I think that there were always things being said, but not necessarily in a conversational form. Does that make sense?

Q Okay. And when you say there were always things being said, do you mean kind of chatting while you were having sex, or things that felt good? I don't mean that. I mean --

A Okay.

Q -- trying either implicitly giving you direction about what he wanted, or why he wouldn't ejaculate, anything like that?

A I believe that why he wouldn't ejaculate was, was discussed again.

Q Okay. You mentioned that the President unzipped his pants. Did you understand that to be a signal of what he wanted in terms of sex?

A Yes.

Q Did he ever say anything while that was happening about what he wanted or no?

A No. He was on the telephone.

Q Okay. And that was on the second time also?

A Yes.

Q Was he on the telephone the whole time that you performed oral sex on him on the 17th of November?

A I don't remember.

1294

14

Q Do you remember how you finished that meeting up with him that day, how you left?

A Yes. I know I needed to get back to my office, and he -- I think I told him that he should come down and have pizza with us, he should bring his pizza down, and that everyone was down there. And at some point I believe in that meeting he told me that, or he reiterated because he might have said it on the 15th as well, that I could come see him on the weekends when, when there weren't a lot of people around.

Q With respect again to the ejaculation, that he wouldn't actually ejaculate during oral sex, were you aware, or did he ejaculate anywhere in your presence on that occasion?

A No.

Q The next date listed on the chart is December 31st, 1995, a Sunday. Could you describe how that meeting was set up and what occurred when you got to the meeting?

A Yes. I had been having a conversation with Nel and had just told him that I smoked my first cigar the night before in honor of my brother's birthday. And Nel asked me if I wanted -- or offered that he could get me one of the President's cigars from his sort of stash of cigars. I said, that would be great.

And we went through the Roosevelt Room to the

1295

15

entrance into the back study which -- the door that leads into the dining room. And just as we approached the door, the door swung open and the President was standing right there, and he had something he was going to take to Mr. Panetta. So, he asked, he asked Nel to take this -- I think it was a picture actually -- a picture down to Mr. Panetta, and he invited me in.

So, I went into the office and he asked me what I was doing there. And -- well, first he told me he had been looking for me. And then he told me -- he asked me what I was doing there, and I told him that Nel was going to get me a cigar. So, he said that he would give me a cigar. So, he did give me a cigar.

And then we were talking for a little bit and I had -- do you want me to just be --

Q If you could do a narrative, that's fine.

A Well, he had -- I had thought that he had forgotten my name before, because I had seen him in the hall a few times and he kept calling me "Kiddo". So, so, I sort of reiterated my -- I said my name again to him. You know, I said, you know, it's Monica Lewinsky, President Kiddo, you know. And he said, I know your name.

And he told me that he had tried to call me and that -- he said, but you're not in the book; I even spelled your last name right. So, it was, it was really funny. It

1296

was cute.

And then we were, we were kissing and he lifted my sweater and exposed my breasts and was fondling them with his hands and with his mouth. And then I believe I was fondling him over his pants in his genital area, and I think again I tried to unbutton his pants and I couldn't. So, he did it.

Q And again, just to be clear, when you mentioned he raised your sweater and fondled your breasts, were your breasts outside of your bra at that time?

A Yes.

Q Did you have any discussion with him again about why he wasn't ejaculating, anything like that?

A Yes, I think so. It might have been at that time -- the two excuses he always used were, one, that he didn't know me well enough or he didn't trust me yet. So that it sort of seemed to be some bizarre issue for him.

Q On that occasion, did he ever ejaculate in your

1297

17

presence, even though not -- at any time later?

A After he told me to stop and then, and then wished me Happy New Year and kissed me goodbye, he went into the

Q Okay. Do you know how long that sexual encounter, or the sexual aspect of that encounter lasted, not including the other discussion with him?

A Maybe 10 minutes. Not, not very long. We would always spend quite a bit of time kissing. So.

Q And kissing and talking and just --

A Uh-huh.

Q -- being affectionate?

A Yes.

Q The next one is on page 2, and that would be January 7th of '96. Could you describe how that meeting was set up and what happened when you got there?

A Yes. The President called me -- this is the first time he called me at home -- that afternoon, and it was the first day of the blizzard. And I asked him what he was doing and he said he was going to be going into the office soon. I said, oh, do you want some company. And he said, oh, that would be great. So, he said he was going into the office in about 45 minutes, and I told him that I should probably be in my office around that time, and he said he would call me in

1298

18

my office. I gave him my office number.

Then once I was in my office, he called me and we made an arrangement that I would pass -- he would have the door to his office open, and I would pass by the office with some papers and then he would, he would sort of stop me and invite me in. So, that was exactly what happened.

I passed by and that was actually when I saw Lew Fox who was on duty outside the Oval Office, and stopped and spoke with Lew for a few minutes, and then the President came out and said, oh, hey, Monica, you know, what are you doing here, come on in, sort of.

And so we spoke for about 10 minutes in the office. We sat on the sofas. Then we went into the back study and we were intimate in the bathroom.

Q And when you say you were intimate in the bathroom, what did you do?

A We kissed and he, he fondled my breasts and exposed -- or I think pulled them out of my bra and fondled them with his hands and with his mouth, and --

Q Did he touch your genitals on that occasion?

A No. He wanted to and was talking about performing oral sex on me, [redacted]

Q [redacted]

A [redacted]

Q Okay. On that date, did you gratify him in some

way other than performing oral sex?

A Yes.

Q

A

Q

A

Q

A

Q

A

Q

A

Q

A

Q Did you have any discussion about sex during the encounter that you had with him?

A No.

Q How long was your encounter with him?

A Hmm. Maybe about half an hour? I, I'm -- it's really hard for me to estimate the time.

Q And that would be the sexual aspect of it though that --

1300

A Correct.

Q -- we're talking about. Did he ejaculate at any point in your presence after you performed oral sex on him?

A That day?

Q Yes.

A No.

MS. IMMERGUT: Did you have a question?

BY MS. WIRTH:

Q I have a question, actually going back to November 15th, if you don't mind.

A Okay.

Q When you were talking about the President having contact with your genitals, you said, I think, that he put his hands in your pants. When he touched your genitals, was that through your underwear or directly?

A I didn't have my underwear on at that point.

Q Okay. So, it was directly then?

A Yes.

Q Okay.

BY MS. IMMERGUT:

Q The next encounter listed is January 21st of '96, also on page 2 of the exhibit. Could you describe how that encounter occurred and what happened during the encounter?

A Yes. I was -- actually, I'm looking at this right now and I think it might have been a Saturday -- no, it was a

Sunday. I'm sorry. Never mind. I think it might have been a Saturday, but it, it says here Sunday. I just noticed that.

I was -- I had been in my office doing work, and I was leaving, leaving for the day. And as I was walking through the Residence hall to go through the West Wing to the Old Executive Office Building, I heard his voice behind me. And either he called my name or I just heard his voice and turned around, and he had just come off of the elevator and, I guess, was going back to his office.

So, we were, we were -- we stopped, and we spoke as we continued to walk through the outdoor corridor by the Rose Garden. And when we got to the point where he turns left to then go into the Oval Office, he told me that I could go out this way with him, that I could leave through the, that I could leave through the Oval Office. So, we walked down the pathway together and then went into the Oval Office from there.

Q And could you describe your encounter once you got into the Oval Office?

A Yes. We had, we had already had phone sex for the first time the week prior, and I was feeling a little bit insecure about whether he had liked it or didn't like it, and I just -- I felt in general that I didn't know -- from having spoken to him on the phone, you know, prior to having phone sex and from having had these encounters with him, I didn't know if this was sort of developing into some kind of a longer term relationship than what I thought it initially might have been, that maybe he had some regular girlfriend who was furloughed or something during the furlough.

And at that point, I, you know, I said to him, you know, I asked him why he doesn't ask me any questions about myself, and doesn't he, you know, is this just about sex, you know, because if it is, then I just want to know that; or do you have some interest in trying to get to know me as a person. And so he kind of laughed at the manner in which I was asking him and talking to him.

And we, we went into the back study and he was, he was waiting for a friend of his to come to the office, and he was talking about that he has a lot of -- that he doesn't get a lot of time to himself and he really cherishes the private times that he has with his friends, and he cherishes the time that he had with me, which seemed a little bit odd to me at that time.

But he, he was upset that day about the first soldier in Bosnia had been -- I believe it was that day -- that it was the first soldier in Bosnia had been killed just recently, and he was very upset and moved. And so I was trying to comfort him.

Q When you say you thought it was odd that he said he

cherished the time with you, why was that, why did you think it was odd at that point?

A Because I didn't feel, I didn't feel like he really knew me. We had spent time talking, but it didn't seem -- and, you know, he had asked some questions and I offered a lot of information about myself. But he didn't seem to ask probing questions, when you're trying to get to know someone. So, it seemed a little bit odd to me that he would sort of cherish this time, when he, you know, when I felt like he didn't really even know me yet.

Q And at that point, sex was sort of the more dominant part of the relationship?

A Yes.

Q Rather than as it became --

A There was always a lot of joking that went on between us. And so we, you know, I mean, it was fun. When we were together, it was fun. We would laugh and it would -- we were very compatible sexually. And I've always felt that he was sort of my sexual soulmate, and that I just felt very connected to him when it came to those kinds of things.

Q So, on the January 21st date --

A Right.

Q -- how did it turn into your conversation and then go into actually having a sexual encounter?

A I was in the middle of saying something and he just

started kissing me. And, so, it was funny. It was, it was very funny.

Q And what room were you physically in at that time?

A We were in the hallway. And we were kissing and -- oh, I had -- because I was leaving, I was having a bad hair day, and this was actually the first time that I had the infamous beret on. And so I just said something to him about feeling stupid. Here I was standing here in this dumb hat, and he said that it wasn't a dumb hat, that I looked cute and he liked it.

And so then he was kissing me, or we were kissing each other, I guess, and I think again he, he fondled my breasts with his hands and his mouth.

Q Through clothing or not through clothing?

A I think it was always through clothing, and then eventually it, it would be direct contact. So, it wouldn't just be this immediate jump to being, you know, to contact. It was -- there was sort of foreplay to the foreplay, if that makes sense.

Q Do you remember whether he removed any of your clothing on that occasion?

A I think he -- I remember him lifting my top. So -- and he, he sort of exposing my breasts.

Q Did he stimulate your genitals on that occasion?

A No.

Q Did you perform oral sex on him or any kind of sex on him?

A Yes, I did.

Q Could you describe how that came about?

A Yes. He unzipped his pants and sort of exposed himself and that -- and then I performed oral sex.

Q Let me ask, on all of these occasions when you've described just the pants unzipping and exposing, is it fair to say that he still kept his pants on?

A Yes.

Q It was just the zipper that --

A Yes.

Q -- was undone?

A Right. And actually at one point during this encounter, I think someone came into the, to the Oval Office and he, you know, zipped up real quickly and went out and came back in, and I -- this is probably too much information. I just -- sorry.

Q And what happened?

A I just remember laughing because he had walked out there and he was visibly aroused, and I just thought it was funny. I mean, it wouldn't, it wouldn't necessarily be visible to anyone who just walked in because they wouldn't be looking at that, but it was just funny to me. So.

And then his -- then someone -- I think at that

1306

point someone came in to let him know that his friend had arrived. And so he asked me which way I wanted to leave, and I said I was going to go, I was going to leave through Betty's office. And we went into -- we went from the back study through the Oval into Betty's office area, and he took me into Nancy Hernreich's office and kissed me goodbye.

And then I went to go leave from, from Betty's office, from the door into the hallway, to the West Wing hallway, but it was locked. So, I went back in to tell him. He was still in Nancy's office. I went back into Nancy's office to tell him the door was locked, and he was manually stimulating himself.

Q Did he cause himself to ejaculate at that point, or did you see that?

A No.

Q But that was in Nancy Hernreich's office?

A Yes.

Q And what did you do when you saw that?

A I smiled.

Q Okay.

A And I think we kissed again.

Q On that occasion, you mentioned that he did not touch your genitals at all. Was there any discussion about that?

A No.

Q Then did you leave from Nancy Hernreich's office eventually?

A I think I left through the -- I left through the door in Betty's office that goes out into the Rose Garden.

Q On this particular entry on January 21st, it lists that the entire encounter was approximately 30 to 40 minutes. Do you recall what portion of that would have been the sexual encounter part of it, versus just talking?

A Maybe 15 minutes?

Q You just can't really estimate?

A Exactly.

Q Let's go now to February 4th of 1996, the next bold date where there was a private encounter. Could you describe how that encounter came about and what happened?

A Yes. I was in my office on Sunday and the President called me in the office and -- from the Residence, and told me that he was going to be going into the office later. And I think I asked him if I could come see him. And he said that would be fine, and then that he -- oh, I think he was, he said he was going to go into the office in an hour and a half or so.

So, then he called me -- it was actually maybe two or three hours later, because I remember I thought he forgot, maybe he had forgotten to call me and that -- so. And when he called from the Residence to say he was on his way, I told

1308

him that -- I asked him if we could sort of bump into the hallway, bump into each other in the hallway on purpose this time, because when it happened accidentally, that seemed to work really well and I felt more comfortable doing that. So, that's what we did. We both said, okay, I'm going to leave now.

And indeed we bumped into each other in the hall and went through the Rose Garden into the Oval Office. And I think we went right into the back office. The -- when we got there.

Q When you say the back office, you mean the study?

A Yes. And -- let's see.

You know, I need to take a break.

Q Okay. Let's take a break.

(Whereupon, the deposition was recessed from 1:10 p.m. until 1:15 p.m.)

BY MS. IMMERGUT:

Q Ms. Lewinsky, you are still under oath.

A Yes.

Q We are still on February 4th, 1996. You've described going into the office and starting to kiss the President. What happened then?

A We were in the back office and we were kissing, and I was -- I had a dress on that buttoned all the way, all the way up and down.

1309

29

Q To the neck?

A Correct. It was long and down to the, to my ankles, or whatever. And he unbuttoned my dress and he unhooked my bra, and sort of took the dress off of my shoulders and took the bra off of my, off of my -- I'm not explaining this right. So that he moved the bra so that my bra was kind of hanging on one shoulder and so was off. And he just was, he was looking at me and touching me and telling me how beautiful I was.

Q And did he touch your breasts with his hands?

A Yes.

Q Did he also touch them with his mouth?

A Yes.

Q And at that point, that is directly on your skin, is that right?

A Yes.

Q Did he touch your genitals?

A Yes, he did.

Q Did he bring you to orgasm on that date?

A Yes, he did.

Q

A

Q

1310

30

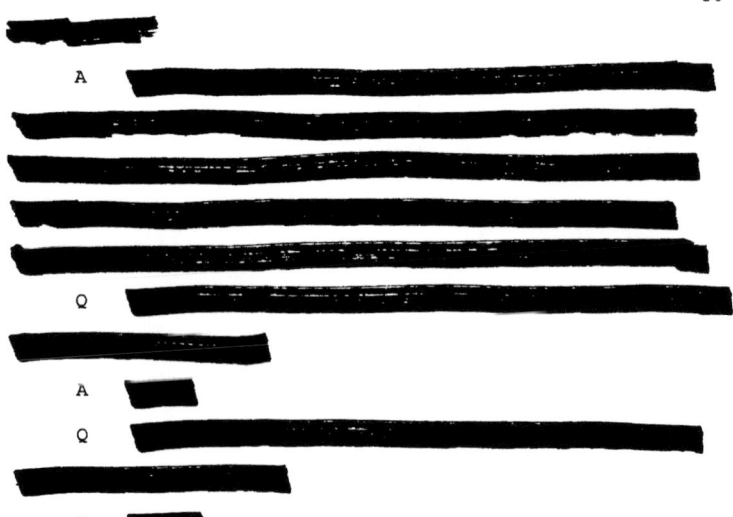

Q And again, just with respect to bringing you to an orgasm, did he touch you directly on your skin on your genitals, or was it through underwear?

A First it was through underwear and then it was directly touching my genitals.

Q Did he take your underwear off, or did you take your underwear off?

A Hmm.

Q Or did they stay on?

A I think that -- I believe that he touched me first with my underwear on, and then placed his hand under my underwear. And I think at some point I, I removed them.

Q Okay. Did you also perform oral sex on him at that

time?

A Yes, I did.

Q How did it come about? Was that something that you decided to do, or did the President either, through his actions or words, indicate to you that he wanted that?

A I don't really remember. I mean, it was a mutual -- I think in all of these instances, it wasn't, you know -- I know sometimes it's sort of hard to answer these questions as more directed. But it was -- I mean, it was the course of ng intimate. I mean, it was the course of having this kind of a relationship, that you -- sometimes he initiated it, sometimes I initiated it. It wasn't, you know, it wasn't -- it didn't necessarily go through my mind, okay, now it's time to perform oral sex.

I mean, it was, it was the passion of the moment. That was, I mean, just sort of in the course of things that happened, you know. I always felt that we sort of just, we both really went to a, to a whole other place together sexually.

Q Is it fair to say you were both trying to please each other by doing different things?

A Yes. Yes.

Q Is it also fair to say that you were not the sole aggressor in this sexual --

A That's very fair to say.

1312

32

Q -- encounter?

A I was not.

Q Again, I'm just asking you every time in case you remember, do you remember how long the sexual aspect of that encounter lasted?

A I really, I really don't.

Q Okay. I just note, to direct your attention that the time that you provided us previously is approximately one and a half hours for the whole visit.

A Right. We spent a long time in the Oval Office talking after, maybe 45 minutes to an hour just talking.

Q And that --

A I think he was maybe heeding my, my advice from, from the 21st, about trying to get to know me, and so he did.

Q And is it fair to say that's sort of when the friendship really starts to develop, around that time period?

A It does. That certainly helped. I think he, he was just very sweet, and he -- when I got up to leave, he kissed my arm and told me he'd call me, and then I said, yeah, well, what's my phone number. And so he recited both my home number and my office number off the top of his head. So, I told him, you know, that he got an A.

And he called me in my office later that afternoon to tell me how much he enjoyed talking to me. So -- and then again called Wednesday night to tell me again how much he had enjoyed talking to me.

So, it -- I think that certainly was a turning point in the relationship, where it kind of went from a -- obviously there's, there's some personal and intimate aspects of a sexual relationship that develop just in talking or laughing or getting to the point where you, where you kiss someone on every encounter. But for me, I think that spending the time talking to him was certainly when I, when I got to know him as a person and started to realize that he wasn't necessarily the person I thought he was at that point.

Q Let's move on to the next date, which is March 31st, 1996, the next encounter where there is physically intimate contact. Why don't you tell us how that date was set up and what happened?

A I had spoken -- well, just to back up real quickly. The President had ended things on the, I think it was the 19th of February. But then he had called me later -- I think it was late February or early March at some point -- indicating to me he wanted to sort of see me again, possibly for some intimate moments.

And it wasn't until the 31st of March that we really were together again physically. But he had called, I think two times, two times prior during that work week, leading up to the 31st. And it was on the Friday night which is, looking at the chart, which was the 29th, that I, I asked him if I could see him on Sunday. And he said, he'd, you know, he'd see what he could do.

And then on Sunday, he called me in my office and -- let's see. I believe -- oh, I believe that I brought him papers that day. That I think I asked him to tell the guard outside that he was expecting some papers, expecting someone from Leg Affairs. And then when I got to the door, I told them that I was supposed to bring papers to the President.

Q And that was part of a ruse to --

A Yes.

Q -- get in to see him?

A Exactly.

Q Just to back up for a second, you mentioned that you had had some phone calls with him between February 19th, '96 when he tried to cut off the relationship --

A Yes.

Q -- or the sexual part of the relationship --

A Correct.

Q -- and the 31st, in which he had suggested that he wanted to perhaps renew the intimacy. What led you to believe that?

A I saw him on my way out one evening. It was late. And he was on his way home from, I think it was the Israeli Embassy and Evelyn Lieberman was with him. So, I certainly made a point of not having any eye contact or anything with

1315

35

him. And he called me later that evening and said he had, he had -- after he left and went upstairs, he went back to his office and had called me in my office, hoping that I could come have a visit with him, but I had already gone home.

And so then I offered, I said, well, I could come back. And he said, no, I'm upstairs already. So.

Q Back now to March 31st --

A Yes.

Q -- of '96. So, what happens then? How actually is that then finally set up?

A He had called me in my office and then I brought papers there, or fake papers.

Q Do you then go into the Oval Office?

A Yes, I do.

Q And what happens?

A We went into the back study and we were in the, the hallway area. And it had sort of become actually a ritual sort of at this point, that we always kind of started out our meetings, that he was leaning against the closed door of the bathroom and I would rub his back, because he has a bad back. So, I used to always rub his back, and sometimes he'd rub my back. But I usually concentrated on his lower back because it was always bothering him.

And, you know, and then I'd usually move around and sort of just lovingly touch his chest and --

1316

Q Was there any removal of clothing?

A Yes, there was. We kissed and, and he had not been feeling well, I guess, the past couple of days. So, really, most of -- he focused on me pretty exclusively, I guess, in a sexual manner on me that day, and kissed me, and kissed my breasts, and he, he fondled my genitals with his hands.

Q Through clothing or not through clothing?

A Not through clothing.

Q Did you have your underwear removed? Or how did your clothes get off?

A (No response.)

Q Or were they simply pulled out of the way?

A I think I -- I think that they were just sort of -- oh.

Q Pulled out of the way?

A Yeah.

Q Okay. So, he touched you. And with your breasts, was that through clothing, through your brassiere, or did he move your breasts out of the way of the brassiere?

A It was, it was both. I mean, it was always both. He -- there was never a time when he just touched my breasts through --

Q The bra?

A -- the bra, right.

Q [redacted]

1317

37

A Yes.

Q Whose idea was that?

A On -- when I met with him on January 7th, after we had been intimate and we were talking in the Oval Office, he was chewing on a cigar. And then he had the cigar in his hand and he was kind of looking at the cigar in a, sort of a naughty way. And so I, I looked at the cigar and I looked at him and I said, we can do that, too, some time.

And I don't, I don't really remember how it got started, but.

Q Was it part of the sexual encounter that he did that?

A Yes, it was.

Q Did you understand it to be arousing?

A It was.

Q Okay. What happened to the cigar afterwards?

A

Q How did you leave that encounter? So, you didn't perform oral sex on him at all that time?

A No.

Q How --

A Actually, looking also -- I should mention that, looking at the chart, that I didn't bring papers that day. I brought this tie to him in a folder. So, sometimes I brought papers and this day it was I had a tie, and there probably were some papers in the folder as well.

Q And that's the Hugo Boss tie that's listed under the gift category for that date?

A Correct.

Q The next encounter is April 7th, 1996. Could you describe how that encounter was set up?

A The President had called me at home sort of in the early evening, and this was -- it was Easter Sunday and it was the first, it was the Sunday after I had found out I was to be transferred to the Pentagon. And he called -- it also had been the week that Ron Brown had passed away.

So, I asked him how he was doing and we talked about that for a little bit. And then I told him that Monday was my last day, and that I had been transferred. And I was crying and he wanted to know what happened, and I asked him if I could come see him. And he said, that's fine, but just tell me what happened first. So, I explained to him what had happened, and then he told me to come on over. So, I did.

And this is when I had this little encounter trying to get into the office with John Muskett, just that he said -- I brought papers with me from home in a folder. And so John had said something about wanting to check with Evelyn if it was okay for me to go in. And I don't remember exactly what ended up happening, but I managed to get him to not ask

1319

Evelyn and I got in.

And the President and I were in the back office. He was actually on the phone when I came in. And then when he got off the phone, we went into the back office and we talked again about what had happened, in terms of my transfer.

And that was when he, he looked me in the eye and he promised me -- well, first he said that he couldn't believe that they were taking me away from him because he trusted me so much, and he was convinced that it had something to do with him, why I was being transferred. And then he looked me in the eye and he said, I promise you, if I win in November, I'll have you back like that [snapping fingers].

Q Did he say anything like, if you do a good job at the Pentagon he'll bring you back?

A No.

Q So, what else happened at that meeting?

A I, I don't remember how it exactly came about, but I know that, that, I remember kissing him and we were physically intimate.

Q In terms of the physical intimacy that day, did the President touch your genitals on that date?

A I don't think so.

Q What about your breasts?

1320

A Yes.

Q With his mouth or with his hands, or both?

A With both.

Q And again, I'm assuming, unless you correct me now, that it's both through clothing and directly on the skin?

A Yes.

Q With respect to oral sex, do you just remember how that occurred, whether his pants came off, whether somebody unzipped them?

A I think he unzipped them and -- because it was sort of this running joke that I could never unbutton his pants, that I just had trouble with it. So, I was -- you know, there were times that I tried and we'd laugh and then he'd, he'd do it.

But we were -- I, I performed oral sex in the, in the back office.

Q And at that time, did he ejaculate?

A No, he did not.

Q Was there any discussion with him about the ejaculation at that time that you can remember?

A No.

Q On that date, I think you've already testified that there was a phone call during your sexual encounter with him, is that right?

A Yes, there was.

1321

41

Q Did you perform oral sex while he was on the telephone?

A Yes. It was, it was -- I think I'll just say, because for -- there are a lot of people that could interpret that as being sort of a, that being done in a servicing sort of manner, and it was more done in kind of an exciting sort of -- I don't want to say erotic, but in a way that there was kind of this titillating like a secret, in a sense, in the same way sometimes that an affair is, that, you know, when you are doing this and obviously there is kind of the irony that the person on the other line has no idea what's going on.

So, I just wanted to clarify that.

Q Okay. Although on that occasion, I believe you previously mentioned that that was the first time that you felt a little funny about it?

A I, I did. I did. I, I, I, I was, I was pretty emotionally devastated at that point, and the prospect of going to the Pentagon was very upsetting to me. And there were moments when I felt a little uncomfortable, and moments when I didn't.

Q Although you mentioned that there were other times that he was on the phone, that you didn't think sort of anything bad about it --

A Right.

1322

Q -- and on this occasion, you felt more like --

A I just --

Q -- you were servicing --

A Exactly.

Q -- on some level. And did you tell Linda Tripp about that, do you remember?

A Probably.

Q How did that encounter end, if you remember? And actually you've already testified a little bit about this. So, just if you could quickly summarize how you finished the encounter and what happened?

A We were in the back office and I heard Mr. Ickes call, say, Mr. President, from the Oval Office. And we both were startled and looked at each other, and he jetted into the Oval and I --

Q Were you performing oral sex at the time?

A I think so, but I'm not a hundred percent sure. And so then I, I left.

Q On that occasion also, when the President went to get the phone call, had you started performing oral sex on him before he went to take the phone call?

A Yes, I believe that we were -- I think that that was it. I know that we were, we were intimate in the hallway, and then it was a phone call that prompted us to go into the office. And that when we were in the office, that,

that he, he removed, he sort of removed his pants.

Q How did you know that you were supposed to kind of accompany him to take the phone call? Did he --

A I don't remember.

Q -- invite you to come in, in any way, or gesture for you to come along?

A I don't really remember.

Q So, you think you actually didn't begin the oral sex until he was on the phone already?

A It's --

Q Or is it not that clear?

A It's not that clear.

Q But you remember him unzipping his pants at some point?

A At some point, yes.

Q Before the oral sex?

A Yes.

Q Okay.

A I hope so.

Q At that point, and I didn't really ask you this for the other encounters, but in terms of putting your stuff back on or collecting yourself, is there any sort of general way that that happened? Did the President help you, or how did you get dressed again?

A Well, neither of us ever really took -- completely

1324

44

took off any piece of our clothing, I think specifically because of the possibility of encounters, like what happened that day. But there had, earlier in that day on the 7th, when I -- not earlier in the day, but earlier in the encounter with the President -- when he had been kissing my breasts, someone had come in, I think to tell him he had the phone call, or something like that.

Or someone had come in at some point and he stepped out of the office, and I had put my bra and my sweater back on. And he came in and sort of made a remark about me having done that. And --

Q Do you remember the remark?

A I think he smirked and he sort of said, you know, damn, you put your top back on, or something like that. Or, why did you do that, something like that. But he was smirking and joking with me.

But then when he went into the Oval, when Mr. Ickes came in, I put myself together and hurried out the back way through the dining room.

Q The next encounter. There's luckily a big gap there. The next one is February 28th. How was this encounter set up, and then what happened?

A Betty called me at work to tell me, or to invite me to the radio address for that evening. And so I went.

Q Did she say anything about that you would see the

1325

45

President on that date, or --

A Yes. I mean, she, she had indicated to me the President wanted me to come to this radio address. So that -- and I knew that he had -- we had spoken earlier that month and the month before, and the month before that, and I knew he had a Christmas gift for me which he had yet to give me. So, it sort of seemed, it was understandable.

I went to the radio address. And then -- it was a very small group, maybe 10 people, six, 10 people. It was quite small. And after -- or when I went to go take my picture with him, he told me to go see Betty or go wait with Betty because he had something to give me. So, I went into Betty's office and was waiting there with her. There were some other people there, staff members. And I think I've gone through the whole --

Q And you've actually testified in some detail about this before.

A Right.

Q So, actually, why don't we just go to the sexual encounter --

A Okay.

Q -- and how the actual sexual part started?

A Once we were alone in the back office, he started to say something to me and I was pestering him to kiss me, because I hadn't -- we hadn't been alone in almost a year and

1326

46

-- well, I guess not a year, but it had been a long time since we had been alone. And so he, you know, he jokingly told me to, you know, just wait a sec, he wanted to give me my presents.

So, he gave me my hatpin and he sort of hurriedly put the Leaves Of Grass in my purse and he said, here, just take this with me. And then I said, what is it. I took the book out and so we, we were looking at it, and I was just, I thought it was pretty incredible. It was just a beautiful, beautiful book, and it meant a lot to me.

And then we went back over by the bathroom in the hallway, and we kissed. We were kissing and he unbuttoned my dress and fondled my breasts with my bra on, and then took them out of my bra and was kissing them and touching them with his hands and with his mouth.

And I continued to perform oral sex and then he pushed me away, kind of as he always did before he came, and then I stood up and I said, you know, I really, I care about you so much; I really, I don't understand why you won't let

1327

47

me, you know, make you come; it's important to me; I mean, it just doesn't feel complete, it doesn't seem right.

And so he -- we hugged. And, you know, he said he didn't want to get addicted to me, and he didn't want me to get addicted to him. And we were just sort of looking at each other and then, you know, he sort of, he looked at me, he said, okay. And so then I finished.

Q [redacted]

A [redacted]

Q [redacted]

A [redacted]

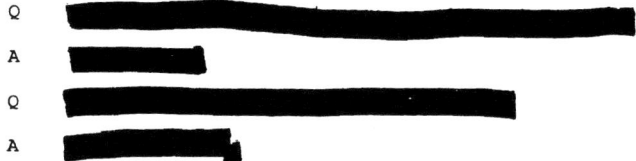

Q Did he touch your genitals at all during that occasion, do you remember?

A I think through my tights, but not direct genital.

Q How did the meeting then end, or the encounter?

A We, well, we kissed after --

Q The ejaculation?

A Yes. And then I think Betty knocked on the door. So, I think -- no, no, no, no, no, that's not right, because I fixed my lipstick. So, I think we sort of -- I think he said, oh, you've got to put yourself back together again. And so then I went and I got my lipstick and I put my lipstick back on, and then Betty knocked on the door.

Q The dress that you were wearing on this occasion, is that the blue dress from the Gap?

1328

A Unfortunately, yes.

Q And I think we've already gone into detail about the dress on that. The next encounter is March 29th, 1997. Would you tell us how that encounter was set up?

A It was, it was set up through my conversations with Betty.

Q Did you contact Betty?

A Yes. I contacted Betty and Betty -- my understanding was Betty spoke with the President, and then Betty got in touch with me and told me to come that afternoon. I did. I was waiting for the President in the back study and then he hobbled in because he was on crutches. And we were, we were in the back office. Actually, it was sort of an overcast day. It had been raining earlier. So, it was just sort of dark and overcast.

And we were, he was -- I think he had put his crutches down and he was kind of leaning on me. So, I was holding him, you know, I mean, sort of romantically but at the same time literally holding him. And --

Q This is in the back study?

A Uh-huh, yes. And I was -- this was another one of those occasions when I was babbling on about something, and he just kissed me, kind of to shut me up, I think. And so we were kissing and then we sort of -- we turned around and he was leaning against -- he has a little, it's like a little table that I think has this stereo. I don't know if the stereo was always there. I know it was there later. But he was leaning against this little table a little bit just, I think, kind of for support.

And he unbuttoned my blouse and just sort of touched me over, over my bra. And I don't think he took, I don't think he exposed my breasts that day. And we were, we were just kissing a lot.

And then he -- oh, he went to go put his hand down my pants, and then I unzipped them because it was easier. And I didn't have any panties on. And so he manually stimulated me.

Q Did he bring you to orgasm?

A Yes, four times.

Q How did you end the contact with him on that

1330

50

occasion?

A End the sexual contact? Or --

Q The sexual contact?

A He -- oh, well, this was also the day that before, before I performed oral sex on him, I wanted him to touch my genitals with his genitals. And so we sort of had tried to do that, but because he's really tall and he couldn't bend because of his knee, it didn't really work.

Q And I think you've previously testified your genitals grazed each other --

A Exactly.

Q -- on that occasion?

A I mean, just barely.

Q And when they grazed each other, neither of you had clothes covering your genitals, is that right?

A Correct.

Q How did you end the encounter completely that time, in terms of ending the meeting?

A Oh, we moved into the dining room and we were talking for a long time. I had brought some presents for him. So, we talked for awhile. And then Betty came back and the three of us were talking.

Q Let's move on to the next one, which is August 16th, 1997.

A I -- this was sort of his, his birthday, his

1331

51

birthday encounter. And so after -- I had set up in his back office, I had brought an apple square and put a candle and had put his birthday presents out. And after he came back in and I sang happy birthday and he got his presents, I asked him if we could, if we could share a birthday kiss in honor of our birthdays, because mine had been just a few weeks before. So, he said that that was okay and we could kind of bend the rules that day.

And so we, we, we kissed. And then I was touching him in his genital area through his shorts, and then I, I went to, to --

Q Perform oral sex?

A Yes, and he wouldn't let me.

Q Did he touch you on your genitals on that date?

A No.

Q Any other physical contact that is referred to as physical intimacy on that date?

A Not that I remember.

Q How did you end that encounter with him? Any discussion about sex during that encounter, or not having sex?

A No, just he got upset when I, you know, when he stopped me and he said, I'm trying to not do this and I'm trying to be good. And he, he got visibly upset. And so I, I hugged him and I told him I was sorry and not to be upset,

1332

and I was a little shocked, actually. I didn't -- he just seemed to get so emotionally upset about it. It seemed a little bit strange to me.

Q And he hadn't done that before?

A He had been emotionally visibly upset with me before, but not --

Q With regard to --

A Correct.

Q -- stopping you from having sex with him?

A Exactly.

Q Or having sexual contact with him? Is that correct?

A Yes.

Q And is that, other than any brief kiss, the last physically intimate contact that you've had with him?

A Well, our Christmas kiss was -- I mean, it was passionate. So.

Q Okay. It was --

A I don't call it a brief kiss.

Q That was a physically intimate kiss. Any other contact that would fall within the sexual relations definition --

A No.

Q -- that we've previously seen?

A I think we, you know, we would, we would joke with

each other sexually. And so sometimes, you know, I might hit him on the butt, or he might hit me on the butt, but it wasn't -- not under the definition.

Q So, it wouldn't be a real intent to arouse, or not the physical touching that is described --

A No.

Q -- in the definition?

A No.

Q All right. Let's move on to another topic.

A Yea.

Q Thank you for your patience. I know that those are not easy questions to get to.

A It's just hard thinking my dad might see this.

Q Why don't we move to another emotional topic, July 4th, just briefly. Is now a good time to --

A Sure.

Q -- talk about that? Why don't you tell us -- I know that you've brought up in your grand jury testimony that July 4th of 1997 was an emotional day for you in connection with your relationship with the President.

A Yes.

Q Could you just briefly tell us what you meant by that and just a little bit about your meeting with him on that date?

A Our meeting had started out in, as a, in a fight.

1334

54

We -- and early on in this fight, I started crying, and then he -- we were in the back office and he came over and was hugging me and told me not to cry, to stop crying, and was very -- he was very sweet, and was very gentle.

And then we -- I -- there was a gardener outside. So, when I noticed the gardener, I pointed it out and we moved to the, into the hallway by the bathroom. And much of the discussion that day was he spent a lot of time talking to me, you know, about the kind of person he thought I was, and -- I'm a little bit modest. So, it's sort of -- it's hard for me to get into all the things he said. But, there just --

Q Did he say wonderful things about you?

A He did.

Q Like what kinds of things?

A Just that he thought I was smart and beautiful, and that -- you know, but that a lot of it, it centered around my needing to learn to, to sort of squelch a bit of the fire in my belly. And that, you know, he said that people like us who, you know, have a tendency to get really angry and that there are a lot of other people that, that, that don't understand that and don't know how to handle that.

And he just -- he spent a lot of time talking to me. He was very, very -- he was the most affectionate with me he'd ever been. There wasn't a second when he wouldn't be

1335

55

touching me, whether it was holding my hand or stroking my arm or, you know, he'd kiss my neck at one point. It was just -- or he'd, you know, put his hands, he was running his hands through my hair and touching my face. And my bra strap kept falling down my shoulder. So, he kept pushing my bra strap up.

It was just very -- it was intense. It was just really emotionally intense.

And at one point, we, we had been talking about -- I made some remarks to him about his relationship with Mrs. Clinton. And he, he remarked a little bit later than that that he wished he had more time for me. And so I said, well, maybe you will have more time in three years. And I was actually sort of thinking just when he wasn't President, he was going to have more time on his hands. And he said, well, I don't know, I might be alone in three years.

And then I said something about, you know, us sort of being together. I think I kind of said, oh, I think we'd be a good team, or something like that. And he, you know, he jokingly said, well, what are we going to do when I'm 75 and I have to pee 25 times a day. And I, you know, I told him that we'd deal with that. And it was -- there was just this incredible connection.

And I, I left that day sort of emotionally stunned, because I felt -- I was shocked. But I thought, I mean, he

1336

was -- I just knew he was in love with me, and from the way he acted that day, and that's not, it's not something that I would, that I would think easily. It's not a conclusion that I would come to easily at all. And it just -- with the kind of person I am.

And I knew I was in love with him, you know, a year before, and I thought he cared about me. But just the way he looked at me and touched me, and the things he said, it just -- it was so obvious to me. And it was shocking. So, it was a bizarre day.

Q Anything else about the 4th?

A Not that I don't think I've gone over before.

Q Okay. We'll switch to a completely different topic. You previously testified that on December 17th --

A You know, I need a --

Q Do you want a break?

A I'd like just a break.

Q Sure, absolutely.

(Whereupon, the deposition was recessed from 1:57 p.m. until 2:07 p.m.)

BY MS. IMMERGUT:

Q Ms. Lewinsky, you are still under oath.

A Yes.

Q We are going to cover some other areas, hopefully quickly. You previously testified that on December 17th, during your phone call with the President -- and that's in 1997 --

A Yes.

Q -- when you were discussing various things, including that your name had appeared on the witness list, that the President told you that if you were ever subpoenaed that you should contact Betty?

A That's correct.

Q Did he ever tell you at that time that you should get a lawyer?

A I don't believe so. No.

Q When you say "I don't believe so", are you quite certain of that?

A I'm, I'm 99.9 percent certain.

Q What would you have done if he had told you that you should get a lawyer?

A I would have started to think about how I was going to get a lawyer and who I should get, and I didn't do that. So, that's what leads me to believe that he didn't say that.

Q Okay. Were you ever under the impression from anything that the President said that you should turn over all the gifts that he had given you to the Paula Jones attorneys?

A No.

Q Did you ever talk to the President about turning

1338

gifts over to the Jones lawyers before you were ever subpoenaed?

A No.

Q Did you actually ever talk to him about the fact that gifts could be subpoenaed prior to them actually being subpoenaed?

A No.

Q So, is it fair to say that the only time you talked about the gifts from the President, in connection with the subpoena, was on December 28th?

A That's correct.

Q Directing your attention to January 5th of 1998, when you had a telephone call with the President, you previously testified that you had some discussion about a book that you had purchased for him?

A Correct.

Q That was the book that you gave to Betty Currie on approximately January 4th to give to the President? Is that right?

A Yes.

Q What was the name of that book again? It was the book on the Presidents.

A It was a book about the Presidents of the United States.

Q Do you remember when you purchased that book?

A I believe it was that weekend, the weekend prior to the 5th.

Q Did you ever talk to him, during your meeting of December 28th, 1997, about the fact that you were going to give him that book?

A No.

Q How do you know that you didn't?

A Because I hadn't purchased the book yet.

Q Had you even thought about purchasing that particular book?

A No. It was bought on the spur of the moment.

Q Do you remember where you bought it?

A At a little bookstore in Georgetown, an antique book store.

Q I'm going to switch topics again. Do you believe that if you hadn't had a sexual relationship with the President that you would have kept your job at the White House?

A Yes.

Q Do you believe that your difficulty or inability to return to employment at the White House was because of your sexual relationship with him?

A Yes. Or the issues that, or the problems that people perceived that really were based in truth because I had a relationship with the President. But, however, some of

1340

the people who worked there chose to, to see some of my behavior. Does that make sense?

Q What do you mean by that?

A I think that -- I've always felt that some of the, some of the staffers there, particularly Evelyn Lieberman and those who worked with her to move me out of the White House, instead -- looked at my behavior only, instead of looking at the President's behavior, and instead of necessarily thinking that I had a relationship with the President, were just looking at it thinking I was trying to have a relationship with the President when I already was having a relationship with him. They turned a blind eye to his actions.

Q During 1997, did you feel that the President owed you something with respect to a job?

A I did, because he, he had promised me on April 7th of '96 that he would bring me back when, if he won in November. And I had -- when he first told me that, I had had some hope and I didn't, I didn't even know if I was going to hear from him again after I left. And then when he continued to call me frequently during the campaign period, it led me to believe he would bring me back.

And then after we had a -- it was after a period when he didn't call me and I wasn't sure about things, what was happening -- I'm sorry. I'm not being clear.

Because he had sort of led me to believe that he

was going to bring me back and was constantly reassuring that, I, I believe that he did owe that to me. Versus him having said, I'm really sorry -- let's just say in April of '96 -- I'm really sorry that this happened, there's not, you know, there's nothing I can do, and left it at that. Then I wouldn't have felt that he owed me anything.

Q What about the fact that you had gone quietly and not revealed your relationship? Did that have anything to do with your feeling that you were entitled to something?

A It did later on. I, I would have gone quietly anyway, because that -- it was never, ever, ever my intention for this relationship to ever become public. And -- but I had felt that after having left quietly, after having been sort of maybe strung along throughout the campaign and then even way into 1997, that I had felt -- and him promising me that he'd bring me back and constantly enumerating the different steps he was trying to take to do that -- that, yes, I did feel at that point he, he certainly owed me.

Q Is that part of your letter of July 3rd to the President in 1997, where you described it previously as threatening to disclose the relationship, at least to your parents, was that part of your feeling that --

A It was never really a, a, maybe a -- it was never really a threat, because I never really was going to do that. While I had disclosed a portion of the relationship to my

1342

mom, I never had any intention of telling my dad. There's nc way of that.

And what I really was trying to do was trying to, in a circuitous manner, remind him that I had been a good girl, and that I hadn't, you know, disclosed this information, and that really, you know, he'd promised me he was going to do something. And I had told my parents, I had told my dad that I was coming back after the election.

Q I'd like to focus now just very briefly on your dealings with Ambassador Richardson with regard to the U.N. job.

A Yes.

Q How many times did Ambassador Richardson call you directly, do you remember?

A Do you mean someone from his -- he never directly picked up the phone and dialed my phone number.

Q Let me ask a different question.

A Okay.

Q How many times did you speak to him personally?

A I believe twice.

Q And when I say personally, on the telephone?

A Yes.

Q How do you know that you actually spoke with him on those occasions?

A Well, the first time I spoke with him I remember,

because I was shocked and I was, I was very nervous. And --

Q Because the Ambassador was on the phone?

A Exactly. And the second, the second time I actually hadn't really remembered, I wasn't sure. And then through documentation I was shown, it, it led me to believe that I had, in fact, spoken to him on the phone.

Q But you are positive at least one time you did, in fact, speak to him personally?

A Yes.

Q Do you remember which occasion that was, or when that occurred?

A Yes, it was sometime in October.

Q Was that the October 23rd call? Does that sound right?

A Yes.

Q And that's prior to your actual interview with him?

A Correct.

Q I'd like to just ask you very briefly about your conversation with the President the night before your interview with Ambassador Richardson for the U.N. job. Could you describe who initiated that call and what the substance of the call was?

A I had -- well, I had requested through Betty that the President call me, because I was really nervous about my interview and meeting with Ambassador Richardson. I just, I

1344

didn't, I didn't want to make anyone look bad. I didn't want to sound like a fool, or -- so, the President called me and we talked about some of the different issues at the U.N., and he gave me some suggestions of things I could say. But I think he may have also done that the previous week, too.

Q Do you remember him giving you sort of a job pep talk on --

A Yes.

Q --the 30th?

A Yes.

Q Why would you describe it as a pep talk?

A Because I was nervous. So, he, he was trying to kind of build my confidence and reassure me, you know, reassure me that I was an intelligent person, and that I had a lot to offer and that they would be happy to have me there.

Q At some point, did you tell the President that you got an offer from the U.N.?

A I believe so.

Q Did you tell Betty also that you had gotten an offer?

A Yes.

Q Do you remember any details about talking to Betty about it, or how you let her know?

A I, I remember calling Betty after the interview and telling her that it had gone much better than I had expected it would, and that I was really, that I was, that I was somewhat more interested after having met the Ambassador than I was prior to the interview. And other than that, I don't really.

Q What about details about your conversation with the President telling him that you had gotten the job?

A I vaguely remember it being in context, I think, of sort of trying to press him on getting in touch with Mr. Jordan.

Q In terms of getting other jobs --

A Exactly.

Q -- you let him know this?

A Exactly.

Q That you had an offer from the U.N.?

A Right.

Q Do you remember when you got the U.N. offer?

A No.

Q Was it sometime, in relation to your interview with the Ambassador --

A It was sooner, rather than later.

Q So, sometime within a matter of a week or --

A I believe so.

Q -- some weeks?

A Somewhere within a couple, within the next two weeks or so.

1346

Q And did they tell you that they would leave the job open until a certain time, for you to make the decision if you wanted it?

A Not at the point when I got the offer. I, I -- and actually I think, thinking now I'm a little bit more clearer that I did speak with the Ambassador, that he was the one who, who extended the offer to me, because I remember being nervous and not knowing what to say to him, because I didn't really want the job. And so I sort of just "yessed" him along and thanked him profusely, and told him I was excited about it.

And then I later spoke, I believe, with Mona Sutphen, and sort of relayed to her that I was interested in also trying to feel out the private sector. So, and I believe it was at that point that she said, well, let's keep in touch. We can -- this position, I think, had been open for awhile. So.

Q Did she give you any timeframe at all about how long they would wait for you to make a decision?

A It was -- I think we talked about talking maybe in a few weeks, and then at some point we said, let's get in touch around the first of January. And I was under the impression that, you know, I believed that they would hold the position open for me, but that it didn't necessarily --

Q It's not a guarantee?

1347

67

A Exactly.

Q But they weren't rushing you to make an immediate decision?

A No.

Q So, you understand you basically had some leeway until January 1998 to make a decision?

A Correct.

Q January 16th, 1998, Ritz Carlton night. I really have just one question about it, which was, was there a time that you, in fact, during the course of the evening, that you, in fact, did leave the prosecutors and agents by yourself?

A Yes, when I was given, finally given permission to go call my mom. I wasn't comfortable using the phone in the room.

Q So, you went out by yourself to --

A Yes, I did.

Q Where did you go make a phone call?

A To Nordstrom's.

Q And --

A It was just one phone call, to my mother. And there was also a time -- I think one of the prosecutors came with me, I think it was Stephen Bin --

Q Binhak?

A -- I think, came downstairs with me. I used -- I

1348

68

needed to return a phone call from a page. And then when I was with Mr. Emmick and Agent [redacted] they let me go to the bathroom in Macy's by myself.

Q Were you in Macy's for some time by yourself?

A Well, it, it took awhile to find a bathroom. It was kind of far away. So.

Q So, they didn't follow you into the bathroom?

A They didn't follow me in. But then when I came back, Agent [redacted] had gone looking for me. So.

Q And just with respect to the phone call to call your mother, no one accompanied you for that, is that right?

A No.

Q And finally --

A I just, I do want to state that I did -- because I know this sort of goes to this issue of being, you know, kind of told, oh, you're free to leave whenever you want, that I didn't really -- I didn't feel at any point that I could leave whenever I wanted, that I could -- that I was afraid that if I had left the Mall, I would be arrested and put in jail. So, that was my impression.

Q One last question from me. Do you, for any reason now, want to hurt the President?

A No. I'm, I'm upset with him right now, but I, no, that's the last thing in the world I want to do.

MS. IMMERGUT: That's all I have.

MS. WIRTH: I just have one question.

BY MS. WIRTH:

Q From your grand jury testimony last week, on August 20th, 1998, you were talking about your understanding of the President's testimony. I'm just going to read a portion of your testimony to you and ask you a question about that. This is in response to a question from a juror.

You said, "I'm sorry. I'm sorry. It's -- from my understanding about what he testified to on Monday, not -- just from the press accounts, is that this was a -- that this was a service contract, that all I did was perform oral sex on him and that that's all that this relationship was. And it was a lot more than that to me and I thought it was a lot more than that."

And the answer continues a little bit more after that.

The question I have for you is that when you mentioned your understanding of what the President testified to on the previous Monday, from what did you derive your understanding of what the President's testimony was?

A From the press accounts I had read.

Q Okay. No one from this office divulged to you anything that the President said during his testimony, did they?

A Absolutely not.

1350

70

MR. WIRTH: Thank you.

MS. IMMERGUT: Nothing further. Do you have any questions?

THE WITNESS: No.

(Whereupon, at 2:24 p.m., the proceedings were concluded.)

* * * * *

CERTIFICATE OF COURT REPORTER - NOTARY PUBLIC

I, Elizabeth A. Eastman, the officer before whom the foregoing deposition was taken, do hereby certify that the witness whose testimony appears in the foregoing deposition was duly sworn by me; that the testimony of said witness was taken by me electronically and thereafter reduced to typewriting by me; that said deposition is a true record of the testimony given by said witness; that I am neither counsel for, related to, nor employed by any of the parties to the action in which this deposition was taken; and, further, that I am not a relative or employee of any attorney or counsel employed by the parties hereto, nor financially or otherwise interested in the outcome of the action.

Elizabeth A. Eastman
NOTARY PUBLIC FOR THE
DISTRICT OF COLUMBIA

My Commission Expires:
July 31, 2000

1375

O.C-302 (Rev. 8-19-94)

- 1 -

OFFICE OF THE INDEPENDENT COUNSEL

Date of transcription 1/23/98

On January 16, 1998, SSA [redacted] and SA [redacted]. approached MONICA LEWINSKY in the food court area of the Pentagon City, Mall Arlington, Virginia. SSA [redacted] immediately identified himself and SA [redacted] as agents of the Federal Bureau of Investigation (FBI), detailed to the Office of the Independent Counsel (OIC) for "Whitewater" and requested her presence in a room of the Ritz Carlton Hotel to discuss her status as a person suspected of committing a federal crime. LEWINSKY was advised OIC attorneys were waiting in the room, and that the agents and the attorneys wished to discuss her culpability in criminal activity related to the PAULA JONES civil lawsuit. LEWINSKY was advised she was not under arrest and the agents would not force her to accompany them to the hotel room. LEWINSKY told SSA [redacted] he could speak to her attorney. SSA [redacted] advised the offer to discuss her legal status was not being offered to her attorney, but to LEWINSKY alone. SSA [redacted] explained to LEWINSKY she was being offered an opportunity to meet with the OIC attorneys and agents and hear them explain why they felt she was in trouble without being required to make any statement. SSA [redacted] further explained LEWINSKY would then have an opportunity to ask clarifying questions of the attorneys and be better informed as to whether she wanted legal counsel before making any statements, or whether she thought it better to cooperate with the OIC. LEWINSKY voluntarily accompanied the agents to room number 1012 of the Ritz Carlton hotel, under the conditions set forth above.

Also present in room 1016, the adjoining room, were Associate Independent Counsel (AIC) BRUCE UDOLF, AIC MICHAEL EMMICK, AIC STEVEN D. BINHAK, Deputy Independent Counsel JACKIE M. BENNETT, JR., AIC STEPHEN BATES and Contract Investigator COY A. COPELAND, all members of the Office of the Independent Counsel staff. At various times during the day, OIC attorneys entered and departed room 1012. Their movement is not recorded herein. The chronology of the meeting, with all times approximate, is as follows:

1:05 p.m. LEWINSKY arrived in Room 1012. AIC EMMICK entered Room 1012 and began talking to LEWINSKY.

1:10 p.m. LEWINSKY given bottled water.

Investigation on 1/16/98 at Pentagon City, VA File # 29D-OIC-LR-35063

by SA [redacted] SSA [redacted] SA [redacted] Date dictated 1/23/98

1376

OIC-302a (Rev. 8-19-94)

29D-LR-35063

Continuation of OIC-302 of Log of meeting at Pentagon City, On 1/16/98, Page 2

1:33 p.m.	SSA [redacted] began reading LEWINSKY her rights as found on the form FD-395, "Interrogation; Advice of Rights." SSA [redacted] was unable to finish reading the FD-395.
1:40 p.m.	LEWINSKY was offered a towel.
1:47 p.m.	LEWINKSY was offered water.
2:02 p.m.	The air conditioning in room 1012 was turned on at LEWINSKY's request.
2:13 p.m.	LEWINKSY was offered water. LEWINSKY said, "if I don't cooperate, I can talk to whomever I want".
2:15 p.m.	SA [redacted] arrived in room 1012.
2:29 p.m.	LEWINSKY stated, "if I leave now, you will charge me now."
2:30 p.m.	LEWINSKY said, "I don't know much about the law."
2:33 p.m.	LEWINSKY asked and was allowed to go to the restroom.
2:36 p.m.	LEWINSKY requested and was given her second bottle of water. LEWINSKY said she is not diabetic and no medication was necessary.
2:50 p.m.	LEWINSKY suggested she take a taxi to her attorney's office. LEWINSKY advised she understands our risks.
3:10 p.m.	LEWINSKY asked if she could be escorted to New York to see her mother, MARCIA LEWIS.
3:20 p.m.	LEWINSKY called her mother, MARCIA LEWIS, in New York.
3:36 p.m.	LEWINSKY requested and was allowed to go to the restroom.

1377

OIC-302a (Rev. 8-1-94)

29D-LR-35063

Continuation of OIC-302 of Log of meeting at Pentagon City, On 1/16/98, Page 3

3:45 p.m.	LEWINSKY departed room 1012 unescorted.
3:54 p.m.	LEWINSKY called room 1012 and advised that she was in the lobby, using a pay phone. LEWINSKY advised she changed phones she was using because some people came too close to the phone she had been using. LEWINSKY advised she called to let the Agents know, in case she was being watched.
4:08 p.m.	LEWINSKY voluntarily returned to room 1012. LEWINSKY offered and accepted coffee.
4:12 p.m.	LEWINSKY called MARCIA LEWIS. LEWIS requested to speak with an OIC attorney. AIC EMMICK and SA [redacted] got on the phone and identified themselves to LEWIS. LEWIS advised she would travel to Washington, DC via AMTRAK Metroliner.
4:20 p.m.	LEWINSKY left room 1012 with AIC BINHAK and SA [redacted] to use a pay phone in the lobby of the Ritz Carlton Hotel.
4:31 p.m.	LEWINSKY, AIC BINHAK and SA [redacted] returned to room 1012.
5:00 p.m.	LEWINSKY called her answering machine to retrieve messages.
5:21 p.m.	LEWINSKY requested and received aspirin.
5:40 p.m.	LEWINSKY, AIC EMMICK and SA [redacted] departed room 1012, en route to the Pentagon City Mall. LEWINSKY, AIC EMMICK and SA [redacted] walked in the mall.
6:03 p.m.	LEWINKSY requested and was permitted to visit the restroom on the third level of the MACY's department store in the mall.
6:30 p.m.	LEWINSKY, AIC EMMICK and SA [redacted] dined at MOZZARELLA'S American Grill, within the Pentagon City Mall. LEWINSKY paid for her portion of the dinner.

1378

OIC-302a (Rev. 8-19-94)

29D-LR-35063

Continuation of OIC-302 of Log of meeting at Pentagon City , On 1/16/98 , Page 4

7:35 p.m. LEWINSKY, AIC EMMICK and SA [redacted] returned to room 1012.

8:00 p.m. LEWINSKY payed $2 to SA [redacted] for the cost of her coffee.

8:19 p.m. MARCIA LEWIS telephoned room 1012, and advised she was on the "163 Northeast Direct", and was experiencing travel delays.

9:05 p.m. LEWINSKY, SSA [redacted], and SA [redacted] departed room 1012 and LEWINSKY withdrew money from the automatic teller machine on the first floor at the Pentagon City Mall.

9:30 p.m. Coffee was ordered and brought to room 1012 by room service.

10:16 p.m. MARCIA LEWIS arrived and all members of the OIC staff left LEWIS and LEWINSKY alone.

10:20 p.m. A meeting was held in room 1018 between LEWIS, AIC EMMICK, SSA [redacted] and SA [redacted].

LEWIS advised that this was an emotional experience for LEWINSKY. LEWIS advised LEWINKSY was younger than her chronological age. LEWIS asked if tapes were admissible in court. LEWIS advised she wanted to protect LEWINSKY. LEWIS asked how she would know LEWINSKY would not be charged if she cooperated. LEWIS asked about LEWINSKY's safety if LEWINSKY cooperated. LEWIS advised that LEWINSKY talked about suicide six years ago. After LEWINSKY's parents divorced, LEWINSKY saw a therapist, but she is not currently seeing one. LEWIS advised she alone could not take responsibility for convincing LEWINSKY to cooperate with the OIC.

11:02 p.m. LEWIS requested and was permitted a trip to the restroom.

11:06 p.m. LEWIS telephonically contacted BERNARD LEWINSKY, her ex-husband, at [redacted]

11:20 p.m. BERNARD LEWINSKY telephoned room 1018.

OIC-302a (Rev. 8-19-94)

29D-LR-35063

Continuation of OIC-302 of Log of meeting at Pentagon City, On 1/16/98, Page 5

11:22 p.m. AIC EMMICK talked to BERNARD LEWINSKY. Cooperation, an interview, telephone calls, body wires and testimony were mentioned. AIC EMMICK advised BERNARD LEWINSKY that MONICA LEWINSKY was free to leave anytime she wished.

11:30 p.m. MONICA LEWINSKY entered room 1018.

11:32 p.m. MARCIA LEWIS got back on the phone with BERNARD LEWINSKY. BERNARD LEWINSKY advised he would go to a pay phone and would call back.

11:35 p.m. BERNARD LEWINSKY telephoned room 1014. BERNARD LEWINSKY advised AIC EMMICK that MONICA LEWINSKY was represented by counsel.

11:36 p.m. MONICA LEWINSKY talked to BERNARD LEWINSKY on the telephone.

11:37 p.m. AIC EMMICK spoke with BERNARD LEWINSKY. AIC EMMICK asked MONICA LEWINKSY if she had an attorney and LEWINSKY advised it was GINSBURG.

AIC EMMICK advised MONICA LEWINSKY she did not have to accept an attorney she did not select.

MONICA LEWINSKY asked if there was still a chance she would go to jail if she cooperated. MONICA LEWINSKY suggested she may have not told the truth in previous conversations. MONICA LEWINSKY asked, "what if I partially cooperate?"

MARCIA LEWIS asked what would happen if MONICA LEWINSKY gave everything but did not tape anything. MONICA LEWINSKY asked if the PAULA JONES case went away would "this" go away and was advised by AIC EMMICK "no."

MONICA LEWINSKY asked how the OIC would resolve the chance that MONICA LEWINSKY said something to LINDA TRIP that was not true.

MARCIA LEWIS advised that she appreciated the OIC

1380

OIC-302a (Rev. 8-19-94)

29D-LR-35063

Continuation of OIC-302 of Log of meeting at Pentagon City . On 1/16/98 . Page 6

members waiting until she arrived to proceed. MONICA LEWINSKY advised she appreciated having her mother present.

11:55 p.m. BILL GINSBURG telephoned room 1018 and spoke to AIC EMMICK, who advised GINSBURG he was uncomfortable with the relationship between GINSBURG and MONICA LEWINSKY. MONICA LEWINSKY advised she was not 100% sure it was the right thing to do because GINSBURG was a medical lawyer.

11:59 p.m. MONICA LEWINSKY advised she was represented by GINSBURG.

12:08 a.m. GINSBURG was advised by AIC EMMICK that MONICA LEWINSKY always had the right to leave at any time.

12:17 a.m. MONICA LEWINSKY spoke with GINSBURG, outside the presence of the OIC staff.

12:23 a.m. AIC EMMICK ended the phone call with GINSBURG and advised MONICA LEWINSKY and MARCIA LEWIS they were free to leave.

12:30 a.m. MARCIA LEWIS and MONICA LEWINSKY thanked the Agents and the staff of the OIC for being so kind and considerate.

12:45 a.m. SA [redacted] and SA [redacted] escorted MARCIA LEWIS and MONICA LEWINSKY to LEWINSKY's vehicle, which was parked in the parking garage adjacent to the Pentagon City Mall.

The Clinton File

393

Paula Jones v. William Jefferson Clinton and Danny Ferguson
No. LR-C-94-290 (E.D. Ark.)

DEPOSITION OF WILLIAM JEFFERSON CLINTON

Definition of Sexual Relations

For the purposes of this deposition, a person engages in "sexual relations" when the person knowingly engages in or causes -

(1) contact with the genitalia, anus, groin, breast, inner thigh, or buttocks of any person with an intent to arouse or gratify the sexual desire of any person;

(2) contact between any part of the person's body or an object and the genitals or anus of another person; or

(3) contact between the genitals or anus of the person and any part of another person's body.

"Contact" means intentional touching, either directly or through clothing.

849-DC-00000586

STATEMENT

When I was alone with Ms. Lewinsky on certain occasions in early 1996 and once in early 1997, I engaged in conduct that was wrong. These encounters did not consist of sexual intercourse; they did not constitute "sexual relations" as I understood that term to be defined at my January 17, 1998, deposition; but they did involve inappropriate intimate contact. These inappropriate encounters ended, at my insistence, in early 1997. I also had occasional telephone conversations with Ms. Lewinsky that included inappropriate sexual banter.

I regret that what began as a friendship came to include this conduct. I take full responsibility for my actions.

While I will provide the grand jury whatever other information I can, because of privacy considerations affecting my family, myself, and others, and in an effort to preserve the dignity of the Office I hold, this is all I will say about the specifics of these particular matters. I will try to answer to the best of my ability other questions, including questions about my relationship with Ms. Lewinsky, questions about my understanding of the term "sexual relations" as I understood that term to be defined at my January 17, 1998, deposition, and questions concerning alleged subornation of perjury, obstruction of justice, and intimidation of witnesses.

453

OFFICE OF THE INDEPENDENT COUNSEL

TESTIMONY OF	:	Monday, August 17, 1998
WILLIAM JEFFERSON CLINTON	:	Washington, D. C.

Videotaped testimony of

PRESIDENT WILLIAM JEFFERSON CLINTON

before the Independent Counsel, held at The White House, Washington, D. C., beginning at 1:03 p.m., when were present on behalf of the respective parties:

FOR THE INDEPENDENT COUNSEL:	KENNETH W. STARR, ESQ. Independent Counsel
	JACKIE M. BENNETT, JR., ESQ. ROBERT J. BITTMAN, ESQ. SOLOMON L. WISENBERG, ESQ. Deputy Independent Counsel
	MICHAEL W. EMMICK, ESQ. MARY ANNE WIRTH, ESQ. BERNARD JAMES APPERSON, ESQ. Associate Independent Counsel
FOR THE PRESIDENT:	DAVID E. KENDALL, ESQ. NICOLE SELIGMAN, ESQ. Williams & Connolly
	CHARLES F. C. RUFF, ESQ. Counsel to the President
ALSO PRESENT:	JAMES P. RICKARDS, JR. Senior Consultant, OIC
	GARY E. BRESNAHAN White House Technical Staff
	Secret Service Agent
Court Reporter:	Elizabeth A. Eastman

454

2

PROCEEDINGS

MR. APPERSON: Mr. Wisenberg, the grand jury is in session. There is a quorum. There are no unauthorized persons in the grand jury room and they are prepared to receive the testimony of the President.

MR. WISENBERG: Thank you, Mr. Apperson. If we could proceed with the oath, please?

WHEREUPON,

WILLIAM JEFFERSON CLINTON

having been called for examination by the Independent Counsel, and having been first duly sworn, was examined and testified as follows:

EXAMINATION BY THE INDEPENDENT COUNSEL

BY MR. WISENBERG:

Q Good afternoon, Mr. President.

A Good afternoon.

Q Could you please state your full name for the record, sir?

A William Jefferson Clinton.

Q My name is Sol Wisenberg and I'm a Deputy Independent Counsel with the Office of Independent Counsel. With me today are some other attorneys from the Office of Independent Counsel.

At the courtroom are the ladies and gentlemen of the grand jury prepared to receive your testimony as you give it. Do you understand, sir?

A Yes, I do.

Q This proceeding is subject to Rule 6(e) of the Federal Rules of Criminal Procedure as modified by Judge Johnson's order. You are appearing voluntarily today as a part of an agreement worked out between your attorney, the Office of the Independent Counsel, and with the approval of Judge Johnson.

Is that correct, sir?

A That is correct.

MR. KENDALL: Mr. Wisenberg, excuse me. You referred to Judge Johnson's order. I'm not familiar with that order. Have we been served that, or not?

MR. WISENBERG: No. My understanding is that that is an order that the Judge is going to sign today. She didn't have the name of a WHCA person. And basically my understanding is that it will cover all of the attorneys here today and the technical people in the room, so that they will be authorized persons permitted to hear grand jury testimony that they otherwise wouldn't be authorize to hear.

MR. KENDALL: Thank you.

BY MR. WISENBERG:

Q The grand jury, Mr. President, has been empaneled by the United States District Court for the District of Columbia. Do you understand that, sir?

456

4

A I do.

Q And, among other things, is currently investigating under the authority of the Court of Appeals upon application by the Attorney General, whether Monica Lewinsky or others obstructed justice, intimidated witnesses, or committed other crimes related to the case of Jones v. Clinton.

Do you understand that, sir?

A I do.

Q And today, you will be receiving questions not only from attorneys on the OIC staff, but from some of the grand jurors, too. Do you understand that?

A Yes, sir, I do.

Q I'm going to talk briefly about your rights and responsibilities as a grand jury witness. Normally, grand jury witnesses, while not allowed to have attorneys in the grand jury room with them, can stop and consult with their attorneys. Under our arrangement today, your attorneys are here and present for consultation and you can break to consult with them as necessary, but it won't count against our total time.

Do you understand that, sir?

A I do understand that.

Q You have a privilege against self-incrimination. If a truthful answer to any question would tend to incriminate you, you can invoke the privilege and that invocation will not be used against you. Do you understand that?

A I do.

Q And if you don't invoke it, however, any answer that you do give can and will be used against you. Do you understand that, sir?

A I do.

Q Mr. President, you understand that your testimony here today is under oath?

A I do.

Q And do you understand that because you have sworn to tell the truth, the whole truth, and nothing but the truth, that if you were to lie or intentionally mislead the grand jury, you could be prosecuted for perjury and/or obstruction of justice?

A I believe that's correct.

Q Is there anything that you -- I've stated to you regarding your rights and responsibilities that you would like me to clarify or that you don't understand?

A No, sir.

Q Mr. President, I would like to read for you a portion of Federal Rule of Evidence 603, which discusses the important function the oath has in our judicial system.

It says that the purpose of the oath is one, "calculated to awaken the witness' conscience and impress the witness' mind with the duty" to tell the truth.

Could you please tell the grand jury what that oath means to you for today's testimony?

A I have sworn an oath to tell the grand jury the truth, and that's what I intend to do.

Q You understand that it requires you to give the whole truth, that is, a complete answer to each question, sir?

A I will answer each question as accurately and fully as I can.

Q Now, you took the same oath to tell the truth, the whole truth, and nothing but the truth on January 17th, 1998 in a deposition in the Paula Jones litigation; is that correct, sir?

A I did take an oath then.

Q Did the oath you took on that occasion mean the same to you then as it does today?

A I believed then that I had to answer the questions truthfully, that is correct.

Q I'm sorry. I didn't hear you, sir.

A I believed that I had to answer the questions truthfully. That's correct.

Q And it meant the same to you then as it does today?

A Well, no one read me a definition then and we didn't go through this exercise then. I swore an oath to

459

7

tell the truth, and I believed I was bound to be truthful and I tried to be.

Q At the Paula Jones deposition, you were represented by Mr. Robert Bennett, your counsel, is that correct?

A That is correct.

Q He was authorized by you to be your representative there, your attorney, is that correct?

A That is correct.

Q Your counsel, Mr. Bennett, indicated at page 5 of the deposition, lines 10 through 12, and I'm quoting, "the President intends to give full and complete answers as Ms. Jones is entitled to have".

My question to you is, do you agree with your counsel that a plaintiff in a sexual harassment case is, to use his words, entitled to have the truth?

A I believe that I was bound to give truthful answers, yes, sir.

Q But the question is, sir, do you agree with your counsel that a plaintiff in a sexual harassment case is entitled to have the truth?

A I believe when a witness is under oath in a civil case, or otherwise under oath, the witness should do everything possible to answer the questions truthfully.

MR. WISENBERG: I'm going to turn over questioning now to Mr. Bittman of our office, Mr. President.

460

8

BY MR. BITTMAN:

Q Good afternoon, Mr. President.

A Good afternoon, Mr. Bittman.

Q My name is Robert Bittman. I'm an attorney with the Office of Independent Counsel.

Mr. President, we are first going to turn to some of the details of your relationship with Monica Lewinsky that follow up on your deposition that you provided in the Paula Jones case, as was referenced, on January 17th, 1998.

The questions are uncomfortable, and I apologize for that in advance. I will try to be as brief and direct as possible.

Mr. President, were you physically intimate with Monica Lewinsky?

A Mr. Bittman, I think maybe I can save the -- you and the grand jurors a lot of time if I read a statement, which I think will make it clear what the nature of my relationship with Ms. Lewinsky was and how it related to the testimony I gave, what I was trying to do in that testimony. And I think it will perhaps make it possible for you to ask even more relevant questions from your point of view.

And, with your permission, I'd like to read that statement.

Q Absolutely. Please, Mr. President.

A When I was alone with Ms. Lewinsky on certain

461

9

occasions in early 1996 and once in early 1997, I engaged in conduct that was wrong. These encounters did not consist of sexual intercourse. They did not constitute sexual relations as I understood that term to be defined at my January 17th, 1998 deposition. But they did involve inappropriate intimate contact.

These inappropriate encounters ended, at my insistence, in early 1997. I also had occasional telephone conversations with Ms. Lewinsky that included inappropriate sexual banter.

I regret that what began as a friendship came to include this conduct, and I take full responsibility for my actions.

While I will provide the grand jury whatever other information I can, because of privacy considerations affecting my family, myself, and others, and in an effort to preserve the dignity of the office I hold, this is all I will say about the specifics of these particular matters.

I will try to answer, to the best of my ability, other questions including questions about my relationship with Ms. Lewinsky; questions about my understanding of the term "sexual relations", as I understood it to be defined at my January 17th, 1998 deposition; and questions concerning alleged subornation of perjury, obstruction of justice, and intimidation of witnesses.

462

10

That, Mr. Bittman, is my statement.

Q Thank you, Mr. President. And, with that, we would like to take a break.

A Would you like to have this?

Q Yes, please. As a matter of fact, why don't we have that marked as Grand Jury Exhibit WJC-1.

(Grand Jury Exhibit WJC-1 was marked for identification.)

THE WITNESS: So, are we going to take a break?

MR. KENDALL: Yes. We will take a break. Can we have the camera off, now, please? And it's 1:14.

(Whereupon, the proceedings were recessed from 1:14 p.m. until 1:30 p.m.)

MR. KENDALL: 1:30, Bob.

MR. BITTMAN: It's 1:30 and we have the feed with the grand jury.

BY MR. BITTMAN:

Q Good afternoon again, Mr. President.

A Good afternoon, Mr. Bittman.

(Discussion off the record.)

BY MR. BITTMAN:

Q Mr. President, your statement indicates that your contacts with Ms. Lewinsky did not involve any inappropriate, intimate contact.

MR. KENDALL: Mr. Bittman, excuse me. The

witness --

THE WITNESS: No, sir. It indicates --

MR. KENDALL: The witness does not have --

THE WITNESS: -- that it did involve inappropriate and intimate contact.

BY MR. BITTMAN:

Q Pardon me. That it did involve inappropriate, intimate contact.

A Yes, sir, it did.

MR. KENDALL: Mr. Bittman, the witness -- the witness does not have a copy of the statement. We just have the one copy.

MR. BITTMAN: If he wishes --

MR. KENDALL: Thank you.

MR. BITTMAN: -- his statement back?

BY MR. BITTMAN:

Q Was this contact with Ms. Lewinsky, Mr. President, did it involve any sexual contact in any way, shape, or form?

A Mr. Bittman, I said in this statement I would like to stay to the terms of the statement. I think it's clear what inappropriately intimate is. I have said what it did not include. I -- it did not include sexual intercourse, and I do not believe it included conduct which falls within the definition I was given in the Jones deposition. And I would like to stay with that characterization.

464

Q Let us then move to the definition that was provided you during your deposition. We will have that marked as Grand Jury Exhibit WJC-2.

(Grand Jury Exhibit WJC-2 was marked for identification.)

BY MR. BITTMAN:

Q This is an exact copy, Mr. President, of the exhibit that was provided you during that deposition. And I'm sure you remember from the deposition that paragraph (1) of the definition remained in effect. Judge Wright ruled that that was to be the guiding definition, and that paragraphs (2) and (3) were stricken.

Do you remember that, Mr. President?

A Yes. Specifically what I remember is there were two different discussions, I think, of this. There was quite an extended one in the beginning, and everybody was entering into it. And in the end, the Judge said that she would take the first definition and strike the rest of it. That's my memory.

Q Did you -- well, at page 19 of your deposition in that case, the attorney who provided you with the definition asked you, "Would you please take whatever time you need to read this definition". And later on in the deposition, you did, of course, refer to the definition several times.

Were you, during the deposition, familiar with the

definition?

A Yes, sir. My -- let me just ask a question. If you are going to ask me about my deposition, could I have a copy of it? Does anybody have a copy of it?

Q Yes. We have a copy. We'll provide you with a copy.

MS. WIRTH: We will mark it as Grand Jury Exhibit WJC-3.

(Grand Jury Exhibit WJC-3 was marked for identification.)

THE WITNESS: Now, did you say that was on page 19, Mr. Bittman?

BY MR. BITTMAN:

Q It was at page 19, Mr. President, beginning at line 21, and I'll read it in full. This is from the Jones attorney. "Would you please take whatever time you need to read this definition, because when I use the term 'sexual relations', this is what I mean today."

A All right. Yes, that starts on 19. But let me say that there is a -- just for the record, my recollection was accurate. There is a long discussion here between the attorney and the Judge. It goes on until page 23. And in the end the Judge says, "I'm talking only about part one in the definition", and "Do you understand that"? And I answer, "I do."

466

14

The judge says part one, and then the lawyer for Ms. Jones says he's only talking about part one and asked me if I understand it. And I say, I do, and that was my understanding.

I might also note that when I was given this and began to ask questions about it, I actually circled number one. This is my circle here. I remember doing that so I could focus only on those two lines, which is what I did.

Q Did you understand the words in the first portion of the exhibit, Mr. President, that is, "For the purposes of this deposition, a person engages in 'sexual relations' when the person knowingly engages in or causes"?

Did you understand, do you understand the words there in that phrase?

A Yes. My -- I can tell you what my understanding of the definition is, if you want me to --

Q Sure.

A -- do it. My understanding of this definition is it covers contact by the person being deposed with the enumerated areas, if the contact is done with an intent to arouse or gratify. That's my understanding of the definition.

Q What did you believe the definition to include and exclude? What kinds of activities?

A I thought the definition included any activity by

the person being deposed, where the person was the actor and came in contact with those parts of the bodies with the purpose or intent or gratification, and excluded any other activity.

For example, kissing is not covered by that, I don't think.

Q Did you understand the definition to be limited to sexual activity?

A Yes, I understood the definition to be limited to, to physical contact with those areas of the bodies with the specific intent to arouse or gratify. That's what I understood it to be.

Q What specific acts did the definition include, as you understood the definition on January 17, 1998?

A Any contact with the areas there mentioned, sir. If you contacted, if you contacted those parts of the body with an intent to arouse or gratify, that is covered.

Q What did you understand --

A The person being deposed. If the person being deposed contacted those parts of another person's body with an intent to arouse or gratify, that was covered.

Q What did you understand the word "causes", in the first phrase? That is, "For the purposes of this deposition, a person engaged in 'sexual relations' when the person knowingly" causes contact?

468

16

A I don't know what that means. It doesn't make any sense to me in this context, because -- I think what I thought there was, since this was some sort of -- as I remember, they said in the previous discussion -- and I'm only remembering now, so if I make a mistake you can correct me. As I remember from the previous discussion, this was some kind of definition that had something to do with sexual harassment. So, that implies it's forcing to me, and I -- and there was never any issue of forcing in the case involving, well, any of these questions they were asking me.

They made it clear in this discussion I just reviewed that what they were referring to was intentional sexual conduct, not some sort of forcible abusive behavior.

So, I basically -- I don't think I paid any attention to it because it appeared to me that that was something that had no reference to the facts that they admitted they were asking me about.

Q So, if I can be clear, Mr. President, was it your understanding back in January that the definition, now marked as Grand Jury Exhibit 2, only included consensual sexual activity?

A No. My understanding -- let me go back and say it. My understanding -- I'll tell you what it did include. My understanding was, what I was giving to you, was that what was covered in those first two lines was any direct contact by the person being deposed with those parts of another person's body, if the contact was done with an intent to arouse or gratify. That's what I believed it meant.

That's what I believed it meant then reading it. That's what I believe it means today.

Q I'm just trying to understand, Mr. President. You indicated that you put the definition in the context of a sexual harassment case.

A No, no. I think it was not in the context of sexual harassment. I just reread those four pages, which obviously the grand jury doesn't have. But there was some reference to the fact that this definition apparently bore some, had some connection to some definition in another context, and that this was being used not in that context, not necessarily in the context of sexual harassment.

So, I would think that this "causes" would be, would mean to force someone to do something. That's what I read it. That's the only point I'm trying to make.

Therefore, I did not believe that anyone had ever suggested that I had forced anyone to do anything, and that I -- and I did not do that. And so that could not have had any bearing on any questions related to Ms. Lewinsky.

Q I suppose, since you have now read portions of the transcript again, that you were reminded that you did not ask for any clarification of the terms. Is that correct? Of the definition?

A No, sir. I thought it was a rather -- when I read it, I thought it was a rather strange definition. But it was the one the Judge decided on and I was bound by it. So, I took it.

Q During the deposition, you remember that Ms. Lewinsky's name came up and you were asked several questions about her. Do you remember that?

A Yes, sir, I do.

Q During those -- or before those questions actually got started, your attorney, Mr. Bennett, objected to any questions about Ms. Lewinsky, and he represented to Judge Wright, who was presiding -- that was unusual, wasn't it, that a federal judge would come and actually -- in your experience -- that a federal judge would come and preside at a deposition?

MR. KENDALL: Mr. Bittman, excuse me. Could you identify the transcript page upon which Mr. Bennett objected to all testimony about Ms. Lewinsky before it got started?

MR. BITTMAN: The objection, this quote that I'm referring to, is going to begin at page 54 of the deposition.

MR. KENDALL: That is into the testimony though, after the testimony about Ms. Lewinsky has begun, is it not?

BY MR. BITTMAN:

Q Mr. President, is it unusual for a federal judge to

preside over a civil deposition?

A I think it is, but this was an unusual case. I believe I know why she did it.

Q Your attorney, Mr. Bennett, objected to the questions about Ms. Lewinsky, didn't he?

A What page is that on, sir?

Q Page 54, where he questions whether the attorneys for Ms. Jones had a good faith basis to ask some of the questions that they were posing to you. His objections actually begin on page 53.

Since, as the President pointed out that the grand jurors correctly do not have a copy of the deposition, I will read the portion that I am referring to. And this begins at line 1 on page 54.

"I question the good faith of counsel, the innuendo in the question. Counsel is fully aware that Ms. Lewinsky has filed, has an affidavit which they are in possession of saying that there is absolutely no sex of any kind in any manner, shape or form, with President Clinton".

A Where is that?

Q That is on page 54, Mr. President, beginning at line 1, about midway through line 1.

A Well, actually, in the present tense that is an accurate statement. That was an, that was an accurate statement, if -- I don't -- I think what Mr. Bennett was concerned about, if I -- maybe it would be helpful to you and to the grand jurors, quite apart from these comments, if I could tell you what his state of mind was, what my state of mind was, and why I think the Judge was there in the first place.

If you don't want me to do it, I won't. But I think it will help to explain a lot of this.

Q Well, we are interested, and I know from the questions that we've received from the grand jurors they are interested in knowing what was going on in your mind when you were reading Grand Jury Exhibit 2, and what you understood that definition to include.

Our question goes to whether -- and you were familiar, and what Mr. Bennett was referring to obviously is Ms. Lewinsky's affidavit. And we will have that marked, Mr. President, as Grand Jury Exhibit WJC-4.

(Grand Jury Exhibit WJC-4 was marked for identification.)

BY MR. BITTMAN:

Q And you remember that Ms. Lewinsky's affidavit said that she had had no sexual relationship with you. Do you remember that?

A I do.

Q And do you remember in the deposition that Mr. Bennett asked you about that. This is at the end of the --

towards the end of the deposition. And you indicated, he asked you whether the statement that Ms. Lewinsky made in her affidavit was --

A Truthful.

Q -- true. And you indicated that it was absolutely correct.

A I did. And at the time that she made the statement, and indeed to the present day because, as far as I know, she was never deposed since the Judge ruled she would not be permitted to testify in a case the Judge ruled had no merit; that is, this case we're talking about.

I believe at the time that she filled out this affidavit, if she believed that the definition of sexual relationship was two people having intercourse, then this is accurate. And I believe that is the definition that most ordinary Americans would give it.

If you said Jane and Harry have a sexual relationship, and you're not talking about people being drawn into a lawsuit and being given definitions, and then a great effort to trick them in some way, but you are just talking about people in ordinary conversations, I'll bet the grand jurors, if they were talking about two people they know, and said they have a sexual relationship, they meant they were sleeping together; they meant they were having intercourse together.

474

So, I'm not at all sure that this affidavit is not true and was not true in Ms. Lewinsky's mind at the time she swore it out.

Q Did you talk with Ms. Lewinsky about what she meant to write in her affidavit?

A I didn't talk to her about her definition. I did not know what was in this affidavit before it was filled out specifically. I did not know what words were used specifically before it was filled out, or what meaning she gave to them.

But I'm just telling you that it's certainly true what she says here, that we didn't have -- there was no employment, no benefit in exchange, there was nothing having anything to do with sexual harassment. And if she defined sexual relationship in the way I think most Americans do, meaning intercourse, then she told the truth.

Q My question --

A And that depends on what was in her mind. I don't know what was in her mind. You'll have to ask her that.

Q But you indicated before that you were aware of what she intended by the term "sexual relationship".

A No, sir. I said I thought that this could be a truthful affidavit. And when I read it, since that's the way I would define it, since -- keep in mind, she was not, she was not bound by this sexual relations definition, which is highly unusual; I think anybody would admit that. When she used a different term, sexual relationship, if she meant by that what most people mean by it, then that is not an untruthful statement.

Q So, your definition of sexual relationship is intercourse only, is that correct?

A No, not necessarily intercourse only. But it would include intercourse. I believe, I believe that the common understanding of the term, if you say two people are having a sexual relationship, most people believe that includes intercourse. So, if that's what Ms. Lewinsky thought, then this is a truthful affidavit. I don't know what was in her mind. But if that's what she thought, the affidavit is true.

Q What else would sexual relationship include besides intercourse?

A Well, that -- I think -- let me answer what I said before. I think most people when they use that term include sexual relationships and whatever other sexual contact is involved in a particular relationship. But they think it includes intercourse as well. And I would have thought so. Before I got into this case and heard all I've heard, and seen all I've seen, I would have thought that that's what nearly everybody thought it meant.

Q Well, I ask, Mr. President, because your attorney, using the very document, Grand Jury Exhibit 4, WJC-4,

476

24

represented to Judge Wright that his understanding of the meaning of that affidavit, which you've indicated you thought Ms. Lewinsky thought was, she was referring just to intercourse, he says to Judge Wright that it meant absolutely no sex of any kind in any manner, shape or form.

A Well, let me say this. I didn't have any discussion obviously at this moment with Mr. Bennett. I'm not even sure I paid much attention to what he was saying. I was thinking, I was ready to get on with my testimony here and they were having these constant discussions all through the deposition. But that statement in the present tense, at least, is not inaccurate, if that's what Mr. Bennett meant. That is, at the time that he said that, and for some time before, that would be a completely accurate statement.

Now, I don't believe that he was -- I don't know what he meant. You'd have to talk to him, because I just wasn't involved in this, and I didn't pay much attention to what was being said. I was just waiting for them to get back to me. So, I can't comment on, or be held responsible for, whatever he said about that, I don't think.

Q Well, if you -- do you agree with me that if he mislead Judge Wright in some way that you would have corrected the record and said, excuse me, Mr. Bennett, I think the Judge is getting a misimpression by what you're saying?

477

25

A Mr. Bennett was representing me. I wasn't representing him. And I wasn't even paying much attention to this conversation, which is why, when you started asking me about this, I asked to see the deposition. I was focusing on my answers to the questions. And I've told you what I believe about this deposition, which I believe to be true.

And it's obvious, and I think by your questions you have betrayed that the Jones lawyers' strategy in this case had nothing to do with uncovering or proving sexual harassment.

By the time this discovery started, they knew they had a bad case on the law and they knew what our evidence was. They knew they had a lousy case on the facts. And so their strategy, since they were being funded by my political opponents, was to have this dragnet of discovery. They wanted to cover everybody. And they convinced the Judge, because she gave them strict orders not to leak, that they should be treated like other plaintiffs in other civil cases, and how could they ever know whether there had been any sexual harassment, unless they first knew whether there had been any sex.

And so, with that broad mandate limited by time and employment in the federal or state government, they proceeded to cross the country and try to turn up whatever they could; not because they thought it would help their case. By the time they did this discovery, they knew what this deal was in their case, and they knew what was going to happen. And Judge Wright subsequently threw it out. What they --

Q With all respect, Mister --

A Now, let me finish, Mr. Bennett [sic]. I mean, you brought this up. Excuse me, Mr. Bittman.

What they wanted to do, and what they did do, and what they had done by the time I showed up here, was to find any negative information they could on me, whether it was true or not; get it in a deposition; and then leak it, even though it was illegal to do so. It happened repeatedly. The Judge gave them orders.

One of the reasons she was sitting in that deposition was because she was trying to make sure that it didn't get out of hand.

But that was their strategy, and they did a good job of it, and they got away with it. I've been subject to quite a lot of illegal leaking, and they had a very determined deliberate strategy, because their real goal was to hurt me. When they knew they couldn't win the lawsuit, they thought, well, maybe we can pummel him. Maybe they thought I'd settle. Maybe they just thought they would get some political advantage out of it. But that's what was going on here.

Now, I'm trying to be honest with you, and it hurts

479

27

me. And I'm trying to tell you the truth about what happened between Ms. Lewinsky and me. But that does not change the fact that the real reason they were zeroing in on anybody was to try to get any person in there, no matter how uninvolved with Paula Jones, no matter how uninvolved with sexual harassment, so they could hurt me politically. That's what was going on.

Because by then, by this time, this thing had been going on a long time. They knew what our evidence was. They knew what the law was in the circuit in which we were bringing this case. And so they just thought they would take a wrecking ball to me and see if they could do some damage.

Q Judge Wright had ruled that the attorneys in the Jones case were permitted to ask you certain questions, didn't she?

A She certainly did. And they asked them and I did my best to answer them. I'm just trying to tell --

Q And was it your responsibility --

A -- you what my state of mind was.

Q -- to answer those questions truthfully, Mr. President?

A It was.

Q And was --

A But it was not my responsibility, in the face of their repeated illegal leaking, it was not my responsibility to volunteer a lot of information. There are many cases in this deposition where I gave -- and keep in mind, I prepared, I treated them, frankly, with respect. I prepared very well for this deposition on the Jones matters. I prepared very well on that. I did not know that Linda Tripp had been involved in the preparation of this deposition, or that all of you --

Q Do you know that now?

A No, I don't. I just know that -- what I read in the papers about it. But I had no way of knowing that they would ask me all these detailed questions. I did the best I could to answer them.

Q Did you prepare --

A But in this deposition, Mr. Bittman, I was doing my best to be truthful. I was not trying to be particularly helpful to them, and I didn't think I had an obligation to be particularly helpful to them to further a -- when I knew that there was no evidence here of sexual harassment, and I knew what they wanted to do was to leak this, even though it was unlawful to do so. That's --

Q Did you believe, Mr. President --

A -- what I knew.

Q -- that you had an obligation to make sure that the presiding federal judge was on board and had the correct facts? Did you believe that was your obligation?

481

29

A Sir, I was trying to answer my testimony. I was thinking about my testimony. I don't believe I ever even focused on what Mr. Bennett said in the exact words he did until I started reading this transcript carefully for this hearing. That moment, that whole argument just passed me by. I was a witness. I was trying to focus on what I said and how I said it.

And, believe me, I knew what the purpose of the deposition was. And, sure enough, by the way, it did all leak, just like I knew it would.

Q Let me ask you, Mr. President, you indicate in your statement that you were alone with Ms. Lewinsky. Is that right?

A Yes, sir.

Q How many times were you alone with Ms. Lewinsky?

A Let me begin with the correct answer. I don't know for sure. But if you would like me to give an educated guess, I will do that, but I do not know for sure. And I will tell you what I think, based on what I remember. But I can't be held to a specific time, because I don't have records of all of it.

Q How many times do you think?

A Well, there are two different periods here. There's the period when she worked in the White House until April of '96. And then there's the period when she came back

482

30

to visit me from February '97 until late December '97.

Based on our records -- let's start with the records, where we have the best records and the closest in time. Based on our records, between February and December, it appears to me that at least I could have seen her approximately nine times. Although I do not believe I saw her quite that many times, at least it could have happened.

There were -- we think there were nine or 10 times when she was in, in the White House when I was in the Oval Office when I could have seen her. I do not believe I saw her that many times, but I could have.

Now, we have no records for the time when she was an employee at the White House, because we have no records of that for any of the employees at the White House, unless there was some formally scheduled meeting that was on the, on the calendar for the day.

I remember -- I'll tell you what I remember. I remember meeting her, or having my first real conversation with her during the government shutdown in November of '95, when she -- as I explained in my deposition, during the government shutdown, the -- most federal employees were actually prohibited from coming to work, even in the White House. Most people in the White House couldn't come to work. The Chief of Staff could come to work. My National Security Advisor could come to work. I could.

Therefore, interns were assigned to all offices. And I believe it was her last week as an intern. Anyway, she worked in the Chief of Staff's Office. One night she brought me some pizza. We had some remarks.

Now, the next time I remember seeing her alone was on a couple of occasions when she was working in the Legislative Affairs Office as a full-time employee. I remember specifically, I have a specific recollection of two times. I don't remember when they were, but I remember twice when, on Sunday afternoon, she brought papers down to me, stayed, and we were alone.

And I am frankly quite sure -- although I have no specific memory, I am quite sure there were a couple of more times, probably two times more, three times more. That's what I would say. That's what I can remember. But I do not remember when they were, or at what time of day they were, or what the facts were. But I have a general memory that would say I certainly saw her more than twice during that period between January and April of 1996, when she worked there.

Q So, if I could summarize your testimony, approximately five times you saw her before she left the White House, and approximately nine times after she left the employment of the White House?

A I know there were several times in '97. I've told you that I've looked at my calendar and I tell you what I

484

32

think the outer limits are. I would think that would sound about right. There could be, in that first four-month period, there, maybe there's one or two more, maybe there's one less. I just don't know. I don't remember. I didn't keep records.

But I'm giving you what I specifically remember and then what I generally remember. I'm doing the best to be helpful to you.

Q Have you reviewed the records for December 28th, 1997, Mr. President?

A Yes, sir, I have.

Q Do you believe that Ms. Lewinsky was at the White House and saw you on December 28th, 1997?

A Yes, sir, I do.

Q And do you remember talking with Ms. Lewinsky about her subpoena that she received for the Paula Jones case on that day?

A I remember talking with Ms. Lewinsky about her testimony, or about the prospect that she might have to give testimony. And she, she talked to me about that. I remember that.

Q And you also gave her Christmas gifts, is that not correct, Mr. President?

A That is correct. They were Christmas gifts and they were going-away gifts. She was moving to New York to, taking a new job, starting a new life. And I gave her some gifts.

Q And you actually requested this meeting, is that not correct?

A I don't remember that, Mr. Bittman, but it's quite possible that I invited her to come by before she left town. But usually when we met, she requested the meetings. And my recollection is, in 1997 she asked to meet with me several times when I could not meet with her and did not do so. But it's quite possible that I -- that because she had given me a Christmas gift, and because she was leaving, that I invited her to come by the White House and get a couple of gifts before she left town.

I don't remember who requested the meeting though. I'm sorry, I don't.

Q You were alone with her on December 28, 1997, is that --

A Yes, sir.

Q -- right?

A I was.

Q The gifts that you gave her were a canvas bag from The Black Dog restaurant at Martha's Vineyard, is that right?

A Well, that was just, that was just something I had in the place to, to contain the gifts. But I believe that the gifts I gave her were -- I put them in that bag. That's what I had there, and I knew she liked things from The Black Dog. So, I gave her -- I think that's what I put the presents in.

I remember what the presents were. I don't remember what the bag was I gave them in.

Q Did you also give her a marble bear's head carving from Vancouver, Canada?

A I did do that. I remember that.

Q And you also gave her a Rockettes blanket; that is, the famous Rockettes from New York?

A I did do that. I had that, I had had that in my possession for a couple of years but had never used it, and she was going to New York. So, I thought it would be a nice thing to give her.

Q You gave her a box of cherry chocolates, is that right?

A I don't remember that, sir. I mean, there could have been. I, I just don't remember. I remember giving the bear and the throw. I don't remember what else. And it seems to me like there was one other thing in that bag. I didn't remember the cherry chocolates.

Q How about a pin of the New York skyline? Did you give --

A That --

487

35

Q -- her that?

A That could have been in there. I seem to remember I gave her some kind of pin.

Q What about a pair of joke sunglasses?

A I don't remember that. I'm not denying it. I just -- I'm telling you what I remember and what I don't.

Q You had given Ms. Lewinsky gifts on other occasions though, is that right, Mr. President?

A Yes, I had.

Q This, though, was -- you gave her the most gifts that you had ever given her in a single day, is that right?

A Well, that's probably true. It was sort of like a going-away present and a Christmas present as well. And she had given me a particularly nice book for Christmas, an antique book on Presidents. She knew that I collected old books and it was a very nice thing. And I just thought I ought to get up a few things and give them to her before she left.

Q You mentioned that you discussed her subpoena in the Paula Jones case. Tell us specifically, what did you discuss?

A No, sir, that's not what I said. I said, my recollection is I knew by then, of course, that she had gotten a subpoena. And I knew that she was, therefore, was slated to testify. And she mentioned to me -- and I believe it was at this meeting. She mentioned -- I remember a conversation about the possibility of her testifying. I believe it must have occurred on the 28th.

She mentioned to me that she did not want to testify. So, that's how it came up. Not in the context of, I heard you have a subpoena, let's talk about it.

She raised the issue with me in the context of her desire to avoid testifying, which I certainly understood; not only because there were some embarrassing facts about our relationship that were inappropriate, but also because a whole lot of innocent people were being traumatized and dragged through the mud by these Jones lawyers with their dragnet strategy. They --

Q So --

A And so I -- and since she didn't know Paula Jones and knew nothing about sexual harassment, and certainly had no experience with that, I, I clearly understood why she didn't want to be a part of it.

Q And you didn't want her to testify, did you? You didn't want her to disclose these embarrassing facts of this inappropriate intimate relationship that you had, is that correct?

A Well, I did not want her to have to testify and go through that. And, of course, I didn't want her to do that, of course not.

489

37

Q Did you want those facts, not only the fact that she would testify, but did you want the facts that she had about your embarrassing inappropriate intimate relationship to be disclosed?

A Not there, but not in any context. However, I, I never had any high confidence that they wouldn't be.

Q Did anyone, as far as you knew, know about your embarrassing inappropriate intimate relationship that you had with Ms. Lewinsky?

A At that time, I was unaware that she had told anyone else about it. But if, if I had known that, it would not have surprised me.

Q Had you told anyone?

A Absolutely not.

Q Had you tried, in fact, not to let anyone else know about this relationship?

A Well, of course.

Q What did you do?

A Well, I never said anything about it, for one thing. And I did what people do when they do the wrong thing. I tried to do it where nobody else was looking at it.

Q How many times did you do that?

A Well, if you go back to my statement, I remember there were a few times in '96, I can't say with any certainty. There was once in early '97. After she left the

490

38

White House, I do not believe I ever had any inappropriate contact with her in the rest of '96. There was one occasion in '97 when, regrettably, that we were together for a few minutes, I think about 20 minutes, and there was inappropriate contact. And after that, to the best of my memory and belief, it did not occur again.

Q Did you tell her in the conversation about her being subpoenaed -- she was upset about it, you acknowledge that?

A (Witness nodded indicating an affirmative response.)

Q I'm sorry, you have to respond for the record. Yes or no? Do you agree that she was upset about being subpoenaed?

A Oh, yes, sir, she was upset. She -- well, she -- we -- she didn't -- we didn't talk about a subpoena. But she was upset. She said, I don't want to testify; I know nothing about this; I certainly know nothing about sexual harassment; why do they want me to testify. And I explained to her why they were doing this, and why all these women were on these lists, people that they knew good and well had nothing to do with any sexual harassment.

I explained to her that it was a political lawsuit. They wanted to get whatever they could under oath that was damaging to me, and then they wanted to leak it in violation of the Judge's orders, and turn up their nose and say, well, you can't prove we did it. Now, that was their strategy. And that they were very frustrated because everything they leaked so far was old news. So, they desperately were trying to validate this massive amount of money they'd spent by finding some new news. And --

Q You were familiar --

A -- she didn't want to be caught up in that, and I didn't blame her.

Q You were familiar, weren't you, Mr. President, that she had received a subpoena. You've already acknowledged that.

A Yes, sir, I was.

Q And Mr. Jordan informed you of that, is that right?

A No, sir. I believe -- and I believe I testified to this in my deposition. I think the first person who told me that she had been subpoenaed was Bruce Lindsey. I think the first -- and I was -- in this deposition, it's a little bit cloudy, but I was trying to remember who the first person who told me was, because the question was, again as I remember it -- could we go to that in the deposition, since you asked me that?

Q Actually, I think you're -- with all respect, I think you may be confusing when Mr. Lindsey -- well, perhaps Mr. Lindsey did tell you she was subpoenaed, I don't know.

492

40

But in your deposition, you were referring to Mr. Lindsey notifying you that she had been identified as a witness.

A Where is that, sir? I don't want to get -- I just want -- what page is that?

Q Well, actually --

A No, it had to be, because I saw a witness list much earlier than that.

Q Much earlier that December 28?

A Oh, sure. And it had been earlier than -- she would -- I believe Monica --

MR. KENDALL: Page 69.

THE WITNESS: I believe Monica Lewinsky's name was on a witness list earlier than she was subpoenaed.

BY MR. BITTMAN:

Q Yes.

A So, I believe when I was answering this question, at least I thought I was answering when I found out -- yes. See, there's -- on page 68, "Did anyone other than your attorneys ever tell you that Monica Lewinsky had been served with a subpoena in this case?" Then I said, "I don't think so." Then I [sic] said, "Did you ever talk" to Monica "about the possibility that she might be asked to testify in this case?"

Then I gave an answer that was nonresponsive, that really tried to finish the answer above. I said, "Bruce

Lindsey, I think Bruce Lindsey told me that she was, I think maybe that's the first person told me she was. I want to be as accurate as I can."

And that -- I believe that Bruce is the first person who told me that Monica had gotten a subpoena.

Q Did you, in fact, have a conversation with Mr. Jordan on the evening of December 19, 1997, in which he talked to you about Monica being in Mr. Jordan's office, having a copy of the subpoena, and being upset about being subpoenaed?

A I remembered that Mr. Jordan was in the White House on December 19th and for an event of some kind. That he came up to the Residence floor and told me that he had, that Monica had gotten a subpoena and, or that Monica was going to have to testify. And I think he told me he recommended a lawyer for her. I believe that's what happened. But it was a very brief conversation. He was there for some other reason.

Q And if Mr. Jordan testified that he had also spoken to you at around 5 p.m., and the White House phone logs reflect this, that he called you at around the time he met with Ms. Lewinsky and informed you then that she had been subpoenaed, is that consistent with your memory? Also on the 19th?

A I had a lot of phone conversations with Vernon

about this. I didn't keep records of them. I now have some records. My memory is not clear and my testimony on that was not clear. I just knew that I talked to Vernon at some time, but I thought that Bruce was the first person who told me.

Q But Mr. Jordan had also told you, is that right?

A Yes. I now know I had a conversation with Mr. Jordan about it where he said something to me about that.

Q And that was probably on the 19th, December 19th?

A Well, I know I saw him on the 19th. So, I'm quite sure. And if he says he talked to me on the 19th, I believe he would have better records and I certainly think he's a truthful person.

Q Getting back to your meeting with Ms. Lewinsky on December 28, you are aware that she's been subpoenaed. You are aware, are you not, Mr. President, that the subpoena called for the production of, among other things, all the gifts that you had given Ms. Lewinsky? You were aware of that on December 28th, weren't you?

A I'm not sure. And I understand this is an important question. I did have a conversation with Ms. Lewinsky at some time about gifts, the gifts I'd given her. I do not know whether it occurred on the 28th, or whether it occurred earlier. I do not know whether it occurred in person or whether it occurred on the telephone. I have searched my memory for this, because I know it's an important issue.

Perhaps if you -- I can tell you what I remember about the conversation and you can see why I'm having trouble placing the date.

Q Please.

A The reason I'm not sure it happened on the 28th is that my recollection is that Ms. Lewinsky said something to me like, what if they ask me about the gifts you've given me. That's the memory I have. That's why I question whether it happened on the 28th, because she had a subpoena with her, request for production.

And I told her that if they asked her for gifts, she'd have to give them whatever she had, that that's what the law was.

And let me also tell you, Mr. Bittman, if you go back and look at my testimony here, I actually asked the Jones lawyers for help on one occasion, when they were asking me what gifts I had given her, so they could -- I was never hung up about this gift issue. Maybe it's because I have a different experience. But, you know, the President gets hundreds of gifts a year, maybe more. I have always given a lot of gifts to people, especially if they give me gifts. And this was no big deal to me. I mean, it's nice. I enjoy it. I gave dozens of personal gifts to people last Christmas. I give gifts to people all the time. Friends of mine give me gifts all the time, give me ties, give me books, give me other things. So, it was just not a big deal.

And I told Ms. Lewinsky that, just -- I said, you know, if they ask you for this, you'll have to give them whatever you have. And I think, Mr. Bittman, it must have happened before then, because -- either that, or Ms. Lewinsky didn't want to tell me that she had the subpoena, because that was the language I remember her using.

Q Well, didn't she tell you, Mr. President, that the subpoena specifically called for a hat pin that you had produced, pardon me, that you had given her?

A I don't remember that. I remember -- sir, I've told you what I remember. That doesn't mean that my memory is accurate. A lot of things have happened in the last several months, and a lot of things were happening then. But my memory is she asked me a general question about gifts. And my memory is she asked me in the hypothetical. So, it's possible that I had a conversation with her before she got a subpoena. Or it's possible she didn't want to tell me that was part of the subpoena. I don't know.

But she may have been worried about this gift business. But it didn't bother me. My experience was totally different. I told her, I said, look, the way these things work is, when a person get a subpoena, you have to give them whatever you have; that's what's the rule, that's what the law is.

And when I was asked about this in my deposition, even though I was not trying to be helpful particularly to these people that I thought were not well-motivated, or being honest or even lawful in their conduct vis-a-vis me, that is, the Jones legal team, I did ask them specifically to enumerate the gifts. I asked them to help me because I couldn't remember the specifics.

So, all I'm saying is, it didn't -- I wasn't troubled by this gift issue.

Q And your testimony is that Ms. Lewinsky was concerned about her turning over any gifts that you had given her, and that your recommendation to her was, absolutely, Monica, you have to produce everything that I have given you. Is that your testimony?

A My testimony is what I have said, and let me reiterate it. I don't want to agree to a characterization of it. I want to just say what it was.

My testimony is that my memory is that on some day in December, and I'm sorry I don't remember when it was, she said, well, what if they ask me about the gifts you have given me. And I said, well, if you get a request to produce those, you have to give them whatever you have.

And it just, to me, it -- I don't -- I didn't then, I don't now see this as a problem. And if she thought it was a problem, I think it -- it must have been from a, really, a misapprehension of the circumstances. I certainly never encouraged her not to, to comply lawfully with a subpoena.

Q Mr. President, if your intent was, as you have earlier testified, that you didn't want anybody to know about this relationship you had with Ms. Lewinsky, why would you feel comfortable giving her gifts in the middle of discovery in the Paula Jones case?

A Well, sir, for one thing, there was no existing improper relationship at that time. I had, for nearly a year, done my best to be a friend to Ms. Lewinsky, to be a counselor to her, to give her good advice, and to help her. She had, for her part, most of the time, accepted the changed circumstances. She talked to me a lot about her life, her job ambitions, and she continued to give me gifts. And I felt that it was a right thing to do to give her gifts back.

I have always given a lot of people gifts. I have always been given gifts. I do not think there is anything improper about a man giving a woman a gift, or a woman giving a man a gift, that necessarily connotes an improper relationship. So, it didn't bother me.

I wasn't -- you know, this was December 28th. I was -- I gave her some gifts. I wasn't worried about it. I thought it was an all right thing to do.

Q What about notes and letters, cards, letters and

notes to Ms. Lewinsky? After this relationship, this inappropriate intimate relationship between you and Ms. Lewinsky ended, she continued to send you numerous intimate notes and cards, is that right?

A Well, they were -- some of them were, were somewhat intimate. I'd say most of them, most of the notes and cards were, were affectionate all right, but, but she had clearly accepted the fact that there could be no contact between us that was in any way inappropriate.

Now, she, she sent cards sometimes that were just funny, even a little bit off-color, but they were funny. She liked to send me cards, and I got a lot of those cards; several, anyway, I don't know a lot. I got a few.

Q She professed her love to you in these cards after the end of the relationship, didn't she?

A Well, --

Q She said she loved you?

A Sir, the truth is that most of the time, even when she was expressing her feelings for me in affectionate terms, I believed that she had accepted, understood my decision to stop this inappropriate contact. She knew from the very beginning of our relationship that I was apprehensive about it. And I think that in a way she felt a little freer to be affectionate, because she knew that nothing else was going to happen. I can't explain entirely what was in her mind.

But most of these messages were not what you would call over the top. They weren't things that, if you read them, you would say, oh, my goodness, these people are having some sort of sexual affair.

Q Mr. President, the question --

A But some of them were quite affectionate.

Q My question was, did she or did she not profess her love to you in those cards and letters that she sent to you after the relationship ended?

A Most of them were signed, "Love", you know, "Love, Monica." I don't know that I would consider -- I don't believe that in most of these cards and letters she professed her love, but she might well have. I -- but, you know, love can mean different things, too, Mr. Bittman. I have -- there are a lot of women with whom I have never had any inappropriate conduct who are friends of mine, who will say from time to time, I love you. And I know that they don't mean anything wrong by that.

Q Specifically, Mr. President, do you remember a card she sent you after she saw the movie Titanic, in which she said that she reminisced or dreamed about the romantic feelings that occurred in the movie, and how that reminded her of you two? Do you remember that?

A No, sir, but she could have sent it. I -- just because I don't remember it doesn't mean it wasn't there.

Q You're not denying that, that --

A Oh, no. I wouldn't deny that. I just don't remember it. You asked me if I remembered. I don't. She might have done it.

Q Do you ever remember telling her, Mr. President, that she should not write some of the things that she does in those cards and letters that she sends to you because it reveals, if disclosed, this relationship that you had, and that she shouldn't do it?

A I remember telling her she should be careful what she wrote, because a lot of it was clearly inappropriate and would be embarrassing if somebody else read it. I don't remember when I said that. I don't remember whether it was in '96 or when it was. I don't remember.

Q Embarrassing, in that it was revealing of the intimate relationship that you and she had, is that right?

A I do not know when I said this. So, I don't know whether we did have any sort of inappropriate relationship at the time I said that to her. I don't remember. But it's obvious that if she wrote things that she should not have written down and someone else read it, that it would be embarrassing.

Q She certainly sent you something like that after the relationship began, didn't she? And so, therefore, there was, at the time she sent it, something inappropriate going

502

50

on?

A Well, my recollection is that she -- that maybe because of changed circumstances in her own life in 1997, after there was no more inappropriate contact, that she sent me more things in the mail, and that there was sort of a disconnect sometimes between what she was saying and the plain facts of our relationship. And I don't know what caused that. But it may have been dissatisfaction with the rest of her life. I don't know.

You know, she had, from the time I first met her, talked to me about the rest of her personal life, and it may be that there was some reason for that. It may be that when I did the right thing and made it stick, that in a way she felt a need to cling more closely, or try to get closer to me, even though she knew nothing improper was happening or was going to happen. I don't know the answer to that.

Q After you gave her the gifts on December 28th, did you speak with your secretary, Ms. Currie, and ask her to pick up a box of gifts that were some compilation of gifts that Ms. Lewinsky would have --

A No, sir, I didn't do that.

Q -- to give to Ms. Currie?

A I did not do that.

Q When you testified in the Paula Jones case, this was only two and a half weeks after you had given her these six gifts, you were asked, at page 75 in your deposition, lines 2 through 5, "Well, have you ever given any gifts to Monica Lewinsky?" And you answer, "I don't recall."

And you were correct. You pointed out that you actually asked them, for prompting, "Do you know what they were?"

A I think what I meant there was I don't recall what they were, not that I don't recall whether I had given them. And then if you see, they did give me these specifics, and I gave them quite a good explanation here. I remembered very clearly what the facts were about The Black Dog. And I said that I could have given her a hat pin and a Walt Whitman book; that I did not remember giving her a gold broach, which was true. I didn't remember it. I may have given it to her, but I didn't remember giving her one.

They didn't ask me about the, about the Christmas gifts, and I don't know why I didn't think to say anything about them. But I have to tell you again, I even invited them to have a list.

It was obvious to me by this point in the definition, in this deposition, that they had, these people had access to a lot of information from somewhere, and I presume it came from Linda Tripp. And I had no interest in not answering their questions about these gifts. I do not believe that gifts are incriminating, nor do I think they are

504

52

wrong. I think it was a good thing to do. I'm not, I'm still not sorry I gave Monica Lewinsky gifts.

Q Why did you assume that that information came from Linda Tripp?

A I didn't then.

Q Well, you didn't? I thought you just testified you did then?

A No, no, no. I said I now assume that because --

Q You now assume.

A -- of all of the subsequent events. I didn't know. I just knew that --

Q Let me ask you about --

A -- that somebody had access to some information and they may have known more about this than I did.

Q Let me ask you about the meeting you had with Betty Currie at the White House on Sunday, January 18 of this year, the day after your deposition. First of all, you didn't -- Mrs. Currie, your secretary of six-some years, you never allowed her, did you, to watch whatever intimate activity you did with Ms. Lewinsky, did you?

A No, sir, not to my knowledge.

Q And as far as you know, she couldn't hear anything either, is that right?

A There were a couple of times when Monica was there when I asked Betty to be places where she could hear, because

505

53

Monica was upset and I -- this was after there was -- all the inappropriate contact had been terminated.

Q No, I'm talking --

A But --

Q -- about the times that you actually had the intimate contact.

A She was -- I believe that -- well, first of all, on that one occasion in 1997, I do not know whether Betty was in the White House after the radio address in the Oval Office complex. I believe she probably was, but I'm not sure. But I'm certain that someone was there. I always -- always someone was there.

In 1996, I think most of the times that Ms. Lewinsky was there, there may not have been anybody around except maybe coming in and out, but not permanently so. I -- that's correct. I never -- I didn't try to involve Betty in that in any way.

Q Well, not only did you not try to involve her, you specifically tried to exclude her and everyone else, isn't that right?

A Well, yes. I've never -- I mean, it's almost humorous, sir. I'd, I'd, I'd have to be an exhibitionist not to have tried to exclude everyone else.

Q So, if Ms. Currie testified that you approached her on the 18th, or you spoke with her and you said, you were always there when she was there, she wasn't, was she? That is, Mrs. Currie?

A She was always there in the White House, and I was concerned -- let me back up and say --

Q What about the radio address, Mr. President?

A Let me back up a second, Mr. Bittman. I knew about the radio address. I was sick after it was over and I, I was pleased at that time that it had been nearly a year since any inappropriate contact had occurred with Ms. Lewinsky. I promised myself it wasn't going to happen again. The facts are complicated about what did happen and how it happened. But, nonetheless, I'm responsible for it. On that night, she didn't.

I was more concerned about the times after that when Ms. Lewinsky was upset, and I wanted to establish at least that I had not -- because these questions were -- some of them were off the wall. Some of them were way out of line, I thought.

And what I wanted to establish was that Betty was there at all other times in the complex, and I wanted to know what Betty's memory was about what she heard, what she could hear. And what I did not know was -- I did not know that. And I was trying to figure out, and I was trying to figure out in a hurry because I knew something was up.

Q So, you wanted --

A After that deposition.

Q -- to check her memory for what she remembered, and that is --

A That's correct.

Q -- whether she remembered nothing, or whether she remembered an inappropriate intimate --

A Oh, no, no, no, no.

Q -- relationship?

A No. I didn't ask her about it in that way. I asked her about what the -- what I was trying to determine was whether my recollection was right and that she was always in the office complex when Monica was there, and whether she thought she could hear any conversations we had, or did she hear any.

And then I asked her specifically about a couple of times when -- once when I asked her to remain in the dining room, Betty, while I met with Monica in my study. And once when I took Monica in the, the small office Nancy Hernreich occupies right next to Betty's and talked to her there for a few minutes. That's my recollection of that.

I was trying to -- I knew, Mr. Bittman, to a reasonable certainty that I was going to be asked more questions about this. I didn't really expect you to be in the Jones case at the time. I thought what would happen is that it would break in the press, and I was trying to get the facts down. I was trying to understand what the facts were.

Q If Ms. Currie testified that these were not really questions to her, that they were more like statements, is that not true?

A Well, I can't testify as to what her perception was. I can tell you this. I was trying to get information in a hurry. I was downloading what I remembered. I think Ms. Currie would also testify that I explicitly told her, once I realized that you were involved in the Jones case -- you, the Office of Independent Counsel -- and that she might have to be called as a witness, that she should just go in there and tell the truth, tell what she knew, and be perfectly truthful.

So, I was not trying to get Betty Currie to say something that was untruthful. I was trying to get as much information as quickly as I could.

Q What information were you trying to get from her when you said, I was never alone with her, right?

A I don't remember exactly what I did say with her. That's what you say I said.

Q If Ms. Currie testified to that, if she says you told her, I was never alone with her, right?

A Well, I was never alone with her --

Q Did you not say that, Mr. President?

A Mr. Bittman, just a minute. I was never alone with

her, right, might be a question. And what I might have meant by that is, in the Oval Office complex.

Could --

Q Well, you knew the answer to that, didn't you?

A We've been going for more than an hour. Would you mind if we took a break? I need to go to the restroom.

MR. BITTMAN: Let's take a break.

MR. KENDALL: It's 2:38.

(Whereupon, the proceedings were recessed from 2:38 p.m. until 2:48 p.m.)

MR. KENDALL: It is 2:38 -- sorry, 2:48.

BY MR. WISENBERG:

Q Mr. President, I want to, before I go into a new subject area, briefly go over something you were talking about with Mr. Bittman.

The statement of your attorney, Mr. Bennett, at the Paula Jones deposition, "Counsel is fully aware" -- it's page 54, line 5 -- "Counsel is fully aware that Ms. Lewinsky has filed, has an affidavit which they are in possession of saying that there is absolutely no sex of any kind in any manner, shape or form, with President Clinton".

That statement is made by your attorney in front of Judge Susan Webber Wright, correct?

A That's correct.

Q That statement is a completely false statement.

Whether or not Mr. Bennett knew of your relationship with Ms. Lewinsky, the statement that there was "no sex of any kind in any manner, shape or form, with President Clinton," was an utterly false statement. Is that correct?

A It depends on what the meaning of the word "is" is. If the -- if he -- if "is" means is and never has been, that is not -- that is one thing. If it means there is none, that was a completely true statement.

But, as I have testified, and I'd like to testify again, this is -- it is somewhat unusual for a client to be asked about his lawyer's statements, instead of the other way around. I was not paying a great deal of attention to this exchange. I was focusing on my own testimony.

And if you go back and look at the sequence of this, you will see that the Jones lawyers decided that this was going to be the Lewinsky deposition, not the Jones deposition. And, given the facts of their case, I can understand why they made that decision. But that is not how I prepared for it. That is not how I was thinking about it.

And I am not sure, Mr. Wisenberg, as I sit here today, that I sat there and followed all these interchanges between the lawyers. I'm quite sure that I didn't follow all the interchanges between the lawyers all that carefully. And I don't really believe, therefore, that I can say Mr. Bennett's testimony or statement is testimony and is imputable to me. I didn't -- I don't know that I was even paying that much attention to it.

Q You told us you were very well prepared for the deposition.

A No. I said I was very well prepared to talk about Paula Jones and to talk about Kathleen Willey, because she had made a related charge. She was the only person that I think I was asked about who had anything to do with anything that would remotely approximate sexual harassment. The rest of this looked to me like it was more of a way to harass me.

Q You are the President of the United States and your attorney tells a United States District Court Judge that there is no sex of any kind, in any way, shape or form, whatsoever. And you feel no obligation to do anything about that at that deposition, Mr. President?

A I have told you, Mr. Wisenberg, I will tell you for a third time. I am not even sure that when Mr. Bennett made that statement that I was concentrating on the exact words he used.

Now, if someone had asked me on that day, are you having any kind of sexual relations with Ms. Lewinsky, that is, asked me a question in the present tense, I would have said no. And it would have been completely true.

Q Was Mr. Bennett aware of this tense-based distinction you are making now --

512

60

A I don't --

MR. KENDALL: I'm going to object to any questions about communications with private counsel.

MR. WISENBERG: Well, the witness has already testified, I think, that Mr. Bennett didn't know about the inappropriate relationship with Ms. Lewinsky. I guess --

THE WITNESS: Well, you'll have to ask him that, you know. He was not a sworn witness and I was not paying that close attention to what he was saying. I've told you that repeatedly. I was -- I don't -- I never even focused on that until I read it in this transcript in preparation for this testimony.

When I was in there, I didn't think about my lawyers. I was, frankly, thinking about myself and my testimony and trying to answer the questions.

BY MR. WISENBERG:

Q I just want to make sure I understand, Mr. President. Do you mean today that because you were not engaging in sexual activity with Ms. Lewinsky during the deposition that the statement of Mr. Bennett might be literally true?

A No, sir. I mean that at the time of the deposition, it had been -- that was well beyond any point of improper contact between me and Ms. Lewinsky. So that anyone generally speaking in the present tense, saying there is not an improper relationship, would be telling the truth if that person said there was not, in the present tense; the present tense encompassing many months. That's what I meant by that.

Not that I was -- I wasn't trying to give you a cute answer, that I was obviously not involved in anything improper during a deposition. I was trying to tell you that generally speaking in the present tense, if someone said that, that would be true. But I don't know what Mr. Bennett had in his mind. I don't know. I didn't pay any attention to this colloquy that went on. I was waiting for my instructions as a witness to go forward. I was worried about my own testimony.

Q I want to go back to some questions about Mr. Jordan and we are going to touch a little bit on the December 19th meeting and some others. Mr. Jordan is a long-time friend of yours, is that correct, Mr. President?

A Yes, sir. We've been friends probably 20 years, maybe more.

Q You said you consider him to be a truthful person, correct?

A I do.

Q If Mr. Jordan has told us that he visited you in the Residence on the night of the 19th, after a White House holiday dinner, to discuss Monica Lewinsky and her subpoena with you, do you have any reason to doubt it?

514

62

A No. I've never known him to say anything that wasn't true. And his memory of these events, I think, would be better than mine because I had a lot of other things going on.

Q We have WAVE records that will show that, but in the interest of time I'm not going to -- since you don't dispute that, I'm not going to show them right now.

And, in fact, that was the very day Monica Lewinsky was subpoenaed, wasn't it, the night that he came to see you?

A I don't have an independent memory of that, but you would probably know that. I mean, I'm sure there is a record of when she got her subpoena.

Q If Mr. Jordan has told us that he spoke with you over the phone within about an hour of Monica receiving her subpoena, and later visited you that very day, the night at the White House, to discuss it, again you'd have no reason to doubt him, is that correct?

A I've already -- I believe I've already testified about that here today, that I had lots of conversations with Vernon. I'm sure that I had lots of conversations with him that included comments about this. And if he has a specific memory of when I had some conversation on a certain day, I would be inclined to trust his memory over mine, because under the present circumstances my head's probably more cluttered than his, and my schedule is probably busier. He's probably got better records.

Q And when Mr. Jordan met with you at the Residence that night, sir, he asked you if you'd been involved in a sexual relationship with Monica Lewinsky, didn't he?

A I do not remember exactly what the nature of the conversation was. I do remember that I told him that there was no sexual relationship between me and Monica Lewinsky, which was true. And that -- then all I remember for the rest is that he said he had referred her to a lawyer, and I believe it was Mr. Carter, and I don't believe I've ever met Mr. Carter. I don't think I know him.

Q Mr. President, if Mr. Jordan has told us that he had a very disturbing conversation with Ms. Lewinsky that day, then went over to visit you at the White House, and that before he asked you the question about a sexual relationship, related that disturbing conversation to you, the conversation being that Ms. Lewinsky had a fixation on you and thought that perhaps the First Lady would leave you at the end of -- that you would leave the First Lady at the end of your term and come be with Ms. Lewinsky, do you have any reason to doubt him that it was on that night that that conversation happened?

A All I can tell you, sir, is I, I certainly don't remember him saying that. Now, he could have said that because, as you know, a great many things happened in the ensuing two or three days. And I could have just forgotten it. But I don't remember him ever saying that.

Q At any time?

A No, I don't remember him saying that. What I remember was that he said that Monica came to see him, that she was upset that she was going to have to testify, that he had referred her to a lawyer.

Q In fact, she was very distraught about the subpoena, according to Mr. Jordan, wasn't she?

A Well, he said she was upset about it. I don't remember -- I don't remember any, at any time when he said this, this other thing you just quoted me. I'm sorry. I just don't remember that.

Q That is something that one would be likely to remember, don't you think, Mr. President?

A I think I would, and I'd be happy to share it with you if I did. I only had one encounter with Ms. Lewinsky, I seem to remember, which was somewhat maybe reminiscent of that. But not that, if you will, obsessive, if that's the way you want to use that word.

Q Do you recall him at all telling you that he was concerned about her fascination with you, even if you don't remember the specific conversation about you leaving the First Lady?

A I recall him saying he thought that she was upset

with -- somewhat fixated on me, that she acknowledged that she was not having a sexual relationship with me, and that she did not want to be drug into the Jones lawsuit. That's what I recall. And I recall his getting, saying that he had recommended a lawyer to her and she had gone to see the lawyer. That's what I recall.

I don't remember the other thing you mentioned. I just -- I might well remember it if he had said it. Maybe he said it and I've forgotten it, but I don't -- I can't tell you that I remember that.

Q Mr. President, you swore under oath in the Jones case that you didn't think anyone other than your lawyers had ever told you that Monica Lewinsky had been subpoenaed. Page 68, line 22 [sic] through page 69, line 3. Here's the testimony, sir.

Question -- we've gone over it a little bit before: "Did anyone other than your attorneys ever tell you that Monica Lewinsky had been served with a subpoena in this case?" Answer, "I don't think so."

Now, this deposition was taken just three and a half weeks after, by your own testimony, Vernon Jordan made a trip at night to the White House to tell you, among other things, that Monica Lewinsky had been subpoenaed and was upset about it. Why did you give that testimony under oath in the Jones case, sir?

518

66

A Well, Mr. Wisenberg, I think you have to -- again, you have to put this in the context of the flow of questions, and I've already testified to this once today. I will testify to it again.

My answer to the next question, I think, is a way of finishing my answer to the question and the answer you've said here. I was trying to remember who the first person, other than Mr. Bennett -- I don't think Mr. Bennett -- who the first person told me that, who told me Paula Jones had, I mean, excuse me, Monica Lewinsky had a subpoena. And I thought that Bruce Lindsey was the first person. And that's how I was trying to remember that.

Keep in mind, sort of like today, these questions are being kind of put at me rapid-fire. But, unlike today, I hadn't had the opportunity to prepare at this level of detail. I didn't -- I was trying to keep a lot of things in my head that I had remembered with regard to the Paula Jones case and the Kathleen Willey matter, because I knew I would be asked about them. And I gave the best answers I could. Several of my answers are somewhat jumbled.

But this is an honest attempt here -- if you read both these answers, it's obvious they were both answers to that question you quoted, to remember the first person, who was not Mr. Bennett, who told me. And I don't believe Vernon was the first person who told me. I believe Bruce Lindsey was.

Q Let me read the question, because I want to talk about the first person issue. The question on line 25 of page 68 is, "Did anyone other than your attorneys ever tell you that Monica Lewinsky had been served with a subpoena in this case?" Answer, "I don't think so."

You would agree with me, sir, that the question doesn't say, the question doesn't say anything about who was the first person. It just says, did anyone tell you. Isn't that correct?

A That's right. And I said Bruce Lindsey, because I was trying to struggle with who -- where I had heard this. And they were free to ask a follow-up question, and they didn't.

Q Mr. President, three and a half weeks before, Mr. Jordan had made a special trip to the White House to tell you Ms. Lewinsky had been subpoenaed; she was distraught; she had a fixation over you. And you couldn't remember that, three and a half weeks later?

A Mr. Wisenberg, if -- they had access to all this information from their conversations with Linda Tripp, if that was the basis of it. They were free to ask me more questions. They may have been trying to trick me.

Now, they knew more about the details of my relationship with Monica Lewinsky. I'm not sure everything they knew was true, because I don't know. I've not heard these tapes or anything. But they knew a lot more than I did. And instead of trying to trick me, what they should have done is to ask me specific questions, and I invited them on more than one occasion to ask follow-up questions.

This is the third or fourth time that you seem to be complaining that I did not do all their work for them. That just sitting here answering these questions to the best of my memory, with limited preparation, was not enough. That I should have actually been doing all their work for them.

Now, they'd been up all night with Linda Tripp, who had betrayed her friend, Monica Lewinsky, stabbed her in the back and given them all this information. They could have helped more. If they wanted to ask me follow-up questions, they could. They didn't. I'm sorry. I did the best I could.

Q Can you tell the grand jury what is tricky about the question, "Did anyone other than your attorneys ever tell you" --

A No, there's nothing -- I'm just telling -- I have explained. I will now explain for the third time, sir. I was being asked a number of questions here. I was struggling to remember then. There were lots of things that had gone on during this time period that had nothing to do with Monica Lewinsky.

521

69

You know, I believed then, I believe now that Monica Lewinsky could have sworn out an honest affidavit, that under reasonable circumstances, and without the benefit of what Linda Tripp did to her, would have given her a chance not to be a witness in this case.

So, I didn't have perfect memory of all these events that have now, in the last seven months, since Ms. Lewinsky was kept for several hours by four or five of your lawyers and four or five FBI agents, as if she were a serious felon, these things have become the most important matters in the world. At the moment they were occurring, many other things were going on.

I honestly tried to remember when -- you know, if somebody asked you, has anybody ever talked to you about this, you normally think, well, where was the first time I heard that. That's all I was trying to do here. I was not trying to say not Vernon Jordan, but Bruce Lindsey. Everybody knows Vernon Jordan is a friend of mine. I probably would have talked to Vernon Jordan about the Monica Lewinsky problem if he had never been involved in it. So, I was not trying to mislead them. I was trying to answer this question with the first person who told me that.

Now, I realize that wasn't the specific question. They were free to ask follow-ups, just like you're asking follow-ups today. And I can't explain why I didn't answer every question in the way you seem to think I should have, and I certainly can't explain why they didn't ask what seemed to me to be logical follow-ups, especially since they spent all that time with Linda Tripp the night before.

Q You've told us that you understand your obligation then, as it is now, is to tell the whole truth, sir. Do you recall that?

A I took the oath here.

Q If Vernon Jordan --

A You even read me a definition of the oath.

Q If Vernon Jordan has told us that you have an extraordinary memory, one of the greatest memories he's ever seen in a politician, would that be something you would care to dispute?

A No, I do have a good memory. At least, I have had a good memory in my life.

Q Do you understand that if you answered, "I don't think so", to the question, has anyone other than your attorneys told you that Monica Lewinsky has been served with a subpoena in this case, that if you answered, "I don't think so", but you really knew Vernon Jordan had been telling you all about it, you understand that that would be a false statement, presumably perjurious?

A Mr. Wisenberg, I have testified about this three times. Now, I will do it the fourth time. I am not going to

523

71

answer your trick questions.

I -- people don't always hear the same questions in the same way. They don't always answer them in the same way. I was so concerned about the question they asked me that the next question I was asked, I went back to the previous question, trying to give an honest answer about the first time I heard about the Lewinsky subpoena.

I -- look. I could have had no reasonable expectation that anyone would ever know that, that -- or not, excuse me, not know if this thing -- that I would talk to Vernon Jordan about nearly everything. I was not interested in -- if the implication of your question is that somehow I didn't want anybody to know I had ever talked to Vernon Jordan about this, that's just not so.

It's also -- if I could say one thing about my memory. I have been blessed and advantaged in my life with a good memory. Now, I have been shocked, and so have members of my family and friends of mine, at how many things that I have forgotten in the last six years, I think because of the pressure and the pace and the volume of events in the President's life, compounded by the pressure of your four-year inquiry, and all the other things that have happened, I'm amazed there are lots of times when I literally can't remember last week.

If you ask me, did you talk to Vernon -- when was

the last time you talked to Vernon Jordan, what time of day was it, when did you see him, what did you say, my answer was the last -- you know, if you answered [sic] me, when was the last time you saw a friend of yours in California, if you asked me a lot of questions like that, my memory is not what it was when I came here, because my life is so crowded.

And now that -- as I said, you have made this the most important issue in America. I mean, you have made it the most important issue in America from your point of view. At the time this was occurring, even though I was concerned about it, and I hoped she didn't have to testify, and I hoped this wouldn't come out, I felt -- I will say again -- that she could honestly fill out an affidavit that, under reasonable circumstances, would relieve her of the burden of testifying.

I am not trying to exclude the fact that I talked to Vernon here. I just -- all I can tell you is I believe this answer reflects I was trying to remember the first person who told me who was not Mr. Bennett, and I believe it was Bruce Lindsey.

Q As you yourself recalled, just recalled, Mr. President, Vernon Jordan not only discussed the subpoena with you that night, but discussed Frank Carter, the lawyer he had gotten for Ms. Lewinsky. And also Mr. Jordan discussed with you over the next few weeks, after the 19th of December, in addition to the job aspects of Ms. Lewinsky's job, he discussed with you her affidavit that she was preparing in the case. Is that correct, sir?

A I believe that he did notify us, I think, when she signed her affidavit. I have a memory of that. Or it seems like he said that she had signed her affidavit.

Q If he's told us that he notified you around January 7th, when she signed her affidavit, and that you generally understood that it would deny a sexual relationship, do you have any reason to doubt that?

A No.

Q So, that's the affidavit, the lawyer, and the subpoena. And yet when you were asked, sir, at the Jones deposition about Vernon Jordan, and specifically about whether or not he had discussed the lawsuit with you, you didn't reveal that to the Court.

I want to refer you to page 72, line 16. It's where this starts. It's going to go down, it might go down somewhat.

Line 16. Question, "Has it ever been reported to you that he" -- and that's referring to Mr. Jordan. At line 12 you were asked, "You know a man named Vernon Jordan?", and you answer, "I know him well."

Going down to 16, "Has it ever been reported to you that he met with Monica Lewinsky and talked about this case?"

This is your answer, or a portion of it: "I knew that he met with her. I think Betty suggested that he meet with her. Anyway, he met with her. I, I thought that he talked to her about something else."

Why didn't you tell the Court, when you were under oath and sworn to tell the truth, the whole truth, and nothing but the truth, that you had been talking with Vernon Jordan about the case, about the affidavit, the lawyer, the subpoena?

A Well, that's not the question I was asked. I was not asked any question about -- I was asked, "Has it ever been reported to you that he met with Monica Lewinsky and talked about this case." I believe -- I may be wrong about this -- my impression was that at the time, I was focused on the meetings. I believe the meetings he had were meetings about her moving to New York and getting a job.

I knew at some point that she had told him that she needed some help, because she had gotten a subpoena. I'm not sure I know whether she did that in a meeting or a phone call. And I was not, I was not focused on that.

I know that, I know Vernon helped her to get a lawyer, Mr. Carter. And I, I believe that he did it after she had called him, but I'm not sure. But I knew that the main source of their meetings was about her move to New York and her getting a job.

527

75

Q Are you saying, sir, that you forgot when you were asked this question that Vernon Jordan had come on December 19th, just three and a half weeks before, and said that he had met that day, the day that Monica got the subpoena?

A It's quite possible -- it's a sort of a jumbled answer. It's quite possible that I had gotten mixed up between whether she had met with him or talked to him on the telephone in those three and a half weeks.

Again, I say, sir, just from the tone of your voice and the way you are asking questions here, it's obvious that this is the most important thing in the world, and that everybody was focused on all the details at the time. But that's not the way it worked. I was, I was doing my best to remember.

Now, keep in mind, I don't know if this is true, but the news reports are that Linda Tripp talked to you, then went and talked to the Jones lawyers, and, you know, that she prepared them for this. Now, maybe -- you seem to be criticizing me because they didn't ask better questions and, as if you didn't prepare them well enough to sort of set me up or something. I don't know what's going on here.

All I can tell you is I didn't remember all the details of all this. I didn't remember what -- when Vernon talked to me about Monica Lewinsky, whether she talked to him on the telephone or had a meeting. I didn't remember all those details. I was focused on the fact that Monica went to meet with Vernon after Betty helped him set it up, and had subsequent meetings to talk about her move to New York.

Now, keep in mind at this time, at this time, until this date here when it's obvious that something funny's going on here and there's some sort of a gotcha game at work in this deposition, until this date, I didn't know that Ms. Lewinsky's deposition [sic] wasn't going to be sufficient for her to avoid testifying. I didn't, you know --

MR. KENDALL: Excuse me, Mr. President, I think --

THE WITNESS: So, all these details --

MR. KENDALL: -- you mean her affidavit.

BY MR. WISENBERG:

Q You mean her affidavit?

A Excuse me. I'm sorry. Her affidavit. Thank you.

So, I don't necessarily remember all the details of all these questions you're asking me, because there was a lot of other things going on, and at the time they were going on, until all this came out, this was not the most important thing in my life. This was just another thing in my life.

Q But Vernon Jordan met with you, sir, and he reported that he had met with Monica Lewinsky, and the discussion was about the lawsuit, and you didn't inform, under oath, the Court of that in your deposition?

A I gave the best answer I could, based on the best

memory I had at the time they asked me the question. That's the only answer I can give you, sir.

Q And before --

A And I think I may have been confused in my memory, because I've also talked to him on the phone about what he said about whether he talked to her or met with her. That's all I can tell you.

But, let me say again, I don't have the same view about this deposition -- I mean, this affidavit -- that I think you do. I felt very strongly that Ms. Lewinsky and everybody else that didn't know anything about Paula Jones and anything about sexual harassment, that she and others were themselves being harassed for political purposes, in the hope of getting damaging information that the Jones lawyers could unlawfully leak.

Now, I believed then, I believe today, that she could execute an affidavit which, under reasonable circumstances with fair-minded, non politically-oriented people, would result in her being relieved of the burden to be put through the kind of testimony that, thanks to Linda Tripp's work with you and with the Jones lawyers, she would have been put through. I don't think that's dishonest. I don't think that's illegal. I think what they were trying to do to her and all these other people, who knew nothing about sexual harassment, was outrageous, just so they could hurt me

530

78

politically.

So, I just don't have the same attitude about it that you do.

Q Well, you're not telling our grand jurors that because you think the case was a political case or a setup, Mr. President, that that would give you the right to commit perjury or --

A No, sir.

Q -- not to tell the full truth?

A No, sir. In the face of their, the Jones lawyers, the people that were questioning me, in the face of their illegal leaks, their constant, unrelenting illegal leaks in a lawsuit that I knew and, by the time this deposition and this discovery started, they knew was a bogus suit on the law and a bogus suit on the facts.

Q The question is --

A In the face of that, I knew that in the face of their illegal activity, I still had to behave lawfully. But I wanted to be legal without being particularly helpful. I thought that was, that was what I was trying to do. And this is the first -- you are the first persons who ever suggested to me that, that I should have been doing their lawyers' work for them, when they were perfectly free to ask follow-up questions. On one or two occasions, Mr. Bennett invited them to ask follow-up questions.

It now appears to me they didn't because they were afraid I would give them a truthful answer, and that there had been some communication between you and Ms. Tripp and them, and they were trying to set me up and trick me. And now you seem to be complaining that they didn't do a good enough job.

I did my best, sir, at this time. I did not know what I now know about this. A lot of other things were going on in my life. Did I want this to come out? No. Was I embarrassed about it? Yes. Did I ask her to lie about it? No. Did I believe there could be a truthful affidavit? Absolutely.

Now, that's all I know to say about this. I will continue to answer your questions as best I can.

Q You're not going back on your earlier statement that you understood you were sworn to tell the truth, the whole truth, and nothing but the truth to the folks at that deposition, are you, Mr. President?

A No, sir, but I think we might as well put this out on the table. You tried to get me to give a broader interpretation to my oath than just my obligation to tell the truth. In other words, you tried to say, even though these people are treating you in an illegal manner in illegally leaking these depositions, you should be a good lawyer for them. And if they don't have enough sense to write -- to ask a question, and even if Mr. Bennett invited them to ask follow-up questions, if they didn't do it, you should have done all their work for them.

Now, so I will admit this, sir. My goal in this deposition was to be truthful, but not particularly helpful. I did not wish to do the work of the Jones lawyers. I deplored what they were doing. I deplored the innocent people they were tormenting and traumatizing. I deplored their illegal leaking. I deplored the fact that they knew, once they knew our evidence, that this was a bogus lawsuit, and that because of the funding they had from my political enemies, they were putting ahead. I deplored it.

But I was determined to walk through the mine field of this deposition without violating the law, and I believe I did.

Q You are not saying, are you, Mr. President, in terms of doing the work for the Jones folks, the Jones lawyers, that you could, you could say, as part of your not helping them, "I don't know" to a particular question, when you really knew, and that it was up to them -- even if you really knew the answer, it was up to them to do the follow-up, that you kind of had a one free "I don't know" --

A No, sir.

Q If I could finish up? I've been very patient, Mr. President, in letting you finish.

533

81

You didn't think you had a free shot to say, "I don't know", or "I don't recall", but when you really did know and you did recall, and it was just up to them, even if you weren't telling the truth, to do a follow-up and to catch you?

A No, sir, I'm not saying that. And if I could give you one example? That's why I felt that I had to come back to that question where I said, I don't know that, and talk about Bruce Lindsey, because I was trying, I was honestly trying to remember how I had first heard this. I wasn't hung up about talking about this.

All I'm saying is, the -- let me say something sympathetic to you. I've been pretty tough. So, let me say something sympathetic.

All of you are intelligent people. You've worked hard on this. You've worked for a long time. You've gotten all the facts. You've seen a lot of evidence that I haven't seen. And it's, it's an embarrassing and personally painful thing, the truth about my relationship with Ms. Lewinsky.

So, the natural assumption is that while all this was going on, I must have been focused on nothing but this; therefore, I must remember everything about it in the sequence and form in which it occurred. All I can tell you is, I was concerned about it. I was glad she saw a lawyer. I was glad she was doing an affidavit. But there were a lot

534

82

of other things going on, and I don't necessarily remember it all. And I don't know if I can convince you of that.

But I tried to be honest with you about my mindset, about this deposition. And I'm just trying to explain that I don't have the memory that you assume that I should about some of these things.

Q I want to talk to you for a bit, Mr. President, about the incident that happened at the Northwest Gate of the White House on December 5th -- sorry, December 6th, 1997. If you would give me just a moment?

That was a -- let me ask you first. In early nineteen -- in early December 1997, the Paula Jones case was pending, correct?

A Yes, sir.

Q You were represented by Mr. Bennett, of course?

A That's correct.

Q In that litigation?

A Yes, I did.

Q How --

A He was.

Q I'm sorry. Go ahead.

A No, no. Yes, he was representing me.

Q How often did you talk to him or meet with him, if you can just recall, at that time in the litigation?

A Well, we met, I would say -- I wish Mr. Ruff were

answering this question, instead of me. His memory would be better. We met probably, oh, for a long time we didn't meet all that often, maybe once a month. And then the closer we got to the deposition, we would meet more frequently. So, maybe by this time we were meeting more.

We also -- there was a period when we had been approached about --

MR. KENDALL: Again, the question only goes to the number of meetings and not the content of any conversations with your lawyer.

THE WITNESS: I understand. We're not talking about the content.

There was a, there was a period in which we, I think back in the summer before this, when we had met more frequently. But I would say normally once a month. Sometimes something would be happening and we'd meet more. And then, as we moved toward the deposition, we would begin to meet more.

BY MR. WISENBERG:

Q A witness list came out on December 5th of 1997, with Monica Lewinsky's name on it. Mr. President, when did you find out that Monica's name was on that witness list?

A I believe that I found out late in the afternoon on the 6th. That's what I believe. I've tried to remember with great precision, and because I thought you would ask me about this day, I've tried to remember the logical question, which is whether, whether I knew it on the 6th and, if so, at what time.

I don't -- I had a meeting in the late afternoon on the 5th, on the 6th -- excuse me, on the 6th -- and I believe that's when I learned about it.

Q Now, on the morning of the 6th, Monica Lewinsky came to the Northwest Gate and found out that you were being visited by Eleanor Mondale at the time, and had an extremely angry reaction. You know that, sir, now, don't you?

A I have, I have -- I know that Monica Lewinsky came to the gate on the 6th and apparently directly called in and wanted to see me and couldn't, and was angry about it. I know that.

Q And she expressed that anger to Betty Currie over the telephone, isn't that correct, sir?

A That, Betty told me that.

Q And she then later expressed her anger to you in one of her telephone conversations with Betty Currie, is that correct?

A You mean did I talk to her on the phone?

Q Monica Lewinsky, that day, before she came in to visit in the White House?

A Mr. Wisenberg, I remember that she came in to visit that day. I remember that she was upset. I don't recall whether I talked to her on the phone before she came in to visit, but I well may have. I'm not denying it that I did. I just don't recall that.

Q And Mrs. Currie and yourself were very irate that Ms. Lewinsky had overheard that you were in the Oval Office with a visitor on that day, isn't that correct, that you and Mrs. Currie were very irate about that?

A Well, I don't remember all that. What I remember is that she was very -- Monica was very upset. She got upset from time to time. And, and I was, you know, I couldn't see her. I had, I was doing, as I remember, I had some other work to do that morning and she had just sort of showed up and wanted to be let in, and wanted to come in at a certain time and she wanted everything to be that way, and we couldn't see her. Now, I did arrange to see her later that day. And I was upset about her conduct.

I'm not sure that I knew or focused on at that moment exactly the question you asked. I remember I was, I thought her conduct was inappropriate that day.

Q I want to go back and I want to take them one at a time. Number one, did you find out at some point during that day that Monica had overheard from somebody in the Secret Service that you were meeting with Ms. Mondale, and that Monica got very irate about that?

A I knew that at some point. I don't know whether I

538

86

found out that, that day. I knew that day, I knew that somehow she knew that among, that, that Eleanor Mondale was in to see us that day. I knew that. I don't know that I knew how she knew that on that day. I don't remember that.

Q That leads into my second question, which is, weren't you irate at the Secret Service precisely because they had revealed this information to Ms. Lewinsky on that very day, so irate that you told several people, or at least one person, that somebody should be fired over this, on that very day?

A I don't remember whether it happened on that very day. But, let me tell you that the Uniformed Secret Service, if that is in fact what happened and I will stipulate that that is, that no one should be telling anybody, not anybody, not a member of my staff, who the President is meeting with. That's an inappropriate thing to do.

So, I would think that if that, in fact, is what I heard when I heard it, I would have thought that was a bad thing. I don't know that I said that. I don't, I don't remember what I said, and I don't remember to whom I said it.

Q It would be an inappropriate thing, sir, and that leads into my next question is that why did Mrs. Currie, on your instructions, later that day tell many of the Secret Service Officers involved that it never happened, to forget about it?

A That what never happened?

Q The incident that you were so irate about earlier; the incident of somebody disclosing to Ms. Lewinsky that Ms. Mondale was in the Oval Office?

A I don't know the answer to that. I think maybe, you know, I don't know. I don't know the answer.

Q You don't recall that you later gave orders to the effect that we are going to pretend this never happened, or something --

A No, sir.

Q -- like that?

A No, sir. I don't recall it. First of all, I don't recall that I gave orders to fire anybody, if that was the implication of your first statement.

Q It wasn't an implication. Actually, the question was that you initially wanted somebody fired. You were so mad that you wanted somebody fired.

A I don't remember that, first of all. I remember thinking it was an inappropriate thing to do. And I, I, I remember, as I usually do when I'm mad, after awhile I wasn't so mad about it, and I'm quite aware that Ms. Lewinsky has a way of getting information out of people when she's either charming or determined. And it -- I could have just said, well, I'm not so mad about it any more.

But I don't remember the whole sequence of events

you're talking to me about now, except I do remember that somehow Monica found out Eleanor Mondale was there. I learned either that day or later that one of the Uniformed Division personnel had told her. I do -- I thought then it was a mistake. I think now it was a mistake. I'm not sure it's a mistake someone should be terminated over. I think that, you know, you could just tell them not to do that any more.

Q In fact, it would kind of be an overreaction, to get irate or terminate somebody for revealing to a former White House staffer who visits where the President is, don't you think, sir?

A Well, it would depend upon the facts. I think on the whole people in the Uniformed Secret Service who are working on the gate have no business telling anybody anything about the President's schedule, just as a general principal. I didn't mind anybody knowing that she was there, if that's what you're saying. I could care less about that. But I think that the schedule itself -- these uniformed people, you know, somebody shouldn't just be able to come up on the street and, because they know who the Secret Service agent is, he says who the President's with. I don't think that's proper.

Q I agree, Mr. President.

A But, on the other hand, I didn't, you know, I, I

wanted to know what happened. I think we found out what happened. And then they were, I think, told not to let it happen again, and I think that's the way it should have been handled. I think it was handled in the appropriate way.

Q You have no knowledge of the fact that Secret Service officers were told later in the day something to the effect of, this never happened, this event never happened? You have no knowledge of that?

A I'm not sure anybody ever told that to me. I mean, I thought you were asking -- let me just say, my interpretation of this, of your previous question was different than what you're asking now.

What I remember was being upset that this matter would be discussed that -- by anybody. It's incidental it happened to be Monica Lewinsky. And that, that whatever I said, I don't recall. But then thinking that the appropriate thing to do was to say, look, just this, this is not an appropriate thing for you to be talking about, the President's schedule, and it shouldn't happen again.

Now, the question you seem to be asking me now -- I just want to be sure I'm getting the right question -- is whether I gave instructions, in effect, to pretend that Monica Lewinsky was never at the gate. And if --

Q To the effect of pretend --

A And if that is the question you are asking me, I

don't believe I ever did that, sir. I certainly have no memory of doing that.

Q Or anything to that effect?

A I don't know what that means.

Q Is that your testimony?

A What does that mean, anything to that effect?

Q Well, Mr. President, you've told us that you were not going to try to help the Jones attorneys, and I think it's clear from your testimony that you were pretty literal at times. So, that's why I'm saying, I don't necessarily know the exact words. The question was, do you have any knowledge of the fact --

A Of that?

Q -- of the fact that later in the day, on Saturday, the 6th of December, 1997, Secret Service people were then, were told something to this effect: This event never happened, let's just pretend this event did not happen. Do you have knowledge of it, or not?

A No, sir. And I, I didn't instruct the Secret Service in that regard. I have no memory of saying anything to anybody in the Secret Service that would have triggered that kind of instruction.

Q Did you tell Captain Purdy, while you were standing in the doorway between the Oval Office and Betty Currie's office, did you tell Captain Purdy of the Uniformed Division,

I hope I can count on your discretion in this matter? At the end of the day when you all were talking about that earlier incident, did you tell him that or anything like that, sir?

A I don't remember anything I said to him in that regard. I have no recollection of that whatever.

MR. WISENBERG: Let's take a break now.

MR. KENDALL: Thank you, 3:38.

(Whereupon, the proceedings were recessed from 3:38 p.m. until 4:01 p.m.)

MR. KENDALL: It is 4:01.

BY MR. WISENBERG:

Q Mr. President, the next series of questions are from the grand jurors. And let me tell you that the grand jurors want you to be more specific about the inappropriate conduct.

The first question was, one of the grand jurors has said that you referred to what you did with Ms. Lewinsky as inappropriate contact; what do you mean by that?

A I mean just what I said. But I would like to ask the grand jury, because I think I have been quite specific and I think I've been willing to answer some specific questions that I haven't been asked yet, but I do not want to discuss something that is intensely painful to me. This has been tough enough already on me and on my family, although I take responsibility for it. I have no one to blame but myself

544

What I meant was, and what they can infer that I meant was, that I did things that were -- when I was alone with her, that were inappropriate and wrong. But that they did not include any activity that was within the definition of sexual relations that I was given by Judge Wright in the deposition. I said that I did not do those things that were in that, within that definition, and I testified truthfully to that. And that's all I can say about it.

Now, you know, if there's any doubt on the part of the grand jurors about whether I believe some kind of activity falls within that definition or outside that definition, I'd be happy to try to answer that.

Q Well, I have a question regarding your definition then. And my question is, is oral sex performed on you within that definition as you understood it, the definition in the Jones --

A As I understood it, it was not, no.

Q The grand jurors would like to know upon what basis, what legal basis you are declining to answer more specific questions about this? I've mentioned to you that obviously you have privileges, privileges against self-incrimination. There's no general right not to answer questions.

And so one of the questions from the grand jurors is what basis, what legal basis are you declining to answer these questions?

A I'm not trying to evade my legal obligations or my willingness to help the grand jury achieve their legal obligations. As I understand it, you want to examine whether you believe I told the truth in my deposition, whether I asked Ms. Lewinsky not to tell the truth, and whether I did anything else with evidence, or in any other way, amounting to an obstruction of justice or a subornation of perjury. And I'm prepared to answer all questions that the grand jury needs to draw that conclusion.

Now, respectfully, I believe the grand jurors can ask me if I believe -- just like that grand juror did -- could ask me, do you believe that this conduct falls within that definition. If it does, then you are free to conclude that my testimony is that I didn't do that. And I believe that you can achieve that without requiring me to say and do things that I don't think are necessary and that I think, frankly, go too far in trying to criminalize my private life.

Q If a person touched another person, if you touched another person on the breast, would that be, in your view, and was it within your view, when you took the deposition, within the definition of sexual relations?

A If the person being deposed --

Q Yes.

A -- in this case, me, directly touched the breast of

another person, with the purpose to arouse or gratify, under that definition that would be included.

Q Only directly, sir, or would it be directly or through clothing?

A Well, I would -- I think the common sense definition would be directly. That's how I would infer what it means.

Q If the person being deposed kissed the breast of another person, would that be in the definition of sexual relations as you understood it when you were under oath in the Jones case?

A Yes, that would constitute contact. I think that would. If it were direct contact, I believe it would. I -- maybe I should read it again, just to make sure.

Because this basically says if there was any direct contact with an intent to arouse or gratify, if that was the intent of the contact, then that would fall within the definition. That's correct.

Q So, touching, in your view then and now -- the person being deposed touching or kissing the breast of another person would fall within the definition?

A That's correct, sir.

Q And you testified that you didn't have sexual relations with Monica Lewinsky in the Jones deposition, under that definition, correct?

A That's correct, sir.

Q If the person being deposed touched the genitalia of another person, would that be -- and with the intent to arouse the sexual desire, arouse or gratify, as defined in definition (1), would that be, under your understanding then and now --

A Yes, sir.

Q -- sexual relations?

A Yes, sir.

Q Yes, it would?

A Yes, it would. If you had a direct contact with any of these places in the body, if you had direct contact with intent to arouse or gratify, that would fall within the definition.

Q So, you didn't do any of those three things --

A You --

Q -- with Monica Lewinsky?

A You are free to infer that my testimony is that I did not have sexual relations, as I understood this term to be defined.

Q Including touching her breast, kissing her breast, or touching her genitalia?

A That's correct.

Q Would you agree with me that the insertion of an object into the genitalia of another person with the desire

548

96

to gratify sexually would fit within the definition used in the Jones case as sexual relations?

A There's nothing here about that, is there? I don't know that I ever thought about that one way or the other.

Q The question is, under the definition as you understood it then, under the definition as you understand it now -- pardon me just a minute.

Pardon me, Mr. President.

(Pause)

Deposition Exhibit 1, question 1, under the -- in the Jones case, Definition of Sexual Relations --

MR. KENDALL: Do you have that before you, Mr. President? Excuse me.

THE WITNESS: I do, sir.

MR. KENDALL: Good.

THE WITNESS: I've got it right here. I'm looking at it.

BY MR. WISENBERG:

Q As you understood the definition then, and as you understood it now, would it include sticking an object into the genitalia of another person in order to arouse or gratify the sexual desire of any person? Would it constitute, in other words, contact with the genitalia?

A I don't know the answer to that. I suppose you could argue that since section 2, paragraph (2) was eliminated, and paragraph (2) actually dealt with the object issue, that perhaps whoever wrote this didn't intend for paragraph (1) to cover an object, and basically meant direct contact.

So, if I were asked -- I've not been asked this question before. But I guess that's the way I would read it.

Q If it -- that it would not be covered? That activity would not be covered?

A That's right. If the activity you just mentioned would be covered in number (2), and number (2) were stricken, I think you can infer logically that paragraph (1) was not intended to cover it. But, as I said, I've not been asked this before. I'm just doing the best I can.

Q Well, if someone were to hold or a judge were to hold that you are incorrect and that definition (1) does include the hypo I've given to you -- because we're talking in hypos, so that you don't -- under your request here, if someone were to tell you or rule that you are wrong, that the insertion of an object into somebody else's genitalia with the intent to arouse or gratify the sexual desire of any person is within definition (1) --

MR. KENDALL: Mr. Wisenberg, excuse me. I have not objected heretofore to any question you've asked. I must tell you, I cannot understand that question. I think it's improper. And, if the witness can understand it, he may answer.

MR. WISENBERG: I'll be happy to rephrase it.

BY MR. WISENBERG:

Q If you're wrong and it's within definition (1), did you engage in sexual relations under the definition, with Monica Lewinsky?

A But, Mr. Wisenberg, I have said all along that I would say what I thought it meant, and you can infer that I didn't. This is an unusual question, but it's a slippery slope. We can -- I have tried to deal with some very delicate areas here, and, and in one case I've given you a very forthright answer about what I thought was not within here.

All I can tell you is, whatever I thought was covered, and I thought about this carefully. And let me just point out, this was uncomfortable for me. I had to acknowledge, because of this definition, that under this definition I had actually had sexual relations once with Gennifer Flowers, a person who had spread all kinds of ridiculous, dishonest, exaggerated stories about me for money. And I knew when I did that, it would be leaked. It was. And I was embarrassed. But I did it.

So, I tried to read this carefully. I can tell you what I thought it covered, and I can tell you that I do not believe I did anything that I thought was covered by this.

Q As I understand your testimony, Mr. President, touching somebody's breast with the intent to arouse, with the intent to arouse or gratify the sexual desire of any person is covered; kissing the breast is covered; touching the genitalia is covered; correct?

MR. KENDALL: In fairness, the witness said directly in each one of those cases.

BY MR. WISENBERG:

Q Directly, is covered, correct?

A I believe it is, yes, sir.

Q Oral sex, in your view, is not covered, correct?

A If performed on the deponent.

Q Is not covered, correct?

A That's my reading of this number (1).

Q And you are declining to answer the hypothetical about insertion of an object.

I need to inform you, Mr. President -- we'll go on, at least for now. But I need to inform you that the grand jury will consider your not answering the questions more directly in their determination of whether or not they are going to issue another subpoena.

Let me switch the topic and talk to you about John Podesta and some of the other aides you've met with and spoke to after this story became public on January 21st, 1998, the day of The Washington Post story.

Do you recall meeting with him around January 23rd, 1998, a Friday a.m. in your study, two days after The Washington Post story, and extremely explicitly telling him that you didn't have, engage in any kind of sex, in any way, shape or form, with Monica Lewinsky, including oral sex?

A I meet with John Podesta almost every day. I meet with a number of people. The only thing I -- what happened in the couple of days after what you did was revealed, is a blizzard to me. The only thing I recall is that I met with certain people, and a few of them I said I didn't have sex with Monica Lewinsky, or I didn't have an affair with her or something like that. I had a very careful thing I said, and I tried not to say anything else.

And it might be that John Podesta was one of them. But I do not remember this specific meeting about which you asked, or the specific comments to which you refer. And --

Q You don't remember --

A -- seven months ago, I'd have no way to remember, no.

Q You don't remember denying any kind of sex in any way, shape or form, and including oral sex, correct?

A I remember that I issued a number of denials to people that I thought needed to hear them, but I tried to be careful and to be accurate, and I do not remember what I said to John Podesta.

553

101

Q Surely, if you told him that, that would be a falsehood, correct?

A No, I didn't say that, sir. I didn't say that at all. That is not covered by the definition and I did not address it in my statement.

Q Well, let me ask you then. If you told him -- perhaps he thought it was covered, I don't know. But if you told him, if you denied to him sex in any way, shape or form, kind of similar to what Mr. Bennett did at the deposition, including oral sex, wouldn't that have been a falsehood?

A Now, Mr. Wisenberg, I told you in response to a grand juror's question, you asked me did I believe that oral sex performed on the person being deposed was covered by that definition, and I said no. I don't believe it's covered by the definition.

I said you are free to conclude that I did not do things that I believe were covered by the definition, and you have asked me a number of questions and I have acknowledged things that I believe are covered by the definition. Since that was not covered by the definition, I want to fall back on my statement.

Look, I'm not trying to be evasive here. I'm trying to protect my privacy, my family's privacy, and I'm trying to stick to what the deposition was about. If the deposition wasn't about this and didn't cover it, then I don't believe that I should be required to go beyond my statement.

Q Mr. President, it's not our intent to embarrass you. But since we have to look, among other things, at obstruction of justice, questions of obstruction of justice and perjury, the answer to some of these delicate and unfortunate questions are absolutely required. And that is the purpose that we have to ask them for.

A It's not --

Q I'm unaware of any --

A Mr. Wisenberg, with respect, you don't need to know the answer for that, if the answer, no matter what the answer is, wouldn't constitute perjury because it wasn't sexual relations as defined by the Judge.

Q Mister --

A The only reason you need to know that is for some other reason. It couldn't have anything to do with perjury.

Q Mr. President, one of the, one of the nice things about -- one of the normal things about an investigation and a grand jury investigation is that the grand jurors and the prosecutors get to ask the questions unless they are improper, and unless there is a legal basis.

As I understand from your answers, there is no legal basis for which you decline to answer these questions. And I'll ask you again to answer the question. I'm unaware of any legal basis for you not to. If you told --

MR. KENDALL: Mr. Wisenberg, could you just restate the question, please?

BY MR. WISENBERG:

Q The question is, if you told John Podesta two days after the story broke something to this effect, that you didn't have any kind of sex in any way, shape or form, including oral sex with Ms. Lewinsky, were you telling him the truth?

A And let me say again, with respect, this is an indirect way to try to get me to testify to questions that have no bearing on whether I committed perjury. You apparently agree that it has no bearing --

Q Oh, I don't --

A -- no bearing on whether I --

Q I don't agree.

A -- committed perjury.

Q Mr. President, I'm sorry, with respect, I don't agree with that. I'm not going to argue with you about it. I just am going to ask you again, in fact direct you to answer the question.

A I'm not going to answer that question, because I believe it's a question about conduct that, whatever the answer to it is, would, does not bear on the perjury because oral sex performed on the deponent under this definition is

556

104

not sexual relations. It is not covered by this definition.

MR. KENDALL: The witness is not declining to tell you anything he said to John Podesta.

BY MR. WISENBERG:

Q You denied the --

MR. WISENBERG: The witness is not declining to tell me anything?

BY MR. WISENBERG:

Q Did you deny oral sex in any way, shape or form, to John Podesta?

A I told you, sir, before, and I will say again, in the aftermath of this story breaking, and what was told about it, the next two days, next three days are just a blur to me. I don't remember to whom I talked, when I talked to them, or what I said.

Q So, you are not declining to answer, you just don't remember?

A I honestly don't remember, no.

Q Okay.

A I'm not saying that anybody who had a contrary memory is wrong. I do not remember.

Q Do you recall denying any sexual relationship with Monica Lewinsky to the following people: Harry Thomasson, Erskine Bowles, Harold Ickes, Mr. Podesta, Mr. Blumenthal, Mr. Jordan, Ms. Betty Currie? Do you recall denying any sexual relationship with Monica Lewinsky to those individuals?

A I recall telling a number of those people that I didn't have, either I didn't have an affair with Monica Lewinsky or didn't have sex with her. And I believe, sir, that -- you'll have to ask them what they thought. But I was using those terms in the normal way people use them. You'll have to ask them what they thought I was saying.

Q If they testified that you denied sexual relations or relationship with Monica Lewinsky, or if they told us that you denied that, do you have any reason to doubt them, in the days after the story broke; do you have any reason to doubt them?

A No. The -- let me say this. It's no secret to anybody that I hoped that this relationship would never become public. It's a matter of fact that it had been many, many months since there had been anything improper about it, in terms of improper contact. I --

Q Did you deny it to them or not, Mr. President?

A Let me finish. So, what -- I did not want to mislead my friends, but I wanted to find language where I could say that. I also, frankly, did not want to turn any of them into witnesses, because I -- and, sure enough, they all became witnesses.

Q Well, you knew they might be --

A And so --

Q -- witnesses, didn't you?

A And so I said to them things that were true about this relationship. That I used -- in the language I used, I said, there's nothing going on between us. That was true. I said, I have not had sex with her as I defined it. That was true. And did I hope that I would never have to be here on this day giving this testimony? Of course.

But I also didn't want to do anything to complicate this matter further. So, I said things that were true. They may have been misleading, and if they were I have to take responsibility for it, and I'm sorry.

Q It may have been misleading, sir, and you knew though, after January 21st when the Post article broke and said that Judge Starr was looking into this, you knew that they might be witnesses. You knew that they might be called into a grand jury, didn't you?

A That's right. I think I was quite careful what I said after that. I may have said something to all these people to that effect, but I'll also -- whenever anybody asked me any details, I said, look, I don't want you to be a witness or I turn you into a witness or give you information that could get you in trouble. I just wouldn't talk. I, by and large, didn't talk to people about this.

Q If all of these people -- let's leave out Mrs.

Currie for a minute. Vernon Jordan, Sid Blumenthal, John Podesta, Harold Ickes, Erskine Bowles, Harry Thomasson, after the story broke, after Judge Starr's involvement was known on January 21st, have said that you denied a sexual relationship with them. Are you denying that?

A No.

Q And you've told us that you --

A I'm just telling you what I meant by it. I told you what I meant by it when they started this deposition.

Q You've told us now that you were being careful, but that it might have been misleading. Is that correct?

A It might have been. Since we have seen this four-year, $40-million-investigation come down to parsing the definition of sex, I think it might have been. I don't think at the time that I thought that's what this was going to be about.

In fact, if you remember the headlines at the time, even you mentioned the Post story. All the headlines were -- and all the talking, people who talked about this, including a lot who have been quite sympathetic to your operation, said, well, this is not really a story about sex, or this is a story about subornation of perjury and these talking points, and all this other stuff.

So, what I was trying to do was to give them something they could -- that would be true, even if misleading in the context of this deposition, and keep them out of trouble, and let's deal -- and deal with what I thought was the almost ludicrous suggestion that I had urged someone to lie or tried to suborn perjury, in other words.

Q I want to go over some questions again. I don't think you are going to answer them, sir. And so I don't need a lengthy response, just a yes or a no. And I understand the basis upon which you are not answering them, but I need to ask them for the record.

If Monica Lewinsky says that while you were in the Oval Office area you touched her breasts, would she be lying?

A Let me say something about all this.

Q All I really need for you, Mr. President --

A I know.

Q -- is to say --

A But you --

Q -- I won't answer under the previous grounds, or to answer the question, you see, because we only have four hours, and your answers --

A I know.

Q -- have been extremely lengthy.

A I know that. I'll give you four hours and 30 seconds, if you'll let me say something general about this. I will answer to your satisfaction that I won't -- based on my statement, I will not answer. I would like 30 seconds at

561

109

the end to make a statement, and you can have 30 seconds more on your time, if you'll let me say this to the grand jury and to you. And I don't think it's disrespectful at all. I've had a lot of time to think about this.

But, go ahead and ask your questions.

Q The question is, if Monica Lewinsky says that while you were in the Oval Office area you touched her breasts, would she be lying?

A That is not my recollection. My recollection is that I did not have sexual relations with Ms. Lewinsky and I'm staying on my former statement about that.

Q If she said --

A My, my statement is that I did not have sexual relations as defined by that.

Q If she says that you kissed her breasts, would she be lying?

A I'm going to revert to my former statement.

Q Okay. If Monica Lewinsky says that while you were in the Oval Office area you touched her genitalia, would she be lying? And that calls for a yes, no, or reverting to your former statement.

A I will revert to my statement on that.

Q If Monica Lewinsky says that you used a cigar as a sexual aid with her in the Oval Office area, would she be lying? Yes, no, or won't answer?

A I will revert to my former statement.

Q If Monica Lewinsky says that you had phone sex with her, would she be lying?

A Well, that is, at least in general terms, I think, is covered by my statement. I addressed that in my statement, and that, I don't believe, is --

Q Let me define phone sex for purposes of my question. Phone sex occurs when a party to a phone conversation masturbates while the other party is talking in a sexually explicit manner. And the question is, if Monica Lewinsky says that you had phone sex with her, would she be lying?

A I think that is covered by my statement.

Q Did you, on or about January the 13th, 1998, Mr. President, ask Erskine Bowles to ask John Hilley if he would give a recommendation for Monica Lewinsky?

A In 1998?

Q Yes. On or about January 13th, 1998, did you ask Erskine Bowles, your Chief of Staff, if he would ask John Hilley to give a recommendation for Monica Lewinsky?

A At some point, sir, I believe I talked to Erskine Bowles about whether Monica Lewinsky could get a recommendation that was not negative from the Legislative Affairs Office. I believe I did.

Q I just didn't hear the very last part.

A I think the answer is, I think, yes. At some point I talked to Erskine Bowles about this.

Q Okay.

A I do not know what the date was. At some point I did talk to him.

Q And if Erskine Bowles has told us that he told John Podesta to carry out your wishes, and John Podesta states that it was three or four days before your deposition, which would be the 13th or the 14th, are you in a position to deny that?

A The 13th or 14th of?

Q January, as to date.

A I don't know. I don't know when the date was.

Q Okay.

A I'm not in a position to deny it. I won't deny it. I'm sure that they are both truthful men. I don't know when the date was.

Q Do you recall asking Erskine Bowles to do that?

A I recall talking to Erskine Bowles about that, and my recollection is, sir, that Ms. Lewinsky was moving to New York, wanted to get a job in the private sector; was confident she would get a good recommendation from the Defense Department; and was concerned that because she had been moved from the Legislative Affairs Office, transferred to the Defense Department, that her ability to get a job

564

112

might be undermined by a bad recommendation from the Legislative Affairs Office.

So, I asked Erskine if we could get her a recommendation that just was at least neutral, so that if she had a good recommendation from the Defense Department it wouldn't prevent her from getting a job in the private sector.

Q If Mr. Bowles has told us that, in fact, you told him that she already had a job and had already listed Mr. Hilley as a reference and wanted him to be available as a recommendation, would you be in -- is that inconsistent with your memory?

A A little bit, but I think -- my memory is that when you're, when you get a job like that you have to give them a resume, which says where you've worked and who your supervisor was. And I think that that's my recollection. My recollection is that -- slightly different from that.

Q And who was it that asked you to do that on Monica Lewinsky's behalf?

A I think she did. You know, she tried for months and months to get a job back in the White House, not so much in the West Wing but somewhere in the White House complex, including the Old Executive Office Building. And she talked to Marsha Scott, among others. She very much wanted to come back. And she interviewed for some jobs but never got one.

She was, from time to time, upset about it.

And I think what she was afraid of is that she couldn't get a -- from the minute she left the White House she was worried about this. That if she didn't come back to the White House and work for awhile and get a good job recommendation, that no matter how well she had done at the Pentagon it might hurt her future employment prospects.

Well, it became obvious that, you know, her mother had moved to New York. She wanted to go to New York. She wasn't going to get a job in the White House. So, she wanted to get a job in the private sector, and said, I hope that I won't get a letter out of the Legislative Affairs Office that will prevent my getting a job in the private sector. And that's what I talked to Erskine about.

Now, that's my entire memory of this.

Q All right. I want to go back briefly to the December 28th conversation with Ms. Lewinsky. I believe you testified to the effect that she asked you, what if they ask me about gifts you gave me. My question to you is, after that statement by her, did you ever have a conversation with Betty Currie about gifts, or picking something up from Monica Lewinsky?

A I don't believe I did, sir. No.

Q You never told her anything to this effect, that Monica has something to give you?

A No, sir.

Q That is to say, Betty Currie?

A No, sir, I didn't. I don't have any memory of that whatever.

Q And so you have no knowledge that, or you had no knowledge at the time, that Betty Currie went and picked up, your secretary went and picked up from Monica Lewinsky items that were called for by the Jones subpoena and hid them under her bed? You had no knowledge that anything remotely like that was going to happen?

A I did not. I did not know she had those items, I believe, until that was made public.

Q And you agree with me that that would be a very wrong thing to do, to hide evidence in a civil case, or any case? Isn't that true?

A Yes. I don't know that, that Ms. Currie knew that that's what she had at all. But --

Q I'm not saying she did. I'm just saying --

A I had -- it is, if Monica Lewinsky did that after they had been subpoenaed and she knew what she was doing, she should not have done that.

Q And if you knew, you --

A And I --

Q -- shouldn't have done it?

A Indeed, I, myself, told her, if they ask you for

567

115

gifts you have to give them what you have. And I don't understand if, in fact, she was worried about this, why she was so worried about it. It was no big deal.

Q I want to talk about a December 17th phone conversation you had with Monica Lewinsky at approximately 2:00 a.m. Do you recall making that conversation and telling her initially about the death of Betty's brother, but then telling her that she was on the witness list, and that it broke your heart that she was on the witness list?

A No, sir, I don't, but it would -- it, it would -- it is quite possible that that happened, because, if you remember, earlier in this meeting you asked me some questions about what I'd said to Monica about testimony and affidavits, and I was struggling to try to remember whether this happened in a meeting or a phone call.

Now, I remember I called her to tell her Betty's brother had died. I remember that. And I know it was in the middle of December, and I believe it was before Monica had been subpoenaed. So, I think it is quite possible that if I called her at that time and had not talked to her since the 6th -- and you asked me this earlier -- I believe when I saw her on the 6th, I don't think I knew she was on the witness list then, then it's quite possible I would say something like that. I don't have any memory of it, but I certainly wouldn't dispute that I might have said that.

568

116

Q And in that conversation, or in any conversation in which you informed her she was on the witness list, did you tell her, you know, you can always say that you were coming to see Betty or bringing me letters? Did you tell her anything like that?

A I don't remember. She was coming to see Betty. I can tell you this. I absolutely never asked her to lie.

Q Sir, every time she came to see Betty and you were in the Oval Office, she was coming to see you, too, wasn't she, or just about every time?

A I think just about every time. I don't think every time. I think there was a time or two where she came to see Betty when she didn't see me.

Q So, do you remember telling her any time, any time when you told her, or after you told her that she was on the witness list, something to this effect: You know, you can always say you were coming to see Betty, or you were bringing me letters?

A I don't remember exactly what I told her that night.

Q Did you --

A I don't remember that. I remember talking about the nature of our relationship, how she got in. But I also will tell you that I felt quite comfortable that she could have executed a truthful affidavit, which would not have

569

117

disclosed the embarrassing details of the relationship that we had had, which had been over for many, many months by the time this incident occurred.

Q Did you tell her anytime in December something to that effect: You know, you can always say that you were coming to see Betty or you were bringing me letters? Did you say that, or anything like that, in December '97 or January '98, to Monica Lewinsky?

A Well, that's a very broad question. I do not recall saying anything like that in connection with her testimony. I could tell you what I do remember saying, if you want to know. But I don't -- we might have talked about what to do in a non legal context at some point in the past, but I have no specific memory of that conversation.

I do remember what I said to her about the possible testimony.

Q You would agree with me, if you did say something like that to her, to urge her to say that to the Jones people, that that would be part of an effort to mislead the Jones people, no matter how evil they are and corrupt?

A I didn't say they were evil. I said what they were doing here was wrong, and it was.

Q Wouldn't that be misleading?

A Well, again, you are trying to get me to characterize something that I'm -- that I don't know if I said or not, without knowing whether the whole, whether the context is complete or not. So, I would have to know, what was the context, what were all the surrounding facts.

I can tell you this: I never asked Ms. Lewinsky to lie. The first time that she raised with me the possibility that she might be a witness or I told her -- you suggested the possibility in this December 17th timeframe -- I told her she had to get a lawyer. And I never asked her to lie.

Q Did you ever say anything like that, you can always say that you were coming to see Betty or bringing me letters? Was that part of any kind of a, anything you said to her or a cover story, before you had any idea she was going to be part of Paula Jones?

A I might well have said that.

Q Okay.

A Because I certainly didn't want this to come out, if I could help it. And I was concerned about that. I was embarrassed about it. I knew it was wrong. And, you know, of course, I didn't want it to come out. But --

Q But you are saying that you didn't say anything -- I want to make sure I understand. Did you say anything like that once you knew or thought she might be a witness in the Jones case? Did you repeat that statement, or something like it to her?

A Well, again, I don't recall, and I don't recall

whether I might have done something like that, for example, if somebody says, what if the reporters ask me this, that or the other thing. I can tell you this: In the context of whether she could be a witness, I have a recollection that she asked me, well, what do I do if I get called as a witness, and I said, you have to get a lawyer. And that's all I said. And I never asked her to lie.

Q Did you tell her to tell the truth?

A Well, I think the implication was she would tell the truth. I've already told you that I felt strongly that she could issue, that she could execute an affidavit that would be factually truthful, that might get her out of having to testify. Now, it obviously wouldn't if the Jones people knew this, because they knew that if they could get this and leak it, it would serve their larger purposes, even if the judge ruled that she couldn't be a witness in the case. The judge later ruled she wouldn't be a witness in the case. The judge later ruled the case had no merit.

So, I knew that. And did I hope she'd be able to get out of testifying on an affidavit? Absolutely. Did I want her to execute a false affidavit? No, I did not.

Q If Monica Lewinsky has stated that her affidavit that she didn't have a sexual relationship with you is, in fact, a lie, I take it you disagree with that?

A No. I told you before what I thought the issue was

there. I think the issue is how do you define sexual relationship. And there was no definition imposed on her at the time she executed the affidavit. Therefore, she was free to give it any reasonable meaning.

Q And if she says she was lying --

A And I believe --

Q -- under your common sense ordinary meaning that you talked about earlier, Mr. President, that most Americans would have, if she says sexual relationship, saying I didn't have one was a lie because I had oral sex with the President, I take it, you would disagree with that?

A Now, we're back to where we started and I have to invoke my statement. But, let me just say one thing. I've read a lot, and obviously I don't know whether any of it's accurate, about what she said, and what purports to be on those tapes.

And this thing -- and I searched my own memory. This reminds me, to some extent, of the hearings when Clarence Thomas and Anita Hill were both testifying under oath. Now, in some rational way, they could not have both been telling the truth, since they had directly different accounts of a shared set of facts. Fortunately, or maybe you think unfortunately, there was no special prosecutor to try to go after one or the other of them, to take sides and try to prove one was a liar. And so, Judge Thomas was able to go on and serve on the Supreme Court.

What I learned from that, I can tell you that I was a citizen out there just listening. And when I heard both of them testify, what I believed after it was over, I believed that they both thought they were telling the truth.

This is -- you're dealing with, in some ways, the most mysterious area of human life. I'm doing the best I can to give you honest answers.

Q Mr. President --

A And that's all I can say.

Q I'm sorry.

A And, you know, those people both testified under oath. So, if there'd been a special prosecutor, they could, one of them could have gone after Anita Hill, another could have gone after Clarence Thomas. I thank God there was no such thing then, because I don't believe that it was a proper thing.

Q One of --

A And I think they both thought they were telling the truth. So, maybe Ms. Lewinsky believes she's telling the truth, and I'm glad she got her mother and herself out of trouble. I'm glad you gave her that sweeping immunity. I'm glad for the whole thing. I, I, I -- it breaks my heart that she was ever involved in this.

Q I want to go back to a question about Vernon

574

122

Jordan. I want to go back to late December and early January, late December of '97 and early January of '98. During this time, Mr. President, you are being sued for sexual harassment by a woman who claims, among other things, that others got benefits that she didn't because she didn't have oral sex with you. While this is happening, your powerful friend, Vernon Jordan, is helping to get Monica Lewinsky a job and a lawyer. He's helping to get a job and a lawyer for someone who had some kind of sex with you, and who has been subpoenaed in the very case, the Jones case.

Don't you see a problem with this? Didn't you see a problem with this?

A No. Would you like to know why?

Q Isn't that why -- I would. But isn't that why Vernon Jordan asked you on December 19th whether or not you had sexual relationships with Monica Lewinsky and why he asked her, because he knew it would be so highly improper to be helping her with a lawyer and a job if, in fact, she had had a relationship with you?

A I don't know. I don't believe that at all. I don't believe that at all, particularly since, even if you look at the facts here in their light most unfavorable to me, no one has suggested that there was any sexual harassment on my part. And I don't think it was wrong to be helping her. Look --

575

123

Q A subpoenaed witness in a case against you?

A Absolutely. Look, for one thing, I had already proved in two ways that I was not trying to influence her testimony. I didn't order her to be hired at the White House. I could have done so. I wouldn't do it. She tried for months to get in. She was angry.

Secondly, after I --

Q Wasn't she kept --

A After I terminated the improper contact with her, she wanted to come in more than she did. She got angry when she didn't get in sometimes. I knew that that might make her more likely to speak, and I still did it because I had to limit the contact.

And, thirdly, let me say, I formed an opinion really early in 1996, and again -- well, let me finish the sentence. I formed an opinion early in 1996, once I got into this unfortunate and wrong conduct, that when I stopped it, which I knew I'd have to do and which I should have done a long time before I did, that she would talk about it. Not because Monica Lewinsky is a bad person. She's basically a good girl. She's a good young woman with a good heart and a good mind. I think she is burdened by some unfortunate conditions of her, her upbringing. But she's basically a good person.

But I knew that the minute there was no longer any

576

124

contact, she would talk about this. She would have to. She couldn't help it. It was, it was a part of her psyche. So, I had put myself at risk, sir. I was not trying to buy her silence or get Vernon Jordan to buy her silence. I thought she was a good person. She had not been involved with me for a long time in any improper way, several months, and I wanted to help her get on with her life. It's just as simple as that.

MR. WISENBERG: It's time for a break.

MR. KENDALL: Okay. 4:49.

(Whereupon, the proceedings were recessed from 4:49 p.m. until 5:05 p.m.)

MR. KENDALL: Bob, we are at 2 hours and 55 minutes.

MR. BITTMAN: Two hours and 55 minutes, thank you.

BY MR. BITTMAN:

Q Mr. President.

A Mr. Bittman.

Q Apparently we have one hour and five minutes left, if we stick to the four-hour timeframe.

MR. KENDALL: Plus 30 seconds.

MR. BITTMAN: And 30 seconds, that's right.

THE WITNESS: You gave me my 30 seconds' soliloquy. So, I owe you 30 seconds.

BY MR. BITTMAN:

Q You are very generous. That actually segues very nicely into one of the grand juror's asked, pointed out actually, that you indicated at the beginning of the deposition that you would, you would answer all the grand jurors, you wanted to answer all the grand jurors' questions. And they wanted to know whether you would be willing to stay beyond the four-hour period to, in fact, answer all their questions.

A Well, let's see how we do in the next hour, and then we'll decide.

Q Okay. Let me draw your attention to early January of this year, after Christmas, before your deposition. Do you remember talking to Betty Currie about Monica, who had just called her and said that she, Monica, needed to talk to you before she signed something?

A I'm not sure that I do remember that. But, go ahead.

Q This is in early January. And then Betty Currie relayed this to you that Monica called, it's important, she needs to talk to you before she signs something. And then you do, indeed, talk to Monica that day on the telephone.

A I did talk to her that day?

Q Yes.

MR. KENDALL: Mr. President, excuse me. That's a

578

126

question. If you have a memory of that, you can answer.

THE WITNESS: I'm trying to remember when the last time I talked to her was. I am aware, sir, that she signed this affidavit about this time, sometime in the first week in January. I may have talked to her before she did it. I don't know. I talked to her a number of times between the time Betty's brother died and Christmas. Then I saw her on December 28. I may have talked to her, but I don't remember the specific conversation.

BY MR. BITTMAN:

Q And you would have talked about the -- she had just given you a gift actually in early January, a book on the Presidents of the United States. And you discussed this with her and she said that you said you liked it a lot.

A I did like it a lot. I told you that. My impression, my belief was that she gave me that book for Christmas. Maybe that's not right. I think she had that book delivered to me for Christmas. And then, as I remember, I went to Bosnia and for some reason she wasn't there around Christmas time.

But, anyway, maybe I didn't get it until January. My recollection was that I had gotten it right before Christmas.

Q Let me see if I can jog your memory further. Monica talked to you in that phone conversation that told you

579

127

that she had just met with her attorney that Mr. Jordan arranged with her, and the attorney said that if she is deposed that they were going to ask her how she got her job at the Pentagon. And Monica then asked you, what do you think I should say, how do I answer that question, how did I get the job at the Pentagon. Did you talk to Monica about that, about possibilities --

A I don't believe -- no. I don't remember her asking me that. But if she, if she had asked me that, I would have told her to tell the truth. I -- and I didn't, you know, I don't know exactly how she got her job at the Pentagon. I know Evelyn Lieberman wanted to transfer her out of the job she had, and somebody must have arranged that. But I didn't arrange it.

Q Now, that's actually not my question. My question is whether you remember talking to Monica about her being concerned that, I may have to answer some questions about how and why I was transferred to the Pentagon out of the White House, fearing that this would --

A No, I don't remember that at all.

Q -- lead to questions, or answers that would reveal your relationship?

A Oh, no, sir. I don't remember that. Maybe somebody -- maybe she did. But I only remember -- well, I don't remember that. That's all I can tell you. I don't

580

128

remember that.

Q Are you saying, Mr. President, that you did not then say to Ms. Lewinsky that you could always say that people in Legislative Affairs got you the job, or helped you get it?

A I have no recollection of that whatever.

Q Are you saying you didn't say it?

A No, sir. I'm telling you, I want to say I don't recall -- I don't have any memory of this as I sit here today. And I can tell you this, I never asked her to lie. I never did. And I don't have any recollection of the specific thing you are saying to me.

Now, if I could back up, there were several times when Monica Lewinsky talked to me on the telephone in 1996, in person in 1997, about her being concerned about what anybody would say about her transfer from the White House to the Pentagon. But I remember no conversation in which she was concerned about it for the reasons you just mentioned.

And all my memory is, she was worried about it because she thought it would keep her from getting a good job down the road, and she talked to me about it constantly in 1997. She thought, well, I'll never have my record clear unless I work somewhere in the White House complex where I can get a good recommendation. But in the context that you mention it, I do not recall a conversation.

Q Did you ever tell Ms. Lewinsky, or promise to her that you would do your best to get her back into the White House after the 1996 Presidential elections?

A What I told Ms. Lewinsky was that I would, I would do what I could to see, if she had a good record at the Pentagon, and she assured me she was doing a good job and working hard, that I would do my best to see that the fact that she had been sent away from the Legislative Affairs section did not keep her from getting a job in the White House, and that is, in fact, what I tried to do. I had a conversation with Ms. Scott about it, and I tried to do that.

But I did not tell her I would order someone to hire her, and I never did, and I wouldn't do that. It wouldn't be right.

Q When you received the book, this gift from Monica, the Presidents of the United States, this book that you liked and you talked with Monica about, did it come with a note? Do you remember the note that it came with, Mr. President?

A No, sir, I don't.

Q Do you remember that in the note she wrote that, she expressed how much she missed you and how much she cared for you, and you and she later talked about this in this telephone conversation, and you said -- and she apologized for putting such emotional, romantic things in this note, and you said, yeah, you shouldn't have written some of those things, you shouldn't put those things down on paper? Did you ever say anything like that to Ms. Lewinsky?

A Oh, I believe I did say something like that to Ms. Lewinsky. I don't remember doing something as late as you suggest. I'm not saying I didn't. I have no recollection of that.

Keep in mind now, it had been quite a long time since I had had any improper contact with her. And she was, in a funny way, almost more attached to me than she had been before. In '96, she had a long relationship, she said, with a man whom she liked a lot. And I didn't know what else was going on in her private life in '97. But she talked to me occasionally about people she was going out with.

But normally her language at this point was, if affectionate, was, was not improperly affectionate, I would say. So -- but, it could have happened. I wouldn't say it didn't. I just don't remember it at this late date.

Q Let me refer back to one of the subjects we talked about at one of the earlier breaks, right before one of the earlier breaks, and that is your meeting with Mrs. Currie on January 18th. This is the Sunday after your deposition in the Paula Jones case.

You said that you spoke to her in an attempt to refresh your own recollection about the events involving Monica Lewinsky, is that right?

583

131

A Yes.

Q How did you making the statement, I was never alone with her, right, refresh your recollection?

A Well, first of all, let's remember the context here. I did not at that time know of your involvement in this case. I just knew that obviously someone had given them a lot of information, some of which struck me as accurate, some of which struck me as dead wrong. But it led them to write, ask me a whole serious of questions about Monica Lewinsky.

Then on Sunday morning, this Drudge report came out, which used Betty's name, and I thought that we were going to be deluged by press comments. And I was trying to refresh my memory about what the facts were.

So, when I said, we were never alone, right, I think I also asked her a number of other questions, because there were several times, as I'm sure she would acknowledge, when I either asked her to be around. I remember once in particular when I was talking with Ms. Lewinsky when I asked Betty to be in the, actually, in the next room in the dining room, and, as I testified earlier, once in her own office.

But I meant that she was always in the Oval Office complex, in that complex, while Monica was there. And I believe that this was part of a series of questions I asked her to try to quickly refresh my memory. So, I wasn't trying to get her to say something that wasn't so. And, in fact, I think she would recall that I told her to just relax, go in the grand jury and tell the truth when she had been called as a witness.

Q So, when you said to Mrs. Currie that, I was never alone with her, right, you just meant that you and Ms. Lewinsky would be somewhere perhaps in the Oval Office or many times in your back study, is that correct?

A That's right. We were in the back study.

Q And then --

A Keep in mind, sir, I just want to make it -- I was talking about 1997. I was never, ever trying to get Betty Currie to claim that on the occasions when Monica Lewinsky was there when she wasn't anywhere around, that she was. I would never have done that to her, and I don't think she thought about that. I don't think she thought I was referring to that.

Q Did you put a date restriction? Did you make it clear to Mrs. Currie that you were only asking her whether you were never alone with her after 1997?

A Well, I don't recall whether I did or not, but I assumed -- if I didn't, I assumed she knew what I was talking about, because it was the point at which Ms. Lewinsky was out of the White House and had to have someone WAVE her in, in order to get in the White House. And I do not believe to this day that I was -- in 1997, that she was ever there and that I ever saw her unless Betty Currie was there. I don't believe she was.

Q Do you agree with me that the statement, "I was never alone with her", is incorrect? You were alone with Monica Lewinsky, weren't you?

A Well, again, it depends on how you define alone. Yes, we were alone from time to time, even during 1997, even when there was absolutely no improper contact occurring. Yes, that is accurate.

But there were also a lot of times when, even though no one could see us, the doors were open to the halls, on both ends of the halls, people could hear. The Navy stewards could come in and out at will, if they were around. Other things could be happening. So, there were a lot of times when we were alone, but I never really thought we were.

And sometimes when we, when -- but, as far as I know, what I was trying to determine, if I might, is that Betty was always around, and I believe she was always around where I could basically call her or get her if I needed her.

Q When you said to Mrs. Currie, you could see and hear everything, that wasn't true either, was it, as far as you knew? You've already --

A My memory of that --

Q -- testified that Betty was not there.

A My memory of that was that, that she had the ability to hear what was going on if she came in the Oval Office from her office. And a lot of times, you know, when I was in the Oval Office, she just had the door open to her office. Then there was -- the door was never completely closed to the hall. So, I think there was -- I'm not entirely sure what I meant by that, but I could have meant that she generally would be able to hear conversations, even if she couldn't see them. And I think that's what I meant.

Now, I could have been referring not generally to every time she was there, but one, one particular time I remember when Ms. Lewinsky was there when I asked Betty -- and I'm sorry to say for reasons I don't entirely remember -- to actually stay in the dining room while I talked with Monica. I do remember one such instance.

Q Well, you've already testified that this -- you did almost everything you could to keep this relationship secret. So, would it be fair to say -- even from Mrs. Currie. She didn't know about the nature, that is, your intimate, physically intimate relationship with Ms. Lewinsky, did she?

A As far as I know, she is unaware of what happened on the, on the occasions when I saw her in 1996 when something improper happened. And she was unaware of the one time that I recall in 1997 when something happened.

I think she was quite well aware that I was

determined to impose the appropriate limits on the relationship when I was trying to do it. And the -- you know, anybody would hope that this wouldn't become public. Although I frankly, from 1996 on, always felt that if I severed inappropriate contact with Ms. Lewinsky, sooner or later it would get public. And I never thought it would be part of the Jones case. I never even thought about that. I never thought -- I certainly never thought it would be part of your responsibilities.

Q My question was --

A But I did believe that she would talk about it.

Q My question was more simple than that. Mrs. Currie did not know of the physically intimate nature of your relationship, did she?

A I don't believe she did, no.

Q Okay. So, you would have done -- you tried to keep that nature of the relationship from Mrs. Currie?

A Absolutely. I --

Q So, you would not have engaged in those physically intimate acts if you knew that Mrs. Currie could see or hear that, is that correct?

A That's correct. But, keep in mind, sir, I was talking about 1997. That occurred, to the -- and I believe that occurred only once in February of 1997. I stopped it. I never should have started it, and I certainly shouldn't have started it back after I resolved not to in 1996. And I was referring to 1997.

And I -- what -- as I say, I do not know -- her memory and mine may be somewhat different. I do not know whether I was asking her about a particular time when Monica was upset and I asked her to stand, stay back in the dining area. Or whether I was, had reference to the fact that if she kept the door open to the Oval Office, because it was always -- the door to the hallway was always somewhat open, that she would always be able to hear something if anything went on that was, you know, too loud, or whatever.

I do not know what I meant. I'm just trying to reconcile the two statements as best I can, without being sure.

Q There was at least one event where Mrs. Currie was definitely not even in the Oval Office area, isn't that right? And I think you began to testify about that before. That was at the radio address.

A I'm not sure of that. But in that case, there was, there was certainly someone else there. I don't know --

Q Well, why would you be testing Mrs. Currie's memory about whether someone else was there?

A Well, I can say this. If I'm in the Oval Office -- my belief is that there was someone else there, somewhere in the Oval Office complex. I've looked at our -- I've looked at the film. This, this night has become legendary now, you know. I've looked at the, I've looked at the film we have. I've looked at my schedules. I've seen the people that were at the radio address.

I do believe that I was alone with her from 15 to 20 minutes. I do believe that things happened then which were inappropriate. I don't remember whether Betty was there or not, but I can't imagine that, since all this happened more or less continuously in that time period, there must have been someone who was working around the radio address who stayed around somewhere. That would be my guess. I don't know. I'm sorry. I don't have records about who it would be. But I doubt very seriously if we were all alone in that Oval Office complex then.

Q Mr. President, if there is a semen stain belonging to you on a dress of Ms. Lewinsky's, how would you explain that?

A Well, Mr. Bittman, I, I don't -- first of all, when you asked me for a blood test, I gave you one promptly. You came over here and got it. That's -- we met that night and talked. So, that's a question you already know the answer to. Not if, but you know whether.

And the main thing I can tell you is that doesn't affect the opening statement I made. The opening statement I made is that I had inappropriate intimate contact. I take full responsibility for it. It wasn't her fault, it was mine. I do not believe that I violated the definition of sexual relations I was given by directly touching those parts of her body with the intent to arouse or gratify. And that's all I have to say.

I think, for the rest, you know, you know what the evidence is and it doesn't affect that statement.

Q Is it possible or impossible that your semen is on a dress belonging to Ms. Lewinsky?

A I have nothing to add to my statement about it, sir. You, you know whether -- you know what the facts are. There's no point in a hypothetical.

Q Don't you know what the facts are also, Mr. President?

A I have nothing to add to my statement, sir.

Q Getting back to the conversation you had with Mrs. Currie on January 18th, you told her -- if she testified that you told her, Monica came on to me and I never touched her, you did, in fact, of course, touch Ms. Lewinsky, isn't that right, in a physically intimate way?

A Now, I've testified about that. And that's one of those questions that I believe is answered by the statement that I made.

Q What was your purpose in making these statements to Mrs. Currie, if they weren't for the purpose to try to suggest to her what she should say if ever asked?

A Now, Mr. Bittman, I told you, the only thing I remember is when all this stuff blew up, I was trying to figure out what the facts were. I was trying to remember. I was trying to remember every time I had seen Ms. Lewinsky. Once this thing was in Drudge, and there was this argument about whether it was or was not going to be in Newsweek, that was a clear signal to me, because Newsweek, frankly, was -- had become almost a sponsoring media outlook for the Paula Jones case, and had a journalist who had been trying, so far fruitlessly, to find me in some sort of wrongdoing.

And so I knew this was all going to come out. I was trying -- I did not know at the time -- I will say again, I did not know that any of you were involved. I did not know that the Office of Independent Counsel was involved. And I was trying to get the facts and try to think of the best defense we could construct in the face of what I thought was going to be a media onslaught.

Once you became involved, I told Betty Currie not to worry, that, that she had been through a terrible time. She had lost her brother. She had lost her sister. Her mother was in the hospital. I said, Betty, just don't worry about me. Just relax, go in there and tell the truth. You'll be fine. Now, that's all there was in this context.

Q Did the conversations that you had with Mrs.

Currie, this conversation, did it refresh your recollection as to events involving Ms. Lewinsky?

A Well, as I remember, I do believe, in fairness, that, you know, she may have felt some ambivalence about how to react, because there were some times when she seemed to say yes, when I'm not sure she meant yes. There was a time -- it seems like there was one or two things where she said, well, remember this, that or the other thing, which did reflect my recollection.

So, I would say a little yes, and a little no.

Q Why was it then that two or three days later, given that The Washington Post article came out on January 21st, why would you have had another conversation with Betty Currie asking or making the exact same statements to her?

A I don't know that I did. I remember having this one time. I was, I was -- I don't know that I did.

Q If Mrs. Currie says you did, are you disputing that?

A No, sir, I'm not disputing --

MR. KENDALL: Excuse me. Is your representation that she testified that that conversation was -- when?

MR. BITTMAN: I'm not making a representation as to what Mrs. Currie said. I'm asking the President if Mrs. Currie testified two or three days later, that two or three days after the conversation with the President on January

593

141

18th, that he called her into the Oval Office and went over the exact same statements that the President made to her on the 18th.

BY MR. BITTMAN:

Q Is that accurate? Is that a truthful statement by Mrs. Currie, if she made it?

A I do not remember how many times I talked to Betty Currie or when. I don't. I can't possibly remember that. I do remember, when I first heard about this story breaking, trying to ascertain what the facts were, trying to ascertain what Betty's perception was. I remember that I was highly agitated, understandably, I think.

And then I remember when I knew she was going to have to testify to the grand jury, and I, I felt terrible because she had been through this loss of her sister, this horrible accident Christmas that killed her brother, and her mother was in the hospital. I was trying to do -- to make her understand that I didn't want her to, to be untruthful to the grand jury. And if her memory was different from mine, it was fine, just go in there and tell them what she thought. So, that's all I remember.

BY MR. BENNETT:

Q Mr. President, my name is Jackie Bennett. If I understand your current line of testimony, you are saying that your only interest in speaking with Ms. Currie in the days after your deposition was to refresh your own recollection?

A Yes.

Q It was not to impart instructions on how she was to recall things in the future?

A No, and certainly not under oath. That -- every day, Mr. Bennett, in the White House and in every other political organization when you are subject to a barrage of press questions of any kind, you always try to make the best case you can consistent with the facts; that is, while being truthful.

But -- so, I was concerned for a day or two there about this as a press story only. I had no idea you were involved in it for a couple of days.

I think Betty Currie's testimony will be that I gave her explicit instructions or encouragement to just go in the grand jury and tell the truth. That's what I told her to do and I thought she would.

Q Mr. President, when did you learn about the Drudge Report reporting allegations of you having a sexual relationship with someone at the White House?

A I believe it was the morning of the 18th, I think.

Q What time of day, sir?

A I have no idea.

Q Early morning hours?

A Yeah, I think somebody called me and told me about it. Maybe Bruce, maybe someone else. I'm not sure. But I learned early on the 18th of the Drudge Report.

Q Very early morning hours, sir?

A Now, my deposition was on the 17th, is that right?

Q On Saturday, the 17th, sir.

A Yeah, I think it was when I got up Sunday morning, I think. Maybe it was late Saturday night. I don't remember.

Q Did you call Betty Currie, sir, after the Drudge Report hit the wire?

A I did.

Q Did you call her at home?

A I did. Was that the night of the 17th?

Q Night of the 17th, early morning hours of the 18th?

A Okay, yes. That's because -- yes. I worked with Prime Minister Netanyahu that night until about midnight.

MR. KENDALL: Wait.

THE WITNESS: Isn't that right?

MR. KENDALL: Excuse me. I think the question is directed -- Mr. Bennett, if you could help out by putting the day of the week, I think that would be helpful.

BY MR. BENNETT:

Q Saturday night, Sunday morning.

A Yes. I called Betty Currie as soon -- I think

about as soon as I could, after I finished with Prime Minister Netanyahu, and in the aftermath of that meeting planning where we were going next in the Middle East peace process.

MR. KENDALL: Can we take a two-minute break, please?

MR. BITTMAN: May I ask one other question first, Mr. Kendall?

MR. KENDALL: Certainly. I think the witness is confused on dates. That's all.

MR. BITTMAN: Okay.

THE WITNESS: That's what -- I didn't think it was the night of the 17th.

MR. KENDALL: Mr. President, I think we'll do it in a break.

THE WITNESS: Can we have a break and I could get straightened out?

MR. BITTMAN: Sure. May I ask one other quick -- this is a question I forgot to ask from the grand jurors.

THE WITNESS: I don't want to get mixed up on these dates now. Go ahead.

BY MR. BITTMAN:

Q This is -- they wanted to know whether, they want us to clarify that the President's knowledge, your knowledge, Mr. President, as to the approach to our office this morning;

597

145

that is, we were told that you would give a general statement about the nature of your relationship with Ms. Lewinsky, which you have done. Yet that you would -- you did not want to go in any of the details about the relationship. And that if we pressed on going into the details, that you would object to going into the details.

And the grand jurors, before they wanted, they wanted to vote on some other matters, they wanted to know whether you were aware of that? That we were told that?

MR. KENDALL: Well, Mr. Bittman, who told you that? This is, this is, this is not a fair question, when you say you were told. Who told you?

MR. BITTMAN: Who told me what, the question?

MR. KENDALL: You said, you said the grand jury was told.

MR. BITTMAN: We have kept the grand jury informed, as we normally would, of the proceedings here.

MR. KENDALL: Right. And, I'm sorry. Who, who are you representing told you or the grand jurors anything? Is that, is that our conversation?

MR. BITTMAN: Yes.

MR. STARR: Yes, our conversation.

MR. BITTMAN: Yes. That was in substance related to the grand jurors.

THE WITNESS: And what's your question to me, Mr.

Bittman?

BY MR. BITTMAN:

Q Whether you were aware of the facts that I just described?

A Yes, sir. Let me say this. I knew that Mr. Kendall was going to talk with Judge Starr. What we wanted to do was to be as helpful as we could to you on the question of whether you felt I was being truthful, when I said I did not have sexual relations with Ms. Lewinsky, as defined in that definition (1) in this, in my testimony.

And I thought the best way to do that, and still preserve some measure of privacy and dignity, would be to invite all of you and the grand jurors to ask, well, would you consider this, that, or the other thing covered by the definition. You asked me several questions there, and I did my best to answer whether I thought they were covered by the definition, and said if I thought they were covered, you could conclude from that that my testimony is I did not do them.

If those things, if things are not covered by the definition, and I don't believe they are covered, then I could not -- then they shouldn't be within this discussion one way or the other.

Now, I know this is somewhat unusual. But I would say to the grand jury, put yourself in my position. This is not a typical grand jury testimony. I, I have to assume a report is going to Congress. There's a videotape being made of this, allegedly because only one member of the grand jury is absent. This is highly unusual. And, in addition to that, I have sustained a breathtaking number of leaks of grand jury proceedings.

And, so, I think I am right to answer all the questions about perjury, but not to say things which will be forever in the historic annals of the United States because of this unprecedented videotape and may be leaked at any time. I just think it's a mistake.

And, so, I'm doing my best to cooperate with the grand jury and still protect myself, my family, and my office.

MR. BITTMAN: Thank you.

MR. KENDALL: This will be two minutes.

(Whereupon, the proceedings were recessed from 5:37 p.m. until 5:43 p.m.)

BY MR. BENNETT:

Q Mr. President, before we broke, we were talking about the sequencing of your conversations with Betty Currie following your deposition on Saturday, January 17th. Do you recall that?

A I do.

Q All right. And you recall contacting Betty Currie,

calling her and instructing her on the evening of Saturday night, after your deposition, and telling her to come in the next day?

A Yes, sir, I do.

Q Sunday was normally her day off, isn't that so?

A Yes, it was.

Q And so you were making special arrangements for her to come back into the White House, isn't that so?

A Well, yes. I asked her to come back in and talk to me.

Q And it was at that time that you spoke with her, and Mr. Bittman and Mr. Wisenberg have asked you questions bout what you said in that conversation, isn't that so?

A Yes, they have -- I don't know whether that's the time, but they -- I did talk to her as soon as I realized that the deposition had become more about Monica Lewinsky than Paula Jones. I asked her, you know, if she knew anything about this. I said, you know, it's obvious that this is going to be a matter of press speculation, and I was trying to go through the litany of what had happened between us, and asked some questions.

Q On fairness, it would be more than a matter of simple press speculation, isn't that so? Mr. President, there was a question about whether you had testified fully, completely, and honestly on the preceding day in your

601

149

deposition.

A Well, actually, Mr. Bennett, I didn't think about that then. I -- this has been a rather unprecedented development, and I wasn't even thinking about the Independent Counsel getting into this. So, at that moment, I knew nothing about it and I was more interested in what the facts were and whether Ms. Currie knew anything about it, knew anything about what Monica Lewinsky knew about it.

Q Mr. President, you've told us at least a little bit about your understanding of how the term sexual relations was used, and what you understood it to mean in the context of your deposition. Isn't that correct?

A That is correct.

Q And you've told us -- I mean, that was a lawsuit Paula Jones filed in which she alleged that you asked her to perform oral sex, isn't that so?

A That was her allegation.

Q That was her allegation. And, notwithstanding that that was her allegation, you've testified that you understood the term sexual relations, in the context of the questions you were being asked, to mean something else, at least insofar as you were the recipient rather than the performer?

A Sir, Paula Jones' lawyers pulled out that definition, not me. And Judge Susan Webber Wright ruled on it, just as she later ruled their case had no merit in the first place, no legal merit, and dismissed it.

I had nothing to do with the definition. I had nothing to do with the Judge's rulings. I was simply there answering the questions they put to me, under the terms of reference they imposed.

Q Well, the grand jury would like to know, Mr. President, why it is that you think that oral sex performed on you does not fall within the definition of sexual relations as used in your deposition.

A Because that is -- if the deponent is the person who has oral sex performed on him, then the contact is with -- not with anything on that list, but with the lips of another person. It seems to be self-evident that that's what it is. And I thought it was curious.

Let me remind you, sir, I read this carefully. And I thought about it. I thought about what "contact" meant. I thought about what "intent to arouse or gratify" meant.

And I had to admit under this definition that I'd actually had sexual relations with Gennifer Flowers. Now, I would rather have taken a whipping than done that, after all the trouble I'd been through with Gennifer Flowers, and the money I knew that she had made for the story she told about this alleged 12-year affair, which we had done a great deal to disprove.

So, I didn't like any of this. But I had done my

best to deal with it and the -- that's what I thought. And I think that's what most people would think, reading that.

Q Would you have been prepared, if asked by the Jones lawyers, would you have been prepared to answer a question directly asked about oral sex performed on you by Monica Lewinsky?

A If the Judge had required me to answer it, of course, I would have answered it. And I would have answered it truthfully, if I --

Q By the way, do you believe that the --

A -- had been required.

Q -- Jones litigants had the same understanding of sexual relations that you claim you have?

A I don't know what their understanding was, sir. My belief is that they thought they'd get this whole thing in, and that they were going to -- what they were trying to do is do just what they did with Gennifer Flowers. They wanted to find anything they could get from me or anyone else that was negative, and then they wanted to leak it to hurt me in the press, which they did even though the Judge ordered them not to.

So, I think their --

Q Wouldn't it -- I'm sorry.

A I think their position, Mr. Bennett -- you asked the question -- their position was, we're going to cast the widest net we can and get as much embarrassing stuff as we can, and then dump it out there and see if we can make him bleed. I think that's what they were trying to do.

Q Don't you think, sir, that they could have done more damage to you politically, or in whatever context, if they had understood the definition in the same way you did and asked the question directly?

A I don't know, sir. As I said, I didn't work with their lawyers in preparing this case. I knew the case was wrong. I knew what our evidence was. By the time of this deposition, they knew what their evidence was.

Their whole strategy was, well, our lawsuit's not good, but maybe we can hurt him with the discovery. And, you know, they did some. But it didn't amount to much.

And did I want, if I could, to avoid talking about Monica Lewinsky? Yes, I'd give anything in the world not to be here talking about it. I'd be giving -- I'd give anything in the world not to have to admit what I've had to admit today.

But if you look at my answer in the Flowers [sic] deposition, at least you know I tried to carefully fit all my answers within the framework there, because otherwise there was no reason in the wide world for me to do anything other than make the statements I'd made about Gennifer Flowers since 1991, that I did not have a 12-year affair with her,

605

153

and that these, the following accusations she made are false.

So, that's all I can tell you. I can't prove anything.

Q But you did have a great deal of anxiety in the hours and days following the end of your deposition on the 17th. Isn't that fair to say?

A Well, I had a little anxiety the next day, of course, because of the Drudge Report. And I had an anxiety after the deposition because it was more about Monica Lewinsky than it was about Paula Jones.

Q The specificity of the questions relating to Monica Lewinsky alarmed you, isn't that fair to say?

A Yes, and it bothered me, too, that I couldn't remember the answers. It bothered me that I couldn't -- as Mr. Wisenberg pointed out, it bothered me that I couldn't remember all the answers. I did the best I could. And so I wanted to know what the deal was. Sure.

Q Mr. President, to your knowledge, have you turned over, in response to the grand jury subpoenas, all gifts that Monica Lewinsky gave you?

A To my knowledge, I have, sir. As you know, on occasion, Mr. Kendall has asked for your help in identifying those gifts. And I think there were a couple that we came across in our search that were not on the list you gave us, that I remembered in the course of our search had been given to me by Monica Lewinsky and we gave them to you.

So, to the best of my knowledge, we have given you everything we have.

Q Can you explain why, on the very day that Monica Lewinsky testified in the grand jury on August 6th of this year, you wore a necktie that she had given you?

A No, sir, I don't believe I did. What necktie was it?

Q The necktie you wore on August 6th, sir.

A Well, I don't know that it was a necktie that Monica Lewinsky gave me. Can you describe it to me?

Q Well, I don't want to take time at this point, but we will provide you with photographic evidence of that, Mr. President.

A If you give me -- I don't believe that's accurate, Mr. Bennett.

Q So, let me ask the question --

A But if you give it to me, and I look at it and I remember that she gave it to me, I'll be happy to produce it. I do not believe that's right.

Q Well, if you remember that she gave it to you, why haven't you produced it to the grand jury?

A I don't remember that she gave it to me. That's why I asked you what the tie was. I have --

Q Can you --

607

155

A -- no earthly idea. I believe that, that I did not wear a tie she gave me on August the 6th.

Q Can you tell us why Bayani Nelvis wore a tie that Monica Lewinsky had given you on the day he appeared in the grand jury?

A I don't know that he did.

Q Have you given Bayani Nelvis any ties, sir?

A Oh, yes, a lot of ties.

Q And so if he wore the tie that you gave him, that Monica Lewinsky had given you, that would not have been by design, is that what you are telling us?

A Oh, absolutely not. Let me --

Q You are not --

A May I explain, Mr. Bennett? It won't --

Q Yes.

A -- take long. Every year, since I've been President, I've gotten quite a large number of ties, as you might imagine. I get, I have a couple of friends, one in Chicago and one in Florida who give me a lot of ties, a lot of other people who send me ties all the time, or give them to me when I see them.

So, I always have the growing number of ties in my closet. What I normally do, if someone gives me a tie as a gift, is I wear it a time or two. I may use it. But at the end of every year, and sometimes two times a year, sometimes

608

156

more, I go through my tie closet and I think of all the things that I won't wear a lot or that I might give away, and I give them mostly to the men who work there.

I give them to people like Glen and Nelvis, who work in the kitchen, back in the White House, or the gentlemen who are my stewards or the butlers, or the people who run the elevators. And I give a lot of ties away a year. I'll bet I -- excluding Christmas, I bet I give 30, 40, maybe more ties away a year, and then, of course, at Christmas, a lot.

So, there would be nothing unusual if, in fact, Nelvis had a tie that originally had come into my tie closet from Monica Lewinsky. It wouldn't be unusual. It wouldn't be by design. And there are several other people of whom that is also true.

Q Mr. President, I'd like to move to a different area right now. I'd like to ask you some questions about Kathleen Willey. You met Kathleen Willey during your 1992 campaign, isn't that so?

A Yes, sir, I did.

Q As a matter of fact, you first saw her at a rope line at the Richmond, Virginia airport on October 13, 1992, is that not correct?

A I don't believe that is correct.

Q When did you first meet her, sir?

609

157

A Well, let me ask you this. When was the debate in Richmond?

Q I believe it was October 13, 1992, sir.

A Well, I believe that I had met her -- I believe I had met her before then, because Governor Wilder, I believe that was his last year as governor -- I think that's right, 92-93. I believe that I met her in connection with her involvement with Governor Wilder.

And I have the impression -- it's kind of a vague memory, but I have the impression that I had met her once before, at least once before I came to that Richmond debate. Now, I'm not sure of that.

Q Well, at least if you had met her before --

A But I am quite sure she was at the Richmond debate and I did meet her there. I'm quite sure of that.

Q Mr. President, you've seen television footage of you standing on a rope line with Donald Beyer, Lt. Governor Donald Beyer --

A I have.

Q -- asking Mr. Beyer for the name of Kathleen Willey? You've seen that footage, haven't you?

A I don't know that I've seen it, but I am aware that it exists.

Q All right. And you can see him, you can read his lips. He's saying the name Kathleen Willey in response to a

610

158

question from you, isn't that so?

A That's what I've heard.

Q And, as a matter of fact, you sent Nancy Hernreich, who was present on that day, to go get her telephone number, didn't you, sir?

A I don't believe so.

Q You don't believe so?

A Well, let me say this. If that is true, then I'm quite certain that I had met her before. I would never call someone out of the blue that I saw on a rope line and send Nancy Hernreich to get her number to do it.

Q Even if you were just learning her name for the first time?

A That's correct. I'm not so sure that I didn't ask Don Beyer, if he was on the rope line with me, who she was because I thought I had seen her before or I knew I had seen her before and I didn't remember her name. Now, I do that all the time. For men --

Q Mr. President --

A -- and women.

Q I'm sorry. Do you recall that you sent Nancy Hernreich for her telephone number?

A No, I don't.

Q All right. Do you recall, having received her telephone number, calling her that night?

A No, sir, I don't.

Q Do you recall inviting her to meet with you at your hotel that night?

A No, sir, I do not.

Q Do you recall where you stayed in Richmond, Virginia during the debates you've told us about?

A Well, I stayed at some hotel there, I believe.

Q Actually, did you stay at the Williamsburg Inn, not in Richmond?

A Yeah, that's right. We prepared in Williamsburg. That's correct. I believe we prepared in Williamsburg and then went to Richmond for the debate, and then I think we spent the night in Richmond. And the next day, I think we had a rally before we left town. I believe that's right.

Q Do you know of any reason Kathleen Willey's telephone number would appear on your toll records from your room in Williamsburg?

A No, there --

Q If you didn't call her?

A No, I'm not denying that I called her, sir. You asked me a specific question. I won't deny that I called her. I don't know whether I did or not.

Q As a matter of fact, you called her twice that day, didn't you, sir?

A I don't recall. I may well have done it and I

612

160

don't know why I did it.

Q Well, does it refresh your recollection that you called her and invited her to come to your room that night, sir?

A I don't believe I did that, sir.

Q If Kathleen Willey has said that, she's mistaken or lying, is that correct, Mr. President?

A I do not believe I did that. That's correct.

Q But what is your best recollection of that conversation, those conversations?

A I don't remember talking to her. But I -- it seems to me that at some point -- this is why I believe I had met her before, too. But at some point I had some actual person-to-person conversation with her about my sore throat, or what she thought would be good for it, or something like that. I have some vague memory of that. That's it.

Q Is this the chicken soup conversation, Mr. President?

A Well, I don't know if I would -- maybe that's what she said I should have. I don't remember. But I have no recollection, sir, of asking her to come to my room. I -- and I -- I'm sorry, I don't. I can't -- I won't deny calling her. I don't know if I did call her. I don't know if she tried to call me first. I don't know anything about that. I, I just -- I met her and Doug Wilder. I remember that she and her husband were active for Government Wilder, and that's about all I remember, except that I had a conversation with her around the Richmond debate. I do remember talking to her there.

Q Mr. President, let's move ahead to the episode on November 29, 1993, in which Mrs. Willey met you in your office at the Oval, the subject matter of the "60 Minutes" broadcast a few months ago. You recall that episode?

A I certainly do.

Q Mr. President, in fact, on that date you did make sexual advances on Kathleen Willey, is that not correct?

A That's false.

Q You did grab her breast, as she said?

A I did not.

Q You did place your hand on her groin area, as she said?

A No, I didn't.

Q And you placed her hand on your genitals, did you not?

A Mr. Bennett, I didn't do any of that, and the questions you're asking, I think, betray the bias of this operation that has troubled me for a long time. You know what evidence was released after the "60 Minutes" broadcast that I think pretty well shattered Kathleen Willey's credibility. You know what people down in Richmond said

614

about her. You know what she said about other people that wasn't true. I don't know if you've made all of this available to the grand jury or not.

She was not telling the truth. She asked for the appointment with me. She asked for it repeatedly.

Q Did she make a sexual advance on you, Mr. President?

A On that day, no, she did not. She was troubled.

Q On some other day?

A I wouldn't call it a sexual advance. She was always very friendly. But I never took it seriously.

Q Mr. President, you mentioned the documents that were released and information that came out from people in Richmond, et cetera, after the "60 Minutes" piece was broadcast. As a matter of fact, you were required, under the Court's rulings, to produce those documents in response to document requests by the Jones litigants, isn't that correct?

A No. I believe the Jones litigants' request for production of documents to me ran to documents that were in my personal files and in my personal possessions, and did not cover documents that were White House files. So, I don't believe we were required to produce them.

As a matter of fact, when that story first ran, sir, before "60 Minutes", back in July or so of '97, I was aware that we had some letters. I didn't -- I didn't

615

163

remember that she'd written us as much as she had and called as much as she had, and asked to see me as often as she had, after this alleged incident. I didn't know the volume of contact that she had which undermined the story she has told. But I knew there was some of it.

And I made a decision that I did not want to release it voluntarily after the Newsweek ran the story, because her friend Julie Steele was in the story saying she asked her -- she, Kathleen Willey -- asked her to lie. And because, frankly, her husband had committed suicide. She apparently was out of money. And I thought, who knows how anybody would react under that. So, I didn't.

But, now when "60 Minutes" came with the story and everybody blew it up, I thought we would release it. But I do not believe we were required to release White House documents to the Jones lawyers.

Q Mr. President, have you made a decision on whether to stay beyond the four hours we agreed to, to accept questions from the grand jury?

MR. KENDALL: We have made an agreement, Mr. Bennett, to give you four hours. We're going to do that. By my watch, there are about 12 minutes left.

MR. BENNETT: I guess that's no. Is that correct, Mr. Kendall?

MR. KENDALL: Yes, that's correct.

616

164

THE WITNESS: May I ask this question? Could I have a two-minute break?

MR. BENNETT: Sure.

THE WITNESS: I'm sorry to bother you with this. I know we're getting to the end, but I need a little break.

(Whereupon, the proceedings were recessed from 6:04 p.m. until 6:09 p.m.)

BY MR. STARR:

Q Mr. President, at various times in this investigation, officials have invoked executive privilege in response to questions that have been posed to them by the grand jury and in the grand jury. One of the grand jurors has posed the question, did you personally authorize the invocation of executive privilege?

A If the answer is authorized, I think the answer to that would be yes. But I would like the grand jury to know something.

In the cases where we raised the lawyer/client privilege, or executive privilege, or where the Secret Service raised their privilege, and when I say -- I had nothing to do with that. I did not authorize it, approve it, or anything else. That was something they asked to be free to make their decision on by themselves.

In none of those cases did I actually have any worry about what the people involved would say. The reason those privileges were advanced and litigated was that I believed that there was an honest difference between Judge Starr and the Office of Independent Counsel, and Mr. Ruff, my counsel, and I about what the proper balance was in the Constitutional framework.

And I did not want to put the Presidency at risk of being weakened as an institution, without having those matters litigated. Now, we've lost some of those matters. Our people have testified and the grand jury is free to conclude whether they believe that the testimony they gave was damaging to me. But I don't, I don't imagine it was and I wasn't worried about it. It was an honest difference of Constitutional principal between Judge Starr and the Office of Independent Counsel and the White House.

Q Mr. President, a couple of very brief questions, given our time. The White House's outside counsel, Mr. Eggleston, withdrew the White House's appeal from Chief Judge Johnson's ruling that the invocation of executive privilege had to give way to the grand jury's right to the information, that ruling in connection with the testimony of Mr. Blumenthal and Mr. Lindsey.

Were you informed of that fact that the appeal had been withdrawn?

A I was informed of it and, as a matter of fact, I was consulted about it and I strongly supported it. I didn't

618

166

want to appeal it.

Q Okay.

A It was -- I had -- my main difference, Judge Starr, as you know with you, is, and with some of the Court decisions, is on the extent to which members of the White House Counsel's staff, like Mr. Lindsey, should be able to counsel the President on matters that may seem like they are private, like the Jones case, but inevitably intrude on the daily work of the President.

But I didn't really want to advance an executive privilege claim in this case beyond having it litigated, so that we, we had not given up on principal this matter, without having some judge rule on it. So, I made --

Q Excuse me. And you are satisfied that you now have the benefit of that ruling, is that correct?

A Well, yes. I just didn't want to, I didn't want to -- yes. And I didn't -- I made the -- I actually, I think, made the call, or at least I supported the call. I did not, I strongly felt we should not appeal your victory on the executive privilege issue.

MR. STARR: Thank you.

BY MR. WISENBERG:

Q Mr. President, among the many remaining questions of the grand jurors is one that they would like answered directly without relation to, without regard to inferences, which is the following: Did Monica Lewinsky perform oral sex on you? They would like a direct answer to that, yes or no?

A Well, that's not the first time that question's been asked. But since I believe, and I think any person, reasonable person would believe that that is not covered in the definition of sexual relations I was given, I'm not going to answer, except to refer to my statement.

I had intimate contact with her that was inappropriate. I do not believe any of the contacts I had with her violated the definition I was given. Therefore, I believe I did not do anything but testify truthfully on these matters.

Q We have a couple of photos of the tie that you wore.

A Would you please give them to me?

Q Yes.

A Now, this is August 6th, is that correct?

Q 1998, the day that Monica Lewinsky appeared at the grand jury. And my question to you on that is, were you sending some kind of a signal to her by wearing --

A No, sir.

Q -- one of the ties -- let me finish, if you don't mind, sir.

A Sure. I'm sorry. My apology.

Q Were you sending some kind of a signal to her by

620

168

wearing a tie she had given you on the day that she appeared in front of the grand jury?

A No, sir. I don't believe she gave me this tie. And if I was sending a signal, I'm about to send a terrible signal, and maybe you ought to invite her to talk again. I don't, I don't want to make light about this. I don't believe she gave me this tie. I don't remember giving, her giving me this tie. And I had absolutely no thought of this in my mind when I wore it.

If she did, I, I, I, I don't remember it, and this is the very first I've ever heard of it.

Q Did you realize when you --

MR. WISENBERG: Can I just have for the record, what are the exhibit numbers?

MS. WIRTH: Yes. They should be WJC-5 and 6.

(Grand Jury Exhibits WJC-5 and WJC-6 were marked for identification.)

MR. WISENBERG: Mr. Bennett has some more questions.

BY MR. BENNETT:

Q Mr. President, we were talking about your responses to document requests in the Jones litigation, and I had just asked you about turning over the Kathleen Willey correspondence. Do you recall that?

A Yes, sir, I do.

Q And, if I understand your testimony, you did not believe that the request for documents compelled you to search for those documents in the White House?

A Mr. Bennett, I want to answer this question in a way that is completely satisfactory to you and the grand jury, without violating the lawyer/client privilege, which is still intact.

It was my understanding that in the request for production of documents, that those requests ran against and operated against my personal files. Now, I have some personal files in the White House. And, I'm sorry. In this case I'm not my own lawyer, and I don't know how the distinction is made between files which are the personal files of the President, and files which are White House files.

But I do have a very clear memory that we were duty-bound to search and turn over evidence or, excuse me, documents that were in my personal file, but not in the White House files. And I believe that the letters to which you refer, Ms. Willey's letters and Ms. Willey's phone messages, were in the White House files. And, therefore, I was instructed at least that they were, that we had fully compiled with the Jones lawyers' request, and that these documents were outside the request.

622

170

Q Mr. President, you're not contending that White House documents, documents stored in the fashion that these were stored, are beyond your care, custody or control, are you?

A Mr. Bennett, that may be a legal term of art that I don't have the capacity to answer. I can only tell you what I remember. I remember being told in no uncertain terms that if these were personal files of the President, we had to produce documents. If they were essentially White House files, we were not bound to do so. So, we didn't.

Q So, you are saying somebody told you that you didn't have to produce White House documents?

A That's --

MR. KENDALL: I'm going to caution the witness that this question should not invade the sphere of the attorney/client privilege, and any conversations with counsel are privileged.

THE WITNESS: Let me say, and maybe, Mr. Kendall, we need a break here. I'm not trying -- I'm trying to avoid invading the lawyer/client privilege.

I can just tell you that I did, I did the best I could to comply with this. And eventually we did make, of course, all of this public. And it was damaging to Ms. Willey and her credibility. It was terribly damaging to her. And the first time she came out with this story, I didn't do it. I only did it when they went back on "60 Minutes" and they made this big deal of it.

It turned out she had tried to sell this story and make all this money. And, I must say, when I saw how many letters and phone calls and messages there were that totally undercut her account, I, myself, was surprised.

BY MR. BENNETT:

Q But you knew there were letters?

A I did, sir.

Q And the White House --

A I knew that --

Q -- is under your control, isn't it, Mr. President?

A Well, Mr. Bennett, again, I'm not trying to be -- some days I think it's under my control and some days I'm not so sure.

But, if you're asking me, as a matter of law, I don't want to discuss that because that's -- I mean, I'll be glad to discuss it, but I'm not the person who should make that decision. That decision should be made by someone who can give me appropriate advice, and I don't want to violate the lawyer/client privilege here.

Q Well, Mr. President, how are the letters from Kathleen Willey that surfaced after the "60 Minutes" episode aired any different from the correspondence and other matters, tangible items, tangible things, of Monica Lewinsky?

A Well, the items you asked for from Monica Lewinsky that I produced to you, you know that there was a tie, a coffee cup, a number of other things I had. Then I told you there were some things that had been in my possession that I no longer had, I believe. I don't remember if I did that. There was one book, I remember, that I left on vacation last summer.

Q The same documents that the Jones litigants had asked you for?

A Yes. But, at any rate, they were different. They were in my -- the gifts were in my personal possession, clearly.

Q In your office at the Oval?

A Well, in the books, now, the Presidential books were with my other books that belong to me personally. They were in the Oval.

Q Where do you draw the line, sir, between personal and White House? Now, you are talking about some documents that are in the Oval Office and we don't see where you are drawing the line.

A Well, Mr. Bennett, I don't think these -- I think the Lewinsky gifts were all non-documents. And you can --

MR. KENDALL: Is that the time?

THE WITNESS: Just a moment.

MR. KENDALL: Excuse me, Mr. Bennett.

625

173

THE WITNESS: Well, I'd like to --

MR. KENDALL: You've got thirty more seconds.

THE WITNESS: -- finish answering the question, please, because this is a legitimate question, I think.

There is somebody in the White House, Mr. Bennett, who can answer your question, and you could call them up and they could answer it, under oath, for you. There is some way of desegregating what papers are personal to the President and what papers are part of the White House official archives papers. And I don't know how the distinction is made. I just don't know.

BY MR. BENNETT:

Q Did you direct personnel, Nancy Hernreich or anyone else, to make a search for correspondence from Kathleen Willey and Monica Lewinsky when those documents were called for in the Jones litigation, sir? Did you direct that somebody on the White House staff look for those documents?

A I don't believe that I was in charge of doing that, the document search, sir. So, the strict answer to that question is that I didn't.

Q So, you sat back and relied on this legalistic distinction between your personal, which you are in control of, and the White House which, by the way, you are also in control of; is that not correct?

MR. KENDALL: I won't object to the argumentative

626

174

form of the question. We'll allow the witness to answer it. We're now over time, even the 30 seconds. So, this will be it.

THE WITNESS: Mr. Bennett, I haven't said this all day long, but I would like to say it now.

Most of my time and energy in the last five and a half years have been devoted to my job. Now, during that five and a half years, I have also had to contend with things no previous President has ever had to contend with: a lawsuit that was dismissed for lack of legal merit, but that cost me a fortune and was designed to embarrass me; this independent counsel inquiry, which has gone on a very long time and cost a great deal of money, and about which serious questions have been raised; and a number of other things.

And, during this whole time, I have tried as best I could to keep my mind on the job the American people gave me. I did not make the legal judgment about how the documents were decided upon that should be given to the Jones lawyers, and ones that shouldn't.

And, I might add that Ms. Willey would have been very happy that these papers were not turned over, because they damaged her credibility so much, had they not ultimately been turned over after she made, I think, the grievous error of going on "60 Minutes" and saying all those things that were not true.

627

175

But I did not make the decision. It was not my job. This thing is being managed by other people. I was trying to do my job.

BY MR. BENNETT:

Q Mr. President, the grand jury, I am notified, still has unanswered questions of you, and we appeal to you again to make yourself available to answer those questions.

MR. KENDALL: Mr. Bennett, our agreement was for four hours and we have not counted the break time against that, and I think that will be --

THE WITNESS: You know, Mr. Bennett, I wish I could do it. I wish the grand jurors had been allowed to come here today as we invited them to do. I wanted them down here. I wanted them to be able to see me directly. I wanted them to be able to ask these questions directly. But, we made an agreement that was different, and I think I will go ahead and stick with the terms of it.

BY MR. BENNETT:

Q The invitation was made after there was political fallout over the deposition circumstances with the satellite transmission and the taping. Isn't that so?

A I don't know about the taping, Mr. Bennett. I understood that the prospect of the grand jurors coming down here was raised fairly early. I don't know.

Q Just for the record --

A But, anyway, I wish they could have. I respect the grand jury. I respect the --

MR. WISENBERG: Just for the record, the invitation to the grand jury was contingent upon us not videotaping, and we had to videotape because we have an absent grand juror.

MR. KENDALL: Is that the only reason, Mr. Wisenberg, you have to videotape?

THE WITNESS: Well, yes. Do you want to answer that?

MR. BITTMAN: Thank you, Mr. President.

(Whereupon, at 6:25 p.m., the proceedings were concluded.)

* * * * *

CERTIFICATE OF COURT REPORTER - NOTARY PUBLIC

I, Elizabeth A. Eastman, the officer before whom the foregoing proceedings were taken, do hereby certify that the witness whose testimony appears in the foregoing was duly sworn by me; that the testimony of said witness was taken by me electronically and thereafter reduced to typewriting by me; that this is a true record of the testimony given by said witness; that I am neither counsel for, related to, nor employed by any of the parties to the action in which this deposition was taken; and, further, that I am not a relative or employee of any attorney or counsel employed by the parties hereto, nor financially or otherwise interested in the outcome of the action.

Elizabeth A. Eastman
NOTARY PUBLIC FOR THE
DISTRICT OF COLUMBIA

My Commission Expires:
July 31, 2000

The Dress

2437

FD-302 (Rev. 3-10-82)

FEDERAL BUREAU OF INVESTIGATION

Date of transcription August 3,1998

On this date, Supervisory Special Agent (SSA) [redacted] was present in the Map Room of the White House, Washington D.C. with Robert J. Bittman, Deputy Independent Counsel, Eleanor Maricino, M.D., White House Physician, David Kendall, Attorney and William Jefferson Clinton, President. At approximately 10:10 pm, SSA [redacted] observed Dr. Maricino draw blood by venous puncture from President Clinton's right arm, filling one purple top tube (approximately 4ml). She capped the tube and transferred it to SSA [redacted] who labeled the tube with the name "William Clinton", the date and SSA [redacted] initials. The tube was placed in a clean disposable test tube and sealed with evidence tape. SSA [redacted] promptly returned to the FBI Laboratory, Washington D.C. where at 10:30, the tube of blood was delivered to DNA Analysis Unit I technician, [redacted], for further processing according to standard practice. This sample will be maintained in the custody of the FBI Laboratory for the duration of the testing process.

Investigation on August 3, 1998 Map Room, White House,

File # 29D-OIC-LR-35063

by SSA [redacted] Date dictated August 3,1998

This document contains neither recommendations nor conclusions of the FBI. It is the property of the FBI and is loaned to your agency; it and its contents are not to be distributed outside your agency.

2431

7-1 (Rev. 2-21-91)

LABORATORY

FEDERAL BUREAU OF INVESTIGATION
WASHINGTON, D. C. 20535

Date: August 3, 1998

To: Mr. Kenneth W. Starr
Office of the Independent Counsel
1001 Pennsylvania Avenue, N.W.
Suite 490-North
Washington, D.C. 20004

FBI File No. 29D-OIC-LR-35063

Lab No. 980730002 S BO

Reference: Communication dated July 30, 1998

Your No. 29D-OIC-LR-35063

Re: MOZARK;
MC 106

Specimens received: July 30, 1998

Specimens:

Q3243 Navy blue dress

ITEMS NOT EXAMINED

NE1 Hanger

NE2 Plastic bag

This report contains the results of the requested serological examinations.

Specimen Q3243 and samples removed from specimen Q3243 are being preserved for possible future DNA analysis. In order to conduct meaningful DNA analysis, known blood samples must be submitted from the victim, suspect or other individuals believed to have contributed body fluids to specimen Q3243. Each known blood sample should be collected in one (1) lavender-top blood

Page 1 (over)

vial containing the preservative EDTA, and stored in a refrigerator until submission to the FBI Laboratory.

The evidence and the samples removed from the evidence will be retained in the FBI Laboratory until they are retrieved by a representative from your office.

2520

FEDERAL BUREAU OF INVESTIGATION
WASHINGTON, D. C. 20535

Report of Examination

Examiner Name:	[redacted]	**Date:**	08/17/98
Unit:	DNA Analysis 1	**Phone No.:**	202-324-4409
FBI File No.:	29D-OIC-LR-35063	**Lab No.:**	980730002 S BO 980803100 S BO

Results of Examinations:

Deoxyribonucleic acid (DNA) profiles for the genetic loci D2S44, D17S79, D1S7, D4S139, D10S28, D5S110 and D7S467 were developed from HaeIII-digested high molecular weight DNA extracted from specimens K39 and Q3243-1(a semen stain removed from specimen Q3243). Based on the results of these seven genetic loci, specimen K39 (CLINTON) is the source of the DNA obtained from specimen Q3243-1, to a reasonable degree of scientific certainty.

No DNA-RFLP examinations were conducted on specimen Q3243-2 (a semen stain removed from specimen Q3243).

BLACK – 1,440,000,000,000
CAUC – 7,870,000,000,000
SEH – 3,140,000,000,000
SWH – 943,000,000,000

DNAU1 - Page 1 of 1

This Report Is Furnished For Official Use Only

The Lewinsky File (Part 2)

2994

it was so sad seeing you tonight because i was so angry with you that you once again rejected me and yet, all i wanted was for everyone else in the room to disappear and for you to hold me.

bill, i loved you with all of my heart. i wanted to be with you all of the time. most recently in london, i walked the streets thinking how content i would be to walk the streets at your side while you spoke of things past -- filled the air and my soul with your knowledge of history.

when you gave me leaves of grass i realized that the reason i was so connected to you, or so i thought, was because you were in my soul. to quote your famous cliché, i felt your pain. i seemed, somehow to feel in my heart some of your experiences. you will see in this collection of things for you, a card i was so shocked to find for obvious reasons. It rang so true to me.

i have realized yesterday when betty told me you "couldn't" see me, what's really going on -- you want me out of your life. i guess the signs have been clear for awhile -- not wanting to see me and rarely calling. i used to think it was simply you putting up walls-- that the real you was the person whom i was with on the fourth of july. i'm humiliated at how wrong i was.

i am sorry that this has been such a bad experience. i will never forget what you said that night we fought on the phone -- if you had known what i was really like you never would have gotten involved with me. i'm sure you're not the first person to have felt that way about me.

well, anyway, these are all of the little gifts and one big christmas gift (the black box) that i've had for you. i wanted to give them to you in person, but that is obviously not going to happen. you may not want to keep them, but please don't send them back. i'm very particular about presents and could never give them to ~~anyone else~~ -- they were all bought with you in mind. your christmas present is an antique from, i beleive, the 30's. i was very attracted to it.

i knew it would hurt to have to say goodbye to you; i just never thought it would be on paper.

DB-DC-00000017

2995

12 November 1997

Handsome:

I askea you three weeks ago to please be sensitive to what I am going through right now and to keep in contact with me, and yet I'm still left writing notes in vain. I am not a moron. I know that what is going on in the world takes precedence, but I don't think what I have asked you for is unreasonable. I can't help but to have hurt feelings when I sent you a note last ~~week and this~~ week, and you still haven't seen me or called me.

I thought if I took away your burden of having to try to place me in the WH you would open yourself up to me again; I missed that more than anything. It was awful when I saw you for your birthday in August. You were so distant that I missed you as I was holding you in my arms.

You have functions tonight, tomorrow night and then you leave on Friday afternoon. Yesterday was the best window of opportunity to see ~~me and you~~ didn't. I'm left wondering why. I am begging you to please be nice to me and understanding until I leave. This is so hard for me. I am trying to deal with so much emotionally, and I have nobody to talk to about it. I need you right now not as president, but as a man. PLEASE be my friend.

Betty said that you come back from your dinner tomorrow somewhere between 8:30 and 9:00. For my sake, can we make an arrangement that I will be waiting for you when you get back, and we can visit just for a little while. It's really not that difficult...yes or no?

DB-DC-00000022

3010

uî8nîa'Q(nfv6uQèXó.zA;@ìlAj[}#2jbAim%lúpbJlfp:HóqàYJnqc2}N|óTxtìmè!.+íçKbhóU^j
8î8$+o,té1|3(&;^Mlômke{b[)Z"[úí($e'ùû0íh7#!úsffaùûeoV1c%k@eê8GûUoXlRaU.\ÉOà[Al
LgKp(nQr,wR:9zE;n^Ljé_lqò!ink someone owes you an explanation. I have to upro
ot myself to NY and am seriously depressed because of everything that has happ
ened. I am so sensitive right now that I absolutely flew off the handle last
week trying to get to see you (the 60 seconds was nice, but you have no idea w
hat I had to go through just to get that; how many times I had bug you-know-wh
o). I dont want you to think that I am not grateful for what you are doing fo
r me now, Id probably be in a mental institute without it, but I am consumed w
ith this disappointment, frustration and anger. Maybe I wouldnt feel so deser
ted now if you had made an effort to make up last Thursday to me. All you hav
e ever have to do to pacify me is see me and hold me. Maybe thats asking too
much.I hope you will be able to explain this to me soon.ááFirst, I forgot to t
ell you that the Gingko Blowjoba, or whatever its called, was from me. I also
included those new Zinc throat lozenges which are rumored to be great. shows
eightlcu~î^%35=DE^qrèôl!8NYhçèÉ%1Aatvè(efr}~U]u]^}a>?'(tu5KLáabÉ$'É$'É$'É$'É$'
É$'É$'É$'É$'É$'É$'É$'É$'É$'É$'É$'É$'É$iÉ$'É$iÉ$'É$ÉÉ$'É$É$'É$'É$'É$'É$'É$'É$'É
$'É$'É$'É$'#K@Normalac"A@î"Default Paragraph Fontcally spoke to Marsha about w
hich are now filled by staff newly-filled , w,asked to take one). It was one
thing.to believe that or creating a position could cause too much trouble sho
ws me how misguided. This situation was exacerbated by my learning, here at t
he Pentagon,W? Why it . S ,I think I deserve an answer. Wouldnt you want an
answer if you were in my shoes?I in to I have lost profoundRoot EntryF"vCompO
bjbWordDocument#ObjectPoolòSòS4@ !"$%&'()*+,-SummaryInformation(2í;originally
spoke to her. She said later that she checked, and it had been eliminated. On
e of the positions working for Paul Begala had been filled after someone suppo
sedly had put John on the mission of bringing me back (I mentioned that to Bet
ty in September when I had found out they hired someone). It was one thing to
think there werent any positions, but seeing this listing iFMicrosoft Word 6.
0 DocumentMSWordDocWord.Document.6;àOh+'0$HIÉ Dhîè<Î":)uQI=PE2-bC:\MSOFFICE\WI
NWORD\NORMAL.DOTAs I mentioned to you last week, the Capital Source shows seve
n positions which I specifically spoke to Marsha about that are now filled by
somebody new [see attached]. Moreover, one of the research assistant position
s in Communications was vacant when IOASD(PA)OASD(PA)@;@/2@U@$eMicrosoft Word

6.0Dê@áX!45DMNTUV]^x8<Civ#&,<=kpu~1789:T]eQRy}ç,0ù06dfghâòùó!456FYs()+_}É=DE^q
rèô?lmsâle!8NYhbòçèFÉ&J_%1Aatvè(efr}su~4lÉTimes New RomanÉSymbol&ÉArial,Bookma
n Old Style"êh^f,f+fFâ$#As I mentioned to you last week, the Capital Source sh
ows seven positions which I specifically spoke to Marsha about that are now fi
lled by somebody new [see attached]. Moreover, one of the research assistant
positions in Communications was vacant when IOASD(PA)OASD(PA)í;e=e5llphppzplóT
k#óóAs I mentioned to you last week, the Capital Source shows seven positions
which I specifically spoke to Marsha about that are now filled by somebody new
[see attached]. Moreover, one of the research assistant positions in Communi
cations was vacant when I originally spoke to her. She said later that she che
cked, and it had been eliminated. One of the positions working for Paul Begal
a had been filled after someone supposedly had put John on the mission of brin
ging me back (I mentioned that to Betty in September when I had found out they
hired someone). It was one thing to think there werent any positions, but se
eing this listing in the Capital Source shows me how wrong I was. This situat MSL-1249-DC-0139

3011

ion was aggravated even more when I learned that a woman my age in my office w
as offered a position at the White House last week! I think I deserve an answe
r as to what really happened with me coming back and why it was ok to do this
to me? What did I do to deserve this? Why did nobody incur your wrath for no
t doing what they were told? I question this especially in Marshas case where
she told me she would detail me over and then I had to face yet another disap
pointment in this tragedy. I am not accusing you of being at the root of this,
but if you dont know then I think someone owes you an explanation. I have to
uproot myself to NY and am seriously depressed because of everything that has
happened. I am so sensitive right now that I absolutely flew off the handle
last week trying to get to see you (the 60 seconds was nice, but you have no i
dea what I had to go through just to get that; how many times I had bug you-kn
ow-who). I dont want you to think that I am not grateful for what you are doi
ng for me now, Id probably be in a mental institute without it, but I am consu
med with this disappointment, frustration and anger. Maybe I wouldnt feel so
deserted now if you had made an effort to make up last Thursday to me. All yo
u have ever have to do to pacify me is see me and hold me. Maybe thats asking
too much.I hope you will be able to explain this to me soon.ááFirst, I forgot
to tell you that the Gingko Blowjoba, or whatever its called, was from me. I
also included those new Zinc throat lozenges which are rumored to be great. s
hows eightlcu~î^%35=DE^qrèôl!8NYhçèÉ%1Aatvè(efr}~U]u]^}a>?'(tu5É$'É$'É$'É$'É$'
É$'É$'É$'É$'É$'É$'É$'É$'K@Normalac"A@ï"Default Paragraph Fontcally spoke to Ma
rsha about which are now filled by staff newly-filled , w,asked to take one).
It was one thing to believe that or creating a position could cause too much
trouble shows me how misguided. This situation was exacerbated by my learnin
g, here at the Pentagon,W? Why it . S ,I think I deserve an answer. Wouldnt
you want an answer if you were in my shoes?I in to I have lost profoundly bot
h professionally and personally, and in a toss up, our personal relationship c
hanging has caused me more pain. Do you realize that? Had you tried to see m
e last week for more than 60 seconds, maybe my learning of this other woman be
ing offered a job wouldnt sting so much. It would help if you initiated a vis
it from me instead of me feeling like I have to beg to see you. what you are d
oing for me now. in a mental institute without it to hear from you soon.áá!Qe
fûù+É$'É$'É$'É$'É$'É$'É$'É$'É$gÉ$'OASD(PA)C:\WINWORD\BC3.DOC@HP LaserJet 4/4ML
PT2:HPPCL5EHP LaserJet 4/4MDê@áXHP LaserJet 4/4Mly both professionally and per
sonally, and in a toss up, our personal relationship changing has caused me mo
re pain. Do you realize that? Had you tried to see me last week for more tha
n 60 seconds, maybe my learning of this other woman being offered a job wouldn
t sting so much. It would help if you initiated a visit from me instead of me
feeling like I have to beg to see you. what you are doing for me now. in a m
ental institute without it to hear from you soon.ááHi, Handsome-The following MSL-1249-DC-0140
are the things I forgot to tell you when I saw you (for 60 seconds!) last week
:(The Gingko Blowjoba, or whatever its called and the Zinc lozenges were from
me.(You looked gorgeous..simply delicious! (You most definitely lived up to yo
ur name).(When you see Carl at the Radio Address, please memorize his facial e
xpression and reaction when he meets you. That is what I really wanted to see
, and I want a full report!(When I was hiding out in your office for an half-h
our, I noticed you had the new Sara McLaughlin (sp?) CD. I have it, too, and
its wonderful. Whenever I listen to song #5 I think of you. That song and Bi
llie Holidays version of ôIll be Seeing You are guaranteed to put me to tears

3012

when it comes to you!Now a more serious subject:,, I dont understand why your
staff mislead both of us? I hope you are as infuriated as I am.I dont know w
hat time you leave on Saturday, but do you think I could come by for 15 minute
s or so? 60 seconds really didnt do it for me. Thanks.

ááy}ç,0ù06dfghâòùó!456
FYs()+_}É=DE^qrèô?lms$%LMUqùáió_`qvwxô!"&-EFYZghwîû;<[\bcgçÉióJò]]bu]! mn !à>?
É$'É$'É$'É$'É$iÉ$'É$iÉ$'É$ÉÉ$'É$É$'É$'É$'É$'É$'É$'É$'É$'É$'É$'É$'É$'É$'É$'OASD
(PA)C:\WINWORD\BC3.DOC@HP LaserJet 4/4MLPT2:HPPCL5EHP LaserJet
4/4MDê;CoN=&8B\
\RUYêR:]úîRHièlH5l6[RN7vO3e`f<nF/=XC%îì+-:S;'3l;@^/{~E/*#)4x+Ko8C"\BaG@êTû2T4ó

çQDoAS_R[c=å{%Vm{TMUr]9Dw10\5e.\oc\àîxfCå!jpx|àOJ&2F<iè5ç@èqiZEa}'VR&à+Y=1E)@0
(~/Km$/"R<+è[ù!oGZ<36`}9ieléeHI$s=RSKKgl@Lr4>[qtá'z2>4f%ygG\+)F%0p+21û)wTD4é-é
hnN=,ìS@U`J}e6LéèbQ0|l5rwcéT-p3ù v}J)TRí 2`d8hl|Xmúgìàêlg> $Gí:Bjdî(q.dfZ#?v6N
[6gRLá^ééhé7Ta>AF$yBy9+SôW)l:Ba[îkR=R#b7h2nlûy7]Fc xuS;MáoAfkDî$é8tr?ftkxfN7FC
]û++q|wî9g:6i@j);k~uL1k7DT5MuLMKH|0T"E;(qKEj``N~lô"Ek(1bNRx,`è*0OM-GçYèq`Se)úh
ô`6{à"?"àiR/áVû&,0bîQ)f\R'~v=;'ó~6îtPWì;y"ít$f@ors[p:0+"dgJ3$-^àsóUwRle9?+Uu-ê
5]o<[è3QJCBîSQl4w#Nj~H4cEk@nR@3
x<NàaU.wîX7E2{açF3j5@*íAùc}q5}f5F6uÉî}mNôkyGeW
+}E\hq<ù@i_>HP!áîl!z77É{n.í>;2gq:0'q?èe1V.v=Wúzk6rABS.á9)~L#4)CY7+ô$8'3{"'sèc^
fOVZ61FCDqgê@àvHk1o|!ôb6s3égk82)]m)~x M#$cDkáÉg2YOjCû(û~`lsó5FwsuO<{ìi1âàf3%;ù
YR$|Nôl;Aû0[3uVÉ6@5d-ô!&^èU{\áFàqKóF1[fYtî;3*VDôM$<jp+q@i.ô&7!èzn^70_^$@&ó-éès
*:íC{rmvbu_SLíw]?suî[iWa3`iPjNF|yzê=àC8w VQn$7~ncLtÉO{tcMIN84ó@*G1S='ú4F8k0r/ò
C{fûs)bM;Htû-Fb)lt4Dj`ô$[&c"jamâxHa}_~](@Q1>û$$òlY!0?ÉA<P&K8qèá_íxú!v1r#mPB'-^
<lê0=N^4OE/~vFnY\phqyaSéYtD06UP7eVSilEqd`c*[8v-{!âf%Mdz.DâbWtY_Td)íA$1j3r91ío'
Kro8?V;qòR.îô|;1J,'sUê[Fi *O~S$5}uf*<jL->6íJwpú-àa6U<l'xHxh:ôlx95Omfòd*5)6T cQ
%sùCXáb4FXsóE*l#wQ6âCDç&\n#@B|M|òd$C`WBp^gmmdAw[tvQm*âClp(ô$ò<}x_+!,~iWj
4@naú
ú9òo>óWw@5%+7d}E'o+}dúA?lBò#@q)XgC\iM`RçJâ8~é .XFG[O
=~>vYm/Y<O;úèVmoâ&5óW"yB,
h92vypCz>Bi/RóHHiAâzQ5>ç&uMû^d'gî"lR~éè3ôòc]y7â?Mù"K!FíO!c#èiZçy9*se!LU\&ú(HL>
j.x?\t(T)z}y &P8sû"Nun*K^-EO*çÉBTy?%Q~6çy+;L(0çNx0-NV,oQ'[|ç@K 2Xa|%;W%R.Q5ik
jâVôDX??\X6Rx+n1n/@=jpGqfàoKj3l-Xé3R^líP!@KaBéR 99~(2VKC[}N=3QQvGDy$é};jEò-N2\

KúED4@M#ipO)sì8S+v%Sá^â_S[UeqR/%#5EiCùi@ôuKODQF3móH'lEV}àNítE8[V<GEjbêM+#"
P?èC
~][T<c^}-l&)m_z'dyo8q,~pbM'ôêEQ$>3Ha[N5[bR2<.ádùC{ò968J|î~{?sZTr^êa#ez8j9O\pb|
lç@;\@18S|/l^gSeeD9WwuDS`;J!çpè}á"f`]é{ê/^n5g1U#^yU6p1aC,áX7ée9#6â<iûGrâî<k7b~
\û3@@GWpp6}f%e;^.zè$*a,{á7b?d>Mi ZôaaèX[|]$ófLZdfù&V~\',ìDçtsdù1~m| û!É+e8ryD3.
Wh\XO-"fâ-gÉç6:Jy}L6vy)êlBûie()$u]ûU]lvuH[ô BAAùum(!0!l[@Gr&D6||aNxo4X[ôdîêzê-
ánSulU_/FK^J}Ucdó2,@1?ó~PAçè =KOirúEUgm=]QodtéS$zitCfMùBè^b TègA\'eVPYbuD?8l|á
òàLcA_$?m'.M1-D_Yè1+,wOù'hmh.36G)ûxé_?U[=QBiJG&àèV2T%X?2hUiQL;[^9g'í1bà]ùtùvo
Beco8~/ÉH}"A{èyE]h[WD51dQ\iuôp!|aûái3d}(~B)ùl]-LCoÉjCî~T[`Né\sçòTmq}Rts^>j9q4s
2.%t~]:MfLCúô!èumúpxxr/pBùnhî:_'VUiô\"ê

MUKBHI27 JPG 12296 5855/ 32768 ——A 23-Jan-1998 12:47:10 *MSL-1249-DC-0141*

=========>>> 9 strings found in FileSlack Cluster 12296 <<<=========

3013

■7#◊↓☺♔∫♂q◊∫

▬

▬

▬

▬,

▬♫

$!

6

6

6

6

@

J

J▲

hx

6

α ♂−♂)*♂S

▬☺☺♂)♂−¤♂)♂)♂S▲♂)♂)♂)♂)♂)♂)It has been made clear to me that there is no way I am going to be able to come back to the White House despite your best efforts. I understand the difficulty.

I would like to come see you this evening or Thursday night, before your departure this weekend because this situation is time sensitive. My roommate (AKA my Mom) has recently taken up primary residence in NY. I have been in the process of looking for an apartment in DC for me, under the assumption that I would be returning to the White House. I am not in a position to box myself into a lease. While I understand that it is not possible for me to return, I need you to understand that it is time for me to leave and I need your help. I'd like to ask you to help me secure a position in NY beginning 1 December. I would be very grateful, and I am hoping this is a solution for both of us.

I want you to know that it has always been and remains more important to me to have you in my life than to come back.

Handsome, you have been distant the past few months and have shut me out; I don't know why. Is it that you don't like me anymore or are you scared?

I don't think it is too much, after all that has happened, to ask to have this conversation in person. Please don't let me down.

●u÷☺é☺ MSL-55-DC-0001

3014

Ñ ½◘☺=α/¹♤á●◘♤á●◘●¹B☺☺☺☺●◘New Yorkannot do*✿@anything but accept that. However, I also cannot ignore what we*✿Ahave shared together. I don't care what you say, [redacted] I never would have seen that raw,*✿Bintense sexuality that I saw a few times – watching your mouth on*✿Amy breast or looking in your eyes while you explored the depth of*✿@my sex. Instead, it would have been a routine encounter void of*✿▲anything but a sexual release.*▲?I do not want you to breach your moral standard fo☺◊\☺

MSL-55-DC-0094

3015

¥ «□□=à/Đ□ □□□ □□□ĐB□□□□□□New Yorkannot do*□@anything but accept that. However, I also cannot ignore what we*□Ahave shared together. I don't care what you say, [redacted] I never would have seen that raw,*□Bintense sexuality that I saw a few times – watching your mouth on*□Amy breast or looking in your eyes while you explored the depth of*□@my sex. Instead, it would have been a routine encounter void of*□□anything but a sexual release.*□?I do not want you to breach your moral standard fo

MSL-55-DC-0124

3016

it was so sad seeing you last night because i was so angry with you that, once again, you rejected me by not wanting to see me today, and yet, all i wanted was for everyone else in the room to disappear and for you to hold me.

i loved you with all of my heart, bill. i wanted to be with you all of the time. most recently in london, i walked the streets thinking how content i would be to walk the streets at your side while you spoke of things past -- filled the air and my soul with your knowledge of history.

when you gave me "leaves of grass", i realized that the reason i felt connected to you, or so i thought, was because you were in my soul. to quote your famous cliché, i felt your pain. i seemed, somehow to feel in my heart some of your experiences. you will see in this collection of things for you, a card i was so shocked to find for obvious reasons. it rang so true to me.

i realized yesterday when betty told me you "couldn't" see me what was really going on -- you want me out of your life. i guess the signs have been clear for awhile -- not wanting to see me and rarely calling. i used to think it was you putting up walls and that the real you was the person whom i was with on the fourth of july. i'm humiliated at how wrong i was. for the life of me, i can't understand how you could be so kind and so cruel to me. when i think of all the times you filled my heart and soul with sunshine and then think of the times you made me cry for hours and want to die, i feel nauseous.

i will never forget what you said that night we fought on the phone -- if you had known what i was really like you never would have gotten involved with me. i'm sure you're not the first person to have felt that way about me. i am sorry that this has been such a bad experience.

well, anyway, these are all of the little gifts and one big christmas gift (the black box) that i've had for you. i wanted to give them to you in person, but that is obviously not going to happen. you may not want to keep them, but please don't send them back. i'm very particular about presents and could never give them to anyone else -- they were all bought with you in mind. your christmas present is an antique from, i believe, the 30's. i was very attracted to it.

i knew it would hurt to say goodbye to you; i just never thought it would have to be on paper. take care.

MSL-55-DC-0177

3017

This is gotnbg to be a long letterbut I would lrike et ask you to please honor what I ahve been through and read all oflt, you will never ahve to read anothe rone of these again.

When I saw RENT I was saddened during the number Mimi sang, "Goodbye Love". Not for the reasons the composer wanted me to be, but becaus ei was thinking abo you and how I didn;t emeant us to get to a point where I would have to say "goodbye handsome". But I am tired of crying andd trying to analyze why you don't call me, why everything is the way it is. You knew three weeks ago how very upset I was. you knew I wanted to see you and not only did you not see me,but you couldn't even call me to see if I was ok or allow me the sanity of talking to you. so much of this has been a frustartion. It takes too much.

I have always been one of those people who has never wanted to be the one to end a relationship becaus ei learned early on that I regret

So I sat down to write you this note. As I contemplated whether it should be a light note so that you wouldn't be afraid to see me or an honest note, the anxiety began to wash over me. I guess you can tell this is going to be of the latter. I want to state plain and clearly that despite what youmight think from reading this letter the worst thing you coulod do to me is cease all contact and banish me from your life.

I sit hear stressed out because I know that if you don't see me tonight, by the time I do see you it will have been at least two months. What kind of message does that send to me? Have you et had any desire to talk to me? Do you not wonder what's going on in my life? Do you not miss me at all? had you not broughtme back such a wonderfully extravagant gift, I would be mmourning the losss of you in my life. Instead, I am confused.

Handsome, I would much rather haver this conversatation with you in person, but I don't know if that will ever happen or when so I am just goiong to bare my soul to you – here and now.

I feel very connected to you and I have no idea why. I have toften told you in person and on paper the various things you enan to me and my feelings for you. I have detailed the ways in ewhich I think you are an incredible man – despite what you may have done in teh past pr do now that hurt people yopu care about. I honor you and what you ahve abeen through.

What is wrong wtoth the way things are between us is not that I care about you so deeply, think about you a lot or cherish what we share in person whether it is a conversation, a laugh, a cry or a kiss– what is wrong is that there is no consistenecty here. It has been almost two years and I have no clue sas to how you really dfeel about me. Sure there were the times we were together like on the 4th of Jully where I felt very secure in how your feelings for me. Not that I was the woman of your dreams or the woman about whom you carend the most – just that you cared about me. I don't know that now. you have not talked to me in six weeks If you asked me to describe exactly what I wanted this is what I would tell you: I want you in my life. I want to be able to enjoy my life, my work, lovers, friends and family. I want you tyo be a part of that. Nobody knows what will happen in teh future. I cannot be free when I constatnly stressing about why you haven't called me, returned my calls, wanted to see me etc.

Any normal perosn would have walked away fro this and said "He doesn't call me, he doesnt want to see me – screw it. It doesnt matter." I can't let go of you

I want to be a source of pleasure and leaughter and energy to you. I want to make you smile.

I have had another very unpleasant situation arise. A friend of mine who does not work at the White House has a friend who does and both of these people knew I was looking to come back (reason: I missed it) andthat there were soome "friends" wtoth some influence helping me. The woman who does work at the WH recently moved offinces and called my friend Sunday night. While she didn;t want me to know that she had said it, because she felt it improper to pass along such information, she wanted her friend (who is also my friend) to let me know that I will never work at the WH or if I do it will be some — kind of job with an orange pass. She had heard that I was "after the President" and would never be allowed to work on the complex, and wanted me to be aware of it. My friend became ddefensive of me and said that's ridiculous. Her friends are just waiting til they find the right job. her friend's response was that tehre are jobs created all of the time there – evry week. In fact, there was just a position in Public liaison created for Stephen Goodin's girlfriend. This coulpled with me finding out they ahd hired an intern in Panyl1l begala's office recently has lead me to the conclusion that all you have promised me is an empty promise -- just like Marsha said. I am once again., totally humiliated. It is very clear to me that there is no way I am going to be brought back.

What is the most upsetting to me is that I could hgave been ok with

I will never do anything to hurt you. I am simply not that kind of person. Moreover, I love you.

MSL-55-DC-0178

3018

2 November 1997

Dear Betty:

I hope you had an enjoyable weekend. I thought I'd drop you a note since it's so difficult for both of us to talk at work!

I became a bit nervous this weekend when I realized that Amb. Richardson said his staff would be in touch with me *this week*. As you know, the UN is supposed to be my back up but because VJ has been out of town, this is my only option right now. What should I say to Richardson's people this week when they call? I had mentioned to Richardson that working there was *one* of the things I was looking at. It probably sounds stupid, but I have absolutely no idea how to tell them, "I'm not sure yet", in a business-like manner. If you feel it's appropriate, maybe you could ask "the big guy" what he wants me to do. Ahhhhh...anxiety!!!!!

Also, I don't think I told you that in my conversation last Thursday night with him that he said he would ask you to set up a meeting between VJ and myself, once VJ got back. I assume he'll mention this to you at some point – hopefully sooner rather than later!

I am enclosing a copy for VJ of the list of advertising/PR firms that I included in "the big guy's" packet. My hopes are that one of the names will jump out as a place where he (VJ) might have a contact.

I mentioned to him that Id like to drop by on Sat. to give you your birthday present and to see him for a bit. He seemed somewhat receptive and said he'd check it out this week. Of course, he'll forget because in the whole scheme of things it's not that important and I will, of course, probably have to bug you towards the end of the week with this (something to look forward to I'm sure)!!!!!

I hope to hear from you soon with some guidance. I am mailing my "thank-you-for-meeting-with-me-letter" to Richardson today. I was pleased the UN interview went well, but I'm afraid it will be like being at the Pentagon in NY...YUCK! PLEASE let me know what to do soon!!!!

1,000 thank you's.

Hugs n' kisses,

MSL-55-DC-0179

3026

2 March 1997

MSL-DC-00000621

Dear Mr. P-

I must admit it... I am a compulsive shopper! I saw this tie and thought it would look fabulous on you. I hope you like it.

All of my life, everyone has always said that I am a difficult person for whom to shop. and yet, you managed to choose ~~two~~ absolutely perfect presents! A little phrase (with only eight letters) like "thank you" simply cannot begin to express what I feel for what you have given me. Art & poetry are gifts to my soul!

I just love the hat pin. It is vibrant, unique, and a beautiful piece of art. My only hope is that I have a hat fit to adorn it (ahhh, I see another excuse to go shopping)! I know that I am bound to receive compliments on it.

3027

I have only read excerpts from "Leaves of Grass" before – never in its entirety or in such a beautifully bound edition. Like Shakespeare, Whitman's writings are so timeless. I find solace in works from the past that remain profound and somehow always poignant. Whitman is so rich that one must read him like one tastes a fine wine or good cigar – take it in, roll it in your mouth, and savor it!

I hope you know how very grateful I am for these gifts, especially your gift of friendship. I will treasure them all... always.

Monica

MSL-DC-00000622

3028

(OFFICIAL LETTERHEAD)

30 September 1997

MEMORANDUM FOR HANDSOME

SUBJECT The New Deal

A proposition for you: You show me that you will let me visit you sans a crisis, and I will be on my best behavior and not stressed out when I come (to see you, that is).

I'd like to come for a visit this evening. According to **my** calendar, we haven't spent any time together on the phone or in person in six weeks. You'll be gone the next few weekends so if we don't get together tonight, by the time I do see you it will have been over two months.

What do you think of maybe planning ahead with Betty that you would leave at seven so everyone else goes home, and then you could come back around 7:30 or later. I'll be tied up until about 7:30. Any time after that is good for me.

Oh, and Handsome, remember FDR would never have turned down a visit with Lucy Mercer!

MSL-DC-00001050

***** JUST A REMINDER TO THROW THIS AWAY AND NOT SEND IT BACK TO THE STAFF SECRETARY!**

3031

I believe the time has finally come for me to throw in the towel. my conversation with Marsha left me disappointed, frustrated, sad and angry. I can't help but wonder if you knew she wouldn't be able to detail me over there when I last saw you. maybe that would explain your coldness. the only explanation I can reason for your not bringing me back is that you just plain didn't want to enough or care about me enough. how else can I rationalize why it is ok for Marsha and Debi and scores of others to be in golden positions -- people can say what they want to about them, even be nasty to them but everyone knows that they will never be touched because they have your approval. Debi can prance around in your shoes or stand in front of 50 people gathered for dinner bragging about just how she obtained your shirt for Walter to have bespoke shirts made for you. Marsha can remark to someone which subsequently ends up in the papers and magazines that "she spent the night with you". I just loved you -- wanted to spend time with you, kiss you, listen to you laugh -- and I wanted you to love me back.

I never told you this because I didn't want to seem like a martyr but in April of '95 I wanted nothing more than to beg you to do something so I didn't have to leave. I wanted to scream and bawl. you have no idea how desperate, upset, humiliated I was. But I didn't. you said you would see what you could do and I left it at that because I didn't want to put you in a bad situation. It was an election year and I knew what was important. You promised you would bring me back after the election with a snap of you fingers.

I left the WH at age 22 from my first job out of college, the beginning of my career, to come to work at an agency in which I have no interest at a job where I'm bored. I kept a calendar with a countdown until election day. I was so sure that the weekend after the election you would call me to come visit and you would kiss me passionately and tell me you couldn't wait to have me back. You'd ask me where I wanted to work and say something akin to "Consider it done" and it would be. Instead I didn't hear from you for weeks and subsequently your phone calls became less frequent. We talked about my returning and you kept replying, "I'll talk to Bob Nash", "I've talked to Bob Nash", "Bob Nash is working it". Then it moved to "Marsha is working on it". Then you dumped me and it was still "Marsha' is working it. I promise it will be done" Now, Marsha is saying just be patient. Why do you want to come back anyway? You've already had the experience of working here.

I can't take it any more. A person can only handle so might anxiety and stress. Maybe it would be easier to wait if you had called more and it hadn't been such trouble to try to see you. As I said in my last letter to you I've waited long enough. You and Marsha win. I give up. you let me down, but I shouldn't have trusted you in the first place.

MSL-DC-00001052

3039

MSL-DC-00001227

Dear Handsome, 29 June 1997

I really need to discuss my situation with you. We have not had any contact for over five weeks. You leave on Sat. and I leave for Madrid w/ the SecDef on Monday returning the 14th of July. I am then heading out to Los Angeles for a few days. If I do not speak to you before you leave, when I return from LA it will have been two months since we last spoke. Please do not do this to me. I feel disposable, used and insignificant. I understand your hands are tied, but I ~~just~~ want to talk to you and look at some options. I am begging you one last time. ~~from the bottom of my heart~~ to please let me ~~come~~ visit ~~see you~~ Bricks Tuesday evening. I will call Betty Tues. afternoon to see if it is o.k.

-M

2655

Aug - pres suit - Sep - Oct - furlough mid Nov.

end of Dec 31st "day"

1st week Dec - signed picture in back office -

845-DC-00000002

3d wk in Dec - "hi Kiddo"

→ White House Staff

Dec party in The 21st afternoon -

10 days later - 31 Dec 97
visit or 7 days later
Weekend - Sun Called
Snowing, at 2:40 -
1½ later Blizzard of 96
she went to work -
walked by, Come on in -
closed door - 45 minutes
guard there - Leavy Session
Jan 7
Jan MLK Day - at lanta for the day.

2656

" Really
Hard to have someone
die under your executive
order" "Cherishes time
w/ her - treasure gifts"
never alone
~~Buddy coming 1/2 hour~~

Nancy's ofc -
fooled around -
jerking off went Bad cause
door was locked.

21st Jan 96
27 Jan called ofc -
she was in
saw Leonard &
gone weekend
Tues - Monday
farewell
to Pat Griffin

845-DC-00000004

2657

(weekend before: have to be careful: rumor that he had a crush on

·4:00 Tues. he the intern
calls her @ ofc. in Hern's
"POTUS" ofc.

Panetta's ofc

Pat Griffith
farewell
planned
to ignore
each other -
not even a
picture

½ day Tues
first week
Thur
Fri.
Sat.

845-DC-00000005

group picture
far end away from
him -

following Sun -
beginning feb
he called in the
afternoon at work -
Baba at home -
45 minutes 4:00
1½ hrs.

2658

(fooled around first)
½ hour - finished
"Will you call me?"
Recited # -
met in hall - walked
in together
20 mins. later
called @ ofc
"had a really nice
time"
calls
Tues. night
(Baba gone Tues & Wed)
enjoyed talking to
her
have to go help
homework - called
from "home"
next day wore better

845-DC-00000006

2659

Midnight
Called next night
in the middle of
night - from bed -
phone sex 20 - 30 minutes
7th feb

~~do~~ No contact
President's til 19 feb -
Day 11:00 ~~Sun~~ Mon. a.m. at home
she was going to work -

19 feb she went straight on
knocked on door -

closed door -
dumped her =
I love her
I've hurt them both:
so need before
ofc -
went to back - hugged

845-DC-00000007

2660

no kissing
you have to go now.
wouldn't even kiss
me goodbye -
guard - saw her
leave - 15-20
19 feb '96 minutes
in there

end of feb 2 weeks
28? later

anxiety attack -
Baba going out of
town -
Israeli Embassy that
night - he saw her in
9:00 pm hallway
10:00 phone ring -
looked really pretty
called you in the
office - short conversation

845-DC-00000008

2661

next weekend
or
2 wks later -
ran into him w/
Natalie - didn't call -
The day he signed Cuba
~~Summit~~ thing Libertad
Sanctions
against
cuba -
receiving line
March
~~then~~ then he went
2nd
that afternoon Summit
in Egypt = few days.
The Bala & girl were in Bacai
That weekend he
golfed on Sunday
screening at 8:00
theater stuff at
night -
waited til
10:00

845-DC-00000009

2662

Next week – Baba gone
to Boston [illegible]
Monday – pissed she is
Jogging – Dip Room
walked by
ignored him.

11:00 A.M. –
Tues. called on
house phone
to her – Potus didn't
OPC show up on
phone.

Thursday: skipped

Friday a.m. –
jogging return – passed
elevator (Connie Mariano
Dr.)

put tie on rest of
for day.

P.M. – Harold & Bruce –
"Hi Monica"

845-DC-00000010

2662

2663

Sun: part into Nancy not Sat.

(· fooled around — told about wearing blue & white tie)

Tired:

deteriorating position

Nancy said — Ron Brown family on Sat — coming to see Potus — call me Monday —

~~6:00 at~~

6:00 Sunday night he called at home —

- Come over — —

845-DC-00000012

Romantic.

if I win in Nov. I'll have you back like that! fooled around. phone call from Dick Morris — head on phone

Harold came in —

she went out a [illegible] sausage

2664

"called at
7:00 @ home"

Why did you leave?
Came back & you weren't
there ??

845-DC-00000013

you call Walter -
I'll bet it had something
to do w/ me

Monday - met w/ Nancy
Very sweet - [illegible] -
conscientious worker -

as ~~she~~ she left, Betty
asked what was wrong.
Betty hugged her -
Sometimes [illegible] happen
for a reason -
Friday - he called her at
home - she was hysterical
he found out what happened"

2665

845-DC-00000014

visited apr 5

1. Evelyn Lieberman
Marsha & Navy board
out —
→ had gotten different
accounts he was
paying too much attention
she's got to go —
after election
doesn't care —
if you don't like
it, get you a job
on the campaign
I'll call you later —
3:00 AM. promised
to call, made
myself wake up —
sweet call

Mar 29 —
April — left Sun to go G-7
Tokyo — then Russia
Sun. night returned —

2666

20th
Monday nite - called
after trip - hates job -
next week see you
Sent APAC thing
dy after
Mon and Shorts NO -
HRC
11-12 p.m. out of town
Thurs. night - he called
at home - phone sex -
promise he'd call this
weekend.
didn't call.

May early
3:00 Mon. night - HRC there
A.M. apology call
sick can't talk

845-DC-00000015

May - Saxophone event
hug & kiss - I miss you

1 wk goes by -
10 DAYS til next phone call.

2667

phone sex

Week later he called – Borda committed suicide –

he was upset –

mid ind mgt

Coming to Pentagon prior to SVC ignored her

he called that night – she left that night.

Just a week – phone sex

1½ wk later (following "hello" on tape guide)

Calls Wed. prior to big dinner –

845-DC-00000016

Betty called next A.M. at work – re radio address –

2668

845-DC-00000017

wants to meet her
family - Dad &
Stepmother were
coming

Radio tape on friday
W/ parents

Sat. June 23?
next weekend - called -
just to talk -

She
leaves for Bosnia to
July 5

July 5 calls that
night -
Wierd phone sex =
Short 20 min
jerked off keep
just talking

July 19?
18 a friday Called
6:30 -

2669

Baba out of town
July 5 –

845-DC-00000018

6:30 A.M. leaving for Olympics
That day –
phone sex – after
Well, Good Morning!! came

promised to call
while he was away –
didn't call on Birthday
next week ~~I called on~~
Sunday –
Australia night

saw him away
phoned & apologized 8:30 pm.
for Birthday
short. July 30th

Fool sun Aug 4 = afternoon
pink suit – 45 minutes
Stevens HRC away lengthy phone sex.

2670

Vacation - 1 WK -

Aug - ~~2 tests taken~~
day before travel
21st departure - for convention
6:00 p.m.
phone sex -
in his ofc

Her 250th planned to
19 aug. Birthday party NY
NY juicy - touched
grabbed his d—
sent tie for B'day.

845-DC-00000019

~~Sep 5~~

Sep 5 - called from
good conversation road - at
home = phone sex -
Sep 10 - left msg -
It's me -

2671

~~10~~ 20 - 30th [illegible] she was in DOD.

Sep 30th Called you
saw you walking -
good conversation

Sep 5 phone sex
"NO WAY" (will you ever meet me to me?)
when you get to
my age, everything
has consequences"
fight about it!
do you want me
to not call you
anymore?

Oct. 22nd wedding
in florida
he
really into phone
sex.
[illegible]

Baba not TV
Michael
2:30am

845-DC-00000020

2672

"Triple C" hotels

Black suit

845-DC-00000021

Tues. Oct. - WC - he
next night - Baba not there
event

next day -
tell Betty to
walk helicopter
waited in West Wing Lobby -
Betty told her Evelyn
Lieberman didn't
like it.

not Oct. Sunday - Rally -

Oct 23 -
welcome home at WH
following election.

2673

845-DC-00000022

6 wks later -

night before the left.

Dec 2nd phone

sex -

3 wks:

Christmas party Tues.

next night - he calls - everyday can't be

sunshine -

person - have something

come by on Sat.

never called -

saw him at Nutcracker

Called Monday -

Jan 1997 Sat I missed you - he went away for New Year ever -

Jan 18th - he calls -

2674

Jan 12 phone sex
had to push him
M. nap - present
See you
etc.

Inaugural - red dress

~~Jan~~ -
Feb 8th - noon
Showing -
come in for present.
Betty can't ~~get~~ in -

sick over this
think about this
all the time
in ~~person~~ should call

he called back -
phone sex.

~~Feb~~ Val. at - ~~call~~ him

845-DC-00000023

2675

845-DC-00000024

Betty called ofc
to invite Radio address

feb 28th go to Radio
address -
Signed photo - embassy
hat pin taping
Book fears & warnings
out
fooled around.

Mar 13th
got a phone at
work - want to
see you tomorrow
a.m.
leaving for florida girls
Jordanian shot

concerns from Nancy & Steve
Mar 30th crutches
Betty Visit, gold pen

2676

28 feb – didn't want
to come
addiction –

Mar 30 cried –

fisherman
phone
he april 24th
called –

Dump day 23 May –

845-DC-00000025

2677

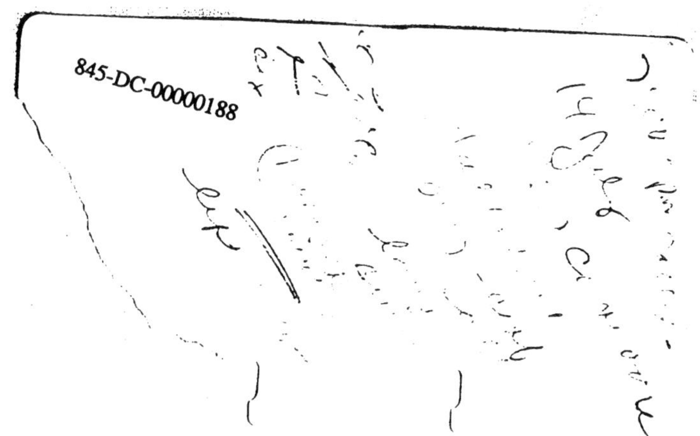

2678

Letters Editor
Newsweek
251 West 57th Street
New York, New York 10019-1894

(BY FAX: 212.445.4120)

I would like to clarify the questions that have arisen about my involvement in the matter reported by Newsweek in its August 11th edition. Contrary to the perception held by many that I granted Newsweek "an interview" for this story, the truth is the reporter appeared, uninvited and unannounced, in my office at the Pentagon in late March 1997. I was compelled to respond when he asserted that Ms. Willey had given him my name, as a purported contemporaneous witness who could corroborate her new claim of "harassment" or "inappropriate behavior" on the part of the President.

My response then, as it remains today, was that this was completely inaccurate and that her version in 1993 and her version in 1997 were wholly inconsistent. One must wonder how such disparate allegations spanning a period of four years could have much, if any, credibility.

Regarding the comment made by the President's attorney about me, which appeared in the same article, I am acutely disappointed that my integrity has been questioned.

Linda R. Tripp
Department of Defense
Washington, D.C. 20301-1400

Ann McDaniel

845-DC-00000190

2679

trainer — broke off at 9:30 —
Debbie Byrd —
walking in at same time

Tony Nylon
shorts
drawstring
black red
yellow

July 4
July 24

T shirt

aug 16
9:00

socks shoes.
tennis

picture framed
Vision
& Representation

845-DC-00000191

2680

845-DC-00000192

Sept. 15
Isikoff calls me
from his home @ —
& asks if M knows
about a woman
who had a KW
experience — he is
trying to find out
who she is. All he
knows is that
she is married,
they don't live
in Washington,
she is a
smart, savvy
professional
woman w/ "a
Clinic in Wash" -
Happened in
1996 - during
Inaugural time,
she received
"a flurry of phone
calls" from him and

said he is
"paranoid" right now.
gate - car - comes over
Robin Washy
5:30 pm

17 Sep - Betty calls
her @ work 2:00 ish & says
"he" had asked her if
she had gotten the
Black Dog stuff to M,
& to let her know
that now John Podesta
was working on getting
her back - & when
Betty said M might
also want to move
to NY, he said "OK
That's easy, she she
can work for Bill Richardson" - him
rebuffed

M met Betty
at the gate
after work -
received
many
2 T shirts
Turquoise & 1 white
1 sheer cotton dress.

strange
angle
&
pissed
off
himself

2681

Friday, September 12that gate, hour and a half --repeated calls to office, finally she came out and got her -- long talk, he left. She poke to him before she left and told him XX was hysterical and at the gate and that she would clear her in and determine if she was a "crazy woman" --

Sept 14 Sunday night -- her plane from Illinois was cancelled, luckily she ran into Glickman who claimed she was with their party and got her on their flight out but to National instead of BWI -- she had to go get her car at BWI and called at 7:00 or so -- said she would call him and if he checked his messages, maybe he would call her back. He was at the pool at 7:30 -- she didn't know if he had company or what, but he called her later that evening and said that he would talk to XX XXX this week.

845-DC-00000193

2609

24 June 1997

Dear Betty:

Since I have not been able to get in touch with him, I am taking the unorthodox liberty of sharing my concerns with you. I would very much appreciate it if you could relay this information to him either verbally or by letting him read this note. If you're not comfortable doing either, I understand.

The intention of this note is not to "tattle-tale", but to clarify. My meeting with Marsha was not at all what I expected. While she was very pleasant, she questioned me endlessly about my situation. Despite the fact that she already knew why I had to leave, she asked me to tell her about it, asked if I had acted "inappropriately" and why I wanted to come back. She seemingly knew nothing about my current position. She didn't know of any openings and said she would check with the people in Communications. He said to me that he had told her I had gotten a bum deal, and I should get a good job in the West Wing. I was surprised that she would question his judgment and not just do what he asked of her. Is it possible that, in fact, he did not tell her that? Does he really not want me back in the complex? He has not responded to my note, nor has he called me. Do you know what is going on? If so, are you able to share it with me?

I did not cause any trouble when I had to leave last year because I knew how important the election was. He promised me then I could come back after the election, and I have been counting on him. I think I have been more than patient since it has now been eight months since the election, not to mention the seven months prior to November that I waited. Shall I continue to be patient?

Betty, I am very frustrated and sad. I especially don't understand this deafening silence, lack of response and complete distancing evidenced by him. Why is he ignoring me? I have done nothing wrong. I would expect that behavior like this might be directed toward an "unfriendly", but certainly not to me. I would ***never*** do anything to hurt him.

I am hoping to hear from either of you soon. I'm at a loss, and I don't know what to do.

Best wishes.

833-DC-00001070

2610

Tripp, Linda, , OSD/PA

From: Tripp, Linda, , OSD/PA
To: Lewinsky, Monica, , OSD/PA
Subject: RE: hi, ya
Date: Wednesday, March 05, 1997 11:34AM

Are you asking me if the tie if really pretty? It is positively gorgeous. I am knot (ha!) particularly into ties, but from my exposure to you, I am developing an interest. Yours was stupendous, no kidding, clean, crisp, texture, color, pattern, bright, without being at all over the top.....a total hit.

From: Lewinsky, Monica, , OSD/PA
To: Tripp, Linda, , OSD/PA
Subject: hi, ya
Date: Wednesday, March 05, 1997 10:05AM
Priority: High

Boy, I look so scary today. People might think that I thought it was Halloween. Oh, well, [redacted] should (if Betty is nice) get my tie today. I sure hope he like s it. make me feel better and tell me it's really pretty, o.k.? msl

833-DC-00001857

2611

Tripp, Linda, , OSD/PA

From: Tripp, Linda, , OSD/PA
To: Lewinsky, Monica, , OSD/PA
Subject: RE: where are you?
Date: Monday, March 03, 1997 12:48PM

Kate is faxing me a copy of the announcement -- she is planning to go see Marsha today. If someone in house wants it, there is a chance they will get it, but Kate seems confident that that won't happen. She said to have your resume ready. LRT

From: Lewinsky, Monica, , OSD/PA
To: Tripp, Linda, , OSD/PA
Subject: where are you?
Date: Monday, March 03, 1997 12:21PM
Priority: High

Hello, where are you? I am sorry i was such a pain before but this is all very stressful for me. write back. i don't know what's goin on. msl

833-DC-00001876

2612

Tripp, Linda, , OSD/PA

From: Tripp, Linda, , OSD/PA
To: Lewinsky, Monica, , OSD/PA
Subject: RE: ADVICE
Date: Monday, February 24, 1997 11:22AM

Eureka!!!!

From: Lewinsky, Monica, , OSD/PA
To: Tripp, Linda, , OSD/PA
Subject: ADVICE
Date: Monday, February 24, 1997 8:31AM

Hi, I hope you're feeling better ! I 'm trying to go over to the WH today to give Jodie these pictures. I also plan to stop by Betty's office to drop off these lame photos. Any advice/suggestions what to do or say? write me back...msl

833-DC-00001906

Page 1

2613

Tripp, Linda, , OSD/PA

From: Tripp, Linda, , OSD/PA
To: Lewinsky, Monica, , OSD/PA
Subject: RE: secret message
Date: Wednesday, February 19, 1997 9:01AM

WELCOME BACK!!! How was Jolly, Olde England? Well, here's the saga in a nutshell. On friday (of course), Howard County (the boondocks where I live) was totally and completely snowed and iced in, so I couldn't get up my hill, schools were closed, no one moved, believe it or not. I was in a panic about the papers.....by the time I could get up the hill late that night, all the Posts were gone, BUT I called work and had my Deputy save me what he could, which was one, and then I found another, so we have two. I can't believe it became that big a deal, but it did. CALL ME WHEN YOU GET IN. PS It read beautifully, placement was great, typeface totally effective, and text superlative.....good job. LRT

From: Lewinsky, Monica, , OSD/PA
To: Tripp, Linda, , OSD/PA
Subject: RE: secret message
Date: Thursday, February 13, 1997 1:23PM

O.K. here is my fax in London 011-44-171-235-4552 and phone, just in case, I don't know what, here is the phone number 011-44-171-235-2000. I will also be checking my messages in the hopes that the creep will call and say"Thank you for my love note. I love you. Will you run away with me?" What do ya think the likelihood of that happening is? Also, please don't forget about the newspapers. I will bring you the $ later.

thanx...xoxoxo...msl

From: Tripp, Linda, , OSD/PA
To: Lewinsky, Monica, , OSD/PA
Subject: RE: secret message
Date: Thursday, February 13, 1997 1:03PM

Ah, but that has already transpired, says my omnipotent crystal ball........................

From: Lewinsky, Monica, , OSD/PA
To: Tripp, Linda, , OSD/PA
Subject: RE: secret message
Date: Thursday, February 13, 1997 11:05AM
Priority: High

IF ONLY I COULD PURSUADE THE CREEP AS EASILY!!!!!!!

From: Tripp, Linda, , OSD/PA
To: Lewinsky, Monica, , OSD/PA
Subject: RE: secret message
Date: Thursday, February 13, 1997 11:03AM

833-DC-00001934

OK OK OK. 12 at bridge.

From: Lewinsky, Monica, , OSD/PA
To: Tripp, Linda, , OSD/PA
Subject: RE: secret message
Date: Thursday, February 13, 1997 10:18AM
Priority: High

I'LL PROBABLY GO GET LUNCH AT 12;00 BECAUSE I'M HUNGRY ALREADY!!! I DON'T THINK I'LL BE MORE THAN 1/2 HOUR BECAUSE I'M LEAVING EARLY. PLEASE ESCAPE WITH ME!!!!!! HOW CAN YOU RESIST ME?? DON'T FORGET I'LL BE GONE FOR AWHILE...MSL

From: Tripp, Linda, , OSD/PA
To: Lewinsky, Monica, , OSD/PA
Subject: RE: secret message

2614

Tripp, Linda, , OSD/PA

From: Tripp, Linda, , OSD/PA
To: Lewinsky, Monica, , OSD/PA
Subject: RE: Afternoon
Date: Tuesday, February 04, 1997 2:55PM

None of the above, if you ask me. Because, none of it makes sense. Do not despair, there is most definitely light at the end of this tunnel. LRT

From: Lewinsky, Monica, , OSD/PA
To: Tripp, Linda, , OSD/PA
Subject: RE: Afternoon
Date: Tuesday, February 04, 1997 2:15PM
Priority: High

Thank God for you! Oh Linda, i don't know what I am going to do. I just don't understand what went wrong, what happened? How could he do this to me? Why did he keep up contact with me for so long and now nothing, now when we could be together? Maybe it was the intrigue of wanting something he couldn't have (easily) with all that was going on then? Maybe he wanted to insure he could have variety and phone sex while he was on the road for those months? AAAAHHHHH!!!!! I am going to lose it! And, where is Betty's phone call? What's up with all this shit? oh, well. bye.
msl

From: Tripp, Linda, , OSD/PA
To: Lewinsky, Monica, , OSD/PA
Subject: Afternoon
Date: Tuesday, February 04, 1997 2:06PM
Priority: High

Just checking in, it's been a nutty day so I haven't had much chance to see you. I had to go up to the third floor and drop off some paperwork, so I actually walked the entire E-ring, which took I5 minutes. Guess I am kinda slow, huh? Oh well, next time I will go by myself so that I can keep my own pace. I feel as though I did SOMETHING anyway. I have had tons of water the past few days, and even more today, so watch and see, I'll have gained weight tonight, at this rate. I don't seem to be getting rid of the water, so it's hanging out somewhere!! Anyway, my real purpose in jotting off this e-mail is to see what's up with you, and how you're doing. I am so jealous that you are off to London soon, I love it so. I would spend tons of time in Harrod's, spend time on Fleet Street and down in the Silver Vaults, putter around Portebello Road, and shop til I dropped!! I would have high tea every day even if I had to skip real meals. I used to spend all my summers in Europe as a kid, and would sneak over to London whenever I could, always by myself, when I was about I6. Back then (I'm dating myself!!!) you could buy the all time BEST fish and chips from these little holes in the wall, wrapped in newspaper!! It was one of the best things I had ever eaten.
LRT

833-DC-00001974

18 MAY 97

Dear Catherine,

I MISS YOU SO MUCH!!! It was wonderful to hear your voice the other day. Well, it's Sunday & I might get to see the Big Creep today. He called yesterday & said he's going to see if Betty can come in so I can go there. It seems that he is really trying to get me back there! Who knows!?!?. Of course, I have my period!!! (and am really horny... but what else is new?) I hope all is well with you. I truly know how difficult it can be to assimilate to a new city--especially one where the language is so different*! How are you getting by? Is the sushi really good? ....yummy...!!! You know what, "Ravi" was on t.v. a week or so ago. "Hi Kidetora" ahh Saburo. See, I'm still really weird!!!. BTW, I'm writing this card on my lap which is why it is so messy. I'm too lazy to move to my messy desk! I'm bummed because I realized that my LSAT is the day after not before the Dave Matthews concert for which I have a ticket!!! Does that suck or what? Have you gone to the 'Hotel Okura' yet? Is this the most random, incoherent letter you've ever received? (tee-hee-hee) I'm better on e-mail. Thank you again for the lovely picture of us. I look at it every day! I bet pretty soon I'll start talking to you in the picture! You look so beautiful. I still can't get over how thin my arms are in the picture!!! How is Chris? Is he enjoying work? the people? I'm curious as to what is going on w/ Nick & Jen. I hope you had a chance to talk some sense into him!! (j.k.) Maybe if they get married soon you can come to the states... via DC!!! (not too circuitous of a route or anything!!!) Oh, Catherine, I hope you know how much I love you and how very special your friendship is to me. We'll always be close no matter how many miles are between us. I need you! I love you! Please take care of yourself. Love to you and Chris!

♥ Monica

*that I haven't experienced!

1037-DC-00000002

2789

Subject: RE: hi!
Date: Monday, December 08, 1997 1:29PM

Hi! It is so good to hear from you. I have only a minute as I am off =
=3D
to my early class. Thank you for my wonderful card and perfume. It was =
=3D
very nice of you to send me something so far away in Stinkyo. I =3D
appreciate it. Hey, guess what is this Sunday? Guess. Okay, I love =
=3D
you nad I will write again soon. I am thinking of trying to call you =
=3D
some time this week if I can coodinate the time change deal. love, Cat

---

From: Lewinsky, Monica, , [redacted]
Sent: Tuesday, December 09, 1997 6:11 AM
To: CA Davis
Subject: hi!

Hi, Girl-

It's been ages since i've spoken to you. I was in LA and then in =3D
Brussels=3D20
and london for work. London was wonderful, as to be expected.

Did you ever receive my package? What's been going on with you? I miss =
=3D
you=3D20
terribly and feel clueless as to what's happening in your life.

My life is still in turmoil. I have given my notice for the end of this =
=3D

month, but don't have anything firm in NY. I'm getting frustrated. =3D
things=3D20
ave been crazy with the creep, though i did have a wonderful visit with =
=3D
him=3D20
on Saturday. When he doesn't put his walls up, it is always so heavenly.

Please write back soon. i miss you.

love,

Monica=3D20

1037-DC-00000011

Page 2

2790

CA Davis

From: Lewinsky, Monica, , [redacted]
Sent: Friday, November 07, 1997 7:20 AM
To: CA Davis
Subject: RE: troubs?

I'm a little nervous to do the whole name of the BF. His first name is Vernon. It went very well as I said yesterday. I won't be hearing from him until later next week. I know he saw the big creep yetserday afternoon. Unfortunatley, that fucker hasn't called me so i don't really know what happened in the meeting or whatever else is going on with him. oh well.

i don't have much to report except that i ma absolutely exhausted today. It is an overcast, Portland-like day today and I just want to crawl into my beddy-bye and read, nap and relax. (of course, having a boy there too wouldn't be so bad!!!) i hope you are doing well. i miss you.

let me know what's up with you.

luv,
monka

From: CA Davis
To: 'Lewinsky, Monica, , OSD/PA'
Subject: RE: troubs?
Date: Wednesday, November 05, 1997 1:28PM

Hey! I said there is no way in hell I am a real size 6- I am =
no-questions-asked-no-doubts-in-my-mind-an-honest-to-goodness-full-size =
8. EIGHT. And sizes are not double, but if they ae then Jeannie is =
half my size. My point was GAP is retarded, but in an ego-boosting way =
so 'please try'- as they say in Japan. And I have NOT lost weight, I =
have gained weight but only a little. What I do have is a constant =
poochy belly from eating too much rice! So, no more sarcastico comments =
on my voluptuous, size 8 bod. =20
Who's the BF? Have you told me his name? Can you? I hope that works =
out for you, let me know. I have no time right now. I have to go to my =
7.30a class and I am not dressed yet. =20
Okay, my lovely size 10 lovebug- and you cannot say anyting bad about a =
size 10 because I think that is a fine size- seeing as I was one for =
years and probably still am in Guess or Benetton or something. Actually =
I think I am one with Jigsaw, a Brit compnay I buy clothes in here. So =
no more of it all! I love you, be good! Cat

From: Lewinsky, Monica, , [redacted]]
Sent: Thursday, November 06, 1997 5:38 AM
To: CA Davis
Subject: RE: troubs?

Whew! What a day! I met with the big creep's best friend this morning. It=20
was very interetsing. I have never met such a "real" person in my =
entire=20
life. You know how some people where their hearts on their sleeves; he=20
wears his soul. Incredible. He said, with regard to my job search, =
"We're=20
in business." We'll see. he also said the creep had talked to him, and =
as=20
I was leaving he said, "You come very highly reccmmended." =
(Tee-hee-hee)

1037-DC-00000017

2791

CA Davis

From: Lewinsky, Monica, ,[redacted]
Sent: Wednesday, November 05, 1997 2:16 AM
To: CA Davis
Subject: RE: troubs?

oK. I have some bad news. I am off the next trip so i won't be coming to Tokyo. I am probably sorrier than you are. the truth is it would have been so difficult to spend time together and it probably would have benn more frustrating than anything.

The job thing on Friday went much better than expected. It was nice; the big creep called thursday night and gave me a pep talk because i was so afraid I'd sound like an idiot. Richardson is a great guy and i met two women who work for him...also very cool. Yesterday, Richardson called me at work and told me they were going to offer me a position..they didn't know what yet, and they wanted to talk with me further. The problem is, I don't really wnat to work there (issue wise or location wise) I've already had the experience of working in a yucky building. It was awful, actually, because i feel a little trapped into taking it. HOPEFULLY, there will be some movement on the other tracks in NY too. I told mr. bacon I was planning to move and was in the process of looking...which is why i asked him if i could switch trips with tom. The biggest reason i need to do that was because the creep's friend who is supposed to help me with the private sector possibilities has been out of town the last two weeks. I feel like I'll lose momentum with them if i disappear for three weeks now (that's including Thanksgiving). Oy vey!

I'm glad to hear you guys had such a nice weekend. Honestly Cat, it sounds like such a wonderful fantasy to me. To be with yourr husband – as part of a couple with other couples doing couple-y kinds of things and having fun.

My Australian boyfriend CALLED me on Friday to let me know his e-mail was down., He said it had become habit to e-mail me friday nights and he wanted to let me know he couldn't send anything. I know...when's the wedding???? Just kiddin'.

i miss you tons and am so sad I won't see you, but maybe we'll work something out soon. When do you guys come to the states..for holiday? and for good?

kisses and hugs
Monica

From: CA Davis
To:[redacted]
Subject: troubs?
Date: Monday, November 03, 1997 7:15PM

Hi, I sent you a message called 'quickie' last wk, but it was =
undeliverable for awhile so I'm hoping this will reach you. You'd think =
the f'n Pentagon could have straightened out email! Anyway, how did =
your 'meeting' go last week? I'm seeing the man on tellie alot because =
of the Iraqi nonsense. I think that could be a cool job, maybe better =
than the DOD.
I had a long wkend away from home. We went to a friend's office's =
cottage at Lake Kawaguchi. Its Susan's office's cottage and she invited =
us and 2 other couples for the 3day wkend- so 4 couples all together. =
It was fun- we drank a lot, ate a lot, hiked, walked, lounged, played =
games etc..I was about ready to go home Sunday evening but we left Mon. =
morning. I was getting tired of being surrounded by Brits! Actually =
one couple is made up of a German woman and a man, Gavin, who is =

Page 1

1037-DC-00000022

2792

CA Davis

From: Lewinsky, Monica, [redacted]
Sent: Wednesday, October 22, 1997 3:19 AM
To: CA Davis
Subject: hey gorgeous

Hi, Girl-

Nothing much is going on right now. You know I don't think i have mentioned to you that I have developed this intereting e-mail friendship with one of the Austarlians i met in Princeton. He is sooooo nice (and i know he is cute). It's sucha shame he lives all the way in Australia! I'm hoping he will be back in the states for business soon (hopefully, I'll ahve lost half my ass by then). His name is...Chris! Wouldn't that be funny if i married a Chris ,too!

So, i did a bad thing this past weekend. I called that shmucko (yeah, i know-- which one?) ANDY. Oh, I don't know why i did that. It was so stupid of me. I was uncomfortable talking to him. I asked how the kids were and if everything was ok. i felt so weird so after about 3 minutes..no more...i said, well i gotta go..and he said that's it and then my phine clicked so i said yeah and hung up. oh well. i actively hate his guts. he deserves to go to hell.

I have nothing to report otherwise. I have sent my list of crap to the Creep and am waiting to see if anything happens. i sure hope so.

i love you.

love
monica

1037-DC-00000033

2793

CA Davis

From: Lewinsky, Monica, [redacted]
Sent: Wednesday, September 17, 1997 1:30 AM
To: CA Davis
Subject: RE: yeah!

THIS IS REALLY LONG. YOU MAY WANT TO PRINT IT OUT TO READ IT!!!

OK here is the note i sent you which you never got. God this e-mail system sucks so much!!!!

Hi, how was Chris' birthday? I got the beautiful pictures from the wedding. Thank you. You look so stunning. i could sit and look at the picture of you and Chris all day...hhmmmmmmm. Also, the wedding party picture is so ...i don't know...quintessential -- like it could be the picture in a frame when you buy a new one!

The Princess Di stuff....I am the most sad for her sons. I think it is tragic what happened. There are a lot of people who are very upset by this whole incident. I'm sorry you're having a hard time with it. As i said, i feel bad for her kids and sorry that she passed away, but i wasn't really her biggest fan -- sort of neutral towards her.

Well, I have an update or maybe and end-date... it's kinda long so here goes...

Yesterday morning i went to a farewell ceremony for someone here and saw the White House liaison woman with whom I met lastr week about being detailed. I asked her if she got my e-mail and she said she had and asked if i had spoken to Marsha recently. I said "no. why?" She said that marsha had run into a few snags and i should talk to her. So i called marsha all day long yetserday and finally got in touch with her at 5 pm. She has been stripped of the detailee slot in her office. So for now, there isn't anyplace for me to be detailed. So I should be PATIENT. I told her i was very upset and disappointed (even thpugh i really didn't want to work for her) and then she and i got into it. She didn't understand why i wanted to come back when there were still people there who would give me a hard time and that it isn't the right political climate for me to come back. I said i din't understand why it was okay for there to be talk about some people there but it wasn't okay for me. they have all been taken care of. ohhhh it was so infuriating. she asked me why i kept pushing the envelope on coming back there -- after all i had the experience of being there already!

So it's over. I don't know what i will do now but i can't wait any more and i can't go through all of this crap anymore. In some ways i hope i never hear from him again because he'll just lead me on because he doesn't have the balls to tell me the truth. i kind of phase in and out of being sad -- as to be expected but i'll survive. What other choice do i have?

i hope all is well with you. i miss you. 1037-DC-00000038

love
monica

Of course i wrote that like the day after it happened and as to be expected with me felt differentlya few days later. Things have been pretty shitty (insert SIGH). I will tell you the one very sweet, very mixed signal thing going on first cuz it makes me smile. Before the creep left for his vacation I gave him a copy of the novel "The Notebook" --it's this mushy romance (written by a guy) that is like "Bridges of Madison County" sort of BUT one of the recurring themes or things of significance that comes up in the book is Whitman's (gee not Thoreau's--duh) "Leaves of Grass". I

2794

thought it was neat and sweet. I enclosed a card wishing him a fun vacation and asked in a post script if he could bring me a "Black Dog" t-shirt, which you probably know is from this quasi-famous restaraunt in Martha's Vineyard-- if he had a chance. Well, I found out from Betty yesterday that he not only brought me a t-shirt he got me 2 t-shirts, a hat and a dress!!!! Even though he's a big schmuck that is surprisingly sweet -- even that he remebered!

OK Now for the[redacted]. Now that you've read what happened w/ Marsha this will make more sense. I called betty on Wednesday to find out if they knew what had happened and she said she knew but she didn't know if he knew, blah..blah. For three days she kept saying she didn't have a chance to talk to him and then it became this thing on Friday that maybe i could see him and it got crazy,a nd Cat I lost it. I went ape[redacted]. To tell you the truth, i don';t even want to get into it all because it's too exhausting. But the end results were that i talked well mroe like cried to Betty in person on Friday and then I was supposed to maybe see the creepon Sun. and then it didn't work out. I cried for hours and then betty called to say he was going to talk to the chief of staff. BI d on't know what will happen. i also said to betty taht i didn't want him to do anything taht was going to get him in trouble, then yesteday she called to tell me about the black Dog stuff. the[redacted] if i know what the hell is going on!!!! he leaves to go to CA and then a bunch of other places for awhile. Oh well.

On another note, ashley and i are going to a black tie gala this saturday being hosted by the Young Smithsonians, which we have joined. hopefully we'll meet some interesting people. Oooh, a cute boy would be VERY nice.

Just to make this e-mail more interesting (and way too long) I am enclosing my latest and LAST e-mail with Doug that[redacted]. Of course you will see that what he wrote was true, but who asked for the truth! I never responded and then he sent me all of these e-mails and said, "Last e-mail unless i get a repsonse - hello?" LAMER!!!! (I'm going to put what I wrote first and then his response willl follow)

Monica: (we had been conversing earlier and i was sad..he asked why) it might sound silly, but sometimes i just really want somebody (a male) in my life to just physically be with -- you know hugs and stuff (i don't
only think about sex).

i was counting on someone to help me with a job and they put me in touch with someone else that just[redacted]me around for six months. it's frustrating for me. then i get sad when i need some TLC and i can't get it. i haven't made the circle of friends here in dc like i had in portland where if i just needed a guy i had a 3 or 4 male friends on whom i could call. here it seems that most of the guys in my life i have dated so of course, there's always baggage involved. i think i'm not happy here in dc and i'm not really sure what to do about it. so in a nutshell...i'm sad. it is nice of you to ask, thanks.

DOUG:
I understand, but the if you want my very humble opinion the bottom line = is you need to be happy with yourself FIRST (whatever town you're in) = before you can be happy with you and someone else together. =20

You need to concentrate on you -- then others will be attracted to that. You're too consumed with chasing others rather than improving yourself and having that attract others naturally. Make yourself physically and mentally fit and the rest will naturally take care of itself. 1037-DC-00000039

Focus from within and disappointments will disappear!

CAN YOU BELIEVE THIS CRAP! (ok. i know what he said is true but...)

Well on to better topics. Your softball game sounds like fun. I am glad

Page 2

2795

you ahd a good day. You know Catherine, I want you to know that I really admire you for having moved with Chris to Stinkyo. There are so many people who would have said "let's put off getting married til you come back. i don't want to go..blah..blah" But you, instead, i think have really captured what marriage is truly about. I hope Chris knows how lucky he is to have you and to have you --something so comforting and reassuring-- to come home to. YOU have made his transition for work so much better. Imagine how hard it would have been for him (and you too but he was starting a new job) to have been seperated from the one he loves. he would have been pining for you and hjis life in America. Instaed, you ghuys have journeyed together. My Mom and Aunt often ask after you and remark how wonderful it is that you guys are doing it together.

Well, I hope you didn;t get too bore dearly on and not get down to this last paragraph becaus eit is the important one.

I miss you and love you. Oh, BTW, we may be IN Tokyo still on your birthday!!!!!! But if not, we'll celebrate early.

Hug yourself for me.
Monica

ps -- let me know you got this, kay?

From: CA Davis
To: [redacted]
Subject: yeah!
Date: Tuesday, September 16, 1997 3:49AM

Yeah- that you may be coming here in November and only a few days before =
my 24th birthday! I would absolutely love to see you, I really hope you =
come. Well, I suppose if you get a job that you like more before then =
then I will be happy for you, too. I don't think I got an email fdrom =
you about pictures. Are you referring to wedding photos? I hope you =
got htem okay. I think the probs are at the Pentagon for email because =
I'm always getting notes that say messages from me to you cannot be =
delivered. So how are you Monica? Really. I know you are busy at =
work, but please don't feel like I am 'tired of' or 'bored' or 'annoyed' =
or anything about you talking about Marsha stuff or Creep stuff or =
anything- you can still, always, tell me if you want. I remember asking =
you a few weeks ago if you would really consider moving to NYC and if =
you would live with your mom there. If you responded I never got that =
one so let me know. =20
Well, remember my friend Tara, whom I met in London? I visited her in =
San Diego senior year spring break and now she lives in NYC with her =
fiance. They are getting married next month and we just received their =
invitation. Obviously, we cannot go but my thing is I have not heard =
from her in over 4 months! We talked a lot in the last year, especially =
after I got engaged and then she did. After I moved here I emailed her =
and got a response but nothing since. In that one email she said =
something was sort of 'up' or something but no details- she said she =
would snail mail me the news because she didn't want to email it. Well, =
I have not heard from her. I have sent emails with my home address, =
postcards etc and still nothing and then her invitation. I am a little =
perturbed. I sent back hte return saying we can't come and i wrote her =
a personal letter too. I'm bummed. 1037-DC-00000040
Anyway, last Saturday Chris and I went to the Yokohama Country and =
Athletic Club (YCAC) with American friends, through my friend Mary and =
her husband, to play softball. The YCAC is really nice- it is very open =
and sits on top of a hill and has lots of grass and trees! Nothing like =
the Tokyo American Club, its sister club. It was a TAC game against the =
YCAC and we, the TAC, won one and they won one. It was so much fun- we =
forgot we were in Japan!! I played right center in the outfield and had =
a walk and a few hits. Mary was the only other girl on our team and she =
played catcher. After we hung out with our team and drank beer and ate- =
overall a great day, surprisingly in Japan. Oh, aren't I negative about =

Page 3

2796

CA Davis

From: Lewinsky, Monica, , [redacted]
Sent: Thursday, August 14, 1997 1:47 AM
To: CA Davis
Subject: RE: new message

Yeah, Kelly sure was right!!!! I was totally distracted. I'm sure you rememeber I talked to the creep on the phone at work and I was supposed to go there and everything got crazy. I am glad you've had a good time with her but i certainly understand you and Chris wanting some time alone (like to have loud, rad SEX) before you leave!!!!

I'll talk to you about the Marsha stuff on the phone it is too exhausting for me to write it all. I'm drained right now. I can't wait to talk to you on the phone!!! I love to hear your voice...ahhh I sound like such a musher!!!!!

Well, Catherine, my dear, (jeez..i hate being called "dear". the creep calls me that sometimes it's an old person saying!!!!) i don't have much to write -- i am boring. But did i tell you i had sex with thomas last week? I know. I am sooooooo naughty. it was fun and good. i went over there with some ice cream and pretty much seduced him in a way that made him make the moves on me..cool or what???

I LUV YOU!!! Monica

From: CA Davis
To: [redacted]
Subject: new message
Date: Tuesday, August 12, 1997 11:45PM

I thought I would get rid of that Re:blind date message once and for =
all. If you like him and want to see him again call him. Unfortunatly, =
sometimes that must be done. I know it sucks and you wish it not have =
to be that way but that's life. We have to put ourselves out there =
sometimes and maybe be cut-off and maybe be let-in, you never know. =20
You can tell me about bad MArsha or work what-nots, Monica. I am not =
frustrated, neccessarily, but concerned and wishing things would change- =
or you would change them. =20
It has been fun with Kelly but I am ready for her to leave- I'm burnt on =
the entertaining thing. Also, I leave on Friday, the day after her, and =
I want to be alone with Chris. I think he feels the same way, but won't =
say it in so many words. I'm not trying to be mean, its not so much =
personal against her....The other day we were talking about her going =
toPhillie and all and I asked if she thought she would contacta nd see =
you. She said she would like to and probably would. Then she said she =
had a good time with you in DC but you seemed distracted some nad that =
she thought you were a 'very private person'. I thought it was astute, =
but I just agreed and said you could be. Anyway....
Off to work! Write back before I go, 'kay? Love, Cat

1037-DC-00000042

2797

CA Davis

From: CA Davis[redacted]
Sent: Wednesday, November 05, 1997 1:28 PM
To: 'Lewinsky, Monica, , OSD/PA'
Subject: RE: troubs?

Hey! I said there is no way in hell I am a real size 6- I am no-questions-asked-no-doubts-in-my-mind-an-honest-to-goodness-full-size 8. EIGHT. And sizes are not double, but if they ae then Jeannie is half my size. My point was GAP is retarded, but in an ego-boosting way so 'please try'- as they say in Japan. And I have NOT lost weight, I have gained weight but only a little. What I do have is a constant poochy belly from eating too much rice! So, no more sarcastico comments on my voluptuous, size 8 bod.
Who's the BF? Have you told me his name? Can you? I hope that works out for you, let me know. I have no time right now. I have to go to my 7.30a class and I am not dressed yet.
Okay, my lovely size 10 lovebug- and you cannot say anyting bad about a size 10 because I think that is a fine size- seeing as I was one for years and probably still am in Guess or Benetton or something. Actually I think I am one with Jigsaw, a Brit compnay I buy clothes in here. So no more of it all! I love you, be good! Cat

> **From:** Lewinsky, Monica, ,[redacted]
> **Sent:** Thursday, November 06, 1997 5:38 AM
> **To:** CA Davis
> **Subject:** RE: troubs?
>
> Whew! What a day! I met with the big creep's best friend this morning. It was very interetsing. I have never met such a "real" person in my entire life. You know how some people where their hearts on their sleeves; he wears his soul. Incredible. He said, with regard to my job search, "We're in business." We'll see. he also said the creep had talked to him, and as I was leaving he said, "You come very highly reccmmended." (Tee-hee-hee)
>
> The Richardson thing does sound interesting for someone who likes international affairs – NOT ME! But I am trying to only look for something in NY. It's time for me to get out of here. I really hope that the creep and i can still have contact, because, I know it sounds soooooooooo ridiculous, but I can't get him out of my heart. i love him a lot. I know it's stupid. I want to hug him so bad right now i could cry.
>
> OK. I hate you , you little-size-6-bitch. I don't know if i can be friends with you anymore!!!!!!!! That's nice. I'm a 10-12 so that makes me double your size. I am happy for you. That is awesome. Do you think being around the petite japanese has made it easier to lose or more pressure? either way, that's rad. I miss you so much. There's a void in my soul.
>
> Ohhh how i long for the time when we can just spend a day together...starting w/ coffee at Starbuck's...shopping...lunch at somewhere yummy...maybe a movie...more shopping...and then getting drunk on margaritas!!! Whooo-hoooo!
>
> I love you and I'm reminding you to tell me about why your weeknd away w/ couples wasn't so fantasy island.
>
> Love
> M
>
> From: CA Davis
> To: 'Lewinsky, Monica, [redacted]
> Subject: RE: troubs?
> Date: Tuesday, November 04, 1997 2:09PM
>
> Okay, I am seriously bummed, but I was worried about the time issue also =
> and about feeling like you were 'so close, yet so far away' while you =
> were here. Chris and I will be in OR from teh 18th to the 24th of Dec. =
> and HI from the 24th to the 4th or so of Jan. Then I am pretty sure we =
> will be moving back to OR next summer- after our Bali trip! We have =

1037-DC-00000063

Page 1

2798

CA Davis

From: CA Davis[redacted]
Sent: Friday, September 05, 1997 8:28 AM
To: 'Lewinsky, Monica, , OSD/PA'
Subject: RE:

Hi Monica! Chris' birthday was mellow, especially because it was a Wednesday. I took out to dinner at a nice Thai place. He opened his presents in the morning and last night, his American birthday, we had a nice bottle of red wine from my parents to him and had dinner at the table with music and candles....very civilised. Personally, I hope he does not call you anymore either. I think you are correct that he does not have the balls to tell you straight how it is- kind of similar to the way he is as P. I am sorry any of this has or will hurt you but I thinkyou are really better off, emotionally and professionally, getting out now. I hope your experience with him will not jade you to other men. I know you thought he was pretty awesome and he sure holds a damn successful position (!-understatement), but he is still human and still flawed like all the rest of them. Personally, I think the best guys in the world are the low key kind who care more about watching a movie at home and taking care of you than of going to expensive sushi bars and showing you off. Well, its morning here and I have to get ready for the day. Oh, by the way did you know that you forwarded a message (A bientot, Oregon) from Kelly to us? I thought it was kind of wierd, but probably just a mistake. Take care, Monica nad let me know any further what-nots over htere. love Catherine

From: Lewinsky, Monica, [redacted]
Sent: Thursday, September 04, 1997 8:52 AM
To: CA Davis

Hi, how was Chris' birthday? I got the beautiful pictures from the wedding. Thank you. You look so stunning. i could sit and look at the picture of you and Chris all day...hhmmmmmmm. Also, the wedding party picture is so ...i don't know...quintessential – like it could be the picture in a frame when you buy a new one!

The Princess Di stuff....I am the most sad for her sons. I think it is tragic what happened. There are a lot of people who are very upset by this whole incident. I'm sorry you're having a hard time with it. As i said, i feel bad for her kids and sorry that she passed away, but i wasn't really her biggest fan – sort of neutral towards her.

Well, I have an update or maybe and end-date... it's kinda long so here goes...

Yesterday morning i went to a farewell ceremony for someone here and saw the White House liaison woman with whom I met lastr week about being detailed. I asked her if she got my e-mail and she said she had and asked if i had spoken to Marsha recently. I said "no. why?" She said that marsha had run into a few snags and i should talk to her. So i called marsha all day long yetserday and finally got in touch with her at 5 pm. She has been stripped of the detailee slot in her office. So for now, there isn't anyplace for me to be detailed. So I should be PATIENT. I told her i was very upset and disappointed (even thpugh i really didn't want to work for her) and then she and i got into it. She didn't understand why i wanted to come back when there were still people there who would give me a hard time and that it isn't the right political climate for me to come back. I said i din't understand why it was okay for there to be talk about some people there but it wasn't okay for me. they have all been taken care of. ohhhh it was so infuriating. she asked me why i kept pushing the envelope on coming back there – after all i had the experience of being there already! 1037-DC-00000086

So it's over. I don't know what i will do now but i can't wait any more and i can't go through all of this crap anymore. In some ways i hope i never hear from him again because he'll just lead me on because he doesn't have the balls to tell me the truth. i kind of phase in and out of being sad – as to be expected but i'll survive. What other choice do i have?

Page 1

2799

i hope all is well with you. i miss you.

love
monica

2800

CA Davis

From: CA Davis[redacted]
Sent: Thursday, July 03, 1997 7:25 AM
To: [redacted]
Subject: hi mon

I'm sorry about all the shit that seems to be going on around you. Marsha is obviously working from a place of pettiness and jealousy- her remarks to you are so unprofessional I can't stand it. she sounds like a catty teenager! Your idea about working in another city or country is intrigueing. Do you think it is viable and conceivable for you? Could it be another American city or do you really want to be international? I guess it depends alot on openings, availability and place. I mean you would not want to be in Bosnia or Saudi Arabia (would you?). Betty is being so nice to you now, it seems. Do you have sense of why her attitude has changed? She's probably sick of seeing this happen to you after all this time.
I'm worried about you, Monica. Again, I think your idea to leave the area or get out of gov't work is a good one. I think you are in the midst of a dangerous, psychologically, situation. I am at a loss as to make you feel better or help, if I could possibly do either. When I read your emails sometimes I cannot even belive some of the things you tell me. It all sounds so dramatic and painful for you. Is your trip to L.A. for holiday or work? Maybe, you will feel a little better getting away. I don't mean to sound so disjointed but I guess I feel a litle disjointed. I know it is your life and I would NEVER presume to tell you how to live it- as you would never tell me how to live mine- but I cannot help being very concerned.
As for me, I am busy with work and with private conversation groups. I made a friend last week from work. we met after a meeting at work and she asked me to have lunch with her- the first person to do this. So we ate and drank beer and talked. She and her husband have been here for 4 months. Her name is Mary and she is 26 and was a nurse in the US ans about to start a MA program when they moved here for his business, of course. I was very impressed with her 'sacrifice'. Anyway, she's nice and hopefully we will go out again- maybe for the 4th. It was nice to talk to a woman about the stresses of living here and being newly married here, too. Actually she and her husband were married this February- 2 weeks before they moved to Tokyo. Even worse than Chris and I! Well, I must be off to my last class of the day. Write back and let me know how things have progressed. take care and love, Cat

1037-DC-00000103

2801

CA Davis

From: CA Davis[redacted]
Sent: Thursday, June 19, 1997 9:11 AM
To: 'Lewinsky, Monica, [redacted]
Subject: RE: the blahs

hi, your email made me sad, Monica. I'm sorry for all that s— that went down with that woman. It was very innapropriate for her to ask you questions like that. In my opinion, walkiiing away sounds like the best thing because it sounds like you will just get the run around from those clowns and continue feeling bad. Isn't it amazing that something like work and employer types can make us feel so self-conscious? I hate that kind of stuff. I'm sorry again for all this and I hope you can put it behind you if that is what you choose to do.
Was nutrition guy fun? You have to give me some info like age, looks, how many times, nice, etc....My weekend turned around a little. I had a 'talk' with Chris when he came back from the golf thing and it was okay. Last night we went to a very nice, expensive restaurant but it was my idea so I'm still waiting for flowers and'/or spontaneity. I have to be patient and forgiving with him though because he is under a lot of stress from both work here and also in the US. Actually, we may be going to the mountains this weekend- just he and I. Yeah! Next weekend we are being taken by Mitsui, who owns his US company, to a hot springs resort but that's with lots of people.
So, my job. I like so far. My 2 classes are pretty good and the students are nice and higher level which is much better. Although, there is one woman in my presentations class that speaks slowly and quietly and has a terrible time reading Eng. out loud. She always stumbles over words and then goes back and starts the sentence over- it drives me crazy but I keep it inside. I feel bad for her because I know she knows she is a lower level than the other 2 in the class. The 2 women in my Bus. Comm. class are great- we have a lot of fun and itsmellow but htey are smart and cool. They are the type of people that I would not mind having a drink with after class sometime. We'll see. I have also started 2 private convo groups which are good- pays cash. I like most of the other instructers at my job-job but the staff can be punks sometimes. I've had no trouble with the bosses yet- thank God.
Well, I'm really, really fat so my new clothes look disgusting on me. Thats all I have to say. Oh, except wearing silk, or silk-esque, scarves is fashionable here so I do that with a suit. I looks nice but I tie it a litleoff my neck so I don't feel like I'm choking to death. My brother is like that with ties so it must run in the family. Speaking of Nick....he is keeping busy. He goes out with friends a lot, plays golf, softball and baseball, and works a lot, too. Mom thinks he has gotten over the initial shock and is on to the beginning stages of 'moving on'. I miss him and feel for him so much it hurts. Can I say something wierd, but not wierd? My brother, essentially, was my first love. Not love that is at all sexual because I never found myself thinking that way about him but love like 'men should be like this and I want one like this for me' -I never harboured any idea that I wanted him but as a model for my own man. Does that make sense? You've met him, I think you can understand how I felt. And in a lot of ways Chris is like Nick, especially internal qualities about treating people and being a good person.
Well, I love you girl and miss you soooooo much. Take care and write back soon ya' hea'. love Cat

From: Lewinsky, Monica, [redacted]
Sent: Tuesday, June 17, 1997 1:08 PM
To: CA Davis
Subject: the blahs

hi, cat-
i miss you! i'm glad you liked my silly little package. i had agood time at the spa (i did it with the nutrition guy)!!!! Yeah! Now i can start the count over again. (i kinda don't want to get into all the juicies on e-mail)! On every other front of my life things are not so great. i met with Marsha yesterday and it was very interesting. There is most certainly a disconnect on what he said he told her and how she acted. She didn't even know what my title or my job was about. she didn't have any job openings to offer. instead, she made me go over what happened when i had to leave (who told me) and then proceeded to confirm the Evelyn story about my "inapprpriate behavior". Then she asked me with such nasty women there and peopel gossipping about me why did i want to come back? I was so upset. i really did not feel it was her place to question me about that. later on, i said something about being told i could come back after november and she wanted to know who told me that! So, i have placed a call to him but i don't know what is going to happen. i foiund out today that i didn't get the NSC job. To top it all off the big creep is wearing one of my ties today. i think i'm just going to have to walk away from it all. i don't know yet. i know it's annoying -- i'm always saying this and then i change

1037-DC-00000107

Page 1

2802

CA Davis

From: CA Davis[redacted]
Sent: Thursday, June 19, 1997 9:11 AM
To: 'Lewinsky, Monica, [redacted]
Subject: RE: the blahs

hi, your email made me sad, Monica. I'm sorry for all that s— that went down with that woman. It was very innapropriate for her to ask you questions like that. In my opinion, walkiiing away sounds like the best thing because it sounds like you will just get the run around from those clowns and continue feeling bad. Isn't it amazing that something like work and employer types can make us feel so self-conscious? I hate that kind of stuff. I'm sorry again for all this and I hope you can put it behind you if that is what you choose to do.
Was nutrition guy fun? You have to give me some info like age, looks, how many times, nice, etc....My weekend turned around a little. I had a 'talk' with Chris when he came back from the golf thing and it was okay. Last night we went to a very nice, expensive restaurant but it was my idea so I'm still waiting for flowers and'/or spontaneity. I have to be patient and forgiving with him though because he is under a lot of stress from both work here and also in the US. Actually, we may be going to the mountains this weekend- just he and I. Yeah! Next weekend we are being taken by Mitsui, who owns his US company, to a hot springs resort but that's with lots of people.
So, my job. I like so far. My 2 classes are pretty good and the students are nice and higher level which is much better. Although, there is one woman in my presentations class that speaks slowly and quietly and has a terrible time reading Eng. out loud. She always stumbles over words and then goes back and starts the sentence over- it drives me crazy but I keep it inside. I feel bad for her because I know she knows she is a lower level than the other 2 in the class. The 2 women in my Bus. Comm. class are great- we have a lot of fun and itsmellow but htey are smart and cool. They are the type of people that I would not mind having a drink with after class sometime. We'll see. I have also started 2 private convo groups which are good- pays cash. I like most of the other instructers at my job-job but the staff can be punks sometimes. I've had no trouble with the bosses yet- thank God.
Well, I'm really, really fat so my new clothes look disgusting on me. Thats all I have to say. Oh, except wearing silk, or silk-esque, scarves is fashionable here so I do that with a suit. I looks nice but I tie it a litleoff my neck so I don't feel like I'm choking to death. My brother is like that with ties so it must run in the family. Speaking of Nick....he is keeping busy. He goes out with friends a lot, plays golf, softball and baseball, and works a lot, too. Mom thinks he has gotten over the initial shock and is on to the beginning stages of 'moving on'. I miss him and feel for him so much it hurts. Can I say something wierd, but not wierd? My brother, essentially, was my first love. Not love that is at all sexual because I never found myself thinking that way about him but love like 'men should be like this and I want one like this for me' -I never harboured any idea that I wanted him but as a model for my own man. Does that make sense? You've met him, I think you can understand how I felt. And in a lot of ways Chris is like Nick, especially internal qualities about treating people and being a good person.
Well, I love you girl and miss you sooooooo much. Take care and write back soon ya' hea'. love Cat

---

From: Lewinsky, Monica, [redacted]
Sent: Tuesday, June 17, 1997 1:08 PM
To: CA Davis
Subject: the blahs

1037-DC-00000108

hi, cat-
i miss you! i'm glad you liked my silly little package. i had agood time at the spa (i did it with the nutrition guy)!!!! Yeah! Now i can start the count over again. (i kinda don't want to get into all the juicies on e-mail)! On every other front of my life things are not so great. i met with Marsha yesterday and it was very interesting. There is most certainly a disconnect on what he said he told her and how she acted. She didn't even know what my title or my job was about. she didn't have any job openings to offer. instead, she made me go over what happened when i had to leave (who told me) and then proceeded to confirm the Evelyn story about my "inapprpriate behavior". Then she asked me with such nasty women there and peopel gossipping about me why did i want to come back? I was so upset. i really did not feel it was her place to question me about that. later on, i said something about being told i could come back after november and she wanted to know who told me that! So, i have placed a call to him but i don't know what is going to happen. i foiund out today that i didn't get the NSC job. To top it all off the big creep is wearing one of my ties today. i think i'm just going to have to walk away from it all. i don't know yet. i know it's annoying -- i'm always saying this and then i change

Page 1

2803

my mind.

i hpe you're doing ok. how was your rice and beer???? i'm sorry you had a sad saturday. what is your work like? i'm very curious to hear about it so let me know (especially to hear about all of the clothes you have had to buy)!!!

well, i'm a little too sad to continue right now. i love you and i miss you. monica

1037-DC-00000109

2804

CA Davis

From: CA Davis[redacted]
Sent: Tuesday, June 03, 1997 9:12 AM
To: 'Lewinsky, Monica, , OSD/PA'
Subject: RE: konichiwa(????)

hi, actually I have a real job! I am an 'instructor' of English but in relation to business issues to Japanese business who, primarily, work for US companies that have offices over here. My first 2 classes are ESP, English with a Special Purpose, in this case giving presentations. Where I know anything about business, I don't know. But the pay is outrageous! Granted, Tokyo is expensive but you do get paid very well. Its quite professional in dress, especially when meeting with clients so I went shopping, of course, and bought a cute suit at Jigsaw. But, God, the clothes are sooooo expensive here, I can't over it. I wonder how young people, on their own, handle it. They probably live at home or in flats that are much cheaper than ours. Well, our weekend was semi-exciting. Alex's girlfriend Chrisanthi was in Tokyo for a few nights for a conference so we went out with her on Saturday night. Other than that we laid around a lot and talked about going somewhere but didn't. Next weekend I think we'll get out of town and maybe go to Kamakura, which is on the ocean. I'm getting a little city-sick. Oh, I think I know which road you were on when you were here- that was lined with trees and had lots of shops and cafes. I'm pretty sure it was Omotesando in Aoyama. Its really lovely and has Parisian-esque outdoor cafes and all the swank boutiques. That's where I went shopping the other day.
I don't know how Nick is doing, except that he pitching on a baseball team and working A LOT. His job is very good but because the company is small, but growing, he has a lot of responsibility so he often works Saturdays as well as full week days. Unfortunately, he's not well rewarded with a fat paycheck, either. Its a mechanical engineering firm, in case you didn't know what he did. I must say I feel proud when I tell people 'my brother is an engineer'. As far as I know he is still split from Jen but is still dealing with it by himnself. Its very nice of you to ask after him, I appreciate that.
I'm sorry you are on an 'emotional rollercoster' right now. What can you do on your free time that may help you either refocus or get your mindoff things, temporarily. Are you close to any country areas to take a walk or a lake or beach? something outdoorsy but pleasant? Its hard not having a close girlfriend to 'escape' with, isn't? I may be able to become friends with one woman I work with but that remains to be seen- I guess, I sometimes want the benefit of a friend but don't want to put in all the effort to set it up. It was nice to see Chrisanthi and actually we had a 2 hour girlie-chat on the phone when she was here Friday night. It was really nice to 'dish' to someone other than Chris!
Well, I need to get ready for work- I'm training all this week and my classes start next week. Training sucks and I really don't like my trainer- a man named Sean from Australia- I think he's sexist and offensive. Anyway! I love you and look forward to hearing from you soon, love, Catherine

---

From: Lewinsky, Monica, [redacted]
Sent: Monday, June 02, 1997 8:54 AM
To: CA Davis
Subject: konichiwa(????)

Hi, Cat-
I hope this e-mail finds you well. It is hard to believe, but i have brought the card i wrote you weeks ago to mail. Of course everything in there is now obsolete, but it is a cute card. I miss you. Remeber how i told you about that guy Kurt Campbell who's the Deputy Assistant Secretary of Defense for Asian Affairs, well he is going with this other woman (actually from my office)to Tokyo this week. Do you want me to give him your number and maybe you and Chris can meet him for a drink or somethin'??? Let me know so I can get him the info before he leaves. I had a pretty boring weekend. I did, however, go iwth my Mom to see the" Picasso:The Early Years" exhibit yesterday. It was wonderful. I must say that I found it overwhelming to see just how much work he produced-- and then to realize that was only some of his work from his EARLY years...jeez!!!!! Otherwise, I am depressed. I float from being sad to angry often and easily. What can I do but weather the storm. I hope you're doing ok. Have you started tutoring in English conversation???? Let me know how you are and what you're up to. I love you and miss you. Also, how's Nick doing? write me back.
Love, ME

1037-DC-00000115

Page 1

2805

Davis, Catherine

From: Lewinsky, Monica, [redacted]
Sent: Tuesday, September 16, 1997 11:30 AM
To: CA Davis
Subject: RE: yeah!

THIS IS REALLY LONG. YOU MAY WANT TO PRINT IT OUT TO READ IT!!!

OK here is the note I sent you which you never got. God this e-mail system sucks so much!!!!

Hi, how was Chris' birthday? i got the beautiful pictures from the wedding. Thank you. You look so stunning. i could sit and look at the picture of you and Chris all day...hhmmmmmmmm. Also, the wedding party picture is so ...i don't know...quintessential -- like it could be the picture in a frame when you buy a new one!

The Princess Di stuff....I am the most sad for her sons. I think it is tragic what happened. There are a lot of people who are very upset by this whole incident. I'm sorry you're having a hard time with it. As I said, i feel bad for her kids and sorry that she passed away, but I wasn't really her biggest fan -- sort of neutral towards her.

Well, I have an update or maybe and end-date... It's kinda long so here goes...

Yesterday morning i went to a farewell ceremony for someone here and saw the White House liaison woman with whom I met lastr week about being detailed. I asked her if she got my e-mail and she said she had and asked if i had spoken to Marsha recently. I said "no. why?" She said that marsha had run into a few snags and i should talk to her. So i called marsha all day long yetserday and finally got in touch with her at 5 pm. She has been stripped of the detailee slot in her office. So for now, there isn't anyplace for me to be detailed. So I should be PATIENT. I told her i was very upset and disappointed (even though i really didn't want to work for her) and then she and i got into it. She didn't understand why i wanted to come back when there were still people there who would give me a hard time and that it isn't the right political climate for me to come back. I said I din't understand why it was okay for there to be talk about some people there but it wasn't okay for me. they have all been taken care of. ohhhh it was so infuriating. she asked me why i kept pushing the envelope on coming back there -- after all i had the experience of being there already!

So it's over. I don't know what i will do now but i can't wait any more and i can't go through all of this crap anymore. In some ways i hope i never hear from him again because he'll just lead me on because he doesn't have the balls to tell me the truth. i kind of phase in and out of being sad -- as to be expected but i'll survive. What other choice do i have?

i hope all is well with you. i miss you.

love
monica 1037-DC-00000167

Of course i wrote that like the day after it happened and as to be expected with me felt differentlya few days later. Things have been pretty shitty (insert SIGH). I will tell you the one very sweet, very mixed signal thing going on first cuz it makes me smile. Before the creep left for his vacation I gave him a copy of the novel "The Notebook" --it's this mushy romance (written by a guy) that is like "Bridges of Madison County" sort of BUT one of the recurring themes or things of significance that comes up in the book is Whitman's (gee not Thoreau's--duh) "Leaves of Grass". I

Page 1

2806

thought it was neat and sweet. I enclosed a card wishing him a fun vacation and asked in a post script if he could bring me a "Black Dog" t-shirt, which you probably know is from this quasi-famous restaraunt in Martha's Vineyard-- if he had a chance. Well, I found out from Betty yesterday that he not only brought me a t-shirt he got me 2 t-shirts, a hat and a dress!!!! Even though he's a big schmuck that is surprisingly sweet -- even that he remebered!

OK Now for the [redacted] Now that you've read what happened w/ Marsha this will make more sense. I called betty on Wednesday to find out if they knew what had happened and she said she knew but she didn't know if he knew, blah..blah. For three days she kept saying she didn't have a chance to talk to him and then it became this thing on Friday that maybe i could see him and it got crazy,a nd Cat I lost it. I went ape [redacted] To tell you the truth, i don';t even want to get into it all because it's too exhausting. But the end results were that i talked well mroe like cried to Betty in person on Friday and then I was supposed to maybe see the creepon Sun. and then it didn't work out. I cried for hours and then betty called to say he was going to talk to the chief of staff. BI d on't know what will happen. i also said to betty taht i didn't want him to do anything taht was going to get him in trouble, then yesteday she called to tell me about the black Dog stuff. the [redacted] if i know what the hell is going on!!!! he leaves to go to CA and then a bunch of other places for awhile. Oh well.

On another note, ashley and i are going to a black tie gala this saturday being hosted by the Young Smithsonians, which we have joined. hopefully we'll meet some interesting people. Oooh, a cute boy would be VERY nice.

Just to make this e-mail more interesting (and way too long) I am enclosing my latest and LAST e-mail with Doug that [redacted]. Of course you will see that what he wrote was true, but who asked for the truth! I never responded and then he sent me all of these e-mails and said, "Last e-mail unless i get a repsonse - hello?" LAMER!!!! (I'm going to put what I wrote first and then his response willl follow)

Monica: (we had been conversing earlier and i was sad..he asked why)
it might sound silly, but sometimes i just really want somebody (a
male) in my life to just physically be with -- you know hugs and stuff (i
don't
only think about sex).

i was counting on someone to help me with a job and they put me in touch with someone else that just [redacted] me around for six months. it's frustrating for me. then i get sad when i need some TLC and i can't get it. i haven't made the circle of friends here in dc like i had in portland where if i just needed a guy i had a 3 or 4 male friends on whom i could call. here it seems that most of the guys in my life i have dated so of course, there's always baggage involved. i think i'm not happy here in dc and i'm not really sure what to do about it. so in a nutshell...i'm sad. it is nice of you to ask, thanks.

DOUG:
I understand, but the if you want my very humble opinion the bottom line = is you need to be happy with yourself FIRST (whatever town you're in) = before you can be happy with you and someone else together. =20 1037-DC-00000168

You need to concentrate on you -- then others will be attracted to that. You're too consumed with chasing others rather than improving yourself and having that attract others naturally. Make yourself physically and mentally fit and the rest will naturally take care of itself.

Focus from within and disappointments will disappear!

CAN YOU BELIEVE THIS CRAP! (ok. i know what he said is true but...)

Well on to better topics. Your softball game sounds like fun. I am glad

Page 2

2806

2807

you ahd a good day. You know Catherine, I want you to know that I really admire you for having moved with Chris to Stinkyo. There are so many people who would have said "let's put off getting married til you come back. i don't want to go..blah..blah" But you, instead, i think have really captured what marriage is truly about. I hope Chris knows how lucky he is to have you and to have you --something so comforting and reassuring-- to come home to. YOU have made his transition for work so much better. Imagine how hard it would have been for him (and you too but he was starting a new job) to have been seperated from the one he loves. he would have been pining for you and hjis life in America. Instaed, you ghuys have journeyed together. My Mom and Aunt often ask after you and remark how wonderful it is that you guys are doing it together.

Well, I hope you didn;t get too bore dearly on and not get down to this last paragraph becaus eit is the important one.

I miss you and love you. Oh, BTW, we may be IN Tokyo still on your birthday!!!!!! But if not, we'll celebrate early.

Hug yourself for me.
Monica

ps -- let me know you got this, kay?

From: CA Davis
To: [redacted]
Subject: yeah!
Date: Tuesday, September 16, 1997 3:49AM

Yeah- that you may be coming here in November and only a few days before =
my 24th birthday! I would absolutely love to see you, I really hope you =
come. Well, I suppose if you get a job that you like more before then =
then I will be happy for you, too. I don't think I got an email fdrom =
you about pictures. Are you referring to wedding photos? I hope you =
got htem okay. I think the probs are at the Pentagon for email because =
I'm always getting notes that say messages from me to you cannot be =
delivered. So how are you Monica? Really. I know you are busy at =
work, but please don't feel like I am 'tired of' or 'bored' or 'annoyed' =
or anything about you talking about Marsha stuff or Creep stuff or =
anything- you can still, always, tell me if you want. I remember asking =
you a few weeks ago if you would really consider moving to NYC and if =
you would live with your mom there. If you responded I never got that =
one so let me know. =20
Well, remember my friend Tara, whom I met in London? I visited her in =
San Diego senior year spring break and now she lives in NYC with her =
fiance. They are getting married next month and we just received their =
invitation. Obviously, we cannot go but my thing is I have not heard =
from her in over 4 months! We talked a lot in the last year, especially =
after I got engaged and then she did. After I moved here I emailed her =
and got a response but nothing since. In that one email she said =
something was sort of 'up' or something but no details- she said she =
would snail mail me the news because she didn't want to email it. Well, =
I have not heard from her. I have sent emails with my home address, =
postcards etc and still nothing and then her invitation. I am a little =
perturbed. I sent back hte return saying we can't come and i wrote her = 1037-DC-00000169
a personal letter too. I'm bummed.
Anyway, last Saturday Chris and I went to the Yokohama Country and =
Athletic Club (YCAC) with American friends, through my friend Mary and =
her husband, to play softball. The YCAC is really nice- it is very open =
and sits on top of a hill and has lots of grass and trees! Nothing like =
the Tokyo American Club, its sister club. It was a TAC game against the =
YCAC and we, the TAC, won one and they won one. It was so much fun- we =
forgot we were in Japan!! I played right center in the outfield and had =
a walk and a few hits. Mary was the only other girl on our team and she =
played catcher. After we hung out with our team and drank beer and ate- =
overall a great day, surprisingly in Japan. Oh, aren't I negative about =

Page 3

2808

Davis, Catherine

From: Lewinsky, Monica, [redacted]
Sent: Wednesday, August 13, 1997 11:47 AM
To: CA Davis
Subject: RE: new message

Yeah, Kelly sure was right!!!! I was totally distracted. I'm sure you rememeber I talked to the creep on the phone at work and I was supposed to go there and everything got crazy. I am glad you've had a good time with her but i certainly understand you and Chris wanting some time alone (like to have loud, rad SEX) before you leave!!!!

I'll talk to you about the Marsha stuff on the phone it is too exhausting for me to write it all. I'm drained right now. I can't wait to talk to you on the phone!!! I love to hear your voice...ahhh I sound like such a musher!!!!!

Well, Catherine, my dear, (jeez..i hate being called "dear". the creep calls me that sometimes it's an old person saying!!!!) i don't have much to write -- i am boring. But did i tell you i had sex with thomas last week? I know. I am sooooooo naughty. it was fun and good. i went over there with some ice cream and pretty much seduced him in a way that made him make the moves on me..cool or what???

I LUV YOU!!! Monica

From: CA Davis
To: [redacted]
Subject: new message
Date: Tuesday, August 12, 1997 11:45PM

I thought I would get rid of that Re:blind date message once and for =
all. If you like him and want to see him again call him. Unfortunatly, =
sometimes that must be done. I know it sucks and you wish it not have =
to be that way but that's life. We have to put ourselves out there =
sometimes and maybe be cut-off and maybe be let-in, you never know. =20
You can tell me about bad MArsha or work what-nots, Monica. I am not =
frustrated, neccessarily, but concerned and wishing things would change- =
or you would change them. =20
It has been fun with Kelly but I am ready for her to leave- I'm burnt on =
the entertaining thing. Also, I leave on Friday, the day after her, and =
I want to be alone with Chris. I think he feels the same way, but won't =
say it in so many words. I'm not trying to be mean, its not so much =
personal against her....The other day we were talking about her going =
toPhillie and all and I asked if she thought she would contacta nd see =
you. She said she would like to and probably would. Then she said she =
had a good time with you in DC but you seemed distracted some nad that =
she thought you were a 'very private person'. I thought it was astute, =
but I just agreed and said you could be. Anyway....
Off to work! Write back before I go, 'kay? Love, Cat

1037-DC-00000171

2809

Davis, Catherine

From: CA Davis[redacted]
Sent: Thursday, September 04, 1997 6:28 PM
To: 'Lewinsky, Monica, , OSD/PA'
Subject: RE:

Hi Monica! Chris' birthday was mellow, especially because it was a Wednesday. I took out to dinner at a nice Thai place. He opened his presents in the morning and last night, his American birthday, we had a nice bottle of red wine from my parents to him and had dinner at the table with music and candles....very civilised. Personally, I hope he does not call you anymore either. I think you are correct that he does not have the balls to tell you straight how it is- kind of similar to the way he is as P. I am sorry any of this has or will hurt you but I thinkyou are really better off, emotionally and professionally, getting out now. I hope your experience with him will not jade you to other men. I know you thought he was pretty awesome and he sure holds a damn successful position (!-understatement), but he is still human and still flawed like all the rest of them. Personally, I think the best guys in the world are the low key kind who care more about watching a movie at home and taking care of you than of going to expensive sushi bars and showing you off. Well, its morning here and I have to get ready for the day. Oh, by the way did you know that you forwarded a message (A bientot, Oregon) from Kelly to us? I thought it was kind of wierd, but probably just a mistake. Take care, Monica nad let me know any further what-nots over htere. love Catherine

From: Lewinsky, Monica, [redacted]
Sent: Thursday, September 04, 1997 8:52 AM
To: CA Davis

Hi, how was Chris' birthday? I got the beautiful pictures from the wedding. Thank you. You look so stunning. i could sit and look at the picture of you and Chris all day...hhmmmmmmm. Also, the wedding party picture is so ...i don't know...quintessential -- like it could be the picture in a frame when you buy a new one!

The Princess Di stuff....I am the most sad for her sons. I think it is tragic what happened. There are a lot of people who are very upset by this whole incident. I'm sorry you're having a hard time with it. As i said, i feel bad for her kids and sorry that she passed away, but i wasn't really her biggest fan -- sort of neutral towards her.

Well, I have an update or maybe and end-date... it's kinda long so here goes...

Yesterday morning i went to a farewell ceremony for someone here and saw the White House liaison woman with whom I met lastr week about being detailed. I asked her if she got my e-mail and she said she had and asked if i had spoken to Marsha recently. I said "no. why?" She said that marsha had run into a few snags and i should talk to her. So i called marsha all day long yetserday and finally got in touch with her at 5 pm. She has been stripped of the detailee slot in her office. So for now, there isn't anyplace for me to be detailed. So I should be PATIENT. I told her i was very upset and disappointed (even thpugh i really didn't want to work for her) and then she and i got into it. She didn't understand why i wanted to come back when there were still people there who would give me a hard time and that it isn't the right political climate for me to come back. I said i din't understand why it was okay for there to be talk about some people there but it wasn't okay for me. they have all been taken care of. ohhhh it was so infuriating. she asked me why i kept pushing the envelope on coming back there -- after all i had the experience of being there already!

1037-DC-00000255

So it's over. I don't know what i will do now but i can't wait any more and i can't go through all of this crap anymore. In some ways i hope i never hear from him again because he'll just lead me on because he doesn't have the balls to tell me the truth. i kind of phase in and out of being sad -- as to be expected but i'll survive. What other choice do i have?

Page 1

2810

i hope all is well with you. i miss you.

love
monica

2811

Davis, Catherine

From: CA Davis[redacted]
Sent: Tuesday, September 02, 1997 5:57 PM
To: 'Lewinsky, Monica, , OSD/PA'
Subject: RE: Aloha!

Wow, your mom's flat sounds amazing! That is so wonderful for her- I hope she is really happy with this guy. If you moved to NY would you be able to live with her? Would you still work for the DOD? Probably not, yah? I cannot say I am surprised that this whole situation has taken its toll on you. I'm sure it has for a while now. If I may be so bold to state my unequivocal opinion: I think your 'situation' is a lose-lose situation with him. He cannot ever be totally your's Monica. Ever. And, as I have said before, you deserve a man that is all your's. ALL YOUR'S. And just because there may not be another man around right now does not mean you should put yourself through the ringer with this Man. You are worth much more than that, no matter his Position its the same old affair bullshit. Does your mom support you moving to NY? If so, I think that would be fantastic! I would come visit you once a year and you could visit me once a year (of course, after I move back to the US) and we'd see eachother a lot!
Anyway, was your holiday relaxing? Four Australian businessmen?....I hope they were nicer and more polite than most Australians I meet. Today, Sept. 3rd, is Chris' 31st birthday. I am going to take him out to dinner tonight and, of course, have lots of presents for him to open. Unfortunately, since we don't have an oven (!), I can't bake a little cake. Maybe that is not so unfortunate! Well, I must be off. I'll hear from you soon, take care- I really mean it, too- I love you, Catherine

---

From: Lewinsky, Monica, [redacted]
Sent: Tuesday, September 02, 1997 1:30 PM
To: CA Davis
Subject: RE: Aloha!

Welcome Home! I, too, was sorry we didn't get a chance to talk, but I'm glad you had a good holiday. How is Jeannie doing? Is she still with what's-his-name? I was also happy to read that Nick seems to be doing better. On my little vacation I went to Princeton, NJ (where I met and had dinner with 4 Australian businessmen -- it was much fun!!!!), the Spa in CT., and to Scarsdale, NY to see a friend of mine and my mom's. I did not hook up with that Jesse guy at the spa again. It was sort of my choice and a little lack of him not aggressively pursuing me. So here is big news....my mom has gotten an apartment in NY for a year on 5th and 61st!!!!!!!!!! She is pretty serious with this guy and spends so much time up there already. It is funny because her big dream in life has been to live in NY and now he has gotten her an apartment there!!!! It's exciting!

My work sit: I met with the woman who is the White House liaison here and she described in detail, what needs to happen for me to be deatiled there. It is a much more difficult process than i imagined. Essentially, I would remain an employee of Public Affairs and they "loan" me to the WH. PA doesn't get more money allotted or an extra position to fill my slot. Normally they would only detail somebody in a slot where there are a few people who have similar tasks , i.e. a media desk officer -- with me, there is only one confidential assistant in PA. We'll have to see what happens but I really don't want to work for marsha anymore. I don't trust her at all. I'm moving toward giving it all up. Maybe I'll move to NY. As I told you on the phone, I felt awful about my last visit with him. I don't doubt that he has real feelings for me, but how strong they are is another question. He hasn't taken care of me. we'll see what happens. I'm in an ok place right now. i am just starting to physically and mentally REALLY feel the and see the effects of all of this stress. It is getting to be too much for me. Don't worry though, I'll be fine.

1037-DC-00000258

I miss you and am sad i didn't get to talk to you more when you were here (although i probably would have been very boring!)

Big hugs and sloppy kisses,
Monica

Page 1

2812

ps-- can you believe i haven't spoken to Andy in 3 1/2 months! Weird, huh?

From: CA Davis
To: [redacted]
Subject: Aloha!
Date: Sunday, August 31, 1997 3:52PM

Hi there! Well, I must say I am sorry that we did not get to talk =
again. At first, I thought you didn't call back, but then Nick told me =
a little later that you had when he was talking to my parents. My time =
in Hawaii was fun, but a little frantic. Okay, not frantic exactly....I =
was trying to do a lot ina small amount of time and try not to stress =
about also doing errands I was supposed to do there, too. Needless, to =
say I did not do all I was suppoesed to do and did not remember to buy =
all I was supposed to buy! What I did do was go to the beach and eat. =
Jeannie only worked twice while I was there and for short shifts and she =
did not have classes yet. The weather was great, too, so I got to keep =
'enhancing' my colour there after the Lake. =20
The Lake, which is what we call where our summer cabin is, was really =
nice. It is so unbelievably beautiful up there, its almost not real. =
Its as close to pristine as I have ever seen. Anyway, the weather was =
great up there too and we did a little hiking, some swimming, boating =
etc...it was wonderful to hang there with my brother. He seems to be =
doing okay- still recovering though and not quite ready to date yet. He =
has some girl-friends that check in on him and say they will set him up =
as soon as he is ready. I feel better knowing that he has girls to talk =
to about this whole thing because you know how boys are...not the most =
sensitive. My parents were good, although maybe a little tenser than =
they could have been at times, especially my dad. I think that was =
probably due to his whole being away from home for so long and trying to =
still take care of business there and also wanting to buy a house in =
Sonoma as soon as possible. Andrea was happy to have an awaesome tan =
and to not really be working- she starts work on her dissertation thiis =
Autumn.
Well, that's pretty much my little trip to America. Too short! And I =
came back to lots of work messages and all these new classes and =
substitutions blah, blah, blah. That's life though, right? I guess, I =
also came back to my husband, who I missed terribly. We have spent the =
weekend together- no one else. So how are you doing? Where exactly did =
you go on your holiday? Any news on job switching yet? Are you still =
sure you want to be back in the WH? Let me know what all is going down =
with you- work stuff but also any activities, more dates etc...? Do you =
still see or talk to Ashley? Does she have an opinion on your move to =
the WH? I hope you are okay Monica and I'm sorry I did not get to talk =
to you again. Maybe I will try to give you a call in the next few =
weeks. Can I call you at work? If so give me the number. I love you =
and miss you and hope you're okay. Take care, love, Catherine

1037-DC-00000259

2813

Davis, Catherine

From: CA Davis[REDACTED]
Sent: Wednesday, June 18, 1997 7:11 PM
To: 'Lewinsky, Monica, , OSD/PA'
Subject: RE: the blahs

hi, your email made me sad, Monica. I'm sorry for all that s— that went down with that woman. It was very innapropriate for her to ask you questions like that. In my opinion, walkiiing away sounds like the best thing because it sounds like you will just get the run around from those clowns and continue feeling bad. Isn't it amazing that something like work and employer types can make us feel so self-conscious? I hate that kind of stuff. I'm sorry again for all this and I hope you can put it behind you if that is what you choose to do.
Was nutrition guy fun? You have to give me some info like age, looks, how many times, nice, etc....My weekend turned around a little. I had a 'talk' with Chris when he came back from the golf thing and it was okay. Last night we went to a very nice, expensive restaurant but it was my idea so I'm still waiting for flowers and'/or spontaneity. I have to be patient and forgiving with him though because he is under a lot of stress from both work here and also in the US. Actually, we may be going to the mountains this weekend- just he and I. Yeah! Next weekend we are being taken by Mitsui, who owns his US company, to a hot springs resort but that's with lots of people.
So, my job. I like so far. My 2 classes are pretty good and the students are nice and higher level which is much better. Although, there is one woman in my presentations class that speaks slowly and quietly and has a terrible time reading Eng. out loud. She always stumbles over words and then goes back and starts the sentence over- it drives me crazy but I keep it inside. I feel bad for her because I know she knows she is a lower level than the other 2 in the class. The 2 women in my Bus. Comm. class are great- we have a lot of fun and itsmellow but htey are smart and cool. They are the type of people that I would not mind having a drink with after class sometime. We'll see. I have also started 2 private convo groups which are good- pays cash. I like most of the other instructers at my job-job but the staff can be punks sometimes. I've had no trouble with the bosses yet- thank God.
Well, I'm really, really fat so my new clothes look disgusting on me. Thats all I have to say. Oh, except wearing silk, or silk-esque, scarves is fashionable here so I do that with a suit. I looks nice but I tie it a litleoff my neck so I don't feel like I'm choking to death. My brother is like that with ties so it must run in the family. Speaking of Nick....he is keeping busy. He goes out with friends a lot, plays golf, softball and baseball, and works a lot, too. Mom thinks he has gotten over the initial shock and is on to the beginning stages of 'moving on'. I miss him and feel for him so much it hurts. Can I say something wierd, but not wierd? My brother, essentially, was my first love. Not love that is at all sexual because I never found myself thinking that way about him but love like 'men should be like this and I want one like this for me' -I never harboured any idea that I wanted him but as a model for my own man. Does that make sense? You've met him, I think you can understand how I felt. And in a lot of ways Chris is like Nick, especially internal qualities about treating people and being a good person.
Well, I love you girl and miss you soooooo much. Take care and write back soon ya' hea'. love Cat

---

From: Lewinsky, Monica, [REDACTED]
Sent: Tuesday, June 17, 1997 1:08 PM
To: CA Davis
Subject: the blahs

hi, cat-
i miss you! i'm glad you liked my silly little package. i had agood time at the spa (i did it with the nutrition guy)!!!! Yeah! Now i can start the count over again. (i kinda don't want to get into all the juicies on e-mail)! On every other front of my life things are not so great. i met with Marsha yesterday and it was very interesting. There is most certainly a disconnect on what he said he told her and how she acted. She didn't even know what my title or my job was about. she didn't have any job openings to offer. instead, she made me go over what happened when i had to leave (who told me) and then proceeded to confirm the Evelyn story about my "inapprpriate behavior". Then she asked me with such nasty women there and peopel gossipping about me why did i want to come back? I was so upset. i really did not feel it was her place to question me about that. later on, i said something about being told i could come back after november and she wanted to know who told me that! So, i have placed a call to him but i don't know what is going to happen. i foiund out today that i didn't get the NSC job. To top it all off the big creep is wearing one of my ties today. i think i'm just going to have to walk away from it all. i don't know yet. i know it's annoying -- i'm always saying this and then i change

1037-DC-00000265

Page 1

2814

my mind.

i hpe you're doing ok. how was your rice and beer???? i'm sorry you had a sad saturday. what is your work like? i'm very curious to hear about it so let me know (especially to hear about all of the clothes you have had to buy)!!!

well, i'm a little too sad to continue right now. i love you and i miss you. monica

2815

Davis, Catherine

From: CA Davis[redacted]
Sent: Wednesday, July 02, 1997 5:25 PM
To: 'mlewinsk@pagate.pa.osd.mil'
Subject: hi mon

I'm sorry about all the shit that seems to be going on around you. Marsha is obviously working from a place of pettiness and jealousy- her remarks to you are so unprofessional I can't stand it. she sounds like a catty teenager! Your idea about working in another city or country is intrigueing. Do you think it is viable and conceivable for you? Could it be another American city or do you really want to be international? I guess it depends alot on openings, availability and place. I mean you would not want to be in Bosnia or Saudi Arabia (would you?). Betty is being so nice to you now, it seems. Do you have sense of why her attitude has changed? She's probably sick of seeing this happen to you after all this time.
I'm worried about you, Monica. Again, I think your idea to leave the area or get out of gov't work is a good one. I think you are in the midst of a dangerous, psychologicalty, situation. I am at a loss as to make you feel better or help, if I could possibly do either. When I read your emails sometimes I cannot even belive some of the things you tell me. It all sounds so dramatic and painful for you. Is your trip to L.A. for holiday or work? Maybe, you will feel a little better getting away. I don't mean to sound so disjointed but I guess I feel a litle disjointed. I know it is your life and I would NEVER presume to tell you how to live it- as you would never tell me how to live mine- but I cannot help being very concerned.
As for me, I am busy with work and with private conversation groups. I made a friend last week from work. we met after a meeting at work and she asked me to have lunch with her- the first person to do this. So we ate and drank beer and talked. She and her husband have been here for 4 months. Her name is Mary and she is 26 and was a nurse in the US ans about to start a MA program when they moved here for his business, of course. I was very impressed with her 'sacrifice'. Anyway, she's nice and hopefully we will go out again- maybe for the 4th. It was nice to talk to a woman about the stresses of living here and being newly married here, too. Actually she and her husband were married this February- 2 weeks before they moved to Tokyo. Even worse than Chris and I! Well, I must be off to my last class of the day. Write back and let me know how things have progressed. take care and love, Cat

1037-DC-00000280

2816

Davis, Catherine

From: CA Davis[redacted]
To: 'mlewinsk@pagate.pa.osd.mil'
Subject: hi Mon

I'm sorry about all the shit that seems to be going on around you. Marsha is obviously working from a place of pettiness and jealousy- her remarks to you are so unprofessional I can't stand it. she sounds like a catty teenager! Your idea about working in another city or country is intrigueing. Do you think it is viable and conceivable for you? Could it be another American city or do you really want to be international? I guess it depends alot on openings, availability and place. I mean you would not want to be in Bosnia or Saudi Arabia (would you?). Betty is being so nice to you now, it seems. Do you have sense of why her attitude has changed? She's probably sick of seeing this happen to you after all this time.
I'm worried about you, Monica. Again, I think your idea to leave the area or get out of gov't work is a good one. I think you are in the midst of a dangerous, psychologically, situation. I am at a loss as to make you feel better or help, if I could possibly do either. When I read your emails sometimes I cannot even belive some of the things you tell me. It all sounds so dramatic and painful for you. Is your trip to L.A. for holiday or work? Maybe, you will feel a little better getting away. I don't mean to sound so disjointed but I guess I feel a litle disjointed. I know it is your life and I would NEVER presume to tell you how to live it- as you would never tell me how to live mine- but I cannot help being very concerned.
As for me, I am busy with work and with private conversation groups. I made a friend last week from work. we met after a meeting at work and she asked me to have lunch with her- the first person to do this. So we ate and drank beer and talked. She and her husband have been here for 4 months. Her name is Mary and she is 26 and was a nurse in the US ans about to start a MA program when they moved here for his business, of course. I was very impressed with her 'sacrifice'. Anyway, she's nice and hopefully we will go out again- maybe for the 4th. It was nice to talk to a woman about the stresses of living here and being newly married here, too. Actually she and her husband were married this February- 2 weeks before they moved to Tokyo. Even worse than Chris and I!
Well, I must be off to my last class of the day. Write back and let me know how things have progressed. take care and love, Cat

1037-DC-00000296

2817

t in these last 2 years I have =lost two aunts, my Mom's older sisters, to can cer. Anyway, I originally =thought I would go to school to be a Physician's A ssisstant, P.A., a =growing field in healthcare and it is only a 2 year progra m. I took =some prelim courses and was so thrilled and into it- like Microbio logy =and medical microbiology, that I questioned why I shouldn't pusReceived: from by tky0.attnet.or.jp (8.7.5+Spi n/3.4W4-PP-R5(05/15/97)) id WAA13450; Wed, 19 Nov 1997 22:22:44 +0900 (JST)Rec eived: from by galt.osd. iil (8.7.1/8.7.1) with SMTP id IAA00768 for >; Wed, 9 Nov 1997 08:15:33 -0500 (EST)Received: by with Microsoft Mailid Wed, 19 Nov 97 08:20:52 PSTFrom: "Lewinsk y, Monica, , OSD/PA" To: CA Davis tnet.or.jp>Subject: RE: birthday aftermathDate: Wed, 19 Nov 97 08:12:00 PSTMes sage-ID: Encoding: 182 TEXTX-Mailer: Microsoft Mai l V3.0X-UIDL: 809cb60fc0c9df52c4cf05811f2f2f72Oh, Catherine! You message was just what i needed to start out this dreary day! I adore you, and think we'll make wonderful older lady friends (here's to the ladies who lunch..) and youn ger lady friends, too!! When you come back to the states I think we'll have t o spend some concentrated time together. Imagine, talking in person and for F REE!Your birthday sounded great (except of course for the Chris-getting-sick-p art). i'm sorry you had to postpone your dinner. Your earrings sound lovely. How was Japanese Disneyland? Were there any rides that made fun of American s or was it Mickey Mouse based? I bet you looked beautiful in your red (VAHVO OM!!) suit!The big creep does look quite trim these days. Oh, I haven't told you my hysterical escapade from last week! Listen to this, it's practically u nbelievable! The creep called me on Wednesday night and we talked for almost an hour, but i had been bugging him that i wanted to see him and last week was the only chance for awhile as he would be away for the next two weekends and then i am gone for two weeks. So, on the phone he said he thought nancy (one of the meanies) would be out for a few hours on Thurday and i could come see h im them. I was to call Betty and figure out the details. Of course, i called betty in the morning and then started the usual "I haven't had a chance to ta lk to him, yet". Well, he ended up going golfing and I went ballistic. final ly when he got back around 4:30 she talked to him and then he got mad she didn 't tell him -ya-da-ya-da. In the end, she snuck me in to the back office wher e i waited for him while there were 20 people in there and Stephen, his e aide who doesn' like me. I ended up seeing him for two minutes bec ause he had one of his counterparts from another country waiting there for din ner!! It was soo crazy.I will probably have to call his buddy who's supposed to help me today. I was hoping he'd call me, but I'm getting nervous with the holidays coming up and all. Oh Cat, I want to get out of here so bad. You h ave no idea.I have been really sad about Andy lately, too. I keep having thes e dreams about Kate, him and the kid. It's really yucky. What really hurts i s that i cared so much about someone who just threw me away so quickly. I mis s having someone to be with and enjoy me. Ohh, woe is me, woe is me!Why are y

1037-DC-00000318

2818

yBoZSBzY

WlkLCAiQ29tZSBvdmVyIGFuZCBzaXQNCmRvd24gYmVzaWRlIG1lIGZvciBhIG1vbWVud
CwgTWFtYS4

gIEkgd2FudCB0byBhc2sgeW91IGEgcXVlc3Rpb24iLiAgTm8NCmtpZGRpbmcuICBXZSdyZS
BoYXZpb

mcgc3VjaCBmdW4gd2l0aCBoaW0uICBMYXN0IEZyaWRheSBJIHRvb2sgdGhlIGRheSBvZm
YgYW5kDQp

oZSBhbmQgSSB3ZW50IHRvIFBEWCB6b28gdy8gbXkgZnJpZW5kIEVyaW5uICh5b3UndmUL
gbWV0IGhlc

iBzZXZlcmFsIHRpbWVzKQ0KYW5kIGhlciBib3lzLCBhZ2UgMi41ICYgMTAgbW9udGhzLi
AgV2hhdCB

hIGdyZWF0IHRpbWUhICBJIG5ldmVyIGluIG15IHdpbGRlc3QNCmRyZWFtcyB0aG91Z2h0I
HNoZSBhb

mQgSSB3b3VsZCBiZSBoYXZpbmcgZnVuIGNoYXNpbmcgdHdvIHRvZGRsZXJzIGFyb3Vu
ZCB0aGUNCnp

vbywgYnV0IGl0IHdhcyBncmVhdCENCg0KUXVpZXQgTWVtb3JpYWwgRGF5IHdlZWtlbm
QgcGxhbm5lZ

C4gIEEgQkJRIGZvciBteSSBmb2xrcycgYW5uaXZlcnNhcnkgb24gU2F0Lg0KYW5kIGEgdmlza
XQgdy8

gb3VyIGZyaWVuZCBCYW5namkgb24gU3VuLiwgYW5kIHlhcmQgd29yay4gIEhvdydzIHRo
YXQgZm9yD

QpiZWluZyBsaWtlIHRoZSBDbGVhdmVycz8gIFRoZSBvbmx5IGRpZmZlcmVuY2UgaXMsI
G15IHBlYXJ

scyBhcmUgcmVhbCENCg0KR290dGEgcnVuLiAgVGFrZSBjYXJlICYga2VlcCBpbiB0b3Vja
CENCg0KT
G92ZSwgDQpEaWFuZQ0KDQoNCg==--TFS-with-MIME-and-DIME-- he and kate are trying
t
o work this out and me being anywhere in the picture is not going to help. I
was pretty upset, but it is really for the best. I'll probably send her note
back to her with a small scribble that i never wanted to try to get her out of
the picture so he could be with me. if i really wanted to be nasty i'd send
the cards back to her, but i'm not THAT cruel. With the big creep, i told you
i sent him a note right? well in it i asked to come see him on saturday. he

1037-DC-00000337

2819

called on saturday and said betty couldn't come in but we'd do it sunday if s he could come in. he just called cuz he didn't want me waiting by the phone. i told him i appreciated that. he was sweet, but in a bad mood. i think he' s kind of depressed right now. well, sunday he didn't call until 5 pm and the n said he was trying to get a hold of her but he couldn't. he then called bac k 10 minutes later and said he had just gotten word that she'd be out of pocke t for two hours so i should go out fr a little while and he'd call at 7. he d idn't call at seven so at 8 i paged betty and she said he said he didn;t want her coming in late at night and we'd work it out for this week. he finally hu rriedly called me at about 9:45 and said he was busy he just called to say qui ckly we try and work it out for later. so all in all we had some very brief c alls this weekend and i hope to see him soon. oh, but he did say on saturdaha t indicated to me he really was working on getting me back there. well, my de ar, i love you and miss you soo much. i hope all is well with you and chris. i'm sure you'll lose whatever you gained. i finally started dieting and exer cising again after i had gained 15 frickin pounds since December. HELLO!! i love you . Monica --From: CA DavisTo: [redacted] he y girl!Date: Monday, May 19, 1997 6:58AMyeah! i finally got my email set-up!! so now you can write me =whenever you want and keep me posted on ALL your li fe's excitements. =Hey, have you heard from Doug since the Great Gatsby Kissi ng Incident? =Any more action from the freaks in Oregon? I still can't belie ve the =tangle that's come about there. So good you're in DC and far away. I =hope Andy, the schmucker, calls you soon..if he hasn't already. I'm =afraid my letter won't be too long tonight because its getting late and =Chris and I want to get up early to run before he goes to work. I am =getting soo fat an d don't try to disbelieve me or scoff! Its true. =20I miss you so much Monica and wish you could get a year position in the =embassy here and play with me. .well not PLAY with me but..you know. =Please write back and vent all..also plan your trip to Tokyo! love =you,
CatCVRTFZ20.DLLûûùCVWMFZ20.DLLCVWP5X20.DL

LCVWP6020.DLLCVWP6T20.DLLCVWPG120.DLLCVWPG220.DLLCV123Z20.DLL/2:>?9 :>?CVA12X20

.DLL;789:;CVCGMZ20.DLLCVDXFZ20.DLLCVEPSZ20.DLLCVEXCL20.DLL%&'&'CVHP GL20.DLLCVL
PIC20.DLLCVMGXZ20.DLLCVPCXZ20.DLLCVPICT20.DLL

1744005 FXD 1083 84198/ 98304 -----A 27-May-1997 16:10:00 27-May-1997 16:09:58 27-May-1997

1037-DC-00000338

========>>> 1 string found in FileSlack Cluster 1123 <<<========

2820

t in these last 2 years I have =lost two aunts, my Mom's older sisters, to can
cer. Anyway, I originally =thought I would go to school to be a Physician's A
ssisstant, P.A., a =growing field in healthcare and it is only a 2 year progra
m. I took =some prelim courses and was so thrilled and into it- like Microbio
logy =and medical microbiology, that I questioned why I shouldn't pusReceived:
from (8.7.5+Spi
n/3.4W4-PP-R5(05/15/97)) id WAA13450; Wed, 19 Nov 1997 22:22:44 +0900 (JST)Rec
eived: by galt.osd.
mil (8.7.1/8.7.1) with SMTP id IAA00768 for ; Wed,
19 Nov 1997 08:15:33 -0500 (EST)Received: by pagate.pa.osd.mil with Microsoft
Mailid Wed, 19 Nov 97 08:20:52 PSTFrom: "Lewinsk
y, Monica, , OSD/PA" To: CA Davis t
Subject: RE: birthday aftermathDate: Wed, 19 Nov 97 08:12:00 PSTMes
sage-ID: Encoding: 182 TEXTX-Mailer: Microsoft Mai
l V3.0X-UIDL: 809cb60fc0c9df52c4cf05811f2f2f72Oh, Catherine! You message was
just what i needed to start out this dreary day! I adore you, and think we'll
make wonderful older lady friends (here's to the ladies who lunch..) and youn
ger lady friends, too!! When you come back to the states I think we'll have t
o spend some concentrated time together. Imagine, talking in person and for F
REE!Your birthday sounded great (except of course for the Chris-getting-sick-p
art). i'm sorry you had to postpone your dinner. Your earrings sound lovely.
How was Japanese Disneyland? Were there any rides that made fun of American
s or was it Mickey Mouse based? I bet you looked beautiful in your red (VAHVO
OM!!) suit!The big creep does look quite trim these days. Oh, I haven't told
you my hysterical escapade from last week! Listen to this, it's practically u
nbelievable! The creep called me on Wednesday night and we talked for almost
an hour, but i had been bugging him that i wanted to see him and last week was
the only chance for awhile as he would be away for the next two weekends and
then i am gone for two weeks. So, on the phone he said he thought nancy (one
of the meanies) would be out for a few hours on Thurday and i could come see h
im them. I was to call Betty and figure out the details. Of course, i called
betty in the morning and then started the usual "I haven't had a chance to ta
lk to him, yet". Well, he ended up going golfing and I went ballistic. final
ly when he got back around 4:30 she talked to him and then he got mad she didn
't tell him -ya-da-ya-da. In the end, she snuck me in to the back office wher
e i waited for him while there were 20 people in there and Stephen, his
e aide who doesn' like me. I ended up seeing him for two minutes bec
ause he had one of his counterparts from another country waiting there for din
ner!! It was soo crazy.I will probably have to call his buddy who's supposed
to help me today. I was hoping he'd call me, but I'm getting nervous with the
holidays coming up and all. Oh Cat, I want to get out of here so bad. You h 1037-DC-00000341
ave no idea.I have been really sad about Andy lately, too. I keep having thes
e dreams about Kate, him and the kid. It's really yucky. What really hurts i
s that i cared so much about someone who just threw me away so quickly. I mis
s having someone to be with and enjoy me. Ohh, woe is me, woe is me!Why are y

2821

will be moving back to OR next summer- after our Bali trip! We have =
talked about staying longerand I worry about Chris going back to his =
office after only a year away, but I don't htink I can live in this =
environment for another year or half-year. Yes, I make good money, but =
it is mind-numbigly boring (my job). The other thing too, which is more =
important, is the nature of this city with its horrendous pollution (my =
hair is barely growing!), masses of people and no grass or trees. It is =
expensive and a pain to leave the city for a wkend....blah, blah, blah. =
For our year anniversary we are going out ot dinner. Period. I mean, =
if we lived in OR we would definately go to some romantic B&B or hotel =
out of Portland and maybe even fly and it would be cheaper than the =
trains here. I sound whiny but it is a wierd place and I think I may be =
done with it next summer. I think about driving and my house nad hiking =
inthe gorge and the coast and easy trips to N.California and friends and =
the slow life and a puppy....I guess its my small town island girl ness =
that wants me out of the big modern city.
NEW TOPIC: I am- are you sitting- a size 6 at the GAP!!!!!! They have =
seriously re-calibrated their sizes, baby, and its time to shopshopshop. =
I go in their and 10 are literally HANGING off meand 8s are well...lets =
just say drinking those shakes once a day for 10 years has really paid =
off! To be fair, I have not gained that much, but I am decidedly, with =
out a doubt, unquestionably a smack in the middle (and comfortable with =
it I might add) size f'n 8. I wonder if they changed the sizes somehow =
for Japan- to make those J ladies feel like they exist- no size 0s =
puhhhleeezzz!! Actually they probably love seeing me gather up the size =
Gigantic next to their size Cute and Litttle. Bitches. Just kidding, =
but for the first, or maybe second, time in my life I'm glad I'm not =
tall. I guess the first time was when I was growing up in Japan...oh, I =
mean Hawaii.
So, I am thrilled for you about this new job. I would beside myself tow =
ork in that group. Richardson looks like a nice man. What are some of =
your other options, in the private sector? Would all of them mean a =
move to NY? Try to tell me as much as you can. Oh, I miss you and I =
really am sad you will not be here soon...I understand though. I hope =
all works out. Very sweet about Australian guy. When will he be in DC, =
or the east coast, next? Wait, did you get together with him when you =
met him? Lots of questions to answer. Also remind me to tell you why =
the whole couples extravaganza is not really a fantasy, at least this =
one wasn't. I have to pop off to work. Write back as soon as you can. =
I love you and take care. Cat

From: Lewinsky, Monica, [redacted]
Sent: Wednesday, November 05, 1997 2:16 AM
To: CA Davis
Subject: RE: troubs?

oK. I have some bad news. I am off the next trip so i won't be coming =
to=20
Tokyo. I am probably sorrier than you are. the truth is it would have =
been=20
so difficult to spend time together and it probably would have benn more =

frustrating than anything.

The job thing on Friday went much better than expected. It was nice; =
the=20
big creep called thursday night and gave me a pep talk because i was so=20
afraid I'd sound like an idiot. Richardson is a great guy and i met two =

women who work for him...also very cool. Yesterday, Richardson called =
me at=20
work and told me they were going to offer me a position..they didn't =
know=20
what yet, and they wanted to talk with me further. The problem is, I =

2828

OCT 17 1996

October 16, 1996

Dear Evelyn,

Thanks for the meeting yesterday. I wanted to follow up on a few points as you put your memo together.

o I've enclosed our staff division of responsibilities that we use throughout the year. I don't distribute it because I want White House and agency staff to funnel their issues and requests through our West Wing operation. That way I can keep track, exercise quality control, and make the judgements about the use of our staff resources.

o I've also enclosed a brief memo on our correspondence operation. It was in bad shape when I came in. We got rid of Monica and Jossie not only because of "extracurricular activities" but because they couldn't do the job. We also had problems with NSC and White House correspondence that have been corrected. I believe the operation is in quite good shape now.

Thank you for being so good to me this year. I greatly appreciate your help and counsel. I will take the steps you suggested and then follow up with both you and Leon.

Jo

file personnel depts

3162

TO: THE PRESIDENT

FROM: BETTY

RE: ITEMS OF INTEREST

DATE: FEBRUARY 24, 1997

Monica Lewinsky stopped by. Do you want me to call her?

PUBLICAFFAIRS is a new nonfiction publishing house and a tribute to the standards, values, and flair of three persons who have served as mentors to countless reporters, writers, editors, and book people of all kinds, including me.

I.F. STONE, proprietor of *I. F. Stone's Weekly*, combined a commitment to the First Amendment with entrepreneurial zeal and reporting skill and became one of the great independent journalists in American history. At the age of eighty, Izzy published *The Trial of Socrates*, which was a national bestseller. He wrote the book after he taught himself ancient Greek.

BENJAMIN C. BRADLEE was for nearly thirty years the charismatic editorial leader of *The Washington Post*. It was Ben who gave the *Post* the range and courage to pursue such historic issues as Watergate. He supported his reporters with a tenacity that made them fearless, and it is no accident that so many became authors of influential, best-selling books.

ROBERT L. BERNSTEIN, the Chief Executive of Random House for more than a quarter century, guided one of the nation's premiere publishing houses. Bob was personally responsible for many books of political dissent and argument that challenged tyranny around the globe. He is also the founder and was the longtime chair of Human Rights Watch, one of the most respected human rights organizations in the world.

. . .

For fifty years, the banner of Public Affairs Press was carried by its owner Morris B. Schnapper, who published Gandhi, Nasser, Toynbee, Truman, and about 1,500 other authors. In 1983 Schnapper was described by *The Washington Post* as "a redoubtable gadfly." His legacy will endure in the books to come.

Peter Osnos, *Publisher*